Christopher Columbus, Richard Henry Major

Select Letters of Christopher Columbus, with other original Documents

Relating to his four Voyages to the New world

Christopher Columbus, Richard Henry Major

Select Letters of Christopher Columbus, with other original Documents
Relating to his four Voyages to the New world

ISBN/EAN: 9783337146320

Printed in Europe, USA, Canada, Australia, Japan

Cover: Foto ©ninafisch / pixelio.de

More available books at **www.hansebooks.com**

SELECT

LETTERS

OF

CHRISTOPHER COLUMBUS,

WITH OTHER ORIGINAL DOCUMENTS,

RELATING TO HIS

FOUR VOYAGES

TO

THE NEW WORLD.

TRANSLATED AND EDITED BY

R. H. MAJOR, F.S.A., ETC.,

KEEPER OF THE DEPARTMENT OF MAPS AND CHARTS IN THE BRITISH MUSEUM,
AND HON. SEC. OF THE ROYAL GEOGRAPHICAL SOCIETY.

Second Edition.

" Tu spiegherai, Colombo, a un novo polo
Lontane sì le fortunate antenne,
Ch' a pena seguirà con gli occhi il volo
La Fama ch' ha mille occhi e mille penne.
Canti ella Alcide e Bacco, e di te solo
Basti a' posteri tuoi ch'alquanto accenne;
Chè quel poco darà lunga memoria
Di poema dignissima e d' istoria."
Tasso.—*Gerusalemme Liberata*. Canto xv, 32.

LONDON:
PRINTED FOR THE HAKLUYT SOCIETY.
M.DCCC.LXX.

T. RICHARDS, 37, GREAT QUEEN STREET.

COUNCIL

OF

THE HAKLUYT SOCIETY.

SIR RODERICK IMPEY MURCHISON, BART., K.C.B., G.C.St.S., F.R.S., F.R.G.S., D.C.L.,
Mem. Imp. Acad. Sc. St. Petersburgh, Corr. Mem. Inst. Fr. etc., etc., PRESIDENT.

REAR-ADMIRAL C. R. DRINKWATER BETHUNE, C.B., } VICE-PRESIDENTS.
THE RIGHT HON. SIR DAVID DUNDAS,

REV. G. P. BADGER, F.R.G.S.
J. BARROW, ESQ., F.R.S.
E. H. BUNBURY, ESQ.
LORD ALFRED CHURCHILL.
REAR-ADMIRAL R. COLLINSON, C.B.
SIR WALTER ELLIOTT, K.S.I.
GENERAL C. FOX.
W. E. FRERE, ESQ.
CAPTAIN J. G. GOODENOUGH, R.N.
CHARLES GREY, ESQ.
EGERTON VERNON HARCOURT, ESQ.
JOHN WINTER JONES, ESQ., F.S.A.
R. H. MAJOR, ESQ., F.S.A.
SIR CHARLES NICHOLSON, BART.
SIR WILLIAM STIRLING MAXWELL, BART.
MAJOR-GENERAL SIR HENRY C. RAWLINSON, K.C.B.
THE LORD STANLEY OF ALDERLEY.

CLEMENTS R. MARKHAM, ESQ., HONORARY SECRETARY.

TO

THE HONOURED AND BELOVED

MEMORY

OF HIS EXCELLENCY

THE COUNT DE LAVRADIO,

LATE

ENVOY EXTRAORDINARY AND MINISTER PLENIPOTENTIARY OF

HIS MOST FAITHFUL MAJESTY

AT THE COURT OF ST. JAMES'S,

ETC., ETC., ETC.,

A WARM APPRECIATOR OF

THE EXALTED MERITS OF

COLUMBUS,

THE FOLLOWING PAGES

ARE REVERENTLY INSCRIBED BY

THE EDITOR.

PREFACE.

IT has been thought desirable by some of the leading members of our Council that I should avail myself of the opportunity offered by this second Edition of the *Select Letters of Columbus*, to lay before the Society a correspondence in which I have endeavoured to vindicate the character of the Society's early productions, and especially the first edition of this work, from a most unjustifiable attack made upon them by Mr. Froude in the *Westminster Review* in 1852, and *repeated* in the second volume of that gentleman's *Short Studies on Great Subjects*, printed in 1867, and *reprinted* in a popular edition in the same year. The letters themselves will convey to the reader the whole of the facts, minus only the bitterness and ferocity of Mr. Froude's attack.

The Athenæum, July 13th, 1867.
" British Museum, July 3rd, 1867.

"Will you allow me to appeal against a wrong done to the Hakluyt Society in general, and to myself in particular, in a work now very extensively read?

"In the second volume of Mr. Froude's *Short Studies on Great Subjects*, at page 102, is an article on 'England's Forgotten Worthies,' in which the author makes an attack on the Hakluyt Society, the bitter expressions of which need not be repeated here. It is headed by the titles of three of the Society's early publications, and the first he states to be *The Observations of Sir Richard Hawkins, Knt., in his Voyage in the South Sea in* 1593. Reprinted from the edition of 1622, and *edited by R. H. Major, Esq., of the British Museum;*

whereas I had nothing to do with the editing of that work. This done, at page 108, Mr. Froude says: '*The Editor of the Letters of Columbus* (which I did edit in 1847) *apologizes for the rudeness of the old seaman's phraseology. Columbus, he tells us, was not so great a master of the pen as of the art of navigation. We are to make excuses for him. We are put on our guard, and warned not to be offended, before we are introduced to the sublime record of sufferings under which a man of the highest order was staggering towards the end of his earthly calamities; although the inarticulate fragments in which his thought breaks out from him, are strokes of natural art, by the side of which literary pathos is poor and meaningless.*' I warmly deny that I apologized for Columbus's language. So far from it, I repeatedly expressed my sympathy with and admiration of his manly and touching record of his sufferings. What I did apologize for was any mischievous result which might possibly have accrued, though I do not think it did accrue, to my own diction from that occasional want of connectedness in the original which I had to contend with in translating. The two things are manifestly different, and it is not pleasant to find the reader's highest sympathies appealed to in order to bring down greater condemnation on me for a fault that I had never committed. But I should not trouble you with such a personal matter, were it not that, having fabricated this handle for censure on me, Mr. Froude makes it a hook for the following criticism on the Hakluyt Society: '*And even in the subjects which they select, they are pursued by the same curious fatality,*' the selection blamed being that of *Drake's Last Voyage in* 1595, edited from the original MSS. Then, after magisterially condemning this elsewhere unblamed selection as a '*fatal*' sin, Mr. Froude proceeds to say, at the foot of page 109, '*But every bad has a worse below it, and more offensive than all these is the Editor of "Hawkins's Voyage to the South Sea,"*'—and if the reader refers to the head of the article for the name of *this most offensive editor*, he will, as I have already said, find my name, who never had anything to do with it. It is true that on page 110 the name of the real editor, Admiral Bethune, occurs; but as Mr. Froude's article is a reprint from the *Westminster Review* of 1852 (not 1853, as Mr. Froude again blunders in saying), there has been time enough for that gentleman to correct the injurious errors into which he had fallen. Although naturally annoyed at this treatment of my name, I left the

offence unnoticed at the time; but now that, after a lapse of fifteen years, it is reprinted, with all faults in a widely-circulated publication, I call on Mr. Froude to correct his mis-statements.

"I am, happily, able to state, from the experience of twenty years, that the estimate of the Hakluyt Society's publications by the literary world is far from supporting Mr. Froude in his supercilious treatment of that Society. Whatever opinion, however, those publications may deserve, it is the duty of a critic to be correct, and the greater the severity, the greater the need of correctness; but when a critic lashes not only one's self, but one's friends, by means of misrepresentations and blunders of his own making, what does that critic deserve?   R. H. MAJOR."

The Athenæum, July 20*th*, 1867.

"5, Onslow Gardens, July 15, 1867.

"I am sorry to have given Mr. Major cause to complain of me. Should my *Essays* be reprinted, the mistake which he points out shall be corrected; and I can only regret the injustice which meanwhile is done to his name. At the same time the only error which I can acknowledge is confined to the title of a work which stands at the head of the article. In the article itself the volumes criticised are assigned to their proper editors.   J. A. FROUDE."

. The Athenæum, July 27*th*, 1867.

"British Museum, July 23, 1867.

"I beg to thank Mr. Froude for his courteous expression of regret for what, I am quite sure, was done inadvertently, and I would thankfully accept his promise of reparation if it were extended to all the mischief that is being done to me. Unfortunately for me, *two editions* of Mr. Froude's *Essays* have been issued this year, *the second this very month*, in a *cheap and popular form*; thus diffusing and prolonging, in the most effectual manner, an injustice to my name which has existed for fifteen years, and postponing indefinitely the chance of reparation in a future edition.

"Under such circumstances, I read with regret that, while acknowledging one error, Mr. Froude does not also acknowledge what everyone else sees clearly and condemns, the injustice of his censure on me with respect to Columbus, and which he makes a ground for censure on the Hakluyt Society. That Society stands too high to need any defence

iv   PREFACE.

from its former Honorary Secretary, but I may be excused for specially asking that this censure may be expunged ; for I have a letter from Mr. Bancroft, who was Ambassador here at the time, in which he eulogizes, in terms so warm that I may not repeat them, the spirit in which I had written both of the sufferings of Columbus, and of the touching language in which he had recorded them. This is exactly the contrary of what Mr. Froude's two editions are telling everybody that I have done.   R. H. MAJOR."

Now that, in revising my translation for this second edition, I have again gone through the texts of Columbus's letters, I uncompromisingly repeat the expression which in 1847 I used *solely* in exculpation of any mischievous result to my own diction from the disconnectedness of the original, viz., that "Columbus was not so great a master of the pen as of the art of navigation." Whether my judgment on this point be of more or less weight than Mr. Froude's is of no moment whatever ; but it is of moment that the mischievous effect of a savage criticism, built up on the critic's own blunders, should be neutralized as far as possible. The reader has the realities of the whole case before him, and may judge for himself.
                                                            R. H. M.

INTRODUCTION.

NEARLY three thousand years have passed since the wisest of men declared that there was nothing new under the sun. The saying has held good to the present day, for men are perpetually finding out that their recent discoveries had been already made, but under circumstances which did not reveal the full value of that which had been discovered. No greater examples of this truth can be adduced than in the history of the Atlantic, of America, and of Australia. Until the days of Prince Henry the Navigator, the Atlantic was so unknown that it justly bore the name of the " Sea of Darkness;" and yet, during the previous two thousand years occasional glimpses of light had in fact been thrown upon the face of that mysterious ocean. " Nil novi sub sole" was still an indisputable proverb. In the researches into the Atlantic originated by Prince Henry, Columbus took part, and hence, as we shall presently more fully see, derived the idea of the great importance of explorations to the West. Within one hundred years of the triumphant rounding by Prince Henry's navigators (in 1434) of Cape Bojador, which till then had been the limit of Atlantic exploration, the Portuguese had discovered both the eastern and western shores of the continental island

of Australia. And yet till recently men knew not that they owed the knowledge either of America or of Australia* to the initiatory efforts of a Prince with whose name, in fact, they were almost entirely unacquainted.

Such facts show the great injustice done to the originators of great explorations who, working with the smallest means, really deserve the highest meed of honour.

Yet in the estimate of merit it must be conceded that priority, immense as are its claims, is not all-absorbent. Columbus, as we shall presently see, was anticipated in the discovery of America, and yet such were the special virtues brought to bear upon the execution of his great achievement, that, as Humboldt has eloquently said, "the majesty of grand recollections seems concentred" on his illustrious name. The peculiar value of the following letters, descriptive of the four important voyages of Columbus, is that the events described are from the pens of those to whom the events occurred. In them we have laid before us, as it were from Columbus's own mouth, a clear statement of his opinions and conjectures on what were to him great cosmical riddles—riddles which have since been solved mainly through the light which his illustrious deeds have shed upon the field of our observation. In these letters also we trace the magnanimity with which

* The Society possesses, in my *Early Voyages to Terra Australis*, printed in 1859, the evidence of these discoveries; and in my *Prince Henry the Navigator*, published in 1868, will be seen the procession of these discoveries from the Prince's efforts.

Columbus could support an accumulated burthen of undeserved affliction. It is impossible to read without the deepest sympathy the occasional murmurings and half suppressed complaints which are uttered in the course of his letter to Ferdinand and Isabella, describing his fourth voyage. These murmurings and complaints were wrung from his manly spirit by sickness and sorrow, and though reduced almost to the brink of despair by the injustice of the king, yet do we find nothing harsh or disrespectful in his language to the sovereign/ A curious contrast is presented to us. The gift of a world could not move the monarch to gratitude; the infliction of chains, as a recompense for that gift, could not provoke the subject to disloyalty. /The same great heart which through more than twenty wearisome years of disappointment and chagrin gave him strength to beg and to buffet his way to glory, still taught him to bear with majestic meekness the conversion of that glory into unmerited shame. /

The translated documents are seven in number. Five of them are letters from the hand of Columbus himself, describing respectively his first, third, and fourth voyages. /Another, describing the second voyage, is by Dr. Chanca, the physician to the fleet during that expedition,/and the seventh document is an extract from the will of /Diego Mendez, one of Columbus's officers during the fourth voyage, who gives a detailed account of many most interesting adventures undertaken by himself, but left undescribed by Columbus. /

I shall not pause here to enter into the important bibliography of these documents, which has no charm for many readers, and is therefore placed at the end of this introduction. A series of original documents of such importance might appear to need but few words of introduction or recommendation, since the entire history of civilisation presents us with no event, with the exception perhaps of the art of printing, so momentous as the discovery of the western world; and, independently of the lustre which the grandeur of that event confers upon the discoverer, there is no individual who has rendered himself, on the score of personal character and conduct, more illustrious than Christopher Columbus. There have, nevertheless, not been wanting those, who, from various motives, and on grounds of various trustworthiness, have endeavoured to lessen his glory, by impeaching his claim to the priority of discovery, or by arguing that the discovery itself has proved a misfortune rather than advantage to the world at large. By way, therefore, of vindicating the value of the original documents here translated, a brief account of such pretensions to prior discovery as have been at different times put forth, may not be thought superfluous.

The oldest story which seems possibly to bear reference to what we call the " new world " is related by Theopompus.

Theopompus lived in the fourth century before the Christian era; in a fragment of his works preserved by Ælian is a conversation between Silenus

and Midas, King of Phrygia, in which the former says that Europe, Asia, and Africa were surrounded by the sea, but that beyond this known world was an island of immense extent, containing huge animals and men of twice our stature, and long-lived in proportion. There were in it many great cities whose inhabitants had laws and customs entirely different from ours. Fabulous as the story is as a whole, we cannot escape from the thought that it suggests, though vaguely, a notion of the real existence of a great western country. This idea is strengthened by the remarkable story related to Solon by a priest of Sais from the sacred inscriptions in the temples, and presented to us by Plato in his Timæus and Critias, wherein he speaks of an island called Atlantis, opposite the Pillars of Hercules, larger than Africa and Asia united, but which in one day and night was swallowed up by an earthquake and disappeared beneath the waters. The result was that no one had since been able to navigate or explore that sea on account of the slime which the submerged island had produced. Many as have been the doubts and conjectures to which this narrative has been subjected by the learned in ancient and modern times, it is a remarkable fact that Crantor, in a commentary on Plato quoted by Proclus, declares that he found this same account retained by the priests of Sais three hundred years after the period of Solon, and that he was shown the inscriptions in which it was embodied. It is also deserving of notice that precisely in that part

of the ocean described in the legend we find the island groups of the Azores, Madeira, the Canaries, and a host of other rocks and sand-banks, while the great bank of varec, or floating seaweed, occupying the middle portion of the basin of the North Atlantic, and covering, according to Humboldt, an area about six times as large as Germany, has been reasonably regarded as explanatory of the obstacle to navigation to which the tradition refers.

Various have been the speculations respecting the original colonisation of the western hemisphere. Athanasius Kircher, in his *Prodromus Coptus and Œdipus Ægyptiacus*, gives the Egyptians the credit of colonising America, as well as India, China, and Japan, grounding his argument upon the religious worship of the sun, moon, stars, and animals. Edward Brerewood, at pages 96 and 97 of his *Enquiries touching the Diversity of Languages*, contends, and he is far from being alone in his opinion, that the Americans are the progeny of the Tartars. Marc Lescarbot, in his *Histoire de la Nouvelle France*, maintains that the Canaanites, when routed by Joshua, were driven into America by storms, and that Noah was born in America, and after the flood showed his descendants the way into their paternal country, and assigned to some of them their places of abode there; while Hornius, in his treatise *De originibus Americanis*, after touching upon the various conjectures here quoted, animadverts on the presumption and folly of Paracelsus, when he states that a second Adam and Eve were created for the peopling of the western world.

INTRODUCTION. vii

The first specific statement, however, of a supposed migration from the shores of the old world to those of the new is that which the elder De Guignes presumes to be demonstrable from the relation given by a Chinese historian, Li-Yen, who lived at the commencement of the seventh century. (See *Mémoires de l'Académie des Inscriptions et Belles Lettres*, vol. 28, p. 504.) The said historian speaks of a country, named Fou-sang, more than forty thousand li* to the East of China. He says that they who went thither started from the province of Leaton, situated to the north of Peking; that after having made twelve thousand li, they came to Japan; that travelling seven thousand li northward from that place, they arrived at the country of Venchin, and at five thousand li eastward of the latter, they found the country of Tahan, whence they journeyed to Fou-sang, which was twenty thousand li distant from Tahan. From this account De Guignes endeavours, by a long chain of argument, to prove that the Chinese had pushed their investigations into Jeso, Kamtschatka, and into that part of America which is situated opposite the most eastern coast of Asia.

This surmise of De Guignes has been answered by Klaproth, in a paper which appeared in the *Nouvelles Annales des Voyages* (tom. 51, 2ª serie, p. 53). His arguments go to show that the country named Fou-sang is Japan; and that the country of Tahan, situated to the west of Asiatic Vinland, can only be

* The *li* is about one-tenth of the common league.

the island of Saghalian. Humboldt observes upon this subject, that the number of horses, the practice of writing, and the manufacture of paper from the Fousang tree, mentioned in the account given by the Chinese historian, ought to have shown De Guignes that the country of which he spoke was not America.

The |presumed discovery of America which comes next in chronological rotation, is that by the Scandinavians, the earliest *printed allusion* to which occurs in Adam of Bremen's *Historia Ecclesiastica Ecclesiarum Hamburgensis et Bremensis*, published at Copenhagen, 1579, 4to. The Baron Von Humboldt has asserted that the merit of first recognising the discovery of America by the Northmen, *belongs indisputably* to Ortelius, who, in his *Theatrum Orbis Terrarum*, with unjust severity says, that Christopher Columbus had done nothing more than to place the new world in a permanently useful and commercial relationship with Europe. The ground upon which the priority is claimed for Ortelius, is that the first edition of his work came out in 1570, although the reference which Humboldt himself gives is to an edition of 1601 which was after the death of Ortelius, and the earlier editions do not contain the chapter on the Pacific Ocean in which the passage occurs. It is true that in the *Bibliotheca Hulthemiana* the edition of 1601 is said to have been revised and augmented by Ortelius before his death in 1598, but, even if the assertion was made by Ortelius, and not by the editor of his work after his death, it still leaves per-

fectly unimpeached the claim to priority of the Copenhagen edition of Adam of Bremen in 1579. Adam of Bremen's work was written soon after the middle of the eleventh century, and was followed in the next half century by the *Historia Ecclesiastica* of Ordericus Vitalis, who also speaks of the country visited by the Scandinavians. Abraham Mylius, in his *Treatise de Antiquitate Linguæ Belgicæ*, Leyden, 1611, makes all Americans to be sprung from Celts; stating that many Celtic words were to be found in use there; and with more reasonable showing affirms that the coast of Labrador was visited by wanderers from Iceland. Hugo Grotius, in his *Dissertatio de Origine Gentium Americanarum*, (Paris, 1642, 8vo.), follows Mylius, and states that America was colonised by a Norwegian race, who came thither from Iceland, through Greenland, and passed through North America down to the Isthmus.

The earliest *printed detail* of these discoveries is given by the Norwegian historian, Thormodus Torfæus, in a work entitled *Historia Vinlandiæ Antiquæ, ex Antiquitatibus Islandicis in lucem producta*, (Hauniæ, 1705, 12mo.) But in the invaluable work by Professor Rafn, published in 1837 by the Danish Royal Society of Antiquaries, under the title of *Antiquitates Americanæ*, the manuscripts which record these discoveries are given at length in the original, accompanied by a Latin translation, and careful and learned geographical illustrations. The following is a summary of the principal events recorded in this highly interesting volume, and the geographical

inferences are those supplied by the professor himself.

Irish Christians were the first Europeans, which we know from well established history, to have migrated into and inhabited Iceland. Close upon the end of the eighth century this island was visited by Irish hermits; but the first discovery of it by the Northmen was made by a Dane named Gardar, of Swedish origin, in the year 863. The regular colonisation of the country was commenced in 874 by Ingolf, a Norwegian, and was carried on continuously for the space of sixty years by some of the most influential and civilised families of Scandinavia. In 877 the mountainous coast of Greenland was for the first time seen by a man named Gunnbiorn, but it was in 983 that this country was first visited by Eric Rauda, or Eric the Red, son of Thorwald, a Norwegian noble, who had been condemned to a banishment of three years for killing Eyolf his neighbour. After three years absence, he returned to Iceland, and in order to hold out an inducement to colonisation, named the newly discovered country Greenland, intending by that name to express the richness of the woods and meadows with which it abounded. Amongst those who had accompanied Eric was a man named Heriulf Bardson, who established himself at Heriulfsnes. Biarne, the son of the latter, finding, on his return home from a trading voyage to Norway, that his father had quitted Iceland, resolved upon following him, though he, as well as those who had accompained him, were quite un-

acquainted with the Greenland sea. Soon after leaving Iceland they met with northerly winds and fogs, and were carried they knew not whither: the weather clearing, they found themselves near a flat woody country, which, not corresponding with the descriptions of Greenland, they left to larboard. After five days' sailing with a south-west wind, they came to a mountainous country, covered with glaciers, which they found to be an island; but as its appearance was not inviting, they bore away from the island, and standing out to sea with the same wind, after four days' sailing with fresh gales, they reached Heriulfsnes in Greenland.

/Some time after this, in the year 1000, Lief, son of Eric the Red, equipped a ship with thirty-five men to make a voyage of discovery, with the view of examining the new found lands more narrowly./ They came to a land were no grass was to be seen, but everywhere there were vast glaciers, while the space intervening between these ice mountains and the shore appeared as one uninterrupted plain of slate. This country they named Helluland, *i. e.* Slate-land (Newfoundland). Thence they stood out to sea again, and reached a level wooded country, with cliffs of white sand. They called this country Markland, *i.e.* Woodland (Nova Scotia). Again they put to sea, and after two days' sail reached an island, to the eastward of the mainland, and passed through the strait between this island and the mainland. They sailed westward, and landed at a place where a river, issuing from a lake, fell into the sea. Here they wintered and built

houses, which were afterwards called Leifsbuder (Leifsbooths.) During their stay, one of their number, named Tyrker, a German, happened to wander some distance from the settlement, and on his return reported that he had found vines and grapes. These proving to be plentiful, Lief named the country Vinland or Vineland (New England), and in the ensuing spring returned to Greenland. In the year 1002, Thorwald, Lief's brother, being of opinion that the country had been too little explored, borrowed his brother's ship, and with the assistance of his advice and instructions, set out on a new voyage. They arrived at Liefsbooths, in Vinland, remained there for the winter, and, in the spring of 1003, Thorwald sent a party in the ship's long boat on a voyage of discovery southwards. They found a beautiful and well-wooded country, with extensive ranges of white sand, but no traces of men, except a wooden shed which they found on an island lying to the westward. They returned to Liefsbooths in the autumn. In the summer of 1004, Thorwald sailed eastward and then northward, past a remarkable headland enclosing a bay, and which was opposite to another headland. They called it Kialarnes (Keel-Cape). Continuing along the east coast, they reached a beautiful promontory, where they landed. Thorwald was so pleased with the place that he exclaimed, " Here is a beautiful spot, and here I should like well to fix my dwelling." He had scarcely spoken before they encountered some Skrellings (Esquimaux) with whom they fell to blows, and a sharp conflict ensuing, Thor-

wald received a mortal wound in his arm from an arrow. He died, and was buried by his own instructions on the spot which had excited his admiring remark, the language of which appeared prophetic of a longer stay there than he had at first contemplated.

The most distinguished, however, of all the first American discoverers is Thorfinn Karlsefne, an Icelander, whose genealogy is carried back in the old northern annals to Danish, Swedish, Norwegian, Scottish, and Irish ancestors, some of them of royal blood. In 1006 this chieftain visited Greenland, and there married Gudrida, the widow of Thurstein (son of Eric the Red), who had died the year before in an unsuccessful expedition to Vinland. Accompanied by Snorre Thorbrandson, also a man of illustrious lineage, Biarne Grimolfson of Breidefiord, and Thorhall Gamlason of Austfiord, he set sail in the spring of 1007 with three ships for Vinland.

They had in all one hundred and sixty men, and as they went with the intention of colonising, they took with them a great variety and quantity of live stock. They sailed, first, to the Tresterbyd, and afterwards to Biarney (Disco); then to Helluland, where they found an abundance of foxes; and thence to Markland, which was overgrown with wood, and plentifully stocked with a variety of animals. Proceeding still in a south-westerly direction, with the land on the right, they came to a place where a frith penetrated far into the country; off the mouth of it was an island, on which they found an immense

number of eyder ducks, so that it was scarcely possible to walk without treading on their eggs. They called the island Straumey (Stream Isle) from the strong current which ran past it, and the frith they called Straumfiordr (Stream Frith). Here Thorhall and eight others left the party in quest of Vinland, but were driven by westerly gales to the coast of Iceland, where some say that they were beaten, and put into servitude. Karlsefne, however, with the remaining one hundred and fifty men, sailed southwards, and reached a place were a river falls into the sea from a lake; large islands were situated opposite the mouth of the river; passing these, they steered into the lake, and called the place Hop. The low grounds were covered with wheat growing wild; and the rising grounds with vines. Here they stayed till the beginning of the year 1008, when finding their lives in constant jeopardy from the hostile attacks of the natives, they quitted the place, and returned to Eric's fiorde. In 1011 a ship arrived in Greenland, from Norway, commanded by two Icelandic brothers named Helge and Finnboge: to these men, Freydisa, a natural daughter of Eric the Red, proposed a voyage to Vinland, stipulating that they should share equally with her the profits of the voyage. To this they assented, and it was agreed that each party should have thirty able-bodied men on board the ship, besides women; but Freydisa secretly took with her five men in addition to that number. They reached Liefsbooths in 1012, and wintered there; when a discussion arising, Freydisa had the subtlety

to prevail on her husband to massacre the brothers and their followers; after the perpetration of which base deed they returned to Greenland in the spring of 1013.

In his expedition to Vinland in 1007, Thorfinn Karlsefne had been accompanied by his wife, Gudrida, who bore him a son, Snorre, who became the founder of an illustrious family in Iceland, which gave that island several of its first bishops. Among these may be mentioned the learned Bishop Thorlak Runolfson, to whom we are principally indebted for the oldest ecclesiastical code of Iceland, written in the year 1123. It is also probable that the accounts of the voyages were originally compiled by him.

The notices given in these old Icelandic accounts, of the climate, soil, and productions of the new country are very characteristic. It is curious that Adam of Bremen, in the eleventh century, though himself not a northman, states, on the authority of Svein Estridson, the King of Denmark, a nephew of Canute the Great, that the country of Vinland got its name from the vine growing wild there, and for the same reason the English re-discoverers gave the name of Martha's Vineyard to the large island close off the coast.

It is fortunate that in these ancient accounts they have preserved the statement of the course steered and the distance sailed in a day. From various ancient Icelandic geographical works it may be gathered that the distance of a day's sailing was estimated at from twenty-seven to thirty geographical miles—

German or Danish—of which fifteen are equal to a degree, and are consequently equivalent to four English miles. From the island of Helluland, afterwards called little Helluland, Biarne sailed to Herjulfsnes (Ikigeit), in Greenland, with strong south-westerly winds, in four days. The distance between that cape and Newfoundland is about one hundred and fifty miles, which, if we allow for the strong south-westerly gales, will correspond with Biarne's voyage; while the well-known barrenness of the flats of Newfoundland corresponds with the Hellue, or slates, which suggested the name the Northmen gave to the island.

/Markland being described as three days' sail south-west of Helluland, appears to be Nova Scotia; and the low and level character of the country, covered with woods, tallies precisely with the descriptions of later writers./

Vinland was stated to be two days' sail to the south-west of Markland, which would be from fifty-four to sixty miles. The distance from Cape Sable to Cape Cod is reckoned at about two hundred and ten English miles, which answers to about fifty-two Danish miles; and in the account given by Biarne of their finding many shallows off the island to the eastward, we recognize an accurate description of Nantucket, and Kialarnes must consequently be Cape Cod. The Straumfiordr of the Northmen is supposed to be Buzzard's Bay, and Straumey, Martha's Vineyard, though the account of the many eggs found there, would seem to correspond more correctly

with Egg Island, which lies off the entrance of Vineyard Sound.

Krossanes is probably Gurnet Point. The Hóp answers to Mount Hope's Bay, through which the Taunton river flows, and it was here that the Leifsbooths were situated.

The ancient documents likewise make mention of a country called Huitramannaland (Whiteman's Land), otherwise Irland it Mikla (Great Ireland) supposed to be that part of the coast of North America, including North and South Carolina, Georgia and Florida. There is a tradition among the Shawanese Indians, who emigrated some years ago from Florida and settled in Ohio, that Florida was once inhabited by white people, who possessed iron instruments. The powerful chieftain, Are Marson of Reykianes, in Iceland,— according to the account given by his contemporary Rafn, surnamed the Limerick trader,—was driven to Huitramannaland by storms in 983, and was baptised there. Are Frode likewise (the first compiler of the Landnama, and a descendant in the fourth degree from Are Marson) states that his uncle, Thorkell Gellerson, had been informed by Icelanders that Are Marson had been recognised in Huitramannaland, and was held in high respect there. This statement therefore shows that there was an occasional intercourse in those days between the Orkneys and Iceland, and this part of America.

It is further recorded in the ancient MSS. that the Greenland bishop Eric went over to Vinland in the year 1121; but nothing more than the fact is stated,

and it simply corroborates the supposition of intercourse between the countries. Again, in the year 1266, a voyage of discovery to the Arctic regions of America is said to have been performed, under the auspices of some clergymen of the bishopric of Gardar in Greenland; and from the recorded observations made by the explorers, would seem to have been carried to regions whose geographical position has been more accurately determined by our own navigators, Parry and the two Rosses. The next recorded discovery was made by Adalbrand and Thorwald Helgason, two Icelandic clergymen, in the year 1285. Contemporaneous accounts state that they discovered a new land to the westward of Iceland, supposed to have been Newfoundland. The last record preserved in the ancient Icelandic MSS. relates a voyage from Greenland to Markland, performed by a crew of seventeen men, in the year 1347. The account written by a contemporary nine years after the event, induces the belief that intercourse between Greenland and America had been maintained as late as the period here mentioned, for he speaks of Markland as a country still known and visited in those days.

The obscurity of many portions of these narratives leaves much to be cleared up with reference to this interesting subject; but their general truthfulness being corroborated by the traces of the residence and settlement of the ancient northmen exhibited in the inscriptions discovered in Kinkigtorsoak, Greenland, and Massachusetts, no room is left for disputing the main fact of the discovery.

Between this period and the date of the first voyage of Columbus, the coast of America is reported to have been visited by the Arabians of the Spanish Peninsula, the Welsh, the Venetians, the Portuguese, and also by a Pole in the service of Denmark.

The Arabian expedition is described both by Edrisi and by Ibn-al-Wardi. It appears to have been undertaken by eight persons of the same family, called the Almagrurins or the Wandering Brothers, who having provided themselves with everything requisite for a long voyage, swore they would not return till they had penetrated to the extreme limits of the Sea of Darkness. They sailed from the port of Aschbona or Lisbon, and steered towards the south-west, and at the end of thirty-five days arrived at the island of Gana or Sheep Island. The flesh of the sheep of this island being too bitter for them to eat, they put to sea again, and after sailing twelve days in a southerly direction, reached an island inhabited by people of a red skin, lofty stature, and with hair of thin growth but long and flowing over their shoulders. The inhabitants of this island told them that persons had sailed twenty days to the west without discovering land, and the Arabian brothers, diverted from the pursuit of their hardy enterprise by this discouraging account, retraced their course, and returned safely to Lisbon. From this description the elder de Guignes inferred that the Arabs had either reached the eastern coast of America, or at least one of the American islands; an opinion, however, which appears to have as little to sanction it, as his above

mentioned conjecture that the Chinese had discovered the west coast of America in the fifth century. The Baron von Humboldt concurs with the opinion expressed by the learned orientalist Tychsen in his *Neue oriental und exegetische Bibliothek*, and repeated by Malte Brun, that the island reached by the Arab wanderers was one of the African islands. This conclusion is drawn from the circumstance that the Guanches, the original people of the Canary group, were a pastoral race, and also possessed the same external characteristics as the islanders here described. Moreover, the fact that the king of the island had an interpreter who spoke Arabic, together with the circumstance that the red men had sailed westward for a month without seeing land, strongly corroborates the opinion advanced. The precise date of this voyage is unknown, but Humboldt presumes that it must have been considerably anterior to the expulsion of the Arabs from Lisbon in 1147; because Edrisi, whose work was finished in 1153, speaks of the occurrence as if it were by no means recent.

It is but upon a slight foundation, that the Welsh have pretended to raise a claim to the discovery; but slight as it is, there is certainly enough to render a decidedly negative assertion on the subject to the full as presumptuous as one decidedly affirmative would be. But as we have no concern with mere conjectures, we must in candour narrate, as succinctly as possible, the grounds upon which these pretensions have been founded.

The first account of this discovery is found in

Humphrey Llwyd's translation of the *History of Wales*, by Caradoc of Llancarvan, published by Dr. Powell in 1584. According to him the occurrence took place as follows:—On the death of Owen Gwynedd, prince of North Wales, in 1169, a contention arose amongst his numerous sons respecting the succession to the crown, when Madawe, or Madoc, one of their number, seeing his native country was likely to be embroiled in a civil war, deemed it more prudent to try his fortune abroad. In pursuance of this object he sailed with a small fleet of ships to the westward, and leaving Iceland on the north, came at length to an unknown country, where everything appeared new and uncommon and the manner of the natives different from all that he had ever seen. The country appearing to him, from its fertility and beauty, to be very desirable for a settlement, he left most of his own men behind him, (amounting, according to Sir Thomas Herbert, to a hundred and twenty), and returning to Wales, persuaded a considerable number of the Welsh to go out with him to the newly discovered country, and so with ten ships he again departed, and bade a final adieu to his native soil. This account of the historian Caradoc of Llancarvan is the only affirmative written document the story has upon which to ground its claim to authenticity, with the exception of an ode, written by a Welsh bard, Meredyth ab Rhys, who died in 1477, fifteen years before Columbus's first expedition, in which an allusion is made to the event.*

* The most strenuous advocate for the truth of the tradition

A circumstance which would appear to confirm the truth of Madoc's voyages, is a peculiar resemblance that has been found between some of the American dialects and the Welsh language; but, as Dr. Robertson reasonably remarks, the affinity has been observed in so few instances, and in some of these is so obscure or so fanciful, that no conclusion can be drawn from the casual resemblance of a small number of words. Dr. Williams adduces in confirmation of his favourite idea the authorities of Lopez de Gomara, Hornius, and Peter Martyr, pretending that they assert that traces of Christianity were found among the Americans by the Spaniards, as well as that there was a tradition among the Mexicans, that many years before a strange nation came amongst them, and taught them a knowledge of God. His references however appear entirely incorrect.

Another pretension to an early discovery of America has been founded upon an account given in a work published in Venice by Francesco Marcolini in 1558, entitled *Dello scoprimento dell' Isole Frislanda, Eslanda, Engrovelanda, Estotilanda, ed Icaria, fatto sotto il Polo Artico da due fratelli Zeni, M. Nicolò il K. e M. Antonio.*" The substance of the account is, that in 1380, Nicolò Zeno, a Venetian noble, fitted out a vessel at his own cost, and made a voyage to the north, with the intention of visiting

that America was discovered by Prince Madoc, was Dr. John Williams of Sydenham, who wrote two tracts on the subject in the year 1791 and 1792, which, if betraying a little of the bias of prejudice, yet manifest a degree of research that does great credit to his industry and zeal.

England and Flanders, but was driven by a storm to Friseland, now proved to be the Færoe Archipelago. Being rescued from the attacks of the natives by Zichmni, a neighbouring prince, Zeno entered into the service of the latter, and assisted him in conquering Friseland and other northern islands. He shortly after dispatched a letter to his brother Antonio, requesting him to find means to join him; whereupon the latter purchased a vessel, and succeeded in reaching Friseland, where he remained fourteen years. During his residence there he wrote to his brother Carlo in Venice, and gave an account of a report brought by a certain fisherman, about a land to the westward. This account stated that about twenty-six years before, the fisherman, when out at sea with four fishing boats, was overtaken by a tempest, which drove them about for many days, and at length cast them on an island called Estotiland, about a thousand miles from Friseland. The inhabitants conveyed them to a fair and populous city, where the king sent for many interpreters to converse with them, but none that they could understand, until a man was found, who had likewise been cast away upon the coast, and who spoke Latin. They remained several days upon the island, which was rich and fruitful, abounding with all kinds of metals, and especially gold. Though much given to navigation, they were ignorant of the use of the compass, and finding the Friselanders acquainted with it, the king of the place sent them with twelve barques to visit a country to the south, called Drogeo. They had nearly perished

in a storm, but were cast away upon the coast of Drogeo. The fisherman described this Drogeo as a country of vast extent, and that the inhabitants were naked and eaters of human flesh. He remained many years in the country, and became rich with trafficking between Estotiland and the main land, and subsequently fitted out a vessel of his own, and made his way back to Friseland. His narrative induced Zichmni to undertake a voyage thither, in which he was accompanied by Antonio Zeno. It was unsuccessful : landing on an island called Icaria, they were roughly treated by the inhabitants, and a storm afterwards drove them on the coast of Greenland.

This account was placed in the hands of Marcolini by Nicolò Zeno, a descendant of the family of the explorers, but it had to be made from fragments, he himself having, when a boy, from ignorance torn up a considerable quantity of the original documents, which were letters written by Antonio Zeno to Carlo his brother. In spite of a considerable amount of fable and exaggeration, defects which enter into the majority of early accounts of travel, it is scarcely to be believed that Nicolò Zeno the younger invented this voyage. He was a man of the highest reputation, as may be seen by the encomium passed on him by Francesco Patrizio ; see *Della Historia dieci Dialoghi di M. Francesco Patrizio*, Venetia, 1560, 4to., p. 30 verso. It is well known that the Venetians had made yearly voyages to the north of Europe for at least two centuries before the period in question, and the most important part of Zeno's publication,

viz., the map, the original of which is stated to have hung up in his palace since the date of the discovery, bears evidence of a knowledge, however imperfect, of Scandinavian geography. The graduation of this map was inserted by Nicolò Zeno the younger himself, and although inaccurate enough to cause much perplexity to geographers, there is no doubt that Greenland was laid down on it with more correctness than on any map preceding the date of its publication. No map before that time shews the Island of Frisland with names thereon tallying with the names of the Færoe islands. No map before 1558 shews the discoveries of the Northmen in America, nor were any of the Sagas known to the Venetians before that time; nor do any books previous to that period set forth the geography of those parts from which Nicolò Zeno could have stolen information. Moreover the correspondence of the Zeno map with surveys much later, as in Davis's Straits, is highly corroborative of its genuineness. Mr. Kohl, in his most valuable *Documentary History of Discovery of the East Coast of North America*, printed by the Maine Historical Society, 1869, 8vo., suggests that Icaria is Helluland or Newfoundland; Estotiland, Markland or Nova Scotia; and Drogeo, Vinland or New England: and he further justly remarks that, assuming that the map is genuine, "it is the first and oldest known to us on which some sections of the continent of America have been laid down."

On an anonymous map in Weimar of the date of

1424, and on a map by Andrea Bianco,* in the library of St. Mark, bearing the date of 1436, is laid down a large extent of land, five or six hundred leagues west of Gibraltar, above which is written the word "Antillia." With reference to this subject, Martin Behaim, on his globe of 1492, says, "In the year 734, after the conquest of Spain by the Mahometans, this island Antillia was discovered and settled by an archbishop from Oporto, who fled to it in ships with six other bishops and other Christian men and women. They built there seven towns, from which circumstance it has also been called Septem Citade, the island of the seven cities. In the year 1414 a Spanish vessel came very near to it." Of the island of S. Brandan also, which is laid down on charts of the fourteenth century, Behaim says, "In the year 565, Saint Brandan, an Irish bishop, arrived with his vessel on this island, saw there most wonderful things, and returned afterwards to his country." Another of these fancied islands in the Atlantic was the island of Brazil. So strong was the belief in the existence of these islands, that we find it stated by Pedro de Ayala, a Spanish envoy in England writing to the sovereigns in 1498, that the Bristol men had sent out every year from 1491 (before Columbus's first great discovery) to 1497, two, three, or four caravels every year in search of the islands of Brazil and the seven cities, at the instigation of John Cabot.

* A copy of this map is given in the second vol. of Sastre's *Mercurio Italico*, Lond. 1789, 8vo., and a photograph of it was published in Venice in 1869 by H. F. and M. Münster.

The following passage occurs in Sir John Barrow's *Chronological History of Voyages in the Arctic Regions*, which, if it stated a defensible truth, would present another claim, anterior to that of Columbus, to the discovery of America. The passage is headed " Cortereals, 1500";—

" The Portuguese, not content with having discovered a route to India, by sailing round the tempestuous extremity to Africa, soon after engaged in an equally dangerous enterprise : that of finding a route to India and the Spice Islands, by sailing westward round the northern extremity of America. This bold undertaking was reserved for the CORTEREALS, the enlightened disciples of the school of Sagres. The first navigator of the name of Cortereal, who engaged in this enterprise, was John Vaz Costa Cortereal, a gentleman of the household of the infant Dom Fernando, who, accompanied by Alvaro Martens Homem, explored the northern seas, by order of king Affonso the Fifth, and discovered the *Terra de Baccalhaos* (the land of cod fish), afterwards called Newfoundland. This voyage is mentioned by Cordeiro,[*] but he does not state the exact date, which however is ascertained to have been in 1463 or 1464 ; for, in their return from the discovery of Newfoundland, or Terra Nova, they touched at the island of Terceira, the captaincy of which island having become vacant by the death of Jacomo Bruges, they solicited the appointment, and in reward for their services the re-

[*] The work quoted is Cordeyro's *Historia Insulana das Ilhas a Portugal sugeytas no Oceano Occidental*, Lisbon 1717.

quest was granted, their patent commission being dated in Evora, 2nd April, 1464."

It will be seen by the wording of this passage, that Sir John Barrow has fallen into the inaccuracy of asserting that, in 1463 or 1464, Cortereal was engaged in the enterprise of finding a route to India and the Spice Islands by sailing westward round the northern extremities of America. We must presume that the Portuguese were aware of the existence of the American continent, before they could conceive the idea of sailing westward round its northern extremity. The patent commission of the appointment of Cortereal and Homem to the government of Terceira does not specify that the service for which it was granted, was the discovery of Newfoundland; and, moreover, at the end of Faria y Sousa's *Asia Portuguesa*, there is a list of all the armadas which sailed from Lisbon on voyages of discovery between 1412 and 1640, and this expedition is passed by in silence; so that the validity of the whole statement hangs on the authority of Cordeiro : but the account is altogether so extremely improbable, from the very silence of Portuguese writers of the time on so important a subject, as to leave Cortereal but small chance of a successful rivalry with Sebastian Cabot.*

The last on the list of those who have been said to

* For a demonstration that the discovery of the east coast of North America was made by Sebastian Cabot in 1497, a year before Columbus reached the terra firma, I must refer the reader to a paper of mine read before the Society of Antiquaries on May 5, 1870, and now being printed for the *Archæologia*.

precede Columbus in the discovery of America is a Polish pilot, named John Szkolny, whose name has been erroneously Latinized by Hornius, Zurla, Malte Brun, Wytfliet, and Pontanus, "Scolvus," or "Sciolvus." He was in the service of Christian II of Denmark in the year 1476. He is said to have landed on the coast of Labrador, after having passed along Norway, Greenland, and the Friseland of the Zeni. Upon this subject Von Humboldt thus expresses himself: " I cannot hazard any opinion upon the statement made to this effect by Wytfliet, Pontanus, and Horn. A country seen *after* Greenland may, from the direction indicated, have been Labrador. I am, however, surprised to find that Gomara, who published his *Historia de las Indias* at Saragossa, in 1553, was cognizant even at that time of this Polish pilot. It is possible that when the codfishery began to bring the seamen of southern Europe into more frequent connexion with those of the north, a suspicion may have arisen that the land seen by Szkolny must have been the same as that visited by John Sebastian Cabot in 1497, and by Gaspar Cortereal in 1500. Gomara says what is in other respects not quite correct, *that the English took much pleasure in frequenting the coast of Labrador, for they found the latitude and climate the same as that of their native land, and the men of Norway have been there with the pilot, John Scolvo, as well as the English with Sebastian Cabot.* Let us not forget that Gomara makes no mention of the Polish pilot with reference to the question of the predecessors of Columbus,

though he is malignant enough to assert that it is in fact impossible to say to whom the discovery of the New Indies is due."*

In the American Philosophical Transactions for 1786, is a letter addressed to Dr. Franklin by Mr. Otto of New York, in which he not only asserts that the illustrious cosmographer Martin Behaim discovered the Azores, but quotes a passage, from what he calls an authentic record, preserved in the archives of Nuremberg, the tenor of which is as follows :— " Martin Behem, traversing the Atlantic Ocean for several years, examined the American Islands, and discovered the strait which bears the name of Magellan, before either Christopher Columbus or Magellan navigated those seas ; and even mathematically.delineated on a geographical chart for the king of Lusitania, the situation of the coast around every part of that famous and renowned strait." He also quotes passages from the *Nuremberg Chronicle*, and from Cellarius, in confirmation of this statement. Don Cristóbal Cladera, in his *Investigaciones Históricas*, says that, in order to refute these statements, he procured from Nuremberg a description of Behaim's globe, together with historical notes on the life and family of that geographer, and upon examining these and the unpublished works of the Academia de las

* Humboldt has fallen into an error in saying that Joachim Lelewel, in his *Pisma pomniejsze geogr. historyczné*, 1814, has recently called up fresh attention to this Polish pilot. The editor has examined the work carefully from beginning to end, and does not find the name even once mentioned, although the page to which reference is made contains allusions to early discoveries.

Ciencias de Lisboa, he became convinced that the observations of Mr. Otto were totally unfounded; and De Murr, who has well investigated the question, assures us that the passage quoted by Mr. Otto from the *Nuremberg Chronicle* was not to be found in the German translation of that work by George Alt in 1493. Moreover, the real globe of Behaim, made in 1492, does not contain any of the islands or shores of the New World; a fact which sets at rest the two questions of Behaim's earlier discovery, or of Colombus gaining his information from Behaim.*

From the series of evidences contained in the preceding accounts, the fact that America had been visited by European adventurers before the time of Columbus is rendered too certain to admit of contradiction even from the most sanguine advocate of the glory of the great discoverer. But, on the other side, it cannot be denied that the discovery of Columbus, however much later in date, deserves the meed of highest honour, as being the result of sagacity, judgment and indomitable perseverance, and as having been carried on with an energetic endeavour to bring into active operation the incalculable advantages which it opened up to the world at large. To vindicate the correctness of this statement, it will be well to give a brief sketch of his eventful life, and to pourtray as briefly as we may the high qualities to which, far more than

---

* A copy of this globe is given in Dr. F. W. Ghillany's *Geschichte des Seefahrers Ritter Martin Behaim*, Nürnberg, 1853, 4to.

to accidental circumstances, the glory of this great discovery is due. The retrospect of his history will at the same time shew, that while every previous discovery was attributable to accident, the greater portion of the accidental or uncontrollable circumstances in the life of Columbus were such as, instead of assisting him, tended to thwart him at every step of his painful career.

It is generally agreed that his father was a wool weaver or carder. There is reason, however, to presume that though his parentage was humble, he was descended from a family of consideration. On this subject his son, Don Ferdinand, denies* with great indignation an assertion which occurs in a curious life of the admiral, inserted in the *Psalterium Octuplex Augustini Justiniani,*" Genoa, 1516, folio, under the comments on the nineteenth psalm, that he was " vilibus ortus parentibus," and complains that he is falsely called a mechanic.

The date of his birth is a "vexata quæstio," which it would be well that we should here examine. For settling a disputed question of the kind no process seems so sure as the comparing of statements made by the same individual, if he be a good authority, at different times and under different circumstances. The following are two statements made by Columbus himself at entirely different periods and in an entirely different shape, and yet both having the same result. They are recorded by his son, Fernando, in the Biography of his father, and are as follows : " In his

* *Historie del S. D. Fernando Colombo*, cap. iv.

book of his first voyage [1492] he says, ' I was upon the sea twenty-three years without being off it any time worth the speaking of, and I saw all the East and all the West, and may say towards the North or England, and have been at Guinea. Yet I never saw harbours for goodness like those of the West Indies,' and a little further he says, ' That he took to the sea at fourteen years of age and ever after followed it.' Now we know for certain that he escaped from Lisbon and came to Andalusia at the close of 1484 ; that during his stay in Portugal he had made many voyages to Guinea, but that from 1484 until his first great voyage in 1492 he was engaged, not at sea, but in endeavouring to secure the interest of the Spanish sovereigns in his important project./ If then we add his twenty-three years of almost constant sea-going to fourteen, his age when he first went to sea, we have thirty-seven years to deduct from 1484, and we find 1447 to be the date of his birth. Again in 1501, many years later, he writes to the Spanish sovereigns as follows: "I went to sea very young and have continued it to this day;...it is now forty years that I have been sailing to all those parts at present frequented." What "very young" meant he had already told us; viz, 14, which added to 40 makes 54; and this total deducted from 1501, the date at which he writes, leaves the same date for his birth as that resulting from his former statement, viz, 1447. But for the sake of attaining as near to accuracy as possible, we must not overlook another statement made in 1503 by Columbus himself in his letter to Ferdi-

d

nand and Isabella, describing his fourth voyage. He there says "I was twenty-eight years old when I came into Your Highnesses service, and now I have not a hair upon me that is not grey." It was in 1484 that he went to Spain, and then, as we have seen, terminated those three-and-twenty years of almost uninterrupted sea-faring life of which he speaks. Now, if he were then only eight-and-twenty, he must have first gone to sea at the age of five instead of fourteen, as he himself informs us. Moreover, by that reckoning he would have been only fifty when he died, in 1506, an age entirely incompatible with the statement of Bernaldez, the Cura de los Palacios, who knew Columbus so well, that he died *in senectute bonâ*, at the age of seventy, more or less. It is intelligible that such a remark should be made of a man of sixty, who had passed through hardships so exhausting to the mind and body as those which had marked the life of Columbus, but scarcely even of him at the age of fifty. It is clear, then, that a mistake has been made in this number 28, but if for it we write 38, it will make the date of Columbus's birth to be 1446. We have, however, to bear in mind that the two statements previously made by him were of a very general character, in which no month or part of a year was specified. It would therefore seem that, on his own showing, we shall be safe in placing the date of his birth 1446-47, which agrees with the inference of the learned and judicious Muñoz, who places it "por los años 1446," although he does not show the process by which he arrives at his conclusion.

With respect to the birthplace of our illustrious navigator, were we to enter into the complex discussions of those who, with different arguments of more or less plausibility, place it in Genoa, Nervi, Savona, Pradello, Cogoleto, Quinto, Bogliasco, Albisola, Chiavara, Oneglia, or the castle of Cuccaro in Monferrato, —we should but launch upon a sea of difficulties, with little hope of a successful voyage. It is difficult to withhold credence from the strong assertion made twice by Columbus in his will, dated 22nd February 1498, that he was born in the city of Genoa; namely, —"I, being a native of Genoa"; and "I desire my said son Diego, or the person who may succeed to the said inheritance, always to keep and maintain one person of our lineage in the city of Genoa...because from thence I came, and there I was born."* But in like manner we know that Leonardo, who was born at Vinci, persisted in calling himself a Florentine.

Having early evinced a strong inclination for the study of geography, geometry, and astronomy, Columbus found at the college of Pavia an excellent opportunity of gaining a more than superficial acquaintance with the principles of those sciences, and at the same time acquired considerable proficiency in the Latin language. The maritime position and commercial engagements of his native city doubtless suggested and

* " *Siendo yo nacido en Genova*"; and "*mando al dicho Don Diego, mi hijo, a la persona que heredare el dicho mayorazgo que tenga y sostenga siempre en la Ciudad de Genova una persona de nuestro linage...pues que della sali y en ella naci.*"

fostered much of that propensity for a nautical life, that he exhibited at so early an age; and although it appears from several historians that for a short time he worked at his father's trade, yet this must have been simply during his earliest boyhood, for by his own account he commenced the life of a mariner at fourteen years of age. The piratical character of the seafaring life of those days necessarily exposed its followers to unceasing hardships and dangers, and the severity of this early discipline must have most materially tended to render available and permanent those distinguished qualities which have subsequently gained for him the admiration of the world: indeed, no career could have been better calculated to develope his peculiar genius, or add fuel to those enthusiastic aspirations which characterised him to the close of his life.

From the period of his going to sea, which was about the year 1460 until the year 1472, we meet with no distinct mention of his name; although in a letter written by him to their Majesties, in 1495, he says: "*It happened to me that king Réné (whom God has taken to himself) sent me to Tunis to capture the galley Fernandina, and on arriving at the island of San Pedro, in Sardinia, I learned that there were two ships and a caracca with the galley, which so alarmed the crew that they resolved to proceed no further, but to return to Marseilles for another vessel and more people; upon which, being unable to force their inclination, I yielded to their wish, and having first changed the points of the compass, spread all sail, for it was evening, and at daybreak we were*

within the cape of Carthagena, while all believed for a certainty that they were going to Marseilles." The date of this occurrence is unknown, but the expedient of Columbus to alter the point of the needle, reminds us of his subsequent stratagem, of altering his reckoning, to appease his discontented crew during his first great voyage of discovery.

In the year 1472, however, we have evidence of his having been in Savona, from the fact of his signature having been found appended to the will of one Nicolò Monleone, under date of the 20th March of that year. The document is preserved in Savona, among the notarial archives.

In 1474 we find his name mentioned in a letter addressed by Ferdinand king of Sicily to Louis king of France, the title of which runs thus: "*Literæ à Ferdinando Rege Siciliæ ad Ludovicum XI, Galliæ Regem, per Fæcialem missæ, quibus quæritur, quod Christophorus Columbus triremes suas deprædatus sit, postulatque sibi ablata restitui. Datum in Terra Fogiæ die 8 Decembr. 1474.*" Then follows a letter in five lengthy clauses, in which it is stated that the said vessels were attacked and taken:—"*A Columbo, qui quibusdam navibus præest, Majestatis vestræ subdito.*"

The title of Louis's reply runs thus: "*Responsio Ludovici XI quibus promittit restitutionem, excusat tamen Columbum, quod jus sit in Oceano capere naves ab hostilibus terris venientes et saltem bona hostium inde auferre.*" These letters are given by Leibnitz, in his *Codex Juris Gentium Diplomaticus*,

Prodromus, art. 16 and 17; but on the correction of Nicolas Toinard, he acknowledges, in the preface to his *Mantissa Codicis*, that he had erroneously inserted the Christian name "Christophorus."

Toinard's correction went to shew that Leibnitz had confounded the name of Guillaume de Caseneuve, surnamed Coulomp, Coulon, or Colon, as the Spaniards called him, with that of the illustrious discoverer. This acknowledgment by Leibnitz of his error might seem to render useless any reference to the letters in question; but as Christopher Columbus is stated by his son, Don Ferdinand, to have been of the same family as the pirate here mentioned, and also to have been engaged at sea with him and his nephew, it becomes interesting to examine what record exists of these illustrious pirates, and to see how far the assertion of Don Ferdinand bears the semblance of correctness. This Caseneuve, or Colon, is called by Duclos, in speaking of the very circumstance which occasioned these letters, in his *Histoire de Louis XI*, " *Vice-Amiral de France, et le plus grand homme de mer de son temps.*" And Zurita, in his *Libro* 19 *de los Anales de Aragon*, calls him, " *Colon, capitan de la Armada del Rey de Francia.*" Garnier, in his *Histoire de France*, thus relates the circumstance: " *Guillaume de Casenove, Vice-Amiral de Normandie, connu dans notre histoire sous le nom d'Amiral Coulon, s'était rendu formidable sur toutes les mers de l'Europe, où il exerçait le métier d'armateur: dans une de ses courses il s'empara de deux riches frégates chargées pour le compte des plus riches*

négocians de Naples, de Florence, et de plusieurs autres villes d'Italie, qui tout sollicitèrent vivement la restitution de cette importante prise."

Another exploit, in which this Colon was successfully engaged, was the taking of eighty Dutch ships returning from the herring fishery, in the Baltic, in 1479. Again, another sea-fight related by Marc Antonio Sabelico, in the eighth book of his tenth Decade, is quoted by Don Fernando, where Columbus the younger (described by Sabelico as the nephew, but by Zurita as Francis, the son of the famous corsair), intercepted, between Lisbon and Cape St. Vincent, four richly laden Venetian galleys, on their return from Flanders. Fernando further asserts that his father (Christopher) was present in this engagement, and that after a desperate contest, which lasted from morning till evening, the hand-grenades and other fiery missiles used in the battle, caused a general conflagration among the vessels, which having been lashed together with iron grapplings, could not be separated, and the crews were compelled to leap into the water to escape the fire. He then goes on to say that "his father, who was a good swimmer, finding himself at the distance of two leagues from the land, seized an oar, and by its aid succeeded in reaching the shore. Whereupon, learning that he was not far from Lisbon, where he knew he should find many natives of Genoa, he went thither, and meeting with a gratifying reception, took up his abode in that city." The engagement here described is shown by various French historians to have taken place in 1485, and as it is certain that

Columbus was in Lisbon prior to 1474 (for in that year he has a letter addressed to him in that city by Paolo Toscanelli, in reply to one written by himself from the same place), this relation by Don Ferdinand assumes a very apocryphal aspect.

With respect to his other statement, that his father was of the same name and family as these two renowned corsairs, it is to be remarked that neither he nor any of the subsequent historians who have claimed this needless honour for the great discoverer, appears to have been acquainted with the real name of the pirates; and as Caseneuve was the strict family name of the latter, and Coulon merely a superadded surname, we may fairly conclude that the claim to consanguinity has no other foundation than the identity in the Spanish language of Columbus's patronymic with the distinguishing surname of the French vice-admiral.

In the *Chronique Scandaleuse* (folio 109) this Caseneuve is said to have had a very handsome mansion, named Gaillart-Bois, in the neighbourhood of Notre Dame d'Escouys, in Normandy, at which Louis XI made a stay of two or three days in the month of June 1475, and returned thither also in the following month and stayed there some time. Spotorno suggests that his name of Coulon may have been derived from a place so called in the province of Berri; so that, in addition to the evidence that he was not of the same name or family with Christopher Columbus, there arises strong reason to believe that he was in

reality a Frenchman:* in which case it becomes probable that an event which has been generally attributed to him, or to his still more renowned relative François Caseneuve, would be with greater correctness ascribed to the Genoese navigator, Christopher Columbus. It appears that, in a letter dated Terra d'Otranto, 2nd October, 1476 (preserved, according to Bossi, in the royal archives at Milan), addressed to the Duke of Milan by two illustrious gentlemen of that city,—the one Guid'Antonio Arcimboldo, and the other Giovanni Giacomo Trivulzio—the following story is related. It says that the captain of the Venetian fleet, when stationed off Cyprus to defend the island, had twice encountered a *Genoese* ship, called the "Nave Palavisina," which he had taken to be a Turkish caracca; and in these two engagements one hundred and twenty of the Turks and Genoese had been killed, and in the Venetian squadron thirty had been killed, and two hundred wounded. The captain appears to have had doubts whether he might not have done wrong, and caused offence to the duke of Milan, who might perhaps be an ally of the Genoese: he therefore goes on to say that his only desire had been to meet with his enemies (the Turks) and plunder them; and adds, in confirmation of that assertion, that "a year before he had met with three times as many galleys, who spoke no evil of his good name, and that he found Columbus with ships and galleys, and

* Another Caseneuve, probably of this family, is said by De Bry to have been captain of the fourth expedition of the French to Mexico, in the year 1567.

had cheerfully let him pass by, upon which the cry was raised of 'Viva San Georgio,' and nothing further passed between them." The Columbus here mentioned is shewn, by the cry of "Viva San Georgio," and by the general tenour of the Venetian captain's letter, to have been a Genoese, and with a Genoese crew; and as it appears probable that the Caseneuves were Frenchmen, and would in all probability sail with French crews, it leaves strong reason to presume that the Genoese captain here mentioned was Christopher Columbus, who is allowed by all his early historians to have been engaged in the Mediterranean about the period referred to.

His son, Ferdinand Columbus, distinctly states that, "it was in Portugal that the admiral began to surmise, that, if the Portuguese sailed so far south, one might also sail westward, and find lands in that direction."

The period of Christopher Columbus's sojourn in Portugal was from 1470 to the close of 1484, during which time he made several voyages to the coast of Guinea in the Portuguese service. ⎧While at Lisbon he married Felipa Moñiz de Perestrello, daughter of that Bartollomeu Perestrello to whom Prince Henry had granted the commandership of the island of Porto Santo.⎫ For some time Columbus and his wife lived at Porto Santo with the widow of Perestrello, who, observing the interest he took in nautical matters, spoke much to him of her husband's expedition, and handed over to him the papers, journals,

maps, and nautical instruments, which Perestrello had left behind him.*

" It was not only," says Ferdinand Columbus (see *Vida*, cap. 8), "this opinion of certain philosophers, that the greatest part of our globe is dry land, that stimulated the admiral; he learned, also, from many pilots, experienced in the western voyages to the Azores and the Island of Madeira, facts and signs which convinced him that there was an unknown land towards the west. Martin Vicente, pilot of the King of Portugal, told him that at a distance of four hundred and fifty leagues from Cape St. Vincent, he had taken from the water a piece of wood sculptured very artistically, but not with an iron instrument. This wood had been driven across by the west wind, which made the sailors believe, that certainly there were on that side some islands not yet discovered. Pedro Correa, the brother-in-law of Columbus, told him, that near the island of Madeira he had found a similar piece of sculptured wood, and coming from the same western direction. He also said that the King of

* Las Casas, in his *History of the Indies*, tells us distinctly that Columbus derived much information from Perestrello's maps and papers, and adds that " in order to acquaint himself practically with the method pursued by the Portuguese in navigating to the coast of Guinea, he sailed several times with them as if he had been one of them." Las Casas says that he learned this from the admiral's son Diego, adding that " some time before his famous voyage Columbus resided in Madeira, where news of fresh discoveries was constantly arriving, and this," he says, " appeared to have been the occasion of Christopher Columbus coming to Spain, and the beginning of the discovery of this great world" (America).

Portugal had received information of large canes having been taken up from the water in these parts, which between one knot and another would hold nine bottles of wine; and Herrera (Dec. 1, lib. 1, cap. 2) declares that the king had preserved these canes, and caused them to be shown to Columbus. The colonists of the Azores related, that when the wind blew from the west, the sea threw up, especially in the islands of Graciosa and Fayal, pines of a foreign species. Others related, that in the island of Flores they found one day on the shore two corpses of men, whose physiognomy and features differed entirely from those of our coasts. Herrera, perhaps from the MSS. of Las Casas, says, that the corpses had broad faces, different from those of Christians. The transport of these objects was attributed to the action of the west winds. The true cause, however, was the great current of the Gulf or Florida stream. The west and north-west winds only increase the ordinary rapidity of the ocean current, prolong its action towards the east, as far as the Bay of Biscay, and mix the waters of the Gulf stream with those of the currents of Davis' Straits and of North Africa. The same eastward oceanic movement, which in the fifteenth century carried bamboos and pines upon the shores of the Azores and Porto Santo, deposits annually on Ireland, the Hebrides, and Norway, the seeds of tropical plants, and the remains of cargoes of ships which had been wrecked in the West Indies.*

While availing himself of these sources of informa-

* Humboldt, *Examen Critique*, vol. ii, p. 246-251.

tion, Columbus studied with deep and careful attention the works of such geographical authors as supplied suggestions of the feasibility of a short western passage to India. Amongst these, the *Imago Mundi* of Cardinal Pierre d'Ailly (Petrus de Aliaco) was his favourite, and it is probable that from it he culled all he knew of the opinions of Aristotle, Strabo, and Seneca, respecting the facility of reaching India by a western route. Columbus's own copy of this work is now in the cathedral of Seville, and forms one of the most precious items in the valuable library, originally collected by his son Ferdinand, and bequeathed to the cathedral on condition of its being constantly preserved for public use. It contains many marginal notes in his own handwriting, but of comparatively little importance.

The fondness of Columbus for the works of Pierre d'Ailly, a Frenchman, has caused a recent French writer, M. Margry, to put forth the empty pretension that the discovery of America was due to the influence of French teaching, whereas, not only was the *Imago Mundi* itself a compilation from ancient authors, but the first edition was not printed till many years after Columbus had devoted himself to the purpose which ended in his great discovery, for his famous correspondence with Toscanelli, of which I shall presently speak, occurred in 1474. M. Margry, indeed, *asserts*, but without giving his authority, that in the Columbian Library at Seville are D'Ailly's treatises *printed at Nuremberg in* 1472. This is in contravention of all the bibliographers — Panzer,

Ebert, Hain, Serna Santander, Lambinet, and Jean de Launoy. The earliest date assigned to the first edition of the *Imago Mundi*, is *about* 1480 by Serna Santander, 1483 (?) by Lambinet, while Jean de Launoy, in his *Regii Navarræ Gymnasii Parisiensis Historia*, Parisiis, 1677, tom. ii, page 478, distinctly gives it the date of 1490. Humboldt, who had Columbus's copy in his hands, and who, as the subject was especially his own, cannot be suspected of sleeping over such an important point, adopts De Launoy's date of 1490, while Lambinet gives the queried date of 1483 from actual collation with another work printed in that year, at Louvain, in the very identical type, by John of Westphalia. In the recently published second volume of the *Ensayo de una bibliotheca de libros españoles raros*, por Don Bartolomé Gallardo, is a list of the books in the Columbian Library, but D'Ailly's *Imago Mundi* is not therein mentioned, although his *Quæstiones*, printed much later by Jean Petit at Paris, a far less important book, is inserted. The omission is to be regretted, as we might have hoped for some illustrative comments from the author.

But perhaps it may be suggested that Columbus may have possessed, or seen, a *manuscript* copy of Pierre d'Ailly at a yet earlier period. We will willingly suppose it for the sake of the argument; but even then the reasoning will fail, for I find that the very portion of the *Imago Mundi*, written in 1410, which is assumed to have supplied the inspiration

for the discovery of America, and which Columbus quoted in his letter to Ferdinand and Isabella from Haiti in 1498, is *taken by Pierre d'Ailly, without acknowledgment, almost word for word, from the " Opus Majus," of Roger Bacon*, written in 1267, a hundred and forty-three years before, as will be seen at page 183 of that work, printed Londini, 1733, fol. See Humboldt, *Examen Critique*, tom. i, pp. 64—70.

Unfortunately Roger Bacon was not a Frenchman, but there remains for M. Margry the consolatory fact that no Englishman is likely to avail himself of the circumstance which I have just enunciated, to claim for his countrymen the honour of having inspired Columbus with the idea which led to the discovery of America, although, by M. Margry's process of reasoning, he might do so if he would. True, Roger Bacon had been a student in the University of Paris; but this fact did not communicate the character of French inspiration to the ancient authors whose statements he quotes. True also (but this is a circumstance either unknown to or unnoticed by M. Margry), Ferdinand Columbus tells us that his father was principally influenced in his belief of the smallness of the space between Spain and Asia, by the opinion of the Arab astronomer, Al Fergani, or Alfragan, to that effect; and it is further true that Alfragan is further treated of by Pierre d'Ailly, in his *Mappa Mundi*. This is a separate work from the *Imago Mundi*, although it happens to have been printed with it, at a period which we have shown to

be posterior to Columbus's correspondence with Toscanelli, in 1474.

It follows, therefore, that either: 1st, the great explorer obtained his knowledge of Alfragan's opinion through one of the Arabo-Latin translations, to which he seems to have had recourse during his cosmographical studies in Portugal and Spain (see Humboldt, *Examen Critique*, tom. i, p. 83), in which case French influence is eliminated; or 2ndly, he derived it from a manuscript of Pierre d'Ailly before 1474, which there is no evidence to show; or 3rdly, he derived it from the printed copy of Pierre d'Ailly, in which case the influence of Alfragan on his mind could not have been primarily suggestive, but only corroborative of conclusions to which he had come several years before that book was printed. And in either of the two latter cases, the information supplied by Alfragan would not become French because adduced by a Frenchman, unless we introduce into serious history a principle analogous to the old conventional English blunder of giving to the toys manufactured in Nuremberg the name of "Dutch toys," because imported through Holland.

The suggestions derived from these works were corroborated by the /narratives of Marco Polo and Sir John Mandeville, whose reports of the vast extent of Asia eastward led to the reasonable inference, that the western passage to the eastern confines of that continent could not demand any considerable length of time. | The natural tendency of his thoughts to nautical enterprise being thus fostered by the works

that he studied, and by the animating accounts of
recent adventurers, as well as by the glorious prospects which the broad expanse of the unknown world
opened up to his view, we find that in the year 1474
his ideas had formed for themselves a determined
channel, and his grand project of discovery was
established in his mind as a thing to be done, and
done by himself. /The combined enthusiasm and
tenacity of purpose which distinguished his character,
caused him to regard his theory, when once formed,
as a matter of such undeniable certainty, that no
doubts, opposition, or disappointment, could divert
him from the pursuit of it./ It so happened that
while Columbus was at Lisbon a correspondence was
being carried on between Fernam Martins, a prebendary of that place, and the learned Paolo Toscanelli, of Florence, respecting the commerce of the
Portuguese to the coast of Guinea, and the navigation of the ocean to the Westward. This came to the
knowledge of Columbus, who forthwith despatched
by an Italian, then at his house, a letter to Toscanelli,
informing him of his project. He received an answer
in Latin, in which, to demonstrate his approbation of
the design of Columbus, Toscanelli sent him a copy
of a letter which he had written to Martins a few
days before, accompanied by a chart, the most important features of which were laid down from the
descriptions of Marco Polo. The coasts of Asia were
drawn at a moderate distance from the opposite
coasts of Europe and Africa, and the islands of Cipango, Antilla, etc., of whose riches such astonishing

accounts had been given by this traveller, were placed at convenient spaces between the two continents.

While all these exciting accounts must have conspired to fan the flame of his ambition, one of the noblest points in the character of Columbus had to be put to the test by the difficulty of carrying his project into effect. The political position of Portugal, engrossed as it was with its wars with Spain, rendered the thoughts of an application for an expensive fleet of discovery worse than useless, and several years elapsed before a convenient opportunity presented itself for making the proposition.

Meanwhile Columbus was not idle. In the year 1477, he tells us, in a letter quoted by his son, Don Ferdinand, that "*he sailed a hundred leagues beyond the island of Thule, the southern part of which is distant from the equinoctial line seventy-three degrees, and not sixty-three, as some assert; neither does it lie within the line which includes the west of Ptolemy, but is much more westerly. To this island, which is as large as England, the English, especially those from Bristol, go with their merchandize. At the time that I was there the sea was not frozen, but the tides were so great as to rise and fall twenty-six fathoms. It is true that the Thule of which Ptolemy makes mention lies where he says it does, and by the moderns it is called Frislanda.*" Whether the Fœroe islands [see ante, page xxiii], or Iceland, was alluded to is uncertain, for nothing more is known of the voyage than is contained in this letter. It is more-

INTRODUCTION.

over supposed by his son, as has been already stated, that he passed a considerable portion of his time at sea, with one or both of the famous pirates of the same name, who were so many years engaged in the Levant; but upon the whole of this portion of his history there rests an impenetrable cloud of obscurity. About the year 1480, by the joint labours of the celebrated Martin Behaim and the prince's two physicians, Roderigo and Josef, who were the most able geographers and astronomers in the kingdom, the astrolabe was rendered serviceable for the purposes of navigation, as by its use the seaman was enabled to ascertain his distance from the equator by the altitude of the sun.

Shortly after this invaluable invention Columbus submitted to the king of Portugal his proposition of a voyage of discovery, and succeeded in obtaining an audience to advocate his cause. He explained his views with respect to the facility of the undertaking, from the form of the earth, and the comparatively small space that intervened between Europe and the eastern shores of Asia, and proposed, if the king would supply him with ships and men, to take the direct western route to India across the Atlantic. His application was received at first discouragingly, but the king was at length induced, by the excellent arguments of Columbus, to make a conditional concession, and the result was that the proposition was referred to a council of men supposed to be learned in maritime affairs. This council, consisting of the above-mentioned geographers, Roderigo

and Josef, and Cazadilla, bishop of Ceuta, the king's confessor, treated the question as an extravagant absurdity. The king, not satisfied with their judgment, then convoked a second council, consisting of a considerable number of the most learned men in the kingdom; but the result of their deliberations was only confirmative of the verdict of the first junta, and a general sentence of condemnation was passed upon the proposition. As the king still manifested an inclination to make a trial of the scheme of Columbus, and expressed a proportionate dissatisfaction with the decisions of these two juntas, some of his councillors, who were inimical to Columbus, and at the same time unwilling to offend the king, suggested a process which coincided with their own views, but which was at once short-sighted, impolitic, and ungenerous. Their plan was to procure from Columbus a detailed account of his design under the pretence of subjecting it to the examination of the council, and then to dispatch a caravel on the voyage of discovery under the false pretext of conveying provision to the Cape Verde Islands. King John, contrary to his general character for prudence and generosity, yielded to their insidious advice, and their plan was acted upon, but the caravel which was sent out, after keeping on its westward course for some days, encountered a storm, and the crew, possessing none of the lofty motives of Columbus to support their resolution, returned to Lisbon, ridiculing the scheme in excuse of their own cowardice. So indignant was Columbus at this unworthy manœuvre, that he re-

INTRODUCTION. liii

solved to leave Portugal and offer his services to some other country, and towards the end of 1484 he left Lisbon secretly with his son Diego. The learned and careful Muñoz states his opinion that he went immediately to Genoa, and made a personal proposition to that government, but met with a contemptuous refusal; at any rate, we are positively informed by Fernando Columbus that his father went to Spain at the close of 1484. A curious surmise is expressed in a note to Sharon Turner's *History of England in the Middle Ages*, in which the supposition is propounded of the possible identity of Christopher Columbus with a person named Christofre Colyns, who is recorded in some grants in the Harleian MSS. to have been military commandant of Queenborough castle, in the isle of Sheppy, in 1484 and 1485. This man is distinctly stated in the same grants to have held that post in April 1485, and it may be reasonably conjectured that the cessation of his office would not take place till the accession of Henry VII, in August in that year, which leaves but little time for his making his way to Genoa, and subsequently reaching Spain, so as to make his application to that court. Moreover, the impoverished condition in which Columbus presented himself at the convent de la Rabida was very incompatible with the probable pecuniary position of a person, who is described by the grants in question not only to have held the prominent station already mentioned, but to have had a ship given him, with an annuity of £100, and an especial grant of money to enable him to supply

himself with habiliments of war. These considerations, combined with the statement of Fernando Columbus just referred to, show that the supposition proposed by Mr. Turner cannot be regarded as tenable.

The interesting story of Columbus's visit to the Franciscan convent of Santa Maria de Rabida forms the first incident that we find recorded of him after his arrival in Spain. It is well known that the lively interest which the worthy prior of that convent, Fray Juan Perez de Marchena, took in his guest, was the means, through the anticipated influence of his friend Fernando de Talavera, of first leading Columbus to the Spanish court, under the hope of obtaining the patronage of the king and queen. Talavera, who was prior of the monastery of Prado, and confessor to the queen, possessed great political interest. Juan Perez took advantage of this influential position of his friend, and addressed him a letter by the hands of Columbus, strongly recommending the project of the latter to his favourable consideration, and requesting his advocacy of it before the sovereigns. It was in the spring of 1486 that Columbus first ventured to the Spanish court in the hope of gaining a favourable audience. On reaching Cordova, however, he had the mortification to find that Talavera, upon whose influence he mainly relied, regarded his design as unreasonable and preposterous. The court also was at that time so engrossed with the war at Granada, as to place any hope of gaining attention to his novel and expensive proposition out

of the question. / At length, at the close of 1486, the theory of Columbus, backed as it was by his forcible arguments and earnest manner, gained weight with the most important personage at court next to the sovereigns themselves. This was Mendoza, archbishop of Toledo, and grand cardinal of Spain; who, pleased with the grandeur of the scheme and the fervent but clear-headed reasoning of Columbus, adopted his cause, and became his staunch protector and friend. Through his means an audience was procured with the sovereigns, and the result of the interview was the expression of a favourable opinion, qualified by the necessity of an appeal to the judgment of the literati of the country. But here again Columbus found himself in a painful predicament, which it required all his knowledge and prudence to escape from with safety. He was examined at Salamanca by a council of ecclesiastics, and had to propound opinions which appeared to be at variance with the descriptions contained in the sacred Scriptures, and that at a period when the expression of any sentiment approaching to heresy exposed its owner to the persecution of the newly established Inquisition. / The ignorance of cosmography, and the blind conclusions drawn from various misinterpreted texts of Scripture, formed mighty impediments to the pleadings of Columbus, and he began to find himself in danger of being convicted not only of error, but of heresy. One learned man of the number, however, Diego de Deza, tutor to prince John, and afterwards archbishop of Seville, appreciated the

eloquent and lucid reasonings of the adventurer, and aiding him with his own powers of language and erudition, not only gained for him a hearing, but won upon the judgments of some of the most learned of the council. Nevertheless, so important a question could not be hastily decided; and the result of the united pedantry and sluggish superstition of the learned body, was to expose the question to protracted argumentation or neglect, while Talavera, who was at its head, and from whom Columbus had hoped to receive the greatest assistance, was too busied with political matters to bring it to a conclusion. At length, in the early part of 1487, the deliberations of the council were brought to a stand-still by the departure of the court to Cordova, and were not resumed till the winter of 1491. During this wearisome period the bustle and excitement of the memorable campaign against the Moors, with its alternations of triumphant festivity, together with the marriage of the princess Isabella to the prince Alonzo, heir apparent of Portugal, were far too engrossing to admit of much attention being given to the schemes of Columbus.* At the close, however, of the year 1491, the learned conclave appears to have recommenced its consultations; but upon being

* It was shortly after this period that Bartholomew Columbus was sent by his brother to king Henry VII, to offer his services in a voyage of navigation; the king is said to have received the offer "con allegro volto"—"with a cheerful countenance"; but his acceptance of the proposition was rendered null by Columbus having in the interim attached himself to the service of queen Isabella.

called upon by the sovereigns for a decision, a report was returned to Talavera that the scheme was considered by the general vote of the junta too groundless to be recommended. Accordingly Talavera was commanded to inform Columbus that the cares and expenses of the war precluded the possibility of their highnesses engaging in any new enterprises, but that when it was concluded, there would be both the will and the opportunity to give the subject further consideration. Regarding this as nothing better than a courteous evasion of his application, he retired wearied and disappointed from the court, and, but for an attachment which he had formed at Cordova which made him reluctant to leave Spain, he would in all probability have repaired to France, under the encouragement of a favourable letter which he had received from that quarter.

The ensuing period till 1492 was spent in a succession of vexatious appeals to the Spanish court, during which he had to contend with every obstacle that ignorance, envy, or a pusillanimous economy could suggest.

At length having overcome all difficulties, he set sail with a fleet of three ships on the 3rd of August 1492, on his unprecedented and perilous voyage. The ordinary difficulties which might be expected to occur in so novel and precarious an adventure were seriously aggravated by the alarming discovery of the variation of the needle, as well as by the mutinous behaviour of his crew, and his life was upon the point of being sacrificed to their impatience, when the fortunate

appearance of land, on the morning of the 12th of October, converted their indignation into compunction, and their despondency into unbounded joy.

With reference to the identity of the first landing place of Columbus in America, I too readily adopted in 1847 the conclusions of Navarrete that the Great Turk, the northernmost of the Turk islands, was the true landfall. I did so under the following process of reasoning. My predecessors in the consideration of the subject had been the learned Juan Bautista Muñoz in 1793, Navarrete in 1825, Washington Irving in 1828, and the Baron Alexander von Humboldt in 1837. It was the opinion of Muñoz that Guanahani was Watling's Island. Navarrete, as just shown, placed it in the Grand Turk, far to the east, while Washington Irving and Humboldt made it to be Cat Island to the west. Such different conclusions, formed by thoughtful men from an examination of the diary of Columbus and other early documents, caused me to set a great value upon any modern reconnaissance of the locality which might throw a fuller light upon these documents and perhaps show which of the conclusions was correct. Now, it so happened that a communication made a short time previously to the New York Historical Society by Mr. Gibbs, a resident on Turk's Island, presented several points of evidence strongly confirmative of the correctness of Navarrete's deductions. The most important of Mr. Gibbs's arguments were the following. Columbus states in his journal that there were several islands in sight from Guanahani.

From the island now called San Salvador, Mr. Gibbs found no land visible. The journal speaks of soundings to the eastward of Guanahani : there were none to the eastward of San Salvador. All the marks wanting at San Salvador were found at Turk's Island. The journal describes Guanahani as well wooded, and having much water ; a large lake in the centre, and two several running streams flowing into the sea. Turk's Island has about one-third of its surface covered with lakes of salt and fresh water ; and a few years before vessels had sailed into one of the ponds. Although the island was now without trees, Mr. Gibbs recollected some remains of a forest existing in his youth. Moreover the journal makes no allusion to the Great Bahama Bank, which must have been passed in approaching San Salvador.* As Mr. Gibbs's personal observation thus appeared to corroborate the deductions of Señor de Navarrete, I yielded to this combination of evidence and so submitted it to the reader. Since that time, however, we have seen other arguments advanced, in which local investigation, as well as the examination of the early documents, have resulted in conclusions as divergent as those which preceded them. Captain Becher, R.N., of our own Hydrographic Office, in his *Landfall of Columbus*, published London, 1856, examining the question from a seaman's point of view, fell in with the opinion formed by Muñoz in 1793, that Guanahani was Watling's Island, while Señor de Varnhagen, in his *La verdadera Guanahani de Colon*,

* Vide *Athenæum* for 1846, page 1274.

published at Santiago, 1864, maintains the unique opinion that it was the island of Mayaguana.

Under these circumstances it has become a duty in me to revise my old opinion; and while the process to which I shall resort will, as I hope, finally settle this much vexed question, it is happily one which will not lay me open to the charge of presumption in giving a judicial verdict where men of such high renown have differed. I congratulate myself on having found a means of enabling the reader to judge for himself by a very simple mode of examination. Annexed is a fac-simile of Herrera's map of the Bahama Islands, as laid down from the original documents in the handwriting of Columbus and his contemporaries, to which, as official historiographer of the Indies in the sixteenth century, Herrera had exclusive access; and side by side with it is a map, reduced from the Admiralty survey, showing those islands as now known, and with their modern names. I indulge the hope that no one will contest the identification* of the respective islands

---

* While agreeing with Captain Becher in the identification of Guanahani with Watling's Island, I find that officer entirely at issue with the Diary of Columbus in making him anchor near the N.E. end of the island, and then sail round its northern point. In a detailed Paper on this subject, read by me on the 16th of September of this year, at the Meeting of the Geographical Section of the British Association at Liverpool, I had the honour of proving for the first time that the first anchorage of Columbus in the New World was off the S.E. point of Watling's Island, a position which entirely tallies with all his movements as mentioned in the Diary.

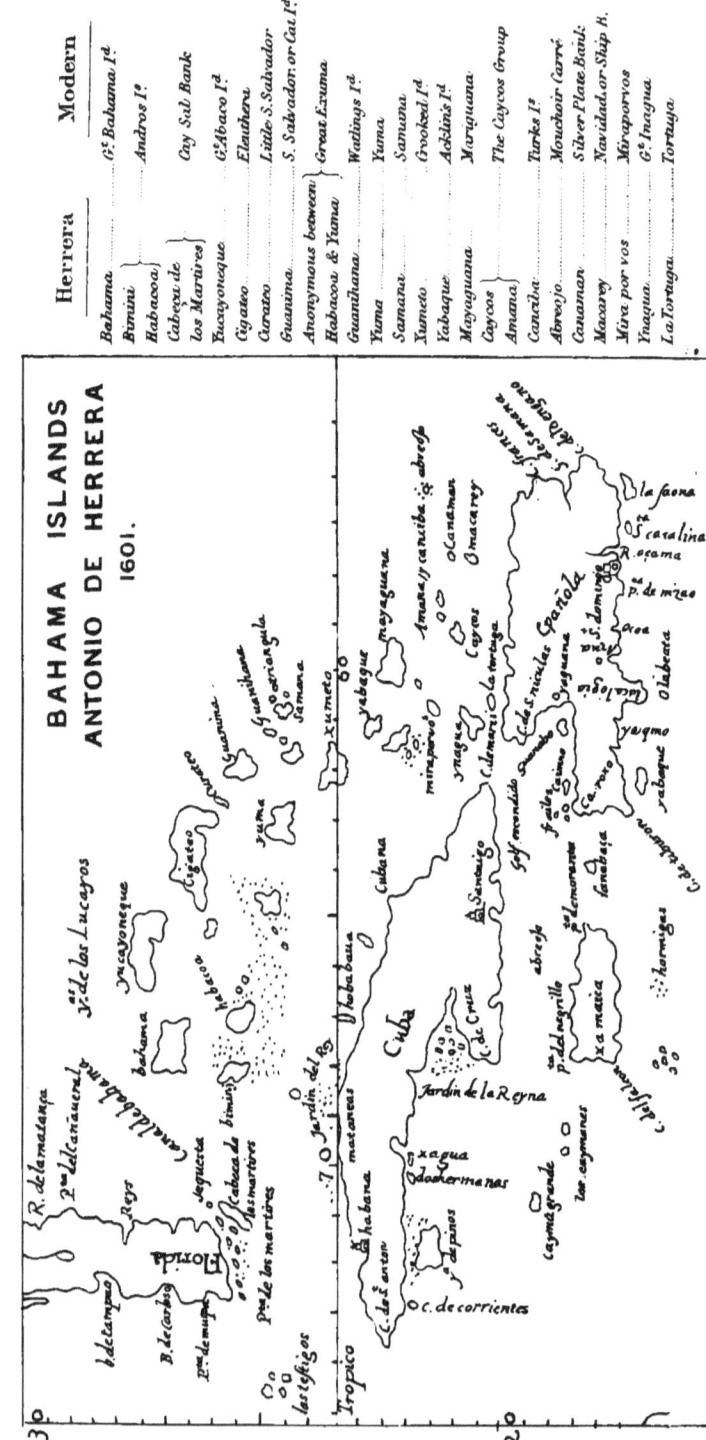

Herrera	Modern
Bahama	G^t Bahama I^d
Bimini	
Habacoa	Andros I^o
Cabeza de los Martires	Cay Sal Bank
Bucayoneque	G^t Abaco I^d
Cigateo	Eleuthera
Curateo	Little S. Salvador
Guanima	S. Salvador or Cat I^d
Anonymous between Habacoa & Yuma	Great Exuma
Guanihana	Watlings I^d
Yuma	Yuma
Samana	Samana
Xumeto	Crooked I^d
Yabaque	Acklins I^d
Mayaguana	Mariguana
Caycos	The Caycos Group
Amana	Turks I^d
Caxiba	Mouchoir Carré
Abreojo	Silver Plate Bank
Cananan	Navidad or Ship B.
Macarey	Mira por vos
Mira por vos	G^t Inagua
Ynagua	Tortuga
La Tortuga	

BAHAMA ISLANDS
ANTONIO DE HERRERA
1601.

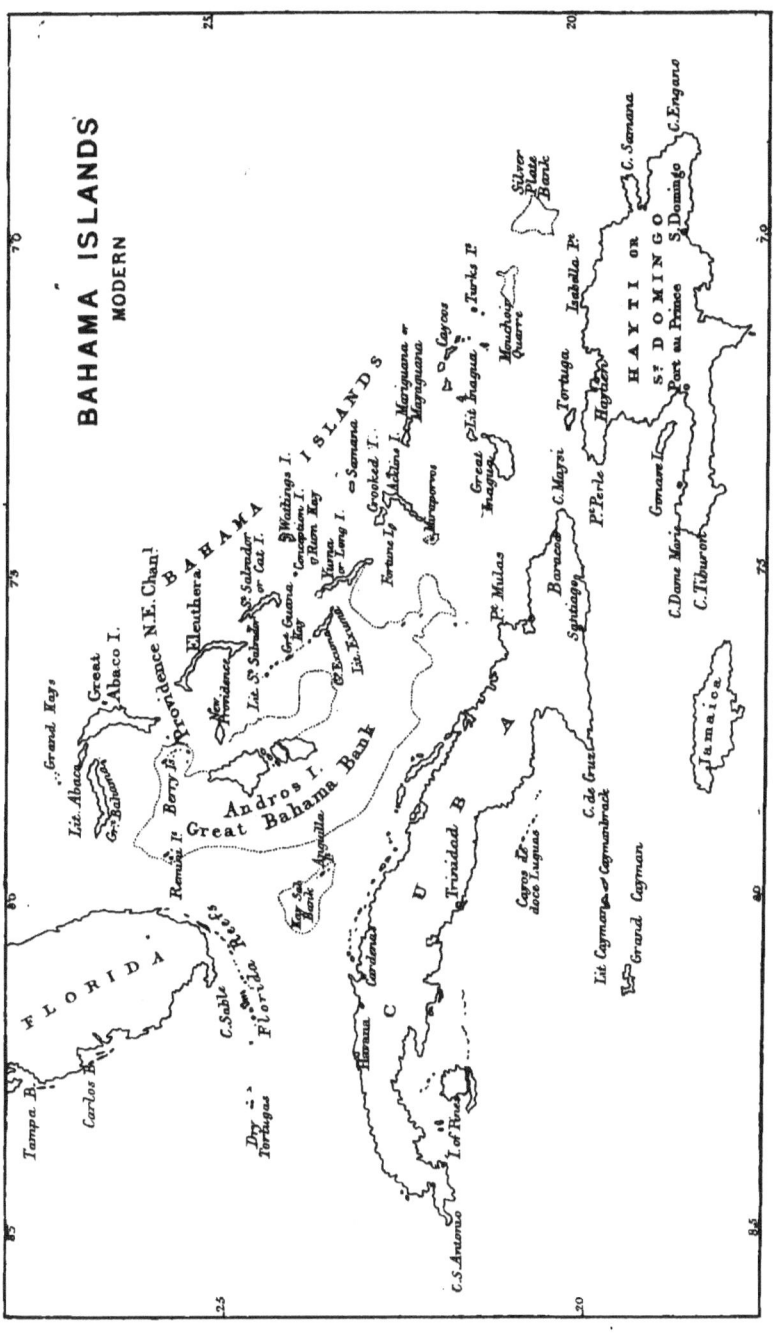

laid down in the old map with those which I have set forth as their correlatives in the modern one, and if so, the Guanahani of Columbus will be plainly seen to be Watling's Island. The correctness of this identification is not only confirmed, but made easily perceptible, by the fact that certain islands of the series have retained their ancient names without change from the beginning, thus affording stations for comparison which reduce the chances of error to a minimum. This map of Herrera's is of especial value for the purpose, because while it embodies the information contained in the map of the pilot Juan de la Cosa, who was with Columbus in his second voyage (1493-96); it has the advantage over the latter in having been made nearly a century later, and so contains the entire chain of islands, many of which had not been explored at the time when De la Cosa laid down his map in 1500. For the satisfaction of the reader, however, a reduction of that part of De la Cosa's map which shows these islands is here given.

But while it is hoped that the identity of Guanahani with Watling's Island will be admitted to be authoritatively established by this comparison, it would be wanting in respect to those who have put forth other claims not to show, I will not say the ground on which these claims were advanced, but rather, for brevity's sake, the points at which their arguments fail. I adopt this plan on the principle that a chain is no stronger than its weakest link. Of all these I fear none occupies so disadvantageous a position as His Excellency Senhor de Varnhagen; for having un-

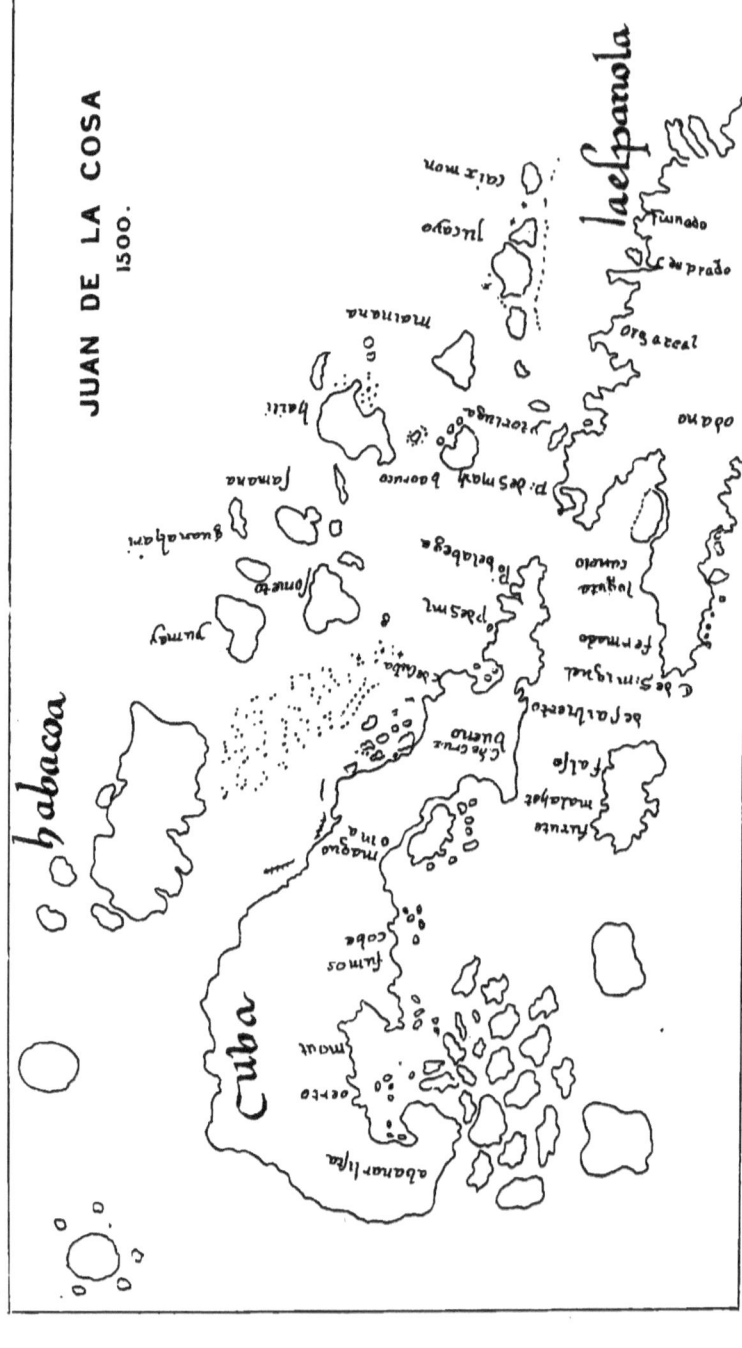

inasmuch as at the period when the name of San Salvador was first continuously applied to Cat Island, viz., the middle of the seventeenth century, both map makers and sailors were possessed of no better materials, nor even so good, as ourselves, for coming to an accurate determination. Humboldt, in accepting the conclusions of Commander Mackenzie as adopted by Irving, thinks them confirmed by the map of Juan de la Cosa, of which I have given an extract. But here I would observe that the attention of the illustrious philosopher was bent on the point to which Mackenzie's paper was directed, viz., the disproval of Turk's Island, and not to a discrimination between Cat Island and Watling's Island for the true landfall. A glance will show that the imperfectness of the Bahama group in Juan de la Cosa's map renders it perfectly inadequate for settling so minute a question.

It is needless to dwell here upon the events which followed this discovery, as they are for the most part described in the letter here translated. The main result of the voyage was the discovery of the islands of St. Salvador, Santa Maria de la Concepcion, Exuma, Isabella, Cuba, Bohio, the Archipelago off the south coast of Cuba (which he names the Jardin del Rey, or King's Garden), the islands of St. Catherine and Hispaniola, on which latter Columbus erected the fortress of La Navidad, and established a colony. Finally, on the 16th of January he began to steer his course for Spain, and he was already near the Azores when, on the 12th February

the wind came on to blow violently, with a heavy sea, and on the following day a frightful tempest broke upon them, which obliged them to scud under bare poles. The storm continuing with unabated violence, on the night of the 14th of February the two caravels parted company, each following the course where the fury of the tempest drove them. The sailors, giving themselves up for lost, offered up prayers and vows; while the admiral, full of gloomy apprehensions that, after all, his discovery might turn to nought, and his two sons be left destitute, wrote upon parchment the account of the voyage, addressed it to the king of Spain, with a promise, written outside, of one thousand ducats to whomsoever would deliver it unopened. He then wrapped the packet up in waxed cloth, and put it into the middle of a cake of wax, and after inclosing it in a barrel well hooped and stopped up, he threw it into the sea. He also placed on the poop of his own vessel a similar barrel, with the same account enclosed, in order that if the ship went to the bottom the barrel might float, and the narrative be saved. During this period Columbus passed three days and nights without sleep, and with scanty and bad food, so that when, on the 18th, he arrived at St. Mary's, one of the Azores, he felt his limbs quite crippled with exposure to the cold and wet. There was a small church there, in a solitary place, dedicated to the Virgin. Columbus, with the view of discharging the vows made during the storm, sent half of his people on shore to the church, but the Portuguese Governor of the island took them all

prisoners, seized their boat, and would have attacked Columbus's own vessel, by orders, as he said, received from his court, but for the firmness with which the latter confronted him. Columbus indignantly asserted his own rank and office, showed his letters patent sealed with the royal seal, and threatened the Governor with the vengeance of the Castilian government. After a few days, during which Columbus was driven from his anchorage and had to beat about in great danger, the Governor, who in the interval had thought better of the matter, liberated the prisoners and allowed the caravel to proceed on her course. The state of the weather was most terrible; the sea ran mountains high; the lightnings rent the clouds, and the violence of the winds was such that the vessel was obliged to scud under bare poles, in which state she arrived, at last, in the Tagus, near Lisbon, on the 4th of March. Columbus immediately wrote a letter to the King of Portugal, then at Valparaiso, informing him that he was not come from Guinea but from the Indies, and requesting protection for his caravel, and permission to bring it up to Lisbon. Not only was this granted, but Columbus was immediately invited to Valparaiso and was received by the monarch and his courtiers with the highest honours. There were not wanting, however, some who would gladly have slain him to prevent his going to Castile as the bearer of such great and glorious news. The magnanimity of the king prevented this injustice, and leaving Portugal in safety, on the 13th of March, Columbus

f

arrived on the 15th at the little port of Palos, from whence he had sailed on the 3rd of August in the preceding year. Meanwhile Pinzon, the captain of the other caravel, who in the late storm had been driven into Galicia, wished to anticipate the admiral, but an express order from the court, forbidding him to come without Columbus, made him actually die of spite and chagrin. The reception of Columbus in Spain was such as the grandeur and dignity of his unrivalled achievement deserved, and his entrance into Barcelona was scarcely inferior to a Roman triumph.*

* The following remark by Mr. George Sumner was kindly supplied to me by that gentleman in 1847, as an interesting item connected with this period of the history of Columbus:—

From the brilliant description given by Irving and Prescott of the arrival of Columbus at Barcelona, and of his reception there by the Catholic sovereigns, it seemed to me as probable that some contemporary account of this arrival and reception, as well as of the sojourn of Columbus, might be found at Barcelona; and, while there in the spring of 1844, I searched the admirably arranged archives of Aragon, and also those of the city of Barcelona, for such notice, but without any success. I could not so much as find a mention of the name of Columbus.

The *Dietaria*, or day book, of Barcelona, notices the arrival of ambassadors, the movements of the king and queen, and even records incidents of as trifling note as those which in our day serve to fill the columns of a court journal; yet not a word appears in regard to Columbus.

How account for this silence? Is it another evidence of the old feeling of jealousy between the Aragonese and Castilians, of which the student of Spanish history meets so many proofs? Such was the opinion to which I was forced, and such I found also was the interpretation given to it by the intelligent Archevero, who had himself gone over this ground a few years since at the request of Navarrete. The voyage of Columbus was un-

INTRODUCTION.

/ Very shortly after his arrival the papal bull was obtained, which fixed the famous line of demarcation, determining the right of the Spanish and Portuguese to discovered lands./ This line was drawn from the north to the south pole, at a hundred leagues west of the Azores and Cape de Verde islands; the discoveries to the westward were to belong to Spain, and those to the eastward to Portugal.

/The seductive adulation of the court and the people did not, however, divert the thoughts of Columbus

dertaken at the expense and for the benefit of the crown of Castile. It was not to Aragon, but to Castilla and Leon, that Columbus gave a new world, and as the Aragonese did not profit directly by this gift, they saw fit to treat it and its donor with scornful silence.

In one of the notes to the great work of Capmany,—*Memorias sobre la ciudad de Barcelona*, 1789—he gives a list of distinguished men who have enjoyed the hospitality of the city, and among them places the name of Columbus, making no allusion however to any contemporary account of his sojourn there.

In the *Dietaria* of Barcelona, under date 15th November 1492, is the following entry:—"The king, queen, and primogenito, entered to-day the city, and lodged in the palace of the bishop of Urgil in the Calle Ancha." This is followed by a description of the festivities which followed. "1493, 4th February.—King and queen went to Alserrat. 14th.—King and queen returned to Barcelona."

As there appears no notice of the king having changed his abode after taking possession of the palace in the Calle Ancha, it was probably there that Columbus recounted to Isabella his adventures and his success. The American pilgrim may still, in the beautiful Alcazar of the Moorish kings, recall the figure of the discoverer of his land, standing in the presence of the Catholic sovereigns of Spain;—in the cotton-spinning town of Barcelona the besom of modern improvement has long since swept away the palace of the bishop of Urgil.

from the preparations for a second expedition. A stay of five months sufficed to make all ready for this purpose; but these preparations gave rise to a malignant feeling towards him on the part of Juan Rodriguez Fonseca, Bishop of Badajos, which eventually led to such disgraceful ill-usage of the admiral as will remain a stain upon the character of Spain while the name of Columbus exists in the memory of man.

On the 25th September 1493, Columbus took his departure from Cadiz, with a fleet of three large ships of heavy burthen, and fourteen caravels, and after a pleasant voyage reached the island of Dominica on the 3rd of November. The letter of Dr. Chanca, here translated, gives an interesting description of a considerable portion of the events of this voyage, but it is to be regretted that his account terminates so abruptly, and the "memorial" of Columbus to the sovereigns adds but few incidents of moment to the narrative. We should be straining the necessary limits of a mere introduction to these translated documents, were we to undertake to lead the reader through the various history of this eventful period of the life of Columbus. Such a task has been rendered perfectly unnecessary by the much admired work of Washington Irving. Suffice it that we state, that the principal geographical information supplied by this voyage consists in the discovery of the Caribbee Islands, Jamaica, an Archipelago (named by Columbus the Queen's Gardens, supposed to be the Morant Keys), Evangelista, or the Isle of Pines; and the island of Mona.

He sailed with his fleet finally for Spain on the 28th of April, 1496, and after nearly two months' struggle against the trade-winds (during which provisions became so reduced, that there was talk of killing, and even eating the Indian prisoners), reached the bay of Cadiz on the 11th of June. The emaciated state of the crew when they disembarked, presenting so mournful a contrast with the joyous and triumphant appearance which they were expected to make, produced a very discouraging impression upon the opinions of the public, and reflected a corresponding depression upon the spirits of Columbus himself. He was reassured, however, by the receipt of a gracious letter from the sovereigns inviting him to the court, which was the more gratifying to him that he had feared he had fallen into disgrace. He was received with distinguished favour, and had a verbal concession of his request to be furnished with eight ships for a third voyage. He was doomed, however, to have his patience severely tried by the delay which occurred in the performance of this promise, which was partly attributable to the engrossing character of the public events of the day, and partly to the machinations of his inveterate enemy, the bishop Fonseca.

It was not till the 30th of May 1498, that he set sail from San Lucar, with six of the eight vessels promised, the other two having been despatched to Hispaniola, with provisions, in the beginning of the year. When off Ferro he despatched three of his six vessels to the same island, with a store of fresh supplies for the colony, while with his remaining three

he steered for the Cape Verde Islands, which he reached on the 27th of June. On the 5th of July he left Boavista, and proceeded southward and westward. In the course of this voyage the crews suffered intensely from the heat, having at one time reached the fifth degree of north latitude, but at length land was descried on the 31st of July,—a most providential occurrence, as but one cask of water remained in the ship. The island they came to formed an addition to his discoveries; and as the first land which appeared consisted of three mountains, united at their base, he christened the island, from the name of the Trinity, La Trinidad. It was in this voyage that he discovered terra firma,* and the islands of Margarita and Cubagua. His supposition that Paria had formed the original abode of our first parents, is curiously described in our translated letter; and to a careful observer the sagacity of his mode of reasoning is perceptible even in a speculation so fanciful as this. On reaching Hispaniola (to which he was drawn by his anxiety on account of the infant colony), he had the mortification to find that his authority had suffered considerable diminution, and that the colony was in a state of organized rebellion. He had scarcely, by his active and at the same time politic conduct, brought matters to a state of comparative tranquillity, when a new storm gathered round him from the quarter of the Spanish court. The hatred of his ancient enemies

/* It is well known that Columbus was preceded in the discovery of terra firma by John Cabot in 1497.

availed itself of the clamour raised against him by some of the rebels who had recently returned to Spain, and charges of tyranny, cruelty, and ambition were heaped unsparingly upon him. The king and queen, wearied with reiterated complaints, at length resolved to send out a judge, to inquire into his conduct,—injudiciously authorizing him to seize the governorship in the place of Columbus, should the accusations brought against him prove to be valid. The person chosen was Don Francisco de Bobadilla, whose character and qualifications for the office are best demonstrated by the fact, that, on the day after his arrival in Hispaniola, he seized upon the government before he had investigated the conduct of Columbus, who was then absent; he also took up his residence in his house, and took possession of all his property, public and private, even to his most secret papers. A summons to appear before the new governor was despatched to Columbus, who was at Fort Concepcion; and in the interval between the despatch of the summons and his arrival, his brother, Don Diego, was seized, thrown into irons, and confined on board of a caravel, without any reason being assigned for his imprisonment. No sooner did the admiral himself arrive, than he likewise was put in chains, and thrown into confinement. The habitual reverence due to his venerable person and exalted character, made each bystander shrink from the task of fixing the fetters on him, till one of his own domestics, described by Las Casas as "a graceless and shameless cook," filled up the measure of ingratitude

that he seemed doomed to experience, by riveting the irons, not merely with apathy, but with manifest alacrity. In this shackled condition he was conveyed, in the early part of October, from prison to the ship that was to convey him home; and when Andreas Martin, the master of the caravel, touched with respect for Columbus, and deeply moved at this unworthy treatment, proposed to take off his irons, he declined the offered benefit, with the following magnanimous reply: "Since the king has commanded that I should obey his governor, he shall find me as obedient in this as I have been to all his other orders; nothing but his command shall release me. If twelve years' hardship and fatigue; if continual dangers and frequent famine; if the ocean first opened, and five times passed and repassed, to add a new world, abounding with wealth, to the Spanish monarchy; and if an infirm and premature old age, brought on by these services, deserve these chains as a reward, it is very fit I should wear them to Spain, and keep them by me as memorials to the end of my life." This in truth he did; for he always kept them hung on the walls of his chamber, and desired that when he died they might be buried with him.

His arrival in Spain in this painful and degraded condition produced so general a sensation of indignation and astonishment, that a warm manifestation in his favour was the immediate consequence. A letter (here translated), written by him to Doña Juana de la Torre, a lady of the court, detailing the wrongs he had suffered, was read to queen Isabella,

whose generous mind was filled with sympathy and indignation at the recital. /The sovereigns hastened to order him to be set at liberty, and ordered two thousand ducats to be advanced, for the purpose of bringing him to court with all distinction and an honourable retinue. / His reception at the Alhambra was gracious and flattering in the highest degree;/ the strongest indignation was expressed against Bobadilla, with an assurance that he should be immediately dismissed from his command, while ample restitution and reward were promised to Columbus, and he had every sanction for indulging the fondest hopes of returning in honour and triumph to St. Domingo. But here a grievous disappointment awaited him; his re-appointment was postponed from time to time with various plausible excuses. Though Bobadilla was dismissed, it was deemed desirable to refill his place for two years, by some prudent and talented officer, who should be able to put a stop to all remaining faction in the colony, and thus prepare the way for Columbus to enjoy the rights and dignities of his government both peacefully and beneficially to the crown. The newly-selected governor was Nicolas de Ovando, who, though described by Las Casas as a man of prudence, justice, and humanity, certainly betrayed a want both of generosity and justice in his subsequent transactions with Columbus. It is possible that the delay manifested by the sovereigns in redeeming their promise might have continued until the death of Columbus, had not a fresh stimulant to

the cupidity of Ferdinand been suggested by a new project of discovering a strait, of the existence of which Columbus felt persuaded from his own observations, and which would connect the New World which he had discovered with the wealthy shores of the east. His enthusiasm on the subject was heightened by an emulous consideration of the recent achievements of Vasco da Gama and Cabral, the former of whom had, in 1497, found a maritime passage to India by the Cape, and the latter, in 1500, had discovered for Portugal the vast and opulent empire of Brazil. The prospect of a more direct and safe route to India than that discovered by da Gama, at length gained for Columbus the accomplishment of his wish for another armament; and, finally, on the 9th of May, 1502, he sailed from Cadiz on his fourth and last voyage of discovery.

It is painful to contrast the splendour of the fleet with which Ovando left Spain to assume the government of Hispaniola, with the slender and inexpensive armament granted to Columbus for the purpose of exploring an unknown strait into an unknown ocean, the traversing of whose unmeasured breadth would complete the circumnavigation of the globe. Ovando's fleet consisted of thirty sail, five of them from ninety to one hundred and fifty tons burden, twenty-four caravels of from thirty to ninety tons, and one bark of twenty-five tons; and the number of souls amounted to about two thousand five hundred. The heroic and injured man, to whose unparalleled combination of noble qualities, the very dignity which called for all

this state was indebted for its existence, had now in the decline of his years and strength, and stripped both of honour and emolument, to venture forth with four caravels,—the largest of seventy, and the smallest of fifty tons burthen—accompanied by one hundred and fifty men, on one of the most toilsome and perilous enterprises of which the mind can form a conception.

On the 20th of May he reached the Grand Canary, and starting from thence on the 25th, took his departure for the west. Favoured by the trade winds, he made a gentle and easy passage, and reached one of the Caribbee Islands, called by the natives Matinino (Martinique), on the 15th of June. After staying three days at this island, he steered northwards, and touched at Dominica, and from thence directed his course, contrary to his own original intention and the commands of the sovereigns, to St. Domingo. His reason was that his principal vessel sailed so ill as to delay the progress of the fleet, which he feared might be an obstacle to the safety and success of the enterprise, and he held this as a sufficient motive for infringing the orders he had received. On his arrival at San Domingo, he found the ships which had brought out Ovando ready to put to sea on their return to Spain. He immediately sent to the governor to explain that his intention in calling at the island was to procure a vessel in exchange for one of his caravels, which was very defective; and further begged permission for his squadron to take shelter in the harbour, from

a hurricane, which, from his acquaintance with the prognostics of the weather, he had foreseen was rapidly approaching. /This request was ungraciously refused; upon which Columbus, though denied shelter for himself, endeavoured to avert the danger of the fleet, which was about to sail, and sent back immediately to the governor to entreat that he would not allow it to put to sea for some days. His predictions and requests were treated with equal contempt, and Columbus had not only to suffer these insulting refusals and the risk of life for himself and squadron, but the loud murmurings of his own crew that they had sailed with a commander whose position exposed them to such treatment. All he could do was to draw his ships up as close as possible to the shore, and seek the securest anchorage that chance might present him with. Meanwhile the weather appeared fair and tranquil, and the fleet of Bobadilla put boldly out to sea. / The predicted storm came on the next night with terrific fury, and all the ships belonging to the governor's fleet, with the exception of one, were either lost, or put back to San Domingo in a shattered condition. The only vessel that escaped was the one which had been freighted with some four thousand gold pieces, rescued from the pillage of Columbus's fortune. Bobadilla, Roldan, and a number of the most inveterate enemies of the admiral, perished in this tremendous hurricane, while his own fleet, though separated and considerably damaged by the storm, all arrived safe at last at Port Hermoso, on the south of San Domingo.

He repaired his vessels at Port Hermoso, but had scarcely left the harbour before another storm drove him into Port Brazil, more to the westward. On the 14th of July he left this port, steering for terra firma, and on the 30th discovered the small island of Guanaga or Bonacca, a few leagues east of the bay of Honduras. He continued an eastern course, and discovered the cape now known as Cape Honduras. While moving along this coast, he experienced one of those frightful tempests to which the tropics are liable, and of which he gives so impressive a description in the letter we have translated. At length, after forty days' struggle to make as much as seventy leagues from the cape of Honduras, he reached a cape, by doubling which he found a direct southward course open, offering at the same time an unobstructed navigation and a favourable wind. To commemorate this sudden relief from toil and danger, Columbus named this point Cape *Gracias a Dios*, or "Thanks to God." A melancholy occurrence took place on the 16th of September, while they were anchored off this coast. The boats had been sent up a large river to procure supplies of wood and water, when, on returning, the encounter of the sea with the rapid current of the river caused so violent and sudden a commotion, that one of the boats was swallowed up, and all on board perished. On the 25th of September he reached Cariay, or Cariari, where he stayed till the 5th of October. The next point was the Bay of Carumbaru, which was the first place on that coast where he met with specimens of pure gold. Leaving this bay on

the 17th of October, he sailed along the coast of Veragua, and here he was informed by the Indians of the wealthy country of Ciguare, which he supposed to be some province belonging to the Grand Khan, and also of a river ten days' journey beyond Ciguare, which he conceived to be the Ganges. On the 2nd of November he discovered Puerto Bello, in which harbour he was detained till the 9th by stormy weather; when, continuing his course eastward, he reached, near the end of the month, a small harbour, to which he gave the name of El Retrete, or the Cabinet. It was here that a continuance of stormy weather, in addition to the murmurs of his crew at being compelled to prosecute an indefinite search, with worm-eaten ships, against opposing currents, determined Columbus on relinquishing his eastward voyage for the present, and to return in search of the gold mines of Veragua. But on altering his course to the westward, he had the mortification to find the wind for which he had long been wishing, come now, as if in direct opposition to his adopted course, and for nine days he was exposed to so terrible a storm that it was a marvel how his crazy vessels could outlive it. At length, after a month's anxiety and suffering, they anchored, on the day of the Epiphany, at the mouth of a river called by the natives Yebra, but which Columbus named Belem, or Bethlehem. Here a settlement was formed, and here occurred the sad disasters and conflicts with the natives, which he describes in his letter from Jamaica, and in which the faithful and zealous Diego Mendez proved an

eminently efficient assistant to his much loved master. The history of this unhappy voyage, the toils and perils of which were aggravated to Columbus by extreme bodily suffering, closes by his reaching Jamaica, where he would in all probability have perished, but for the devotedness and activity of Mendez. The highly interesting description of that brave man's exploits on behalf of Columbus, has been quoted by Navarrete from his will, and is here translated. When at length, through the agency of Mendez, two ships arrived from Hispaniola to the assistance of the admiral, he was enabled, on the 28th of June, 1504, to leave his wrecked vessels behind him, and start with revived hopes for San Domingo, which he reached on the 13th of August. His sojourn there was not, as may be judged, calculated to afford him satisfaction or pleasure. The overstrained courtesy of the governor offered but a poor alleviation to the rush of rankling feelings which the past associations and present desolation of the place summoned up to his mind.

On the 12th of September he set sail for Spain, and the same tempestuous weather which had all along tended to make this his last voyage the most disastrous, did not forsake him now. The ship in which he came home sprung her mainmast in four places in one tempest, and in a subsequent storm the foremast was sprung, and finally, on the 7th of November, he arrived, in a vessel as shattered as his own broken and care-worn frame, in the welcome harbour of San Lucar.

The two years which intervened between this

period and his death present a picture of black ingratitude on the part of the crown to this distinguished benefactor of the kingdom, which it is truly painful to contemplate. We behold an extraordinary man, the discoverer of a second hemisphere, reduced by his very success to so low a state of poverty that, in his prematurely infirm old age, he is compelled to subsist by borrowing, and to plead, in the apologetic language of a culprit, for the rights of which the very sovereign whom he has benefited has deprived him. The death of the benignant and high-minded Isabella, in 1505, gave a finishing blow to his hope of obtaining redress, and we find him thus writing subsequently to this period to his old and faithful friend Diego de Deza:—"It appears that his majesty does not think fit to fulfil that which he, with the queen, who is now in glory, promised me by word and seal. For me to contend for the contrary, would be to contend with the wind. I have done all that I could do: I leave the rest to God, whom I have ever found propitious to me in my necessities." The selfish and cold-hearted Ferdinand beheld his illustrious and loyal servant sink, without relief, under bodily infirmity, and the palsying sickness of hope deferred; and at length, on the 20th of May 1506, the generous heart which had done so much without reward and suffered so much without upbraiding, found rest in a world where neither gratitude nor justice is either asked or withheld.

His body was in the first instance buried at Valladolid, in the parish church of Santa Maria de la

Antigua, but was transferred, in 1513, to the Cartuja de las Cuevas, near Seville, where a monument was erected over his grave with the memorable inscription,—

A CASTILLA Y A LEON
NUEVO MUNDO DIÓ COLON.

In the year 1536, both his body, and that of his son Diego, who had been likewise buried in the Cartuja, were transported to St. Domingo, and deposited in the cathedral of that city. From hence they were removed to Havannah in 1795, on the cession of Hispaniola to the French, and the ashes of the immortal discoverer now quietly repose in the cathedral church of that city.*

* I am indebted to Mr. George Sumner for the following copy of the inscription on the tomb of Fernando Columbus, in the pavement of the cathedral of Seville, and for the note which accompanies it:—

"Aqui yaze el M. Magnifico S. D. Hernando Colon, el qual aplicó y gastó toda su vida y hazienda en aumento de las letras, y juntar y perpetuar en esta ciudad todos sus libros de todas las ciencias, que en su tiempo halló y en reducirlo a quatro libros. Falleció en esta ciudad a 12 de Julio de 1539 de edad de 50 años 9 meses y 14 dias, fue hijo del valeroso y memorable S. D. Christ. Colon primero Almirante que descubrió las Yndias y nuevo mundo en vida de los Cat. R. D. Fernando y D. Ysabel de gloriosa memoria a 11 de Oct. de 1492 con tres galeras y 90 personas, y partió del puerto de Palos a descubrirlas a 3 de Agosto antes, y Bolvió a Castilla con victoria a 7 de Maio del Año Siguiente y tornó despues otras dos veces ā poblar lo que descubrió. Falleció en Valladolid à 20 de Agosto de 1506 años.

"ROGAD A DIOS POR ELLOS."

Beneath this is described, in a circle, a globe, presenting the western and part of the eastern hemispheres, surmounted by a

lxxxii   INTRODUCTION.

But injustice, unhappily, was not buried with Columbus in the tomb. It was but one twelvemonth after his death that an attempt was made, and only too successfully, to name the new world which he had discovered, after another, who was not only his inferior, but his pupil in the school of maritime enterprise. In an obscure corner of Lorraine, at the little cathedral town of St. Dié, a cluster of learned priests, who had there established a printing-press under the auspices of René II, Duke of Lorraine, suggested to give to the newly discovered continent the name of the Florentine, Amerigo Vespucci, whose nautical career did not commence till after Columbus had returned from his second voyage to the western hemisphere. The first time that the name of Amerigo came into notice was in the year 1504, when Johann Ottmar published at Augsburg the *Mundus Novus*, a description of Vespucci's third voyage, now extremely rare, embodied in a letter addressed by Ves-

---

pair of compasses. Within the border of the circle is the same inscription as that which was placed over Columbus himself at the Cartuja, with the exception of the word "mundo" being placed before, instead of after, the word "nuevo".

Throughout all Spain I know of no other inscription to the memory of Columbus. At Valladolid, where he died, and where his body lay for some years, there is none that I could discover, neither is there any trace of any at the Cartuja, near Seville, to which his body was afterwards transferred, and in which his brother was buried.

It is a striking confirmation of the reproach of negligence, in regard to the memory of this great man, that in this solitary inscription in old Spain, the date of his death should be inaccurately given.   G. S.

pucci himself to Lorenzo di Pier Francesco de' Medici. In this voyage, which occupied from May 1501 to September 1502, he was in the service of Portugal, and explored the coasts of South America as far as beyond the fifty-second degree. But it was not till May, 1507, when Columbus had been a twelvemonth dead, that the world was informed of four voyages professed to have been made by Vespucci, of which the one just mentioned was only the third, the two former having been made, as he states, in the service of Spain. As the first of these was asserted to have taken place between May 20th, 1497, and October, 1499 [say 1498], and, if correct, would involve the discovery by him not only of the north coasts of South America, but a large extent of the coast of North America also, and that in priority of the claims both of Cabot and Columbus as regards the discovery of the American continent, it has been a matter of keen interest to many to examine minutely the correctness of Vespucci's claim to having made this voyage.

It would be out of place here to enter into the complicated arguments in which this question is involved ; but I have elsewhere shown* on how frail a tenure the claim in question is founded. In the same place I have also traced in detail the mode adopted for giving to the New World the name of Vespucci instead of that of Columbus, who, by the exercise of such transcendently superior qualities had earned for himself that honour. I will here sketch

* See *Life of Prince Henry the Navigator*, pp. 367 to 379.

it in brief. Vespucci was an intimate friend of the Giocondi family, one of whom, the celebrated architect, Fra Giovanni Giocondi, who built the bridge of Nôtre Dame at Paris, was the translator into Latin of Vespucci's letter to Lorenzo di Pier Francesco de' Medici describing his third voyage. A young Alsatian, named Mathias Ringmann, who was at this time pursuing his studies in Paris, appears to have made the acquaintance of this Giocondi and to have carried back with him into Alsace an admiration for Vespucci and his achievements, which showed itself in his editing at Strasbourg in 1505, Giocondi's translation of Vespucci's letter, accompanied by some laudatory verses in Latin by himself. Now in the neighbouring province of Lorraine, one of the canons of the cathedral at St. Dié, Walter Lud, who was secretary to René II, Duke of Lorraine, had already for many years established a gymnasium or college under the duke's auspices, and also a printing-press. Ringmann, better known in literature by the pseudonym of Philesius, became professor of Latin at the college and corrector of the press in the printing-office. On the 25th of April, 1507, *a year after the death of Columbus*, one of the members of this little clique, named Martin Waldseemüller, otherwise known as Hylacomylus, produced from this press a small work entitled *Cosmographiæ Introductio*, to which was appended a Latin translation of Vespucci's four voyages, as described by himself and addressed to Duke René II, although it can be shown by the contents to have been really intended for

Pietro Soderini, Gonfaloniere of Florence, who had been Vespucci's schoolfellow. In my *Life of Prince Henry the Navigator*, I have ventured to suggest the process by which these letters, intended for another, came to be addressed to Duke René, and that suggestion supplies the solution of some riddles, there treated of, which it would be out of place to speak of here. We have seen the connection of the Giocondi with Vespucci. We have seen, also, the connection of Ringmann with the work of Fra Giovanni Giocondi and his interest in the glory of Vespucci. This interest he infuses into the little circle of St. Dié, and we can imagine their pleasure at having the opportunity of blazoning forth to the world, from their own printing-press, a story which would throw so bright a reflection on the obscurity of their secluded valley. But in the little book thus issued, not only were printed for the first time four voyages of Vespucci, but also a suggestion was made that from his name, Amerigo, should be given the name of "Amerige" or "America" to the newly-discovered western world. In September of the same year, 1507, appeared a re-issue of the same book; and in 1509 a new edition of it was issued from the printing-press of Johann Grüninger of Strasburg. In this same year, 1509, three years before the death of Vespucci, the name of America appears, as if it were already accepted as a well-known denomination, in an anonymous work entitled *Globus Mundi*, printed also at Strasburg. But although this work is anonymous, it was my good fortune to detect from the colophon,

in which occur the words "Adelpho Castigatore," that the source of the suggestion of the name of America in the one case, and of the adoption of the suggestion in the other, are either identical or in close proximity, inasmuch as the already mentioned re-issue of the *Cosmographiæ Introductio* in 1509, has in the colophon, "Johanne Adelpho Mulicho Argentinensi Castigatore." Now, Mulicho merely means native of Muhlingen, near Strasburg, and this Adelphus, so named, was a physician established in that city, and reviser of both the one work and the other.

The first place in which we find the name of America used a little further a-field, is in a letter dated Vienna, 1512, from Joachim Vadianus to Rudolphus Agricola, and inserted in the *Pomponius Mela* of 1518, edited by the former. The expression used is " America discovered by Vesputius."* But although this Vadianus, whose real name was Joachim Watt, writes from Vienna in 1512, I find that he was a native of St. Gall, whence in 1508, being then twenty-four years old, he went to the High School of Vienna. His learned disputations and verses gained him the chair of the professorship of the liberal arts at that school, and he subsequently studied medicine, of which faculty he obtained the doctorate. This attachment to the study of medicine recalls to my mind a fact which awakens a suspicion that he may have been a personal friend of John Adelphus, just referred to, and if so, of the little confraternity of St. Dié. Before Adelphus established himself in Strasburg, he

* " Americam a Vespuccio repertam."

had practised as a physician at Schaffhausen, and this at the time when Joachim Watt was a young man, still resident at St. Gall, which is distant from Schaffhausen seventy English miles, a distance which would offer very little hindrance to Swiss intercommunication. Whether this suspicion be worth anything or no, I advance it as a possible clue to yet further researches which may show the process by which this spurious appellation of America became adopted, through the efforts of a small cluster of men in an obscure corner of France.

The earliest engraved map of the new world yet known as bearing the name of America, is a mappemonde by Appianus, bearing the date of 1520, annexed to the edition by Camers of the Polyhistoria of Julius Solinus (*Viennæ Austr.*), 1520), and a second time to the edition of *Pomponius Mela* by Vadianus, printed at Basle in 1522. The earliest manuscript map hitherto found bearing that name, is in a most precious collection of drawings by the hand of Leonardo da Vinci, now in Her Majesty's collections at Windsor, to which, from an examination of its contents, I have assigned the date of 1513-14.*

I have thus endeavoured to unravel the intricate story of a great and irreparable injustice. No one can deny to Vespucci the credit of possessing courage, perseverance, and a practical acquaintance with the art of navigation; but he had never been the commander of an expedition, and had it not been for the great initiatory achievement of Columbus, we

* See *Archæologia*, vol. xl, 1866.

have no reason to suppose that we should ever have heard his name.

" To say the truth," as has been well remarked by the illustrious Baron von Humboldt, " Vespucci shone only by reflection from an age of glory. When compared with Columbus, Sebastian Cabot, Bartolomé Dias, and Da Gama, his place is an inferior one. The majesty of great memories seems concentrated in the name of Christopher Columbus. It is the originality of his vast idea, the largeness and fertility of his genius, and the courage which bore up against a long series of misfortunes, which have exalted the Admiral high above all his contemporaries."

A tardy tribute has been at length paid to his memory by his fellow-citizens of Genoa, and the first stone of a monument in commemoration of his achievements was laid in that city on the 27th of September, 1846, and completed in 1862. There is now serious talk of his canonization.

Among the many so-called portraits of Columbus, too numerous to be detailed here, but for elaborate notices of which the reader is referred to the works mentioned at foot,* there is not one that can be regarded as unquestionably authentic. It was at the

---

* Carderera (Valentin): Informe sobre los retratos de Cristóbal Colon, su trage y escudo de Armas. Imprenta de la Real Academia de la historia. Madrid. 1851. Small 4to.

Feuillet de Conches (F). " Portraits de Christophe Colomb," extrait de la Revue contemporaine, T. xxv, 95me livraison in 8°, and in the " Revue Archéologique," an article by Mr. Isidore de Lœwenstern, on the Mémoires of MM. Jomard et Carderera respecting the portraits of Columbus.

suggestion of my friend M. Ferdinand Denis, the distinguished Librarian of the Ste. Geneviève in Paris, that I have inserted as the frontispiece to this volume a chromolithograph fac-simile of the St. Christopher on the famous map of Juan de la Cosa, Columbus's pilot, made in 1500. My friend most reasonably suggests that, in this case, St. Christopher represented Christopher Columbus carrying the Christian faith across the Atlantic, and that the face would be a portrait. In corroboration of his idea, I may quote the words of Herrera, whose possession of the Columbian documents enabled him to speak with accuracy. He says, "Columbus was tall of stature, with a long and imposing visage. His nose was aquiline; his eyes blue; his complexion clear, and having a tendency to a glowing red; the beard and hair red in his youth, but his fatigues early turned them white." The cap and costume seem also less those of the saint than of the sailor. It is to my late revered and dear friend, His Excellency the Count de Lavradio, that I am indebted for procuring the coloured photograph from the original map on his visit to Madrid in 1869. The chromolithograph has been prepared in Berlin.

A POEM

COMPOSED BY GIULIANO DATI IN 1493,

[FROM COLUMBUS'S FIRST LETTER,]

And sung in Florence to announce the discovery of the New World.

LA LETTERA DELLISOLE CHE HA TROVATO NUOVAMENTE
IL RE DISPAGNA.

Omnipotente idio, che tucto regge,
donami gratia chio possa cantare
allaude tua & di tu sancta legge,
cosa che piaccia achi stara ascoltare
maxim al popol tuo & alla tua grege,
el qual nō resta mai magnificare,
como al p̃sēte ha fatto nella Spagna,
delle isole trovate cosa magna.

Io ho gia lecto degli antichi regi
& principi signori stanti in terra,
del re della soria & facti egregi,
& lebactaglie loro & la gran guerra,
& delle giostre gli acquistati pregi
di Bello lessi & selmio dir nō erra,
de persi, medi, & degli ateniensi,
Dāfinione & gli altri egregi immēsi.

Et de lacedemoni le grandi entrate,
di Labores di Oreste & daltri assai,
del Principe Gisippo cose late,
come si legge so che inteso lhai,
di Tholomeo piu cose smisurate,
& del gran Faraone come saprai.
di judici & de regi de giudei,
che afaccia parlavano con lei.

Et de latini lessi, & degli albani,
& di quel fiesolano Re Atalante,
de regi & consolati de romani,
& de tribuni lessi cose tante,
dedeci viri electi tanti humani,
& degli īmperadori potrei dir quāte
cose chi tengo nel mio pecto fisse.
p che sarian nel dir troppo plisse.

che sio volesse tucti efacti dire
disopra nominati & altri assai,
certo farei latua mente stupire
maximi alcuni che nō ludiron mai,
q̃ste cose alte degne magne et mire
che se tu leggi tu letroverrai
invernacula lingua & ī latino,
si come narra un decto dagostino.

Ma chi potessi leggere nel futuro
duno Alexādro magno papa sexto,
della sua creatione il modo puro,
grato a ciascūo anessū mai molesto,
& del primanno suo il magno muro,
che nō glipuo nessuno esser infesto
sesto alexādro pappa borgia ispano,
justo nel giudicare & tucto humano.

Et chi leggesi poi del sua Ferrādo
christianissimo rege xp̃iani
che lisabella tiene al suo comādo,
unica sposa sua, che nelle mani
tanti reami indota allui donando,
gliha dati ītendi ben cō pēsier sani,
che glie re della spagna & di castella
& di leon tolecto villa bella.

Simile re di cordube chiamato,
& poi dimutia re mipar che sia
& digalitia re incoronato,
dalgarbe re & tienla in sua balia,
re digranata sai che conquistato
diragona signor & divalēzia pia
conte mipar che sia dibarzalona,
& disicilia re isola buona.

Di quāta altura principe mipare
& disardigna tien la signoria,
& di corsica sifa simil chiamare,
di q̃lla parte che glha in sua balia
& conte di serdeina appellare,
& dirosello conte par che sia
simile re mi pare che dimaiorica,
l'altro reame e poi della minorica.

Et poi signor dibiscaia & molina,
delalsesiras signor chiamato,
dellasturias terra peregrina,
p tucto il mondo q̃sto e nominato,
tucto fedele della legge divina,
chi altro crede e mal dallui trattato
come sivede che nō e mai satio,
dimarrani giudei far ogni stratio.

Pero il signore lha semp̃ Ivicto facto,
che si puo uno agusto nominare,
ogni sua lega triegua legge o pacto,
mai nō sividde dallui maculare
lui nō derise mai savio ne macto
limosine per dio sempre fa fare
della chiesa zeloso a tucte lhoro
come fedel, xp̃iano, & pio signore.

Come mōstra lamagna ābascieria,
che glha mandato adar lubidiēza
al suo sesto Alexādro anima pia
che mai sivide tal magnificenza
in tucte cose la sua signoria
dimōstrā aver fra gli altri grā potēza
ī q̄sti magni ābascidor sispechi
chi nol credessi nōcti p̄sti orecchi.

Se io volessi e sua titoli dire,
o auditore io ti potrei tediare,
de sua reame io ti farei stupire,
sol que che lisabelela volse dare
indota a q̄sto Re o questo sire,
quando luso p marito pigliare
q̄sta isabella e dispagna Regina,
honesta doña savia & peregrina.

Hor vo tornar almio primo tractato
dellisole trovate incognite a te
in q̄sto anno presente q̄sto e stato
nel millequatrocento novūtatre,
uno che xp̄ofan colōbo chiamato,
che e stato in corte del prefato Re
ha molte volte questo stimolato,
el Re ch'cerchi acrescere il suo stato.

Dicendo, signor mio, io vo cercare
p che comprēdo che ce molta terra
che nostri antichi nō seppō trovare
& spero dacquistarle senza guerra,
se vostra signoria si vuol degnare
ajuto darmi che so que non erra
lamente mia spera nel signore
chimbrieve cidara rengo & honore.

Voi mectetē la roba io la persona
non sara vostra signoria disfacta,
ispesse volte la fortuna dona
p̄ picol prezo assai & non e macta
che sua sperāza tucto il mōdo sprona
savio e colui che dicercar sadacta
p̄ che dice elvāgelio ī legge nuova
che chicercādo va spesso truova.

Hō poi ch' lebbe ilre piu volte udito
& facto carisposta sorridendo
xp̄ofano ripigliando come ardito
q̄sto āno il re secōdo ch' io cōprēdo
prese di dargli aiuto per partito
& disse il tuo sperare oggi cōmēdo
piglia una nave cō due carovelle
di q̄ste mie armate le piu belle.

Et comādo de poi che gli sia dato
danari & roba q̄l che fa mestiero,
& poi dimolta gēte acompagnato
divotamente & cō buō pensiero,
al sommo dio che fu racomandato,
& alla madre sua & sancto piero,
& prese q̄ste cose, & poi licentia
dalre & laregina & sua clementia

Et navico piu giorni per perduto,
cō pena, con affanni & grūde stento,
pensa che ua in mare no e mai tuto,
ma semp̄ cōbactēdo ī acqua & uēto
p̄desi spesso elguadagno eltrebuto,
& nōgli gioua dire io menepento
ma come piacq̄ adio ch' mai nōerra
in trentatre giornate pose in terra.

Et messe dua desua huomini armati
a cercar ple terre che han trouate,
seforce siscoprissin qualche aguati,
ma caminaron ben per tre giornate
che nōsi furon mai indrieto uolti,
& nō trouaron mai uille o brigate,
si che simarauiglia che camina
& piu chi e restato alla marina.

Ma niēte di manco quella terra
era di uari fructi molto ornata,
se chi ha scripto i qua neldir nōerra,
mōtagne e ue daltura ismisurata,
& molti fiumi lacircūda & serra,
doue trouorun poi molta brigata,
sēza pāni, uestite, o arme, o scudi
ma tucti emēbri loro si erano nudi.

Saluo chalcuna donna che coperte
tiene leparte genitale immonde,
cō bambagia tessuta, & di po certe
lhauen coperte con diuerse frōde,
& come uidon questi lediserte
forte fuggendo ciascun fina scōde,
& questi dua in drieto si tornauano,
& axp̃ofano lo facto racontauano.

Et xp̃ofano & glialtri dismontati
armati tucti il paese cercando
isole molte & huomini trouati
come tu intenderai qui ascoltando
& glistendardi del Re ha rizati,
& a ciascuno il suo nome mutando,
come dira questa pistola magna,
da xp̃ofano scripta al Re di spagna.

Perchio so, signor mio, ch' grā piacer̃
hara la uostra magna signoria
quando potra intendere o sapere,
delle cose che io presi in mia balia,
p uirtu del signore & suo potere,
& simil della madre sua maria,
dal partir mio a trētatre giornate,
molte isole & grū gēte iho trouate.

Lisola prima chio trouai, signore,
io lho p nome facta nominare
isola magna di san Saluadore,
& la seconda poi feci chiamare
conceptio Marie a suo honore,
di poi laterza feci baptezare
per uostra signoria ch' tūto ornata
isola ferrandina lho nominata,

Et la quarta Isabella fo chiamare,
p la Regina che tūnto honorata,
& alla quinta il nome uolsi dare
che lisola Giouanna fia chiamata,
& la festa dun nome uolsi ornare
che cōgruo miparse a q̄lla fiata,
che Laspagnuola qlla sichiamasse,
per che mipar che cosi meritasse.

Enomi son dellisole trouate
nel india, signor mio, como uiscriuo,
& questa & laltre sopra nominate
notitia auoi nedo signor mio diuo
trecōto uc̄tun miglio ho caminate,
& peruenuto alfin colsancto uliuo
dalla giouūna alla spagnuola elmar̃
cīquātaquattro miglia largo apare.

Et per septentrione lanauicai
cinquantaquattro miglia dimarina,
doue che alla spagna io arriuai,
inuerso loriente sauicina,
& per lalinea recta io caminai
da onde la spagnuola li confina
son c̄iquec̄esessantaquattro miglia,
e lalargheza che q̄sta isola piglia.

Et q̄sta & tucte laltre e molto forte,
ma q̄sta sopra laltre par fortissima,
potresi inanzi dare a tucte morte
ch' una parte sacquisti piccolissima,
certo questo eildestino qsto e lesorte,
ch' uostra signoria fan felicissima,
e dotata di fructi molte & uarie,
& liti, & porti, & cose necessarie,

Et molti fiumi, & maxime mōtagne,
che son dalteza molto smisurate,
arbori, fonte, uccegli, & cose magne,
chauostri tempi nō san mai trouate,
certo lamente mia signor ne piagne,
per lalegreza delle cose ornate,
di tucte cose cie se io non erro,
saluo ch' nōsi truoua acciaio o ferro.

Sonci di septe o uer docto ragioni
di palme che mifan marauigliare,
& se alzando gliocchi poni
pini uison che laria par toccare,
passere lusignuoli & altri doni,
che nonsi potre mai tucto narrare,
della bambagia un pondo ce infinito
& daltre cose assai ce inquesto lito.

Arbori cison duna ragion fioriti
del mese di novembre chenoi siano
come ī ispagna, & ne suo degno liti,
liarberi sō elmagio, elmōte, elpiano,
si che no altri stiano tucti stupiti
p labōdantia che trouata habbiano,
sonci gli arberi uerdi & and lelor foglie,
chi credo che nō pdā mai lespoglie.

Di reubarbaro ce tanta abōdantia,
& dicenamo daltra spetieria,
loro & largento, el metallo ciauūza,
maxime un fiume che per q̄sta uia,
che nō puo questa terra farne senza,
doue ho trouato cō mia fantasia,
che dimoltoro e piena quella rena,
sicome lacqua di quel fiume mena.

Simil, signore, io uiuoglio auisare,
che inq̄stisola ce molta pianura,
doue difizi molti sipuon fare,
& castelle cipta cō magne mura,
che nō bisogna poi di dubitare,
ne dhauer chi cista nulla paura,
molte terre cison da feminare,
& depascer lebestie & nutricare.

Ho po trouati certi fiumicelli,
ch' tucti menano oro & nō gia poco,
& molti porti grādi & da far belli,
che abōdanza ce dacqua diloco,
lherbe & leselue facte co pennelli
nō son si belle & nō cisusa foco,
glhuomini sono affabile formati,
timidi semp̃ & alfuggir parati.

Sonci assai uille ma son picoolecte,
dhuomini & dōne son tucte calcate,
glihabitacoli qui son capānecte
semplici sono & credule brigate,
& ben che sieno nudi stāno necte,
si che signor dibuona uoglia state,
& credon che no siā di cielo ī terra,
mādati per cāpargli dogni guerra.

Portano alcun certe cāne appuntate,
socto lebraccia come noi lespade,
archi cō frecce dicanne tagliate,
& uāno īsieme assai come lesquadř
di capegli & di barbe molto ornate,
nō son micidial persone o ladre,
ma tucto q̃l ch' glhiāno ī lor potere
celodarebbon p̄ farci piacere.

Et parmi che cifia grā diferenza
da questa isola a q̃lla di Giouāna
darbori, fructi, and dherbe & dip̃sēza,
nōci manca senon la sancta māna,
doro ce tanto cha uostra potenza
chi guerra far sipensa ī uan safāna
oltre alla roba acquistate lhonore.
tucti son prōti acreder al signore.

Questi popoli grādi & infiniti,
come p̄ segni ciāno dimōstrato,
ledōne & lor figluoli & lor mariti
ciascuno spera desser baptezato,
priego il signor iesu che puo glīuiti
apossedere el suo regno beato
di quāto ben cagion signor sarete
coluostro auxilio che dato mhauète.

Iho menati qui certi indiani
ch' cōpredū di q̄sta alcun līguaggio
tal che parlando con cēni dimani
q̄lcū diq̄sti ch'e piu sperto & saggio
dicon di farsi a noi tucti xp̃iani
tal chiho p̃so signor mio uātaggio
& di legname una bastia fo fare
& lagente uimecto per guardare.

Et forniti glilascio per uno anno
darme diuectouaglia ben chi spero
che nō haranno molestia ne dāno
p̄ che gli lascio cō un buon pensiero,
humili mansueti tucti stanno,
sich' auxilio iluostro signor chiero,
mandimi uostra signoria piacente
allaude del signore omnipotente.

Chi nō uede signor lisole degne,
& lericheze o nobil creatura,
& lauarieta darbori & legne,
& deglhuomini & dōne lor figura,
nō sa ch' sia delmōdo lesue ī segno,
chi nō esce delcerchio di sua mura,
nō puo perfectamente idio laudare
chi nō gusta lecose che sa fare.

Signor mio dolce, lapiaceuoleza
di q̄sta gente io non saprei narrare,
per una stringa che poco sipreza
uolson tanto oro aun diquesti dare
ch' tre ducati & mezo o che richeza
hare potuto inqueste parte fare,
ma io ho comādato alla mia gente
che ciascun doni & nō pigli niēte.

Per far lor grata uostra signoria
dimolta roba io ho facto donare
di quella dimie gente & della mia,
come scodelle & piacti damāgiare,
& uetri & pauni chera in mia balia,
senza riserbo alcuno per me fare
p chio glho conosciuti tante grati,
iglho come fedeli & buō tractati.

Vero e ch' sono assai prōti alfugire
per che non sono usati di uedere
gente che usin panni da uestire,
ma per che uegan noi tucto sapere,
ciascun diloro ciadora come sire,
& lalor roba da mangiare o bere,
nō ho ueduto fare ne tuo ne mio,
ma lauita comune alparer mio.

Volsano ancora p una bocte trista,
& per un pezo darco che nō uale,
tre once doro darmi & similmista,
tanta bambagia che mezo quintale,
ma poi chi hebbi questa cosa uista
parsemi dipigliar niente male,
& ho cōmesso aciaschedun de mia
chedipigliare niente ardito sia.

Nō e fra loro alcuna briga o secta,
ma pacifici tucti insieme stanno,
di parole & ni facti mai saspecta,
di far uēdecta alcūa īgiuria o dāno,
beato a qˀllo che seguir sidilecta,
acompagnati abraccio sempˀ uāno,
io glho uisti si buoni recti & grati,
che abuō fine idio glhara chiamati.

Nō e fra loro idolatria nessuna,
tucti lemani al ciel tengono alzate,
nō adoran pianeti, o sole, o luna,
ma lelor mente al ciel tucte leuate.
dicon la gloria ī ciel esser sol una,
dellaqual patria credon ch' mādate
ienostre barche siano & noi ī terra,
a far pace colciel dogni lor guerra.

Io nho cō meco semp̃ alcū menato
equali feci per forza pigliare,
q̃ndo alprĩcipio ī terra fui smōtato,
non potendo inaltra forma fare
pelueloce fuggir mai ascoltato
nō era lemie uoci olmio parlare,
& q̃sti che per forza allhor pigliai,
son per amor uenuti sempre mai.

Semp̃ mangiare, o bere, & adormire,
acanto a me io glho si ben tractati,
ch' gliaferman p̃ certo & usan dire
ch' dalregno del ciel no siā mūdati,
uanocci inanzi gridando uenire,
debba ciascuno auedere ebeati,
si chalpresente ognū corre auedere
& portan tucti damāgiare & bere.

Da luna isola allaltra q̃sti uāno
cō certe barche che inquesta isola e,
lequal dun legno solo facte stanno,
& son chiamate queste canoe,
sō lūghe strecte & par quasi uolādo
andare achiunche messo dētro ce,
bench' sien grossamente lauorate
cō sassi & legni & ossi son cauate.

Et hōne uista alcuna tāto grāde
che octanta persone cista dentro,
& ciascūo hal suo remo & leumāde
nauica q̄sti & con buon sētimeto
la roba luno allaltro li sispande
q̄l chio uscriuo signor nulla mēto
& uanno baractando tucti quāti
come sefussin quasi mercatanti.

Inqueste isole tucte nominate
nō ho ueduta nulla differenza
dincarnati diuisi o dibrigate,
ma tucti quasi son duna presenza
& dun cōstume tucti cōstumate
huomini & dōne sō pie dicremēza,
tucti hāno una loquela & un parlař
che uifarē, signor, marauigliare.

Che par che util cosa questa sia
acōuerrirgli a nostra sancta fede.
che come scriuo auostra signoria
ciascun disposto ce, & gia lacrede
dique che han uista lapresenza mia
no glho tucti ueduti de siuede
ch'glie margior giouāna senza sotia
che nōe linghilterra con lascotia.

Son duo puincie chio nō ho certate,
secondo che q̄sti altri decto hāno,
una cene la qual queste brigate
dican che quelle gente che uistāno
son con le code tucte quante nate
& Anaan elnome posto lehanno,
poi caminai p la spagnuola ciglia
p cinquecēsessantoquattro miglia.

Doue e lauilla laqual io pigliai,
doue io feci larocca o uer bastia
che la piu bella che io uedessi mai,
come iho scripto a uostra signoria
non miricorda se adir uimandai
inquesta brieue epistolecta mia
elnōe ch' io lho posto & forse auisto
natiuita del nostro Iesus Xp̃o.

In queste isole tucti questi stāno
contenti duna dōna ciascheduno,
ma q̄sti principali tucti mhanno
uēti lequal son date lor per uno,
& luno allaltro mai torto nō fanno,
che a cio far nō ce pronto nessuno,
& nelle cose tucte da mangiare
nulla diuision uiueggo fare.

Et ben che i q̄ste parti caldo sia,
lastate eluerno ce digran freddura,
ma p che mangiā molta spetieria
lacarne loro alfreddo molto dura
inquesta parte nulla cosa ria,
sitruoua diche questi habbin paura,
saluo che ce unisola allentrare
dellindia per uoler qui arriuare.

In nella quale sta gente uillana
da q̄sti nō mipar che siano amati,
p ch' dice māgiā carne humana,
pero nō son da questi qui prezati,
hanno assai legni q̄sta gente strana,
da nauicare & hanno gia rubati,
aquesti di scorrendo dogni banna
cō archi ī mano & cō frecce dicāna.

Non e da q̄sti a quegli differenza,
senō innecapegli che q̄gli hanno
lunghi come ledōne & dipresenza
son come q̄sti & fāno molto dūno,
aq̄ste ch' son ppro essa clemenza,
si che ingelosia sempre nestanno,
ma spero che lauostra signoria
sapra purgare una tal maltaia.

Una isola cie decta mactanino,
nella qual le donne sole stanno,
& questo iniquo popol glie uicino,
& ausar con q̄ste spesso uanno,
ma q̄sto popol tucto feminino
exercitio di dōne mai nō fanno,
ma cō gliarchi trahēdo tuctauia,
che par per certo una grū fantasia.

Et uanno queste ben tucte coperte,
nō gia di pāni lini, o lani, o ueli,
ma derbe & giūchi, & q̄ste cose certe
son che di qua nq̄e lēzuoli o teli
unaltra isola poi legente offerte,
femine & maschi nascō senza peli,
manzi uoglia cōfuso esser nel dire
chi uoglia alcuna cosa preterire.

Et dove q̄sti senza peli sono,
piu oro cie chihabbia ācor trouata
di q̄l chi scriuo o parlando ragiono,
signore, io ne son ben giustificato
auostra signoria un magno dono
iho per portar meco preparato
di tucti q̄sti luoghi iuo menare
gente che possin cio testificare.

Pero, giusto signor, di Spagna degno,
stia uostra signoria dibuona uoglia
chĩho cresciuto tãto iluostro regno,
ch' chi ua ĩuida po crepar didoglia
doro & dargento passarete el segno
tel ch' trarra elnimico di sua soglia,
ma q̃l chi so ch' molto piu prezate
son queste gẽte a xp̃o preparate.

Reubarbero assai & aloe,
Mastice, cinamono, & spetierie,
tanta richeza, signor mio, qui e
che discaccia da me leuoglie rie,
piu allegreza, signor mio, fare,
si fussi certo che per tucte uie
q̃sta scripta uenissi asaluamento
nel mõdo nõ sare huom piu-cõtẽto.

Nõ miacascaltro degno mio signore
scriuere auostra magna signoria,
raccomandomi a q̃lla a tucte lhore,
laqual cõserui ilfigluol di Maria
parato semp̃mai per uostro amore
amecter q̃sta breue uita mia
aquindici de febraio q̃sta sife
nel mille quattrocento nouãta tre.

Magnifici & discreti circũstanti
q̃sta e gran cosa certo da pensare,
ch'l nostro redẽptor̃ cõ tucti esancti
nõ resta mai legratie sue mandare
douerebbon di q̃sto tucti quanti
ebaptizati a x̃po festa fare,
chi ue chi uimãdo & chi ue andato
prepari dio alsuo regno beato.

Questa ha cōposto de dati Giuliano
apreghiera del magno caualiere
messer Giouanphilippo ciciliano,
che fu di Sixto quarto suo scudiero
& commessario suo & capitano,
a q̄lle cose che fur di mestiere
allaude del signor sicanta & dice
che ciconduca al suo regno felice.

¶ FINIS LAUS DEO.

¶ Finita lastoria della iūctione delle nuoue isole dicūnaria
īdiane tracte duna pistola dixp̃ofano colōbo, & p̃messer
Giuliano dati tradocta dilatino ī uersi uulgari allaude
della christiana religione & ap̃ghiera delmagnifico
caualiere messer Giouāfilippo del ignamine
domestico familiare dello illustrissimo
Redispagna xp̃ianissimo a
di. xxvi. doctobre.
14.93.

Florentie.

BIBLIOGRAPHY.

In this bibliographical notice I do not propose to deal with any editions of the first letter of Columbus beyond the "Incunabula," which I arrange in the order of their publication, as ascertained from an examination of the documents themselves.

1. ¶ Epistola Christofori Colom: cui etas nostra multū debet: de | Insulis Indie supra Gangem nuper inuētis. Ad quas perqren- | das octauo antea mense auspiciis & ere invictissimor' Fernādi & | Helisabet Hispaniar' Regū missus fuerat: ad magnificum dñm | Gabrielem Sanchis eorundē serenissimor' Regum Tesaurariū | missa : quā nobilis ac litteratus vir Leander de Cosco ab Hispa | no ideomate in latinum cōuertit tertio kal's Maii m.cccc.xciii | Pontificatus Alexandri Sexti Anno primo.

Small 4to. This edition, which, as I shall presently show, is the *editio princeps*, was printed by Stephen Plannck at Rome in 1493. It consists of four leaves, printed in gothic type, and has 33 lines in a full page. Copies are in the Grenville and King's Libraries in the British Museum.

2. ¶ Epistola Christofori Colom: cui etas nostra multum debet: de | Insulis Indie supra Gangem nuper inuētis. Ad quas perquiren | das octauo antea mense auspiciis & ere inuictissimorum Fernandi | ac Helisabet Hispaniar' Regū missus fuerat: ad Magnificū dñm | Gabrielem Sanches: eorundem serenissimorum Regum Tesau | rariū missa: Quā generosus ac litteratus vir Leander de Cosco ab | Hispano

idiomate in latinū cōuertit : tertio Kalen' Maij M.cccc. | xc.iij. Pontificatus Alexandri Sexti Anno Primo. | 4to.

End :—¶ Impressit Rome Eucharius Argenteus [Silber] Anno dñi. M.ccccxciij.

Three leaves, printed in gothic letter. 40 lines in a page. A copy is in the Grenville Library.

3. ¶ Epistola Christofori Colom : cui etas nostra multū debet : de | Insulis Indie supra Gangem nuper inuentis. Ad quas perqui | rendas octauo antea mense auspicijs & ere invictissimi Fernan | di Hispaniarum Regis missus fuerat : ad Magnificum dñum Ra | phaelem Sanxis : eiusdem serenissimi Regis Tesaurariū missa : | quam nobilis ac litteratus vir Aliander de Cosco ab Hispano | ideomate in latinum conuertit : tertio kal's Maij. M.cccc.xciij. | Pontificatus Alexandri Sexti Anno Primo.

Small 4to. Gothic letter; four leaves, 34 lines in a full page. This edition is supposed to have been printed by Stephen Plannck at Rome, about 1493. 3 or 4 copies are known ; two are in the General Library and Grenville Library, British Museum.

4. De Insulis inuentis | Epistola Cristoferi Colom (cui etas nostra | multū debet : de Insulis in mari Indico nup' | inuētis. Ad quas perquirendas octauo antea | mense : auspicijs et ere Invictissimi Fernandi | Hispaniarum Regis missus fuerat | ad Magnificum dñm Raphaeleƺ Sanxis : eiusdē sere | nissimi Regis Thesaurariū missa. quam nobi | lis ac litterat' vir Aliander đ Cosco : ab His | pano ydeomate in latinū conuertit: tercio k'ls | Maij. M.cccc.xciij. Pontificatus Alexandri | Sexti Anno Primo.

Small 8vo. Gothic character; ten leaves, 26 and 27 lines in a page. The title above given is preceded by a leaf bearing on the recto the arms of Spain, "Regnū hyspanie"—on the verso the cut of the "Oceanica Classis". There are 6 woodcuts—the

"Oceanica Classis", being repeated. A copy is in the Grenville Library.

5. Epistola de insulis de | nouo repertis. Impressa | parisius in cāpo gaillardi.

Small 4to. Gothic letter; four leaves, 39 lines in a full page. This edition was printed by Guy Marchand about 1494. Brunet states that the only copy known is that formerly belonging to M. Ternaux-Compans, now the property of Mr. John Carter Brown.

This edition was reprinted in 1865, "Lettre de Christophe Colomb sur la découverte du Nouveau-Monde, publiée d'après la rarissime version latine conservée à la Bibliothèque Impériale. Traduite en Français, commentée et enrichie de notes puisées aux sources originales par Lucien de Rosny. 8vo., Paris, 1865."

6. Epistola de Insulis noui | ter repertis. Impressa parisius In campo gaillardi.

Small 4to. Gothic letter; four leaves, 39 lines in a page. The above title is in two lines, the first printed in a larger character. Underneath is the device of the printer, "Guiot Marchant"—two cobblers at work, one cutting the leather, the other making it up. This edition was printed by Guy Marchand at Paris, about 1494.

A copy is in the Bodleian Library. A facsimile made by Mr. John Harris, sen., is in the British Museum; the impression was limited to five copies.

All the foregoing editions have at the end the Latin Epigram in eight verses of R. L. de Corbatia, (a pseudonym for Leonardus de Carninis, Bishop

of Monte Peloso in Naples). In this edition, below the epigram, on the same page, is a woodcut of the Angel appearing to the Shepherds. Mr. Lenox has given a facsimile of this in the Appendix to *Syllacius*. The title on the recto of the following leaf (sig. a, ij) is the same as in the Roman editions, having the name of Ferdinand without that of Isabella. It ends with the words: " Vale. Ulisbone pridie Idus Marcij."

A " pictorial" edition of the Latin letter, in 4to., was printed in 1494. It is appended to a work by Carolus Verardus, "In laudem Serenissimi Ferdinandi Hispaniar' regis.... Et de Insulis in mari Indico nuper inuentis."

The work is printed on fifteen pages in Roman characters, and probably at Basle, by B. de Olpe. The woodcuts are the same as those used in the small 8vo. edition printed about 1493 (see No. 4).

No sooner did this letter make its appearance in print in the year 1493, than the narrative it contained was put forth in Italian ottava rima by Giuliano Dati, one of the most popular poets of the day; and there is reason to believe that it was sung about the streets to announce to the Italians the astounding news of the discovery of a new world. (See *ante*, p. xc.)

The only copy of this curious and valuable poem known at the time of the issue of the first edition of this work in 1847 is that which I now reprint.

¶ La lettera dellisole che ha trouato nuovamente il Re dispagna.
End:

¶ Finita lastoria della iuctione del | le nuoue isole dicū-
naria īdiane trac | te duna pistola dixp̄ofano colōbo & |
pmesser Giuliano dati tradocta di la | tino ī uersi uulgari
allaude della ce | lestiale corte & aconsolatione della |
christiana religione & ap̄ghiera del magnifico caualiere
messer Giouā | filippo del ignamine domestico fa | mīliare
dello illustrissimo Re dispa | gna xp̄ianīssimo a di. xxvi.
docto | bre. 14.93. Florentie.

4to. Printed in Roman characters on four leaves, in double columns. The poem consists of 68 stanzas in *ottava rima*. Beneath the single-line title is a woodcut representing the landing of Columbus, and King Ferdinand seated on his throne on the *opposite shore*. This is the only copy known.

Since 1847 another edition has been acquired by the British Museum, bearing the following title :—

¶ Questa e la hystoria della inuentiōe delle diese Isole
di Cannaria In | diane extracte duna Epistola di Chris-
tofano Colombo & per messer Giu | liano Dati traducta
de latino in uersi uulgari a laude e gloria della cele |
stiale corte & a consolatione della christiana religiōe &
apreghiera del ma | gnifico Caualier miser Giouanfilippo
Delignamine domestico familia | re dello Sacratissimo Re
di spagna Christianissimo a di. xxv. doctobre. |
M.ccccbxxxxiii. |
End : FINIS
    Joannes dictus Florentinus.

4to. Printed in gothic characters, in double columns, and, without doubt, at Florence. A complete copy should contain four leaves. The copy in the British Museum, the only one of this edition hitherto discovered, is, unfortunately, deficient in two leaves—viz., the second and the third. It is printed

in a very rude type on coarse paper, and was evidently a popular edition, sold at a very small price. This edition presents many variations from the other, both in the orthography and language ; *e.g.*, the opening stanza, which may be compared with that given in the present edition.

> LOīpotente idio ch'l tulto regge
> mi presti gr̃a chi possa cantare
> allaude sua e di sua sancta legge
> cosa che piaza achi stara ascoltaro
> maxime alpopul suo & a sua greggo
> elqual non cessa mai magnificare
> come al presente afacto nela spagna
> delle isole trouate cosa magna.

This edition omits the final stanza, which is little else than the colophon of the other versified :—

> Questa ha cōposta de' dati Giuliano
> etc.   etc.   etc.

Eyn schön hübsch lesen von etlichen insslen | dīe do in kurtzen zyten funden synd durch dē | künig von hispania. vnd sagt vō grossen wun | derlichen dingen die in dē selbē insslen synd.

End:

Getruckt zŭ strassburg vff gruneck vō meīster Bartlomess | küstler ym iar. M.cccc.xcvij. vff sant Jeronymus tag.—

Small 4to. Seven leaves, 30 lines in a page. Beneath the title is a woodcut representing the apprehension of Christ in the garden ; this is repeated on the verso of the last leaf. This edition is very rare. A copy is in the Grenville Library.

Besides the foregoing we are in possession of a photo-zincographic facsimile published at Milan in 1866, by the Marquis Gerolamo d'Adda, of an early

i

printed edition of the Spanish original, in the Ambrosian Library in that city. It bears no printer's name or place or date of publication, but it is unquestionably of the fifteenth century, and is considered by bibliographers to be of the date of 1493. Señor Pascual de Gayangos (in a valuable paper, entitled "La Carta de Cristóbal Colon al Escribano Luis de Santangel", printed in the Madrid Journal, *La America*, under date of 13th April, 1867) suggests that it was printed in Lisbon.

We have also in Navarrete's *Coleccion de Viages*, printed at Madrid 1825, vol. i, pp. 167-175, what professes to be an attested literal rendering of a copy of Columbus's letter in Spanish to the Escribano de Racion (whom we know from Argensola's *Anales de Aragon* to be Luis de Santangel), in the Archives at Simancas.

And, further, we have a printed version of a copy of the first letter in Spanish MS., discovered by His Excellency Senhor de Varnhagen in Valencia, and published by him in that city in 1858, under the title of *Primera Epistola del Almirante Don Christobal Colon...a D. Gabriel Sanchez Tesorero de Aragon*. As editor, Senhor de Varnhagen assumed the pseudonym of D. Genaro H. de Volafan; and last year His Excellency published at Vienna a little work, the nature and contents of which are explained by its title, which is as follows :—" Carta de Cristóbal Colon enviada de Lisboa a Barcelona en Marzo de 1493. Nueva Edicion Critica: Conteniendo las variantes de los diferentes textos, juicio sobre estos, re-

flexiones tendentes a mostrar a quien la Carta fue escrita, y varias otras noticias, por el Seudónimo de Valencia."

Be it observed that in all these the *titles* are supplied by the respective editors, and consequently have no authority beyond the weight of each editor's individual opinion. I have carefully collated the three documents, and the result is a certain conclusion that neither one nor the other is a correct transcript of the original letter. The grounds for this conclusion are, that while no two of them entirely agree *inter se*, every one of them exhibits certain special errors which, as I shall presently demonstrate, *could* not have been in the original. The apparent rashness of this assertion will disappear if the reader will accompany me in my effort to detect which of the printed Latin editions which we possess is to receive the distinction of *editio princeps*. Various have been the opinions on this subject. Mr. Lenox, following Brunet, has given the lead to the edition which I have ventured to place *fourth*. Mr. Harrisse, in his elaborate *Notes on Columbus*, gives the first place to that which stands *third* in my series, and His Excellency Senhor de Varnhagen assigns priority to the edition which I make to be the *second*. That to which I assign the distinction of taking the lead has the *second* place given to it by Senhor de Varnhagen, and the *third* by Brunet, Mr. Lenox, and Mr. Harrisse. In offering a conclusion so much at variance with my predecessors, my only means of escaping the charge of presumption (but that I hope is an effectual one),

is neither to adopt the opinion of any one else nor to offer any opinion of my own, but to reduce the matter to demonstration by facts either within or connected with the documents themselves.

On examination of the titles it will be seen that the six editions resolve themselves by several very strongly marked features into two distinct groups. One of these groups, embracing four of the editions, is characterized by remarkable inaccuracy in three separate points—all four exhibiting all these inaccuracies in common ; while the remaining two, being free from them, stand clearly defined into a distinct group by themselves.

Thus ; the titles of the editions numbered 3, 4, 5, 6, all speak of Columbus being sent out under the auspices and at the expense of Ferdinand, King of Spain, without reference to the name of Queen Isabella. They all describe the letter as addressed to the Treasurer "Sanxis," instead of "Sanchez," whose Christian name they pervert from "Gabriel" to "Raphael." Furthermore, they all convert the Christian name of the translator from "Leander" to "Aliander."

The titles of the editions numbered 1 and 2, on the contrary, give the names of both the sovereigns, call the Treasurer in No. 2 Sanches, in No. 1 " Sanchis," but not Sanxis, and rightly name the translator " Leander de Cosco."

Now there is no difficulty in showing which of these groups has the merit of correctness, or which the demerit of incorrectness.

It is perfectly well known that in 1493 Ferdinand

and Isabella held the common title of *Reyes de España*. Whether "Sanches" or "Sanxis" should be the correct form of spelling the name of a Spaniard who was treasurer to the Spanish sovereigns, it would be waste of time to question, and that his Christian name was Gabriel and not Raphael, we have clear evidence from an independent document in the Archives of Simancas, dated December 1495, for which the reader is referred to Navarrete's *Coleccion de Viages*, vol. iii, p. 76, line 16, where he is called "El tesorero Gabriel Sanchez". His name is also mentioned more than once by Zurita in his *Anales de Aragon*.

The question then arises whether the palm of priority is to be conceded to the correct or to the incorrect form. Now all these six titles agree in stating that the original Spanish letter of Columbus was *sent* to the Treasurer Royal. But for a letter to be sent, it must carry an address, and if Columbus inserted in such address the Treasurer's name, he, who knew Spanish so well, would not have insulted that dignitary by converting his surname of Sanchez into Sanxis, or his Christian name of Gabriel into Raphael. But even if we suppose that he omitted the name altogether, as is probable, and simply superscribed his letter with the title of the Treasurer, the fact still remains that the translator or editor of the first edition derived the information that the letter was so sent, directly from the Treasurer himself, who at least knew his own name and would not allow it to be transmitted for publication (if Columbus

had been guilty of the blunder) under the form of "Raphael Sanxis." Nor would he, holding a high official post, have been guilty of the *maladresse* of omitting the name of the queen in the description of his own title. Now of our two groups of printed letters it is indisputable that that one must take precedence which comes immediately in connection with the original source, and as that source is at the same time the head-quarters of correctness, it follows that correctness must be the criterion of priority.

We thus find our six candidates for the glory of "editio princeps" reduced to two. Now these two issued from two different printing presses. One of them is printed by Argenteus, *i.e.*, Silber, and bears his name with the imprint, "Rome, 1493." The other is without printer's name or place or date of publication, but is indisputably from the printing press of Stephanus Plannck, as may be seen by comparing it with a work of Benedictus de Nursia of the same date, entitled "*Incipit libellus de conservatione sanitatis secundum ordinem alphabeti distinctus per eximium doctorem magistrum Benedictum compositus.*" *Impressum Rome per magistrum Stephanum Planck. Anno Domini mccccxciii, quarto nōn Maii.* In this and other works from the same press the form and type precisely correspond with those of our letter.

Now these two editions of Plannck and Silber were either printed simultaneously or not. Instances of the same work being printed by two different printers on the same day do occur. One example is before me of this happening in this very year 1493. The

work is entitled, "*Illustris et Reverendi Domini Nicolai Mariæ Estensis Episcopi Hadriensis oratio pro consanguineo suo inclyto Hercule Estensi Ferrariæ duce secundo.*" One edition in Roman character bears the colophon, *Romæ impressa per mgrm Plannck : Julio Campello Spoletino procurante. Anno Salvatoris mcccclxxxiii. Nonis Januariis.* The other, in Gothic character, bears precisely the same title and the same colophon, with the difference of the words, *impressa per magistrum Andream Fritag.* Both are small quarto, of the size of our two editions of the letter of Columbus.

But here it must be observed that there was apparently a special object in resorting to this exceptional procedure, viz., the production simultaneously of one edition in Roman and another in Gothic types, to suit the tastes of purchasers. In the case before us, however, the question of this motive does not arise, for both Plannck's and Silber's editions are in Gothic type; and any way it is clear that, in a case of the kind, the same text would be handed to each printer to set up, as any patent discrepancies between the two would be to the self-stultification of the editor. Now, in the case of the Columbus letter, such patent discrepancies do occur; by which I mean no mere printer's blunders, but deliberate alterations of Latin expressions, as for example "ambularunt" in Plannck is "ambulaverunt" in Silber; "serenissimos Reges nostros," correct Latin in Plannck, is "serenissimorum regum nostrorum," making bad grammar, in Silber. This fact of itself I contend dis-

proves simultaneity of production. But side by side with these discrepancies we observe the repetition in the one, of eccentricities or inaccuracies occurring in the other, as in the words "quom," "benivolentia," and "nanque." The former, though not incorrect, is quaint and unusual, but the two latter are faulty peculiarities, and their occurrence, in both editions, side by side with deliberate alterations, proves the one to be copied from the other either by the hand of the transcriber or of the compositor. This fact once established, I have to call attention to the following remarkable difference between the two editions. In the Plannck edition the distance sailed by Columbus along the north coast of Hispaniola is stated as DLXIIII miles. In Silber's the same figures occur minus the D, and with no space left for the letter to have fallen out. Now it being understood that one of these is a copy from the other, whether through a transcriber's or a compositor's hand, if we suppose that the Silber edition, which was minus the D, appeared first, we must perceive that the error is one which no special knowledge could enable the editor or printer of the other to suspect, much less to rectify, and yet in the Plannck edition we should find it so rectified. Whereas if the Plannck edition be supposed to be the first, we have no such difficulty to encounter, but simply meet (in the Silber edition) with a negligent omission of a letter, which may so easily happen. The next enquiry, of course, is, which number is right, 564 or 64 miles? Fortunately we have the means of answering this question with cer-

tainty, for as we possess two copies, or copies of copies, of the original Spanish letter, we find that the translator, Leander de Cosco, converted the leagues of the Spanish original into miles by multiplying them, though ignorantly, by three; and in one of these two copies, which can in other respects be shown to be far more correct than its fellow, these leagues are stated as 188, which correspond exactly with 564 miles. It must be clear, then, that the edition containing the number 564 was derived from the original accounts, while that which contained the number 64 had allowed the D to be lost. The result I submit to be that Plannck's edition must claim the palm to priority.

To this conclusion it has been objected by a friend that the argument is not complete, inasmuch as Cosco the translator, may have sent his translation to Rome, with instructions that a copy thereof should be made, and that, as the work was of importance, two printers should at once be employed in printing from the two copies; that the copyist may have thought fit to make the alterations which appear between the two, or, failing him, that these alterations may have been made by the compositor of one of them. To which I reply that the deviations in the Silber edition are all on the side of ignorance, and not such as could have been made by an original translator. To take the most notable example: in Plannck's edition occurs this passage, already slightly referred to, "quæ res perutilis est ad id quod Serenissimos Reges nostros exoptare præcipue reor." "Which thing is very useful for the object which I think that our most serene

Sovereigns principally desire." Here we find the right grammatical construction of the accusative before the infinitive mood, just as the translator would write it. In Silber's edition the sentence stands thus: "quæ res perutilis est ad id quod Serenissimorum regum nostrorum exoptare præcipue reor," a change showing such ignorance of grammatical construction that it could not have been the work of the translator. I contend that, under such circumstances, even if it should be assumed (though there is no warranty for such assumption) that the two editions were printed simultaneously, Plannck's edition would justly take the lead on account of its more immediate derivation from the original translation.

But before I leave this subject I must call attention to a notable fact, which opens up the question whether the real *editio princeps* has perished, or not as yet come to our knowledge. It happens that the length of the north coast of Hispaniola is *twice* stated by Columbus in this letter. The *first* mention of it is given correctly in Plannck's edition as "milliaria dlxiiii," which I have already shown to be a right number, while in Silber the "d" is lost, and the number stands "lxiiii." The *second* mention of the length of the coast is given *alike incorrectly by both* as dxl. This fact, brought into combination with those evolved by our comparison of the two texts, not only corroborates the non-originality and secondary position of Silber's edition, but it raises a question as to whether Plannck's was not preceded by another which has never come to our knowledge, in which both numbers were

BIBLIOGRAPHY.   cxxiii

correctly given. It might be conjectured that Columbus himself wrote the second number incorrectly, but here the different Spanish texts come valuably to our aid, and the curious circumstance that the translator Cosco converted the leagues of the Spanish into miles in the Latin, supplies a most welcome means of solving the riddle. Another document, the contemporaneous rhythmical version of the letter by Giuliano Dati, will also be of great service in the examination of the subject. For the sake of clearness I will tabulate them, and distinguish the correct numbers, where they occur, by italics.

	Ambrosian text.	Valencia MS.	Simancas MS.	Plannck's edition.	Silber's edition.	Dati.
First mention.	clxxviii leguas.	*ciento e ochenta y ocho leguas.*	ciento e setenta y ocho leguas.	milliaria dlxiiii.	milliaria lxiiii.	*cinquecensessanta quattro miglia.*
Second mention.	clxxxviii leguas.	ciento treinta y ocho leguas.	ciento treinta y ocho leguas.	milliaria dxl.	milliaria dxl.	*cinquecensessanta quattro miglia.*

From this table it will be seen that the erroneous one hundred and thirty-eight leagues do not tally with the erroneous five hundred and forty miles; but the most striking fact that this table presents to our notice is that the *Dati poem* is the only one of these documents that has the number right in both places; and it might at first sight appear a very simple and easy thing for Dati to see that what was right measurement in the one case must be the right measurement in the other, even although the other copyists had failed to realise this fact. But not so. Dati composed his poem from the Latin translation, and if the edition from which he worked had been as faulty as that of Plannck, now under notice, he could have had

no means of deciding which number was right, the dlxiiii of the first mention, or the dxl of the second. We have the means of knowing, but only because we possess the various copies of the Spanish, which state the distance in leagues. The necessary conclusion then is that Dati worked from a copy either MS. or printed, in which the number was right in both places; and this conclusion is corroborated by the fact that, of the Spanish documents, the Valencia MS. shows the number right in the first mention, and the Ambrosian text shows it right in the second. Furthermore, I observe that Dati, who distinctly states that his poem was "tradocta di latino," gives the letter the date of Feb. 15th, a date which occurs in the Spanish, but not in the Latin texts which we possess. It follows, therefore, that if he worked from a printed text, that edition is lost to us.

But there remains the alternative that he worked from the MS. Latin translation, and that the latter had been fully rendered from the original Spanish, but was afterwards modified by the compositor in setting it up in type. That such was in reality the case the reader will find proved beyond all dispute at the close of this disquisition. It therefore remains that, while there is no reason to suppose that an edition is lost, the edition by Plannck, consisting of four leaves, with thirty-three lines to the page, must take the lead among those which are known to us.

But now we come to the very interesting subject of the original Spanish. Columbus's manuscript letter is lost, and the only representatives of it with

which we are acquainted are the manuscript copies already mentioned at Simancas and Valencia, published respectively by Navarrete and Senhor de Varnhagen, and the valuable printed text in the Ambrosian Library, for the reproduction of which by photozincography all who are interested in the subject are so deeply indebted to the enlightened liberality of the Marquis d'Adda. The two former transcripts are confessedly made at a much later date, while to the latter bibliographers give the credit of the date of 1493. At the end of the Simancas copy is the expression : " Esta carta envio Colon al Escribano de Racion de las islas halladas en las Indias e otra de sus altezas." This office of Escribano de Racion was held by Luis de Santangel. The Valencia copy had no such sentence at the end, but simply bore the title : " Carta del Almirante á D. Gabriel Sanches." The Ambrosian text photo-zincographed by the Marquis d'Adda bore a similar expression at the end to that of the Simancas copy, but with a difference ; thus : " Esta carta embio Colon al Escrivano de Racion de las Islas halladas en las Indias. Contenida a otra de sus altezas." Under these circumstances the Marquis d'Adda, accepting the pre-supposed fact that Columbus had addressed two similar letters to the two above-named officials, very naturally regarded the Ambrosian text as derived from the Simancas MS. A collation of the three texts, *inter se*, and with the Latin translation of Cosco, exhibits, however, the following results :—the Valencia MS. addressed to Gabriel Sanchez is almost a verbatim repetition of the Si-

mancas text addressed to the Escribano de Racion, while the Ambrosian text also addressed to the Escribano de Racion agrees with the Latin text addressed to Gabriel Sanchez in certain forms of expression, which are entirely different from those used in common in the Valencia and Simancas MSS. to describe the same thing. This perplexing result has been stated by Senhor de Varnhagen in the little work published last year already referred to, and I can confirm it by actual careful collation of all the four documents. The *prima facie* inference from this fact would, I think, be that the Escribano de Racion and Gabriel Sanchez, either really were, or by some mistake had been taken to be, identical. A very high authority on such a subject, Senor de Gayangos, in the learned article already referred to, distinctly maintains the dispatch of two letters to the said two officials, whereas Senhor de Varnhagen not only limits the dispatch to one single address, but goes so far as to conclude that the Spanish printed text, from which he believes the Latin to be translated, is in fact the letter addressed to the sovereigns, with the change only of "vuestras" into "sus." But as his Excellency has given much careful thought to this matter, and has, under the guidance of a most judicious criticism, supplied an amended text, derived from a collation of the different texts, it is but justice to him and to the subject itself to give a literal translation of his remarks. This is the more requisite as I shall have to submit some facts which seem to me to lead to conclusions differing from some of those arrived at by my learned friend.

His Excellency says : " We hold it for certain that the said *primitive* edition (the Ambrosian) which we have had the opportunity of seeing in Milan, *must have given origin* to the text published in Rome the 25th April* of that same year (1493) by Cozco, who perhaps from not being able to transfer easily to the Latin the last part of it, cut it off. The said fact is principally *shown* by the mistake of the date of 14th (instead of 4th) of March, which could not be in the letter of Columbus, as he had left Lisbon before that day ; nor would it be reasonable to suppose that the error would be repeated in the same manner, if said original had been kept in sight. Still less could the repetition of such a mistake be conceived, if the original manuscript were different."

Now, before we proceed to an examination of this matter, the first thing requisite is to lay before the reader a specific difference which exists between the Spanish and the Latin texts. In the Spanish (I quote from the Ambrosian text) the letter closes thus : "Esto segun el fecho asi en breve. Fecha en la calavera sobre las Yslas de Canaria a xv de Febrero mil et quatrocientos et noventa y tres años."

Then comes a
"Nyma que venia dentro en la carta."

" Despues desta escripto y estando en mar de Castilla salyo tanto viento conmigo sul y'sueste que me ha fecho descargar la navios por cosi (correr ?) aqui en este puerto de Lysbona oy, que fue la mayor maravilla del mundo. Adonde acordé escrivir a sus altezas. En

* It should be 29th. The mistake is copied from Navarrete.

todas las Yndias he siempre hallado los tenporales como en Mayo, adonde yo fuy en xxxiii dias et volvi en xxviii, salvo questas tormentas me han detenido xiiii dias corriendo por esta mar. Dizen aqua todos los honbres de la mar que jamas ovo tan mal yvierno no ni tantas perdidas de naves, fecha a xiiii dias de marco.

"Esta carta embio Colon al Escrivano de racion de las Islas halladas en las Indias. Contenida a otra de sus altezas."

For those who need it, the translation will be found in our printed text at page 18.

The Latin translation ends very differently; thus: "Hæc ut gesta sunt sic breviter enarrata. Vale. Ulisbone, pridie Idus Martii."

Now the reader will observe that in the above "nyma" or postscript, Columbus states that on the day of his reaching Lisbon he resolved to write to their Highnesses, and we know from his diaries that that day was the 4th of March, and yet at the end the postscript is dated the 14th of March, a day on which we know, from the said diaries, that he was off Cape St. Vincent on his way from Lisbon to Spain, which he was then on the point of reaching at the harbour of Palos.

The Latin, it will be perceived, repeats this discrepancy in a more distinct shape, by bringing the name of Lisbon immediately into connection with the 14th of March, of which the words: "pridie Idus Martii" are the equivalent.

With these specialities in his mind, the reader will

be able with greater clearness to follow the following disquisition :—

The perfectly sound piece of criticism by Senhor de Varnhagen, which we have just read, is based upon the accepted premiss that it was on the 4th of March that Columbus dispatched to the King and Queen the letter describing his voyage, with the nema attached. The words of the "nema" itself make such an inference highly reasonable. It states that "el viento me ha fecho descargar los navios por correr aqui en este puerto de Lisbona *hoy* . . . adonde acordé de escribir a sus altezas."—" The wind made me unload the ships to run into this port of Lisbon to-day . . . where I resolved to write to their Highnesses." The diary shows that this day was the 4th of March, and hence, *prima facie*, the date of "14th of March"in the nema would appear to be not written by Columbus, but a blunder of the printer of the Ambrosian text. This natural inference *appears* confirmed, I find, by the distinct statement of Ferdinand Columbus that on his father's arrival in Lisbon on the 4th —" Subito espedì un corriero a' Re Catolici con la nuova della sua venuta"—"he immediately dispatched a courier to the Catholic Sovereigns with the news of his arrival."

Now, supposing, for I do not take it for granted, that this statement of Fernando's, written many years after, was correct, and that his father carried out his intention of writing to the Sovereigns from Lisbon, that statement does not tell us that he then *sent on the account of his voyage*; and if we inquire a little

k

further, we have good reason to suppose that he did *not* forward it on that day. There is no mention in his Diary of his so doing, although the act would be of sufficient importance to call for mention. He was in a country where his success in the cause of Spain was regarded with intense animosity. He was ignorant of the whereabouts of the Sovereigns, and in prospect of an early arrival in Spain, when he both would gain the necessary information, and could send on his precious missive in perfect safety. In harmony with these suggestions of mine, I find that Herrera, the historiographer, who had in his charge all the Columbian documents, states that on Wednesday, the 13th March, Columbus left Lisbon for Seville in his caravel. On Thursday, the 14th, before daybreak, he was off Cape St. Vincent. On Friday, the 15th, at mid-day, he entered the port of Palos, whence he had sailed on the 3rd of August of the previous year. *And having learned that the Catholic Sovereigns were at Barcelona*, he at first thought of going there in his caravel ; but subsequently resolving not to go to Barcelona by sea, he *announced his arrival to the Catholic Sovereigns, and sent a summary of what had happened to him, reserving the more complete narrative for their immediate presence.* The *reply* reached him in Seville, and contained expressions of joy at his safe arrival and at the success of his voyage, offered him rewards and honours, and commanded him to make haste to go to Barcelona. Now, it will be remembered that Columbus's narrative was already written, and dated February 15th or

18th, and only waiting to be despatched, and had attached to it the nema, which Mr. Gayangos tells us was a piece of paper placed on the outside of a letter like a padlock, and over which the seal was put. On this nema, beyond all question, was the date of March 4th ; and if, as I gather from Herrera's statement, Columbus dispatched this narrative of his voyage, not from Lisbon on the 4th March, but from Palos on the 15th, or the 16th, it is not unlikely that on the 14th, when he was nearing the Spanish harbour from which he was looking forward to be able to dispatch it in safety, he should have altered the remote date of the 4th, which agreed with the wording of the nema at the time of writing it, into the later date of the 14th, which was more in accordance with the date of dispatch. We know that the letter to the Sovereigns was enclosed in the letter to the Escribano de Racion ; and the sentence printed at the end of the Ambrosian text bears the aspect of an endorsement of the letter by that officer's secretary. The date of the Sovereigns' reply from Barcelona, March 30th, is in entire harmony, as regards lapse of time, with the dispatch of Columbus' letter from Palos on the 15th or 16th of the month. The Latin translation was completed on the 29th April, a full month after the arrival of the letter in Barcelona. There was plenty of time, therefore, it is true, for the letter to have been printed in Spanish, and for that Spanish to have served for the translation into Latin; but if my suggestion, as derived from the above data, be correct, that the alteration of 4 to 14 on the nema was made by Columbus him-

self, my friend Senhor de Varnhagen's conclusion that the Spanish printed text *must* have served for that translation becomes a *non sequitur*. Such alteration by Columbus would naturally lead to the erroneous "ulisbone, pridie idus Martii" in the Latin text, without the intervention of the Spanish printed text, in which that alteration would of course also be copied.

I have stated these facts to show that the occurrence of March 14th both in the Ambrosian text and the Latin translation, does not, as Senhor de Varnhagen concluded, prove of necessity that the latter was derived from the former, but from a common origin, to wit, in all probability the original MS. of Columbus. But now that I have shown that the Latin *need not* have been derived from the Ambrosian, I proceed to show that it *could not* have been so.

In the Ambrosian we find Guanahani spelt Guanaham; the island of Matinino called Matremonio, etc., while in the Latin text we find the first name correctly written Guanahani, Matinino is more nearly correctly written Mateunin; and we have the name of an island, Charis, which is left out in the Spanish altogether. But as the Latin translator possessed no special knowledge by which he could make such corrections, it is clear that the Ambrosian text could not have served as the basis for the Latin; whereas if the two were derived from a common source, the errors of the Ambrosian text would be those of its copyist, while the accurate rendering of the corresponding passages in the Latin would be the result, not of correction, as Senhor de Varnhagen suggests, but of attention to the original.

Upon this head Senhor de Varnhagen writes as follows :—

"The Latin texts contain a correction of the words Guanahanin, Charis (Caribes or Caraibes), and Mateunin (Matinino); but these corrections, if perchance it should be proved that they were made at the time of the first edition, and not afterwards (which we cannot here examine, not having the different editions at hand), may have been pointed out by the editor himself in sight of the original after the publication of the printed text; or by Columbus himself, on receiving it on his road to Barcelona, in order that some correct copies might be sent to Rome, by way of communicating the news of the discovery that had been made, with the view of obtaining the famous Bull from Alexander VI."

Now it is pretty clear that the Latin translation had nothing in the world to do with the Papal bull. The name of *De* Cosco indicates that the translator was a Spaniard—and it is reasonable to assume that a Spaniard would be selected to translate from Spanish into Latin—; therefore we may fairly suppose that the translation was made in Spain. It was not completed till the 29th of April—tertio kalendas maii —(not the 25th, an error of Navarrete's, which Senhor de Varnhagen has adopted), and the first bull was issued on the 3rd of May. The interval of four days is scarcely sufficient to allow of the formal dispatch of the document to Rome, its presentation and the drawing up of the bull, much less if it had to undergo revision by Columbus, still less if it be a question

of correction of printed proofs set up in type at Rome in that short interval. It is tolerably evident, then, that the Latin was sent to Rome, not to the Pope, but only for printing. If, therefore, the missive to the Pope was in Spanish, and included this letter, the corrections by Columbus or by Sanchez, suggested by Senhor de Varnhagen, would have been far better applied to the Spanish than to the Latin, instead of the reverse, as suggested.

It should, however, be borne in mind that in those days proofs were not sent out for revision : but as a doubt may reasonably be entertained on this point, on the score of the many imaginable possibilities that may not have been foreseen or taken into consideration in this criticism, I will now proceed to demonstrate that the Spanish and the Latin printed texts certainly are derived from different, though similar, documents. That they should be similar is natural, the one being written by Columbus from the other, with such trivial changes as may have dropped from his pen in transcribing.

First : we have a Spanish text, the endorsement of which shows it to have been sent to the Escribano de Racion. That this officer was Luis de Santangel we know for certainty from Argensola's *Anales de Aragon*, lib. 1, cap. 10, p. 99, *et seq.*, where he tells us that when the King looked coldly on Columbus's proposals, because the royal finances had been drained by war, Isabella offered her jewels for the enterprise ; but this was rendered needless, as " Luis de Santangel, Escrivano de Racion de Aragon, advanced

seventeen thousand florins for the expenses of the Armada." This leaves no room for doubt that Columbus should immediately send a copy of his letter to Santangel. In it was enclosed the copy addressed to the Sovereigns.* This text sent to Santangel consisted of a letter dated February 15th, and a postscript, announcing the arrival off Lisbon on the 4th, subsequently altered to the 14th March.

Secondly : we have a Latin text, distinctly stated to have been translated from a letter addressed to the Royal Treasurer, Gabriel Sanchez. We have thus clearly two letters addressed to two persons, but to annihilate this duality Senhor de Varnhagen suggests " Why not suppose that this last name, Gabriel Sanxis, which Cosco thought it necessary to announce, was the result of his own verifications ? He would inquire in Rome of the Catholic delegates the name of the Escribano de Racion, and they would give him that of the Treasurer General." But this is inventing *one surmise* to fortify *another*, whereas Senhor de Varnhagen's own zealous research had provided evidence to prove a contrary *fact*. The Marquis d'Adda

* In pursuance of his idea that not two, but only one letter, was despatched to head-quarters, Senhor de Varnhagen has translated the words of the endorsement " Contenida a otra de Sus Altezas."—" Contenida *en* otra, etc." and then, reasoning from the impossibility of Columbus showing such familiarity with the Sovereigns, argues, that the letter was in fact addressed to them only. With all respect I submit that the natural rendering is " Contenida la otra de Sus Altezas" ; Angl. " Contained the other of their Highnesses"; or, as it would be clearer in French, " Y contenue l'autre de Leurs Altesses ;" and Santangel appropriately appears as bearer of the missive to the Sovereigns.

has kindly sent me a photo-lithograph of a fragment of an Italian version of this letter, of which His Excellency Senhor de Varnhagen had found the title in the catalogue of the Ambrosian Library. This fragment distinctly states it to have been a copy of one "sent by the Grand Treasurer to his brother, Joane Sanxis."

Thus, beyond all question, it is proved that Columbus addressed these two several letters to these two different persons, from one of which the Spanish text was printed, and from the other the Latin translation was made and subsequently printed. And having reached this point, we see clearly that my suggestion of Columbus having altered the date of 4th March to 14th *must* have been correct; and, furthermore, that he copied the date of "14th," on whichever of these two letters was written last, because, while it stands March 14th *in totidem verbis* in one, it is rendered "pridie idus Martii" (which means the same thing) in the translation from the other. We see in this date " Ulisbone, pridie idus Martii," a proof that the copy from which the Latin was made, consisted, like the original of the Ambrosian Spanish text, of a complete letter with the "nema" added, because the place Lisbon is derived from the language at the beginning of the nema, and the date from Columbus's alteration at the end. Although the printer, Plannck, inserted nothing of the "nema" beyond the said place and date, which he placed at the end of the body of the letter in lieu of February 15th, we have a clear proof that De Cosco had really translated the letter

and nema as they stand in the Spanish, for when we come to look into Dati's poem, which he distinctly states to be translated from the Latin, we find *the date of February 15th retained, but no allusion to the contents of the nema, which, being detached, had evidently not reached his hands.* This fact, and others observable in his text, especially when examined in combination with the Italian, which also came from the Sanchez original, show that Dati worked from Cosco's manuscript translation. As to whether of the two printed texts, the Ambrosian Spanish or Plannck's Latin, can claim priority, we have no present means of deciding, but that the preference is due to the Spanish under critical correction is manifest, since it has been exposed to modifications from a compositor only, while the Latin has passed through the two ordeals of a translation and a compositor's alterations. For this reason I have adopted the Spanish in my text, observing that it replaces the very worst Latin text which I could have adopted, viz., that taken by Navarrete from the *España Illustrada*. The faults in the Ambrosian text are many and great, and this has led Señor de Gayangos to suggest that it was printed, not in Spain, but in Portugal, probably Lisbon. An opinion from one so eminent has great weight, but while yielding to none in sincere respect for the judgment of my distinguished friend, I confess I think that the circumstances of the letter point, as Senhor de Varnhagen has stated, to Barcelona for the place of printing. Mr. Winter Jones, the Principal Librarian of the British Museum, and late Keeper of

the Department of Printed Books, whose bibliographical knowledge is so well known, tells us that he recollects having seen the initial letter S, which commences the Ambrosian text, but, in spite of great research, I have failed to find it or the corresponding type in any work in our vast library. It is here well to remark that no kind of *fac-simile* is so baulking to bibliographic comparison as the photographic. The respective sizes of the letters are altered, and the outline is rendered broken and rotten. A *fac-simile* of this same letter, done by the hand, was published in Milan in 1863, in the sixteenth volume of the *Biblioteca Rara* of G. Daelli, and gives the type a far firmer appearance than that in the photograph. It is obvious that an opportunity is afforded of correcting the mistakes in the Ambrosian text from the other texts which we possess. This has been done with great skill and judgment by Senhor de Varnhagen by collation with the Simancas, the Valencia, and the Latin texts; to these aids I have added the Italian poem of Giuliano Dati, and the Italian fragment, for which I have been indebted to the kindness of the Marquis d'Adda.

We possess no detailed description of the second voyage of Columbus from his own hand. That which is here printed is the translation of a letter addressed to the Chapter of Seville by Dr. Chanca, a native of that city, who was physician to the fleet in this voyage, and was an eye-witness of the events that he related. For this reason it is preferred to two other accounts in Latin which are in existence, but which

have both been made up from hearsay. One of these occurs in the second book of the *Decades* of Peter Martyr of Anghiera, published first at Seville (Hispali) in 1511, and afterwards at Alcala de Henares (Compluti) in 1516, and often subsequently printed. The other is a compilation by Nicolò Scillacio, of Messina, who, while studying philosophy at Pavia in 1494 (?), and living with Giovanni Antonio Biretta, received from Spain, from a certain nobleman named Guglielmo Coma, a description of the recent discoveries of Columbus. This, as Mr. Lenox tells us, he translated into Latin, and inserted such other accounts as were then universally current, but without changing or adding anything. Mr. James Lenox, of New York, who is the possessor of one of the only two copies of this work known (the other being in the possession of the Marquis Trivulzio of Milan), and who states that it was first published in 1494, or early in 1495, reprinted it in 1859, with a translation by the Rev. John Mulligan, giving as an appendix my translation of Doctor Chanca's letter, as printed in the first edition of the present work in 1847. It is obvious that this work of Scillacio's, which is a pedantic compilation, cannot compare for authenticity with the account of Dr. Chanca ; while the latter contains more incidents, and is more agreeably written than the narrative of Peter Martyr.

This letter by Dr. Chanca was copied by Navarrete (as he himself says at the end of the letter in his work) from a manuscript in the possession of the Royal Academy of History at Madrid, written in the middle of the

sixteenth century, and was amongst the collection of papers referring to the West Indies, collected by Father Antonio de Aspa, a monk of the order of St. Jerome, of the monastery of the Mejorada, near Olmedo.—This document was unpublished previous to Navarrete's compilation. A copy was taken from the original by Don Manuel Avella, and deposited in the collection of Don Juan Bautista Muñoz, and from that copy, after collation with the original manuscript, the transfer was made by Navarrete into his valuable work. This letter is followed by a Memorial respecting the second voyage, addressed to the sovereigns by Columbus, through the intervention of Antonio de Torres, governor of the city of Isabella. At the close of each chapter or item is affixed their highness's reply. The document was taken by Navarrete from the Archives of Seville.

The two letters next in order in the present translation, are from the hand of Columbus himself, and are descriptive of the events of the third voyage. The first, addressed to the Sovereigns, was taken by Navarrete, under careful collation by himself and Muñoz, from a manuscript in the handwriting of the bishop Bartolomé de la Casas, found in the archives of the duke del Infantado. The second, addressed to the nurse of Prince John, is taken from a collection of manuscripts, relating to the West Indies, made by Muñoz, and deposited in the Real Academia de la Historia at Madrid. The text was collated by Navarrete with a copy inserted in the Codice Colombo-

Americano, said to have been written in the monastery of Santa Maria de las Cuevas in Seville.

The letter by Columbus, descriptive of his fourth voyage, was taken by Navarrete from a manuscript in the king's private library at Madrid, written in the handwriting of the middle of the sixteenth century, and probably the same copy as that which Pinelo, at page 61 of his *Biblioteca Occidental*, 4to., 1629, describes as having been made by Don Lorenzo Ramirez de Prado, from an edition in 4to., which does not appear to be now in existence. It was translated into Italian by Constanzo Bayuera of Brescia, and published at Venice in 1505, and, on account of its extreme scarcity, was republished, with some learned comments, by Morelli, the librarian of St. Mark's at Venice, in 1810.

That it had been printed in Spanish is asserted both by Pinelo and by Fernando Columbus.

It is presumed that the manuscript from which Navarrete made his copy was that made by Ramirez de Prado, because it had been removed to the king's library, from the Colegio Mayor de Cuenca, in Salamanca, where the papers of Ramirez had been deposited.

I must not close this bibliographical notice without tendering my warmest thanks to my friends, William Brenchley Rye, Esq., the learned Keeper of the Printed Books in the British Museum; and Robert Edmund Graves, Esq., one of the most accomplished of his Assistant-Librarians;—to the former for most kindly making out the foregoing list of incunabula of

the first letter, and the latter for very valuable help in my search for collateral texts by which to fortify my conclusions in the toilsome examination which I have here brought to a termination.

SELECT LETTERS

OF

CHRISTOPHER COLUMBUS.

ETC.

FIRST VOYAGE OF COLUMBUS.[1]

A Letter sent by Columbus to [Luis de Santangel] Chancellor of the Exchequer [of Aragon], respecting the Islands found in the Indies, enclosing another for their Highnesses.

SIR,—Believing that you will take pleasure in hearing of the great success which our Lord has granted me in my voyage, I write you this letter, whereby you will learn how in thirty-three days'[2] time I reached the Indies with the fleet which the most illustrious King and Queen, our Sovereigns, gave to me, where I found very many islands thickly peopled, of all which I took possession without resistance, for

Esta Carta embió Colon al Escrivano de Racion de las Islas halladas en las Indias. Contenida la otra de Sus Altezas.

Señor, por que se que aureis[3] plazer de la grand victoria que nuestro señor me ha dado en mi vyaie, vos escriuo esta por la qual sabreys commo en xxxiij dias pase a las jndias[4] con la armada que los illustrissimos Rey et reyna, nuestros señores, me dieron, donde yo falle muy muchas Islas pobladas con gente syn numero. Y dellas todas he tomado posession por sus altezas con pregon y

---

[1] The original spelling of the Ambrosian text, with all its faults, is here preserved, with the exception of the separation of words fused together, and the addition of punctuation and capitals for the sake of clearness. Suggested corrections from the other texts will be placed at the foot of each page, V. standing for Valencian text; S. for Simancas text; I. for Italian text; L. for Latin; D. for Dati. Such misspellings as a Spanish scholar will readily recognize as the blunders of the Spanish printer I have not thought it necessary to notice.

[2] From the 8th of September when Columbus sailed from the Canaries, to the 11th of October when he first saw land, was thirty-three days.

[3] Habreis. [4] V. "pasé de las Islas de Canaria a las Indias."

their Highnesses by proclamation made and with the royal standard unfurled. To the first island that I found I gave the name of *San Salvador*,[1] in remembrance of His High Majesty, who hath marvellously brought all these things to pass; the Indians call it *Guanaham*. To the second island I gave the name of *Santa-Maria de Concepcion*;[2] the third I called *Fernandina*;[3] the fourth, *Isabella*;[4] the fifth, *Juana*;[5] and so to each one I gave a new name. When I reached *Juana*, I followed its coast to the westward, and found it so large that I thought it must be the mainland,—the province of *Cathay*; and, as I found neither towns nor villages on the sea-coast, but only a few hamlets, with the inhabitants, of which I could not hold conversation, because they all immediately fled, I kept on the same route, thinking that I could not fail to light upon some large cities and towns. At length, after the proceeding of many leagues, and finding that nothing new presented itself, and that the coast was leading

---

vandera real estendida, y non me fue contradicho. A la primera que yo falle puse nombre Sant Saluador, a comemoracion de Su Alta Magestad, el qual marauillosamente todo esto andado;[6] los jndios la llaman Guanaham. A la segunda puse nombre la ylsa de santa Maria de Concepcion. A la tercera Ferrandina. A la quarta la Ysabella. A la quinta la isla Juana, et asy a cada vna nombre nueuo. Quando yo llegue a la Juana segui yo la costa della al poniente y la falle tan grande que pense que seria tierra firma, la prouincia de Catayo, y como no falle asi[7] villas y lugares en la costa de la mar, salvo pequeñas poblaciones, conla gente de las quales non podia hauer fabla, por que luego fuyan todos, andaua yo adelante por el dicho camino, pensando de no errar grandes Ciudades o villas, y al cabo de muchas leguas visto que no hauia innovacion y que la costa me leuaua al setentrion, de adonde mi voluntad era contraria, por que el yuierno era ya encarnado,[8] yo

[1] Watling's Island.   [2] Long Island.   [3] Great Exuma.
[4] Saometo or Crooked Island.   [5] Cuba.
[6] V. and S. "ha dado."   [7] V. "ahi."
[8] So in all the texts. Senhor de Varnhagen suggests "entrado" for "encarnado"

me northwards (which I wished to avoid, because winter had already set in, and it was my intention to move southwards; and because moreover the winds were contrary), I resolved not to wait for a change in the weather, but returned to a certain harbour which I had remarked, and from which I sent two men ashore to ascertain whether there was any king or large cities in that part. They journeyed for three days and found countless small hamlets with numberless inhabitants, but with nothing like order; they therefore returned. In the meantime I had learned from some other Indians whom I had seized, that this land was certainly an island; accordingly, I followed the coast eastward for a distance of one hundred and seven leagues, where it ended in a cape. From this cape, I saw another island to the eastward at a distance of eighteen leagues from the former, to which I gave the name of La Española.[1] Thither I went,

tenia proposito de hazer del[2] al austro y tanbien el viento me dio adelante, determine de no aguardar otro tiempo, y bolui atras fasta un señalado puerto da donde enbie dos hombres por la tierra para saber si auia rey o grandes ciudades. Andouieron tres iornadas y hallaron infinitas poblaciones pequeñas y gente sin numero, mas no cosa de regimiento, por lo qual se boluieron. Yo entendia harta de otros jndios que ya tenia tomados commo continuamente esta tierra era isla, et asi segui la costa della al oriente ciento y siete leguas faste donde fazia fin : del qual cabo vi[3] otra isla al oriente, distincta[4] de esta diez o ocho leguas, a la qual luego puse nombre la Spañola, y fui alli y segui la parte del setentrion asi commo de la Juana al oriente, clxxviij[5] grandes leguas[6] por linia recta del

[1] Hispaniola or San Domingo.
[2] So in all the texts. Senhor de Varnhagen suggests "hacerme."
[3] V. and S. "habia otra isla;" L. "aliam insulam prospexi."
[4] V. and S. "distante."
[5] V. "ciento e ochenta y ocho." S. "ciento e setenta y ocho." I. "cento otanta otto leghe." L. "miliaria dlxiiii." D. "cinquecensessantaquattro miglia."
[6] V. "leguas la cual y todas. S. "leguas por via reta del oriente asi como de la Juana, la cual y todos." I. "leghe por la dritta linea del oriente cosi como de la Zouana."

and followed its northern coast to the eastward (just as I had done with the coast of *Juana*), one hundred and seventy[1]-eight full leagues due east. This island, like all the others, is extraordinarily large, and this one extremely so. In it are many seaports with which none that I know in Christendom can bear comparison, so good and capacious that it is wonder to see. The lands are high, and there are many very lofty mountains with which the island of *Cetefrey* cannot be compared. They are all most beautiful, of a thousand different shapes, accessible, and covered with trees of a thousand kinds of such great height that they seemed to reach the skies. I am told that the trees never lose their foliage, and I can well understand it, for I observed that they were as green and luxuriant as in Spain in the month of May. Some were in bloom, others bearing fruit, and others otherwise according to their nature. The nightingale was singing as well as other birds of a thousand different kinds; and that, in November, the month in which I myself was roaming amongst them. There are palm-trees of six or eight

---

oriente asi commo de la Juana, la qual y todas las otras son fortissimas[2] en demasiado grado, y esta en estremo; en ella ay muchos puertos enla costa dela mar, sin comparacion de otros que yo sepa en christianos, y sartos, y buenos, y grandes, que es marauilla. Las tierras della son altas y en ella muy muchas sierras y montañas altissimas sin comparacion de ysla de centre.[3] Son todas fermossimas de mill. fechuras y todas andabiles y llenas de arboles de mil maneras y altas y pareçen que llegan al cielo; y tengo por dicho que jamas pierden la foia, segun lo puede comprehender que los vi tan verdes y tan hermosos commo son por Mayo en Spaña, y dellos stavan floridos, dellos con fruto, y dellos en otro termino segun es su calidad; y cantaua el ruiseñol[4] y otros paxaricos[5] de mil maneras en el mes de nouienbre por alli donde yo andaua. Ay

[1] It should be 188 leagues. See Bibliographical Notice.
[2] V. "fertilisimas." S. "fortisimas." I. "feralissime."
[3] V. "Teneryfe." S. "Cetrefrey." I. "Santaffer." L. omitted.
[4] V. and S. "ruiseñor."   [5] V. and S. "pajaros."

kinds, wonderful in their beautiful variety; but this is the case with all the other trees and fruits and grasses; trees, plants, or fruits filled us with admiration. It contains extraordinary pine groves, and very extensive plains. There is also honey, a great variety of birds, and many different kind of fruits. | In the interior there are many mines of metals and a population innumerable./ *Española* is a wonder. /Its mountains and plains, and meadows, and fields, are so beautiful and rich for planting and sowing, and rearing cattle of all kinds, and for building towns and villages. The harbours on the coast, and the number and size and wholesomeness of the rivers, most of them bearing gold, surpass anything that would be believed by one who had not seen them. There is a great difference between the trees, fruits, and plants of this island and those of *Juana*./ In this island there are many spices and extensive mines of gold and other metals. | The inhabitants of this and of all the other islands I have found or gained intelligence of, both men and women, go as naked as they were born, with the

---

palmas de seys[1] o de ocho maneras, que es admiracion verlas por la disformidad fermosa dellas; mas asi commo los otros arboles y frutos et yeruas. En ella ay pinares a marauilla, e ay canpiñas grandissimas et ay mjel, y de muchas maneras, de aues y frutas muy diversas. En las tierras ay muchas minas de metales et ay gente inestimable numero. La spañola es marauilla; las sierras y las montañas y las uegas y las campiñas y las tierras tan fermosas y gruesas para plantar et senbrar, para criar ganados de todas suertes para hedificios de villas y lugares. Los puertos de la mar aqui no hauria creancia sin vista, et delos rios muchos y grandes y buenas aguas, los mas delos quales traen oro. En los arboles et frutos et yeruas ay grandes diferencias de aquellas de la Juana. En esta ay muchas specierias[2] y grandes minas de oro y d'otros metales. La gente desta jsla et de todas las otras que he fallado y hauido,[3] in aya hauido noticia, andan todos desnudos, hombres et mugeres, asi

[1] V. and S. "seis." I. "setto." L. "septem." D. "septe."
[2] V. and S. "especies."
[3] V. and S. "y ha havido. I. "ho travado ho inteso."

exception that some of the women cover one part only with a single leaf of grass or with a piece of cotton, made for that purpose. They have neither iron, nor steel, nor arms, nor are they competent to use them, not that they are not well-formed and of handsome stature, but because they are timid to a surprising degree. / Their only arms are reeds cut in the seeding time,[1] to which they fasten small sharpened sticks, and even these they dare not use; for on several occasions it has happened that I have sent ashore two or three men to some village to hold a parley, and the people have come out in countless numbers, but, as soon as they saw our men approach, would flee with such precipitation that a father would not even stop to protect his son; and this not because any harm had been done to any of them, for, from the first, wherever I went and got speech with them, I gave them of all that I had, such as cloth and many other things, without receiving anything in return,

commo sus madres los paren, avnque algunas mugeres se cobijan vn solo lugar con vna sola foia de yerua o vna cosa[2] de algodon que para ellos fazen. Ellos no tienen fierro ni azero ni armas, ni son para ello; no porque no sea gente bien dispuesta et de fermosa estatura, saluo que son muy temerosos a marauilla. No tienen otras armas saluo las armas de las cañas, quando estan con la simiente, a la qual ponen al cabo vn palillo agudo, et no osan usar de aquellas, que muchas vezes me ha acaescido enbiar a tierra dos o tres honbres alguna villa para hauer fabla, y salir a ellos dellos sin numero, et despues que los veyan llegar, fuyan a no aguardar padre a hijo, y esto no porque a ninguno se aya fecho mal; antes a toda cabo a donde yo ay estado et podido auer fabla, les he dado de todo lo que tenia, asi paño commo otras cosas muchas, sin recebir por ello cosa alguna; mas son asi temerosos sin remedio. Verdad es que despues que aseguran y pierden esta miedo, ellos son tanto sin engaño y tan liberales delo que tienen que no lo

[1] These canes are probably the flowering stems of large grasses, similar to the bamboo or to the arundinaria used by the natives of Guiana for blowing arrows.
[2] V. "cofia." S. "cosa." I. "cosa."

but they are, as I have described, incurably timid. /It is true that when they are reassured and have thrown off this fear, they are guileless, and so liberal of all they have that no one would believe it who had not seen it. They never refuse anything that they possess when it is asked of them; on the contrary, they offer it themselves, and they exhibit so much loving kindness that they would even give their hearts; and, whether it be something of value or of little worth that is offered to them, they are satisfied./ I forbade that worthless things, such as pieces of broken porringers and broken glass, and ends of straps, should be given to them; although, when they succeeded in obtaining them, they thought they possessed the finest jewel in the world. It was ascertained that a sailor received for a leather strap a piece of gold weighing two *castellanos*[1] and a half, and others received for other objects of far less value, much more. For new *blancas*[2] they would give all that they had, whether it was two or three *castellanos* in gold or one or two arrobas[3] of spun cotton. They took even bits of the broken hoops of the wine barrels,

---

creerian sino el que lo viese. Ellos de cosa que tengan pidiendo gela, iamas dizen de no; antes conuidan la persona con ello, y muestran tanto amor que darian los coraçones, et quieren sea cosa de valor quien sea de poco precio luego por qualquiera cosica de qualquiera manera que sea que sele de por ello, sean contentos. Yo defendi que no se les diesen cosas tan siuiles commo pedaços de escudillas rotas, y pedaços de vidrio roto, y cabos de agugetas: aunque quando ellos esto podran llegar,[4] los parescia auer la mejor joya del mundo: que se açerto auer vn marinero por vna agugeta de oro de peso de dos castellanos y medio, y otros de otras cosas que muy menos valian, mucho mas. Ya por blancas nueuas dauan por ellas todo quanto tenian auer que[5] fuesen dos ni tres castellanos de oro o vna arroua[6] o dos de algodon fylado.

[1] An old Spanish coin, equal to the fiftieth part of a mark of gold.
[2] Small copper coins, equal to about the quarter of a farthing.
[3] One *arroba* weighs twenty-five pounds.
[4] V. "llevar."   [5] V. and S. "aunque."   [6] V. and S. omitted.

and gave, like fools, all that they possessed in exchange, insomuch that I thought it was wrong, and forbade it. I gave away a thousand good and pretty articles which I had brought with me in order to win their affection; and that they might be led to become Christians, and be well inclined to love and serve their Highnesses and the whole Spanish nation, and that they might aid us by giving us things of which we stand in need, but which they possess in abundance. /They are not acquainted with any kind of worship, and are not idolaters| but believe that all power and, indeed, all good things are in heaven; and they are firmly convinced that I, with my vessels and crews, came from heaven, and with this belief received me at every place at which I touched, after they had overcome their apprehension. /And this does not spring from ignorance, for they are very intelligent, and navigate all these seas, and relate everything to us, so that it is astonishing what a good account they are able to give of everything; but they have never seen men with clothes on, nor vessels like ours. / On my reaching the Indies,

---

Fasta los pedaços delos arcos rotos de las pipas tomauan y dauan lo que tenian commo bestias, asy que me parescia mal. Yo lo defendi y daua yo graciosas mil cosas buenas que yo leuaua, por que tomen amor y allenda desto se faran[1] cristianos, que se jnclinan al amor y servicio de sus altezas y de toda la nacion castellana, y procuran de aiuntar[2] de nos dar de las cosas que tienen en abundancia que nos son neçessarias. Y no conocian ninguna seta nin ydolatria, saluo que todos creen que las fuerças y el bien es en el cielo. Y creyan muy firme que yo con estos nauios y gente venia del cielo, y en tal catamiento me recibian[3] en todo cabo despues de auer perdido el miedo. Y esto no precede porque sean ygnorantes, saluo de muy sotil ingenio y hombres que nauegan todas aquellas mares, que es marauilla la buena cuenta quellos dan de todo, salvo porque nunca vieron gente vestida ny semejantes nauios. Y luego que legue a las jndias en la primera ysla que halle, tome por fuerça algunos dellos para que depren-

[1] V. "façan." [2] V. and S. "ayudar." [3] V. and S. "reciben."

I took by force, in the first island that I discovered, some of
these natives, that they might learn our language and give me
information in regard to what existed in these parts; and it
so happened that they soon understood us and we them, either
by words or signs, and they have been very serviceable to us.
They are still with me, and, from repeated conversations that
I have had with them, I find that they still believe that I come
from heaven. And they were the first to say this wherever
I went, and the others ran from house to house and to the
neighbouring villages, crying with a loud voice: "Come,
come, and see the people from heaven!" And thus they all,
men as well as women, after their minds were at rest about
us, came, both large and small, and brought us something
to eat and drink, which they gave us with extraordinary
kindness. They have in all these islands very many canoes
like our row-boats: some larger, some smaller, but most of
them larger than a barge of eighteen seats. They are not so
wide, because they are made of one single piece of timber,
but a barge could not keep up with them in rowing, because
they go with incredible speed, and with these canoes they

---

diesen y me diesen notia delo que auia en aquellas partes, et asy
fue que luego entendiron, y nos a ellos, quando por lengua o señas,
y estos han aprouechado mucho. Oy en dia los traygo que siempre
estan de proposito que vengo del cielo por mucha conuersacion
que ayan auido conmigo, y estos eran los primeros a pronunciarlo
adonde yo llegaua; y los otros andauan corriendo de casa en
casa, y alas villas çercenas con bozes altas, venid, venid a ver la
gente del cielo. Asi todos, hombres commo mugeres, despues de
aner el coraçon seguro de nos, venian[1] que no quedauan grande ni
pequeño, y todos trayan algo de comer y de beuer que dauan con
un amor marauilloso. Ellos tienen todas las yslas muy muchas
canoas a manera de fustes[2] de remo, dellas maioras, dellas menores
y algunas y muchas son mayoras que vna fusta de diez et ocho
bancos. No son tan anchas porque son de vn solo madero, mas
vna fusta no terna con ellas al remo porque van que no es cosa
de creer, y con estas nauegan todas aquellas yslas que son

[1] V. and S. "venieron." [2] "fustas."

navigate among these islands, which are innumerable, and carry on their traffic. I have seen in some of these canoes seventy and eighty men, each with his oar. In all these islands I did not notice much difference in the appearance of the inhabitants, nor in their manners nor language, except that they all understand each other, which is very singular, and leads me to hope that their Highnesses will take means for their conversion to our holy faith, towards which they are very well disposed. I have already said how I had gone one hundred and seven leagues in following the sea-coast of *Juana* in a straight line from west to east: and from that survey I can state that the island is larger than England and Scotland together, because, beyond these one hundred and seven leagues, there lie to the west two provinces which I have not yet visited, one of which is called *Avan*, where the people are born with a tail. These two provinces cannot be less in length than from fifty to sixty leagues, from what can be learned from the Indians that I have with me, and who are acquainted with all these islands. The other,

---

jnnumerables, y traten sus mercaderias. Algunas destas canoas he visto con. lxx. y lxxx. honbres en ella, y cada vno con su remo. En todas estas yslas no vide mucha diuersidad de la fechura dela gente ni en las costumbres ni en la lengua, saluo que todos se entienden, que es cosa muy singular, para lo que espero que determinaren sus altezas para la conversacion[1] dellos de nuestra santa fe a la qual son muy dispuestos. Ya dixe commo yo hauia andada c.vij. leguas por la costa de la mar por la derecha liña de ocidente a oriente por la ysla Juana, segun el qual camino puedo desir que esta isla es mayor que inglaterra y escosia juntas por que allen de destas c.vij. leguas, me queda de la parte de poniente dos prouincias que yo no he andado; la vna de las quales llaman Auan,[2] adonde nascen la gente con cola, las quales prouincias no pueden tener en longura menos de l. o lx. leguas, segund puede[3] entender destos jndios que yo tengo, los quales saben todas las

[1] V. and S. "conversion." L. "conversionem."
[2] V. "Nhan." S. "Cibau." L. "Anan." [3] V. and S. "puedo."

Española, has a greater circumference than all Spain, from Catalonia by the sea-coast to Fuenterabia in Biscay, since on one of its four sides I made one hundred and eighty-eight great leagues in a straight line from west to east. This is something to covet, and when found not to be lost sight of. Although I have taken possession of all these islands in the name of their Highnesses, and they are all more abundant in wealth than I am able to express; and although I hold them all for their Highnesses, so that they can dispose of them quite as absolutely as they can of the kingdoms of Castile, yet there was one large town in *Española* of which especially I took possession, situated in a locality well adapted for the working of the gold mines, and for all kinds of commerce, either with the main land on this side, or with that beyond which is the land of the great Khan, with which there will be vast commerce and great profit. To that city I gave the name of *Villa de Navidad*, and fortified it with a

---

yslas. Esta otra española en cierco tiene mas que la españa toda desde colunya[1] por costa de mar fasta fuente rauia en vi scaya pues en vna quadra anduue clxxxviij.[2] grandes leguas por recta linia de occidente a oriente. Esta es para desear, et vista, es para nunca dexar; enla qual puesto que de todas tenga tomada possesion por sus altezas, y todas sean mas abastadas delo que yo se y puedo dezir, y todas las tengo por de sus altezas qual dellas pueden disponer commo y tan complidamente commo delos Reynos de castilla. En esta española en el lugar[3] mas conuenible y meyor comarca para las minas del oro y de todo trato, asi dela tierra firme de aqua commo de aquella de alla del grand can, adonde aura[4] grand trato et grand gananç̧a, he tomado possession de vna villa grande, ala qual puse nombre la villa de Nauidad. Y en ella he fecho fuerç̧a y fortaleza que ya a estas horas estara del

---

[1] V. "Colibre." S. "Colunia." L. "Colonia." Misread from an abridged word in the original, which the sense of the passage would make "Catalonia."

[2] V. and S. "ciento treinta y ocho." L. "miliaria dxl." D. "cinquecensessantoquattro miglia."

[3] V. and S. "en lugar."   [4] V. and S. "habra."

fortress, which by this time will be quite completed, and I have left in it a sufficient number of men with arms,[1] artillery, and provisions for more than a year, a barge, and a sailing master skilful in the arts necessary for building others. I have also established the greatest friendship with the king of that country, so much so that he took pride in calling me his brother, and treating me as such. Even should these people change their intentions towards us and become hostile, they do not know what arms are, but, as I have said, go naked, and are the most timid people in the world; so that the men I have left could, alone, destroy the whole country, and this island has no danger for them, if they only know how to conduct themselves. In all those islands it

todo acabada, y he dexada en ella gente que abasta para semejante fecho, con armas y artellarias et vituallas por mas de un año; y fusta y maestro de la mar en todas artes para fazer otras, y grande amistad con el rey de aquella tierra en tanto grado que se preciaua de me llamar y tener por hermano; y aunque le mudasse[2] la voluntad a offender esta gente, el ni los suyos no saben que sean armas y andan desnudos commo ya he dicho: son los mas temerosos que ay en el mundo, asi que solamente la gente que alla queda, es para destroir toda aquella tierra, y es ysla syn peligro de sus personas sabiendo se regir. En todas estas yslas me parece que todos los honbres sean contentos con vna muger, y a su mayoral

[1] There appears to be a doubt as to the exact number of men left by Columbus at Española, different accounts variously giving it as thirty-seven, thirty-eight, thirty-nine, and forty. There is, however, a list of their names included in one of the diplomatic documents printed in Navarrete's work, which makes the number amount to forty, independent of the governor Diego de Arana, and his two lieutenants Pedro Gutierrez and Rodrigo de Escobedo. All these men were Spaniards, with the exception of two; one an Irishman named William Ires, a native of Galway, and one an Englishman, whose name was given as Tallarte de Lajes, but whose native designation it is difficult to guess at. The document in question, was a proclamation to the effect that the heirs of those men should, on presenting at the office of public business at Seville, sufficient proof of their being the next of kin, receive payment in conformity with the royal order to that purpose, issued at Burgos, on the twentieth of December, 1507.   [2] V. and S. "mudasen."

seems to me that the men are content with one wife, except their chief or king, to whom they give twenty. The women seem to me to work more than the men. I have not been able to learn whether they have any property of their own. It seemed to me that what one possessed belonged to all, especially in the matter of eatables. I have not found in those islands any monsters, as many imagined; but, on the contrary, the whole race is very well-formed, nor are they black, as in Guinea, but their hair is flowing, for they do not dwell in that part where the force of the sun's rays is too powerful. It is true that the sun has very great power there, for the country is distant only twenty-six degrees from the equinoctial line. In the islands where there are high mountains, the cold this winter was very great, but they endure it, not only from being habituated to it, but by eating meat with a variety of excessively hot spices. As to savages, I did not even hear of any, except at an island which lies the

---

o rey dan fasta veynte. Las mugeres me parece que trabaian mas que los honbres, ni he podido entender si tenien bienes propios, que me parecio ver que aquello que vno tenia todos hazian parte, en especial de las cosas comederas. En estas yslas fasta aqui no he hallado honbres mostrudos, commo muchos pensauan; mas antes es toda gente de muy lindo acatamiento, ny son negros commo en guinea, saluo con sus cabellos corredios,[1] y no se crian adonde ay jnpeto[2] demasiado delos rayos solares. Es verdad quel sol tiene alli grande fuerça, puesto que es didistinta[3] dela linia inquinocial xxvi. grandes. En estas islas adonde ay montañas, ay tenida[4] a fuerça el frio este yuierno, mas ellos lo sufren por la costumbre que con la ayuda delas viandas que comen con[5] especias muchas y muy calientes en demasia. Asy que mostruos no he hallado jnnoticia,[6] saluo de una ysla[7] que es aqui en la segunda a la entrada

[1] V. and S. "correndios."
[2] V. "effeto." S. "espeto." Navarrete says that in old Spanish "espeto" meant a "spit."   [3] V. and S. "distante."
[4] V. and S. "ahi tenia fuerza."
[5] V. and S. "como son." L. "quibus vescuntur."
[6] V. and S. "ni noticia."
[7] V. "isla de Quarives." L. "insula Charis nuncupata."

second in one's way in coming to the Indies.¹ It is inhabited by a race which is regarded throughout these islands as extremely ferocious, and eaters of human flesh. These possess many canoes, in which they visit all the Indian islands, and rob and plunder whatever they can. They are no worse formed than the rest, except that they are in the habit of wearing their hair long, like women, and use bows and arrows made of reeds, with a small stick at the end, for want of iron, which they do not possess. They are ferocious amongst these exceedingly timid people; but I think no more of them than of the rest. These are they which have intercourse with the women of Matenino,² the first island one comes to on the way from Spain to the Indies, and in which there are no men. These women employ themselves in no labour suitable to their sex ; but use bows and arrows made of reeds like those above described, and arm and cover themselves with plates of copper, of which metal they have a

---

de las jndias, que es poblada de vna gente que tienen en todas las yslas por muy ferozes, los quales comen carne humana.³ Estos tienen muchas canoas, con las quales corren todas las yslus de jndia: roban y toman quanto pueden. Ellos no son mas difformes que los otros, saluo que tienen en costumbre de traer los cabellos largos commo mugeres, y vsan arcos y flechas de las mismas armas de cañas con vn palillo al cabo, por defecto de fierro, que no tienen. Son feroses entre estos otros pueblos que son en demasiado grado couardes, mas yo no lo tengo a nada mas que a los otros. Estos son aquellos que tratan con las mugeres de matremonio,⁴ que es la primera ysla partiendo despaña para las jndias que se falla, enla qual no ay honbre ninguno. Ellas no vsan exercicio femenil, saluo arcos y flechas commo los sobredichos de cañas, y se arman y cobijan con lamines de arambre, de que tienen mucho. Otra ysla me seguran mayor que la española, en que las

¹ Dominica.   ² Martinique.
³ V. and S. "viva."   L. "humana."
⁴ V. "que tomaban las mugeres de Matinino."   S. "que trocaban las mugeres de matrimonio."   L. "qui coeunt cum quibusdam feminis quæ insulam Mateunim habitant."   D. "isola decta Matanino."

great quantity. They assure me that there is another island larger than *Española*, in which the inhabitants have no hair. It is extremely rich in gold; and I bring with me Indians taken from these different islands, who will testify to all these things. Finally, and speaking only of what has taken place in this voyage, which has been so hasty, their Highnesses may see that I shall give them all the gold they require, if they will give me but a very little assistance; spices also, and cotton, as much as their Highnesses shall command to be shipped; and mastic, hitherto found only in Greece, in the island of Chios, and which the Signoria[1] sells at its own price, as much as their Highnesses shall command to be shipped; lign aloes, as much as their Highnesses shall command to be shipped; slaves, as many of these idolators as their Highnesses shall command to be shipped. I think also I have found rhubarb and cinnamon, and I shall find a thousand other valuable things by means of the men that I have left behind me, for I tarried at no point so long

personas no tienen ningun cabello. En esta ay oro sin cuenta, y desta y de las otras traigo comigo jndios para testimonio. Y conclusion a fablar desto solamente que sea fecho este viage, que fue si de corrida que pueden ver sus altezas que yo les dare oro quanto ovieren[2] menester con muy poquita ajuda que sus altezas me daran, agora specieria y algodon quanto sus altezas mandaran cargar, y almastica[3] quanta mandaran cargar, et dela qual fasta oy no se ha fallado, saluo en grecia enla ysla de xio, y el señorio la vende commo quiere, y liguñaloe quanto mandaran cargar, y esclavos quanto mandaran cargar et seran delos ydolatres.[4] Y creo auer hallado ruybarno y canela y otras mil cosas de sustancia fallare, que auran fallado la gente que yo alla dexo, por que yo no me he detenido ningun cabo, en quanto el viento me aya dado lugar de

[1] Of Genoa. The island of Chios belonged to the Genoese Republic from 1346 to 1566.
[2] V. and S. "hobieren."   [3] V. and S. "almasiga."
[4] In the corrupt edition of the Latin translation reprinted by Navarrete from the *España Illustrada*, this word is rendered "hydrophilatorum."

as the wind allowed me to proceed, except in the town of *Navidad,* where I took the necessary precautions for the security and settlement of the men I left there. Much more I would have done if my vessels had been in as good a condition as by rights they ought to have been. This is much, and praised be the eternal God, our Lord, who gives to all those who walk in his ways victory over things which seem impossible; of which this is signally one, for, although others may have spoken or written concerning these countries, it was all mere conjecture, as no one could say that he had seen them—it amounting only to this, that those who heard listened the more, and regarded the matter rather as a fable than anything else. But our Redeemer hath granted this victory to our illustrious King and Queen and their kingdoms, which have acquired great fame by an event of such high importance, in which all Christendom ought to rejoice, and which it ought to celebrate with great festivals and the offering of solemn thanks to the Holy Trinity with many solemn prayers, both for the great exaltation which

---

nauegar, solamente en la villa de Nauidad en quanto dexe asegurado et bien asentado; y ala verdad mucho mas ficiera si los nauios me siruieran commo razon demandaua. Esto es harto[1] y eterno dios nuestro señor el qual da a todos aquellos que andan su camino victoria de cosas que parecen inposibles : y esta señaladamente fue la vna; porque avnque destas tierras ayan fallado o escripto,[2] todo va por conlectura sin allegar devista, saluo comprendiendo a tanto que los oyentes los mas escuchauan y juzgauan mas por fabla que por poca[3] cosa dello.

Asy que pues nuestro redentor dio victoria a nuestros illustrissimos rey et reyna y a sus reynos famosos de tan alta cosa, adonde toda la christianidad deve tomar alegria y fazer grandes fiestas, y dar gracias solennes a la santa trinidad con muchas oraciones solennes por el tanto enxalçamiento que auran, en

---

[1] V. and S. " cierto."
[2] V. and S. " fablado otros." L. " scripserunt vel locuti sunt."
[3] V. and S. " otra." L. " prope videbatur fabula."

may accrue to them in turning so many nations to our holy faith, and also for the temporal benefits which will bring great refreshment and gain, not only to Spain, but to all Christians. This, thus briefly, in accordance with the events.

Done on board the caravel, off the Canary Islands, on the fifteenth of February, fourteen hundred and ninety-three.

At your orders.   THE ADMIRAL.

After this letter was written, as I was in the sea of Castille, there arose a south-west wind, which compelled me to lighten my vessels and run this day into this port of Lisbon, an event which I consider the most marvellous thing in the world, and whence I resolved to write to their High-

---

tornandose[1] tantos pueblosa nuestra santa fe, y despues por los bienes temporales; que no solamente a la españa mas a todos los cristianos ternan aqui refrigerio y ganancia. Esto segun el fecho asi en breue[2]. Fecha enla calauera[3] sobre las yslas de canaria[4] a xv.[5] de febrero, Mill. y quatrocientos y nouenta y tres años.

Fara[6] lo que mandereys[7].

EL ALMIRANTE.

Nyma[8] que venia dentro en la carta.

Despues desta escripto:[9] y estando en mar de Castilla salyo tanto viento conmigo sul y sueste que me ha fecho descargar los nauios por cori[10] aqui en esto puerto de lysbona oy, que fue la mayor marauilla del mundo. Adonde acorde escriuir a sus altezas.

[1] V. and S. "ayuntandose."
[2] V. and S. "esto segundo ha fecho ser muy breve." L. "hæc ut gesta sunt sic breviter enarrata."   [3] V. and S. "carabela."
[4] V. "la isla de Sa. Maria."
[5] V. "18." This latter date is the only one which corresponds with the fourteen days, mentioned in the postscript, during which Columbus was detained at sea by the weather previously to his reaching Lisbon on the 4th of March.
[6] V. "Para."   [7] V. "mandaredes."
[8] S. "Anima." V. The entire nema wanting. The same in L. and D.   [9] S. "escrita."   [10] S. "correr."

nesses. In all the Indies I have always found the weather like that in the month of May. I reached them in thirty-three days, and returned in twenty-eight, with the exception that these storms detained me fourteen days knocking about in this sea. All seamen say that they have never seen such a severe winter nor so many vessels lost.

Done on the fourteenth day of March.

En todas las yndias he siempre hallado los tenporales[1] commo en mayo. Adonde yo fuy en xxxiij.[2] dias y bolui en xxviij.[3] salvo questas tormentas me han detenido xiiij.[4] dias corriendo por esta mar. Dizen aqua todos los honbres dela mar que jamas ouo tan mal yuierno, no ni tantas perdidas de naues.[5] Fecha a. xiiij dias de marco.

Esta carta embio Colon al escrivano Deracion delas Islas halladas en las Indias. Contenida a otra[6] de sus Altezas.

[1] S. "tiempos."   [2] S. "noventa y tres."
[3] S. "setenta y ocho." Both are wrong. It should be forty-eight, from January 16 to March 4.   [4] S. "trece."
[5] S. "los quatro." Columbus really arrived at Lisbon on the 4th of March. For an explanation of this discrepancy, see Biographical Notice.
[6] S. "Indias e otra."

SECOND VOYAGE OF COLUMBUS.

A Letter addressed to the Chapter of Seville by Dr. Chanca,[1] *native of that city, and physician to the fleet of Columbus, in his second voyage to the West Indies, describing the principal events which occurred during that voyage.*

MOST noble sir,—Since the occurrences which I relate in private letters to other persons, are not of such general interest as those which are contained in this epistle, I have resolved to give you a distinct narrative of the events of our voyage, as well as to treat of the other matters which form the subject of my petition to you. The news I have to communicate are as follows: The expedition which their Catholic

---

SEGUNDA VIAGE DE COLON.

La Carta del Doctor Chanca, que escribió a la Ciudad de Sevilla.

Muy magnífico Señor: Porque las cosas que yo particularmente escribo á otros en otras cartas no son igualmente comunicables como las que en esta escritura van, acordé de escribir distintamente las nuevas de acá y las otras que á mi conviene suplicar á vuestra Señoría,é las nuevas son las siguientes: Que la flota que los Reyes

---

[1] Doctor Chanca was appointed physician to Columbus's fleet by a dispatch of the 23rd of May, 1493; and on the 24th, the chief accountants were instructed to pay him salary and rations as scrivener in the Indies. Señor de Navarrete, who saw the manuscript, "Historia de la Reyes Católicos," says that its author, Andres Bernaldez, Cura de los Palacios, makes mention of Dr. Chanca, and had this same narration before him, as may be seen in the one hundred and twentieth chapter of his history.

c 2

Majesties sent, by Divine permission, from Spain to the Indies, under the command of Christopher Columbus, admiral of the ocean, left Cadiz on the twenty-fifth of September, of the year ,[1] with wind and weather favourable for the voyage. This wind lasted two days, during which time we managed to make nearly fifty leagues. The weather then changing, we made little or no progress for the next two days; it pleased God, however, after this, to restore us fine weather, so that in two days more we reached the Great Canary. Here we put into harbour, which we were obliged to do, to repair one of the ships which made a great deal of water; we remained all that day, and on the following set sail again, but were several times becalmed, so that we were four or five days before we reached Gomera. We had to remain at Gomera one day to lay in our stores of meat, wood, and as much water as we could stow, preparatory to the long voyage which we expected to make without seeing land: thus through the delay at these two ports, and being calmed the day after leaving Gomera, we were nineteen or

---

Católicos, nuestros Señores, enviaron de España para las Indias é gobernacion del su Almirante del mar Océano Cristóbal Colon por la divina permision, parte de Caliz á veinte y cinco de Setiembre del año de   años con tiempo é viento convenible á nuestro camino, é duró este tiempo dos dias, en los cuales pudimos andar al pie de cincuenta leguas: y luego nos cambió el tiempo otros dos, en los cuales anduvimos muy poco ó no nada; plogó á Dios que pasados los dias nos tornó buen tiempo, en manera que en otros dos llegamos á la Gran Canaria donde tomamos puerto, lo cual nos fue necesario por reparar un navío que hacia mucha agua, y estovímos ende todo aquel dia, é luego otra dia partimos é fizonos algunas calmerías, de manera que estovímos en llegar al Gomero cuatro ó cinco dias, y en la Gomera fue necesario estar algun dia por facer provisiones de carne, leña é agua la que mas pudiesen, por la larga jornada que se esperaba hacer sin

---

[1] A similar gap in the original: it should say *of the year* 1493.

twenty days before we arrived at the Island of Ferro. After this we had, by the goodness of God, a return of fine weather, more continuous than any fleet ever enjoyed during so long a voyage; so that leaving Ferro on the thirteenth of October, within twenty days we came in sight of land : and we should have seen it in fourteen or fifteen days if the ship *Capitana* had been as good a sailer as the other vessels; for many times the others had to shorten sail, because they were leaving us much behind. During all this time we had great good fortune, for throughout the voyage we encountered no storm, with the exception of one on St. Simon's eve, which for four hours put us in considerable jeopardy/

On the first Sunday after All Saints, namely, the third of November, about dawn, a pilot of the ship *Capitana* cried out "The reward, I see the land!"

The joy of the people was so great, that it was wonderful to hear their cries and exclamations of pleasure; and they had good reason to be delighted, for they had become so wearied of bad living, and of working the water out of the

---

ver mas tierra: ansi que en la estada destos puertos y en un dia despues de partidos de la Gomera, que nos fizo calma, que tardamos en llegar fasta la isla del Fierro, estovimos diez y nueve ó veinte dias: desde aqui por la bondad de Dios nos tornó buen tiempo, el mejor que nunca flota llevó tan largo camino, tal que partidos del Fierro á trece de Octubre dentro de veinte dias hobimos vista de tierra: y vieramosla á catorce ó quince si la noa Capitana fuera tan buena velera comos los otros navíos, porque muchas veces los otros navíos sacaban velas porque nos dejaban mucho atras. En todo este tiempo hobimos mucha bonanza, que en él ni en todo el camino no hobimos fortuna, salvo la víspera de S. Simon que nos vino una que por cuatro horas nos puso en harto estrecho. El primero domingo despues de Todos Santos, que fue á tres dias de Noviembre, cerca del alba, dijó un piloto de la nao Capitana: albricias, que tenemos tierra. Fue el alegría tan grande en la gente que era maravilla oir las gritas y placeres que todos hacian, y con mucha razon, que la gente venian ya tan fatigados de mala vida y

ships, that all sighed most anxiously for land. The pilots of the fleet reckoned on that day, that between leaving Ferro and first reaching land, we had made eight hundred leagues; others said seven hundred and eighty (so that the difference was not great), and three hundred more between Ferro and Cadiz, making in all eleven hundred leagues; I do not therefore feel as one who had not seen enough of the water. On the morning of the aforesaid Sunday, we saw lying before us an island, and soon on the right hand another appeared: the first[1] was high and mountainous, on the side nearest to us; the other[2] flat, and very thickly wooded: as soon as it became lighter, other islands began to appear on both sides; so that on that day, there were six islands to be seen lying in different directions, and most of them of considerable size. We directed our course towards that which we had first seen, and reaching the coast, we proceeded more than

de pasar agua, que con muchos deseos sospiraban todos por tierra. Contaron aquel dia los pilotos del armada desde la isla de Fierro hasta la primera tierra que vimos unas ochocientas leguas, otros setecientas ó ochenta, de manera que la diferencia no ere mucha, ó mas trescientas que ponen de la isla de Fierro fasta Caliz, que eran por todos mil ó ciento; ansí que no siento quien no fuese satisfecho de ver agua. Vimos el Domingo de mañana sobredicho, por proa de los navíos, una isla y luego á la man derecha parecio otra: la primera era la tierra alta de sierras por aquella parte que vimos, la otra era tierra llana, tambien muy llena de árboles muy espesos, y luego que fue mas de dia comenzó á parecer á una parte ó á otra islas; de manera que aquel dia eran seis islas á diversas partes, y las mas harto grandes. Fuimos enderezados para ver aquella que primero habiamos visto, ó llegamos por la costa andando mas de una lagua buscando puerto para sorgir, el cual todo aquel espacio nunca se pudo hallar. Era en todo aquello que parecia desta isla

[1] The island of Dominica, so called from having been discovered on a Sunday.
[2] The island Marigalante, so called from the name of the ship in which Columbus sailed.

a league in search of a port where we might anchor, but without finding one :/all that part of the island which met our view, appeared mountainous, very beautiful, and green even up to the water, which was delightful to see, for at that season there is scarcely any thing green in our own country/ When we found that there was no harbour there,[1] the admiral decided that we should go to the other island, which appeared on the right, and which was at four or five leagues distance: one vessel however still remained on the first island all that day seeking for a harbour, in case it should be necessary to return thither. /At length, having found a good one, where they saw both people and dwellings, they returned that night to the fleet, which had put into harbour at the other island,[2] and there the admiral, accompanied by a great number of men, landed with the royal banner in his hands, and took formal possession on behalf of their Majesties. This island was filled with an astonishingly thick growth of wood; the variety of unknown trees, some bearing fruit and some flowers, was surprising, and indeed every spot was covered

---

todo moutaña muy hermosa y muy verde, fasta el agua que era alegria en mirarla, porque en aquel tiempo no hay en nuestra tierra apenas cosa verde. Despues que allí no hallamos puerto acordó el Almirante que nos volviesemos á la otra isla que parescia á la mano derecha, que estaba desta otra cuatro ó cinco leguas. Quedó por entonces un navío en esta isla buscando puerto todo aquel dia para cuando fuese necesario venir á ella, en la cual halló buen puerto ó vido casas é gentes, é luego se tornó aquella noche para donde estaba la flota que habia tomado puerto en la otra isla, donde decendió el Almirante é mucha gente con él con la bandera Real en las manos, adonde tomó posesion por sus Altezas en forma de derecho. En esta isla habia tanta espesura de arboledas que era maravilla, é tanta diferencia de árboles no conocidos á nadie que era para espantar, dellos con fruto, dellos con flor, ansí que todo

---

[1] Dominica has no harbours, but there are several good roadsteads on the western side.   [2] Marigalante.

with verdure. We found there a tree whose leaf had the finest smell of cloves that I have ever met with; it was like a laurel leaf, but not so large: but I think it was a species of laurel. There were wild fruits of various kinds, some of which our men, not very prudently, tasted; and upon only touching them with their tongues, their countenances became inflamed,[1] and such great heat and pain followed, that they seemed to be mad, and were obliged to resort to refrigerants to cure themselves. We found no signs of any people in this island, and concluded it was uninhabited; we remained only two hours, for it was very late when we landed, and on the following morning we left for another very large island,[2] situated below this at the distance of seven or eight leagues. We approached it under the side of a great mountain, that seemed almost to reach the skies, in the middle of which rose a peak higher than all the rest of the mountain, whence many streams diverged into different channels, especially towards the part at which we arrived. At three leagues distance,

---

era verde. Allí hallamos un arbol, cuya hoja tenia el mas fino olor de clavos que nunca ví, y era como laurel, salvo que no era ansi grande; yo ansí pienso que era laurel su especia. Allí habia frutas salvaginas de diferentes maneras, de las quales algunos no muy sabios probaban, y del gusto solamente tocándoles con las lenguas se les hinchaban las caras, y los venia tan grande ardor y dolor que parecian que rabiaban, los cuales se remediaban con cosas frias. En esta isla no hallamos gente nin señal della, creimos que era despoblada, en la cual estovimos bien dos horas, porque cuando allí llegamos era sobre tarde, ó luego otro dia de mañana partimos para otra isla que parescia en bajo desta que era muy grande, fasta la cual desta que habria siete ú ocho leguas, llegamos á ella hácia la parte de una gran montaña que parecia que queria llegar al cielo, en medio de la cual montaña estaba un pico mas alto que toda la otra montaña, del cual se vertian á diversas partes muchas aguas,

[1] The fruit of the manchineal, which apparently produces similar effects.   [2] Guadaloupe.

we could see an immense fall of water, which looked of the breadth of an ox, and discharged itself from such a height that it appeared to fall from the sky; it was seen from so great a distance that it occasioned many wagers to be laid on board the ships, some maintaining that it was but a series of white rocks, and others that it was water. When we came nearer to it, it showed itself distinctly, and it was the most beautiful thing in the world to see from how great a height and from what a small space so large a fall of water was discharged. As soon as we neared the island the admiral ordered a light caravel to run along the coast to search for a harbour; the captain put into land in a boat, and seeing some houses, leapt on shore and went up to them, the inhabitants fleeing at sight of our men; he then went into the houses and there found various household articles that had been left unremoved, from which he took two parrots, very large and quite different from any we had before seen; he found a great quantity of cotton, both spun and prepared for spinning, and articles of food, of all of which he brought away a portion; besides these, he also brought away four or five bones of human arms and legs. On seeing these we suspected that

---

en especial hácia la parte donde ibamos: de tres leguas paresció un golpe de agua tan gordo como un buey, que se despeñaba de tan alto como si cayera del cielo: parescia de tan lejos, que hobo en los navíos muchas apuestas, que unos decian que eran peñas blancas y otros que era agua. Desque llegamos mas á cerca vídose lo cierto, y era la mas hermosa cosa del mundo de ver cuan alto se despeñaba é de tan poco logar nacia tan gran golpe de agua. Luego que llegamos cerco mandó el Almirante á una carbela ligera que fuese costeando á buscar puerto, la cual se adelantó y llegando á la tierra vido unas casas, é con la barca saltó el Capitan en tierra é llegó á las casas, en las cuales halló su gente, y luego que los vieron fueron huyendo, é entró en ellas, donde halló las cosas que ellos tienen, que no habian llevado nada, donde tomó dos papagayos muy grandes y muy diferenciados de cuantos se habian visto. Halló mucho algodon hilado é por hilar, é cosas de sus mantenimientos,

we were amongst the Caribbee islands, whose inhabitants eat human flesh; for the admiral, guided by the information respecting their situation which he had received from the Indians of the islands discovered in his former voyage, had directed his course with a view to their discovery, both because they were the nearest to Spain, and because this was the direct track for the island of Española, where he had left some of his people. Thither, by the goodness of God and the wise management of the admiral, we came in as straight a track as if we had sailed by a well known and frequented route. This island is very large, and on the side where we arrived it seemed to us to be twenty-five leagues in length. We sailed more than two leagues along the shore in search of a harbour. On the part towards which we moved appeared very high mountains, and on that which we left extensive plains; on the sea coast there were a few small villages, whose inhabitants fled as soon as they saw the sails. At length after proceeding two leagues we found a port late in the evening. That night the admiral resolved that some of the men should land at break of day in order to confer with the natives, and

ó de todo trajo un poco, en especial trajo cuatro ó cinco huesos de brazos é piernas de hombres. Luego que aquello vimos sospechamos que aquellas islas eran las de Caribe, que son habitadas de gente que comen carne humana, porque el Almirante por las señas que le habian dado del sitio destas islas, el otro camino, los indios de las islas que antes habian descubierto, habia enderezado el camino por descubrirlas, porque estaban mas cerca de España, y tambien porque por allí se hacia el camino derecho para venir á la isla Española, donde antes habia dejado la gente, á los cuales, por la bondad de Dios y por el buen saber del Almirante, venimos tan derechos como si por camino sabido ó seguido vinieramos. Esta isla es muy grande, y por el lado nos pareció que habia de luengo de costa veinta ó cinco leguas: fuimos costeando por ella buscando puerto mas de dos leguas; por la parte donde ibamos eran montañas muy altas, á la parte que dejamos parecian grandes llanos, á la orilla de la mar habia algunos poblados pequeños, ó

learn what sort of people they were; although it was suspected, from the appearance of those who had fled at our approach, that they were naked, like those whom the admiral had seen in his former voyage. In the morning several detachments under their respective captains sallied forth; one of them returned at the dinner hour, with a boy of about fourteen years of age, as it afterwards appeared, who said that he was one of the prisoners taken by these people. The others divided themselves, and one party took a little boy, whom a man was leading by the hand, but who left him and fled; this boy they sent on board immediately with some of our men; others remained, and took certain women, natives of the island, together with other women from among the captives who came of their own accord. One captain of this last company, not knowing that any intelligence of the people had been obtained, advanced farther into the island and lost himself, with the six men who accompanied him: they could not find their way back until after four days, when they lighted upon the sea shore, and following the line of coast returned to

---

luego que veian las velas huian todos. Andadas dos leguas hallamos puerto y bien tarde. Esa noche acordó el Almirante que á la madrugada saliesen algunos para tomar lengua ó saber que gente era, no embargante la sospecha é los que ya habian visto ir huyendo, que era gente desnuda como la otra que ya el Almirante habia visto el otro viage. Salieron esa madrugada ciertos Capitanes; los unos vinieron á hora de comer é trageron un mozo de fasta catorce años, á lo que despues se sopo, é él dijo que era de los que esta gente tenian cativos. Los otros se dividieron, los unos tomaron un mochacho pequeño, al cual llevaba un hombre por la mano, ó por huir lo desamparó. Este enviaron luego con algunos dellos, otros quedaron, ó destos unos tomaron ciertas mugeres naturales de la isla, é otras que se vinieron de grado, que eran de las cativas. Desta compañía se apartó un Capitan no sabiendo que se habia habido lengua con seis hombres, el cual se perdió con los que con él iban, que jamas sopieron tornar, fasta que á cabo de cuatro dias toparon

the fleet.[1] We had already looked upon them as killed and eaten by the people that are called Caribbees; for we could not account for their long absence in any other way, since they had among them some pilots who by their knowledge of the stars could navigate either to or from Spain, so that we imagined that they could not lose themselves in so small a space. / On this first day of our landing several men and women came on the beach up to the water's edge, and gazed at the ships in astonishment at so novel a sight; and when a boat pushed on shore in order to speak with them, they cried out "tayno tayno," which is as much as to say, "good," and waited for the landing of the sailors, standing by the boat in such a manner that they might escape when they pleased. The result was, that none of the men could be persuaded to join us, and only two were taken by force, who were secured

---

con la costa de la mar, ó siguiendo por ella tornaron á topar con la flota. Ya los teniamos por perdidos é comidos de aquellas gentes que se dicen los Caribes, porque no bastaba razon para creer que eran perdidos de otra manera, porque iban entre ellos pilotos, marineros que por la estrella saben ir é venir hasta España, creiamos que en tan pequeño espacio no se podian perder. Este dia primero que allí decendimos andaban por la playa junto con el agua muchos hombres é mugeres mirando la flota, ó maravillándose de cosa tan nueva é llegándose alguna barca á tierra á hablar con ellos, diciéndolos *tayno tayno*, que quiere decir *bueno*, esperaban en tanto que no salian del agua, junto con él moran, de manera que cuando ellos querian se podian salvar: en conclusion, que de los hombres

---

[1] It was Diego Marquez, the caterer, who with eight other men went on shore into the interior of the island, without permission from the admiral, who caused him to be sought for by parties of men with trumpets, but without success. One of those who were sent out with this object, was Alonzo de Hojeda, who took with him forty men, and on their return they reported that they had found many aromatic plants, a variety of birds, and some considerable rivers. The wanderers were not able to find their way to the ships until the eighth of November. (M. F. Navarrete's note, from Bartholomeo de las Casas' Manuscript History, chap. 84.)

and led away. More than twenty of the female captives were taken with their own consent, and other women natives of the island were surprised and carried off: several of the boys, who were captives, came to us fleeing from the natives of the island who had taken them prisoners. We remained eight days in this port in consequence of the loss of the aforesaid captain, and went many times on shore, passing amongst the dwellings and villages which were on the coast; we found a vast number of human bones and skulls hung up about the houses, like vessels intended for holding various things. There were very few men to be seen here, and the women informed us that this was in consequence of ten canoes having gone to make an attack upon other islands. These islanders appeared to us to be more civilised than those that we had hitherto seen; for although all the Indians have houses of straw, yet the houses of these people are constructed in a much superior fashion, are better stocked with provisions, and exhibit more evidences of industry, both on the part of the men and the women. They had a considerable quantity of cotton, both spun and prepared for spinning, and many

---

ninguno se pudo tomar por fuerza ni por grado, salvo dos que se seguraron é despues los trajeron por fuerza allí. Se tomaron mas de veinte mugeres de las cativas, y de su grado se venian otros naturales de la isla, que fueron salteadas é tomadas por fuerza. Ciertos mochachos cabtivos se vinieron á nosotros huyendo de los naturales de la isla que los tenian cabtivos. En este puerto estovimos ocho dias á causa de la perdida del sobredicho Capitan, donde muchas veces salimos á tierra andando por sus moradas é pueblos, que estaban á la costa, donde hallamos infinitos huesos de hombres, ó los cascos de las cabezas colgados por las casas á manera de vasijas para tener cosas. Aquí no parescieron muchos hombres; la causa era, segun nos dijeron las mugeres, que eran idas diez canoas con gentes á saltear á otras islas. Esta gente nos pareció mas pulítica que la que habita en estas otras islas que habemos visto, aunque todos tienen las moradas de paja; pero estos las tienen de mucho mejor hechura, é mas proveidas de mantenimientos, é parece en

cotton sheets, so well woven as to be no way inferior to those of our country. We inquired of the women, who were prisoners in the island, what people these islanders were: they replied that they were Caribbees. As soon as they learned that we abhorred such people, on account of their evil practice of eating human flesh, they were much delighted; and, after that, if they brought forward any woman or man of the Caribbees, they informed us (but secretly), that they were such, still evincing by their dread of their conquerors, that they belonged to a vanquished nation, though they knew them all to be in our power.

We were enabled to distinguish which of the women were natives, and which were captives, by the Caribbees wearing on each leg two bands of woven cotton, the one fastened round the knee, and the other round the ankle; by this means they make the calves of their legs large, and the above-mentioned parts very small, which I imagine that they regard as a matter of prettiness: by this peculiarity we distinguished them. The habits of these Caribbees are brutal. There are three islands: the one called Turuqueira; the other, which

---

ellas mas industria ansi veril como femenil. Tenian mucho algodon hilado y por hilar, y muchas mantas de algodon tan bien tejidas que no deben nada á las de nuestra patria. Preguntamos á las mugeres, que eran cativas en esta isla, que qué gente era esta; respondieron que eran Caribes. Despues que entendieron que nosotros aborreciamos tal gente por su mal uso de comer carne de hombres, holgaban mucho, y sí de nuevo traian alguna muger ó hombre de los Caribes, secretamente decian que eran Caribes, que allí donde estaban todos en nuestro poder mostraban temor dellos como gente sojuzgada, y de allí conocimos cuáles eran Caribes de las mugeres é cuáles nó, porque las Caribes traian en las piernas en cada una dos argollas tejidas de algodon, la una junto con rodilla, la otra junto con los tobillos; de manera que les hacen las pantorrillas grandes, ó de los sobredichos logares muy ceñidas, que esto me parece que tienen ellos por cosa gentil, ansi que por esta diferencia conocemos los unos de los otros. La costumbre desta gente de Caribes es bestial: son tres islas, esta se llama Turuqueira,

was the first that we saw, is called Ceyre;[1] the third is called Ayay : there is a resemblance among the natives of all these, as if they were of one race, and they do no injury to each other; but each and all of them wage war against the other neighbouring islands, and for the purpose of attacking them, make voyages of a hundred and fifty leagues at sea, with their numerous canoes, which are a small kind of craft made out of a single trunk of a tree. Their arms are arrows, in the place of iron weapons, and as they have no iron, some of them point their arrows with tortoise-shell, and others make their arrow heads of fish spines, which are naturally barbed like coarse saws: these prove dangerous weapons to a naked people like the Indians, and may cause death or severe injury, but to men of our nation they are not very formidable. In their attacks upon the neighbouring islands, these people capture as many of the women as they can, especially those who are young and beautiful, and keep them as concubines; and so great a number do they carry off, that in fifty houses no men were to be seen; and out of the number of the captives, more

---

la otra que primero vimos se llama Ceyre, la tercera se llama Ayay; estos todos son conformidad como si fuesen de un linage, los cuales no se hacen mal : unos ó otros hacen guerra á todas las otras islas comarcanas, los cuales van por mar ciento ó cincuenta leguas á saltear con muchas canoas que tienen, que son unas fustas pequeñas de un solo madero. Sus armas son frechas en lugar de hierros; porque no poseen ningun hierro, ponen unas puntas fechas de huesos de torgugas los unos, otros de otro isla ponen unas espinas de un pez fechas dentadas, que ansi lo son naturalmente, á manera de sierras bien recias, que para gente desarmada, como son todos, es cosa que les puede matar ó hacer harto daño ; pero para gente de nuestra nacion no son armas para mucho temer.

[1] This island, called further on Cayre, is most probably the " Charis" or " Carib" referred to on page 14, which the log of the first voyage makes to be next to and westward of Matenin, which latter all evidence shows to be Martinique. Dominica, therefore, will be Charis or Ceyre. Turuqueira and Ayay, probably the two islands which form Guadaloupe.

than twenty were young girls. These women also say that the Caribbees use them with such cruelty as would scarcely be believed; and that they eat the children which they bear to them, and only bring up those which they have by their native wives. Such of their male enemies as they can take alive, they bring to their houses to make a feast of them, and those who are killed they devour at once. They say that man's flesh is so good, that there is nothing like it in the world; and this is pretty evident, for of the bones which we found in their houses, they had gnawed everything that could be gnawed, so that nothing remained of them but what was too tough to be eaten: in one of the houses we found the neck of a man, undergoing the process of cooking in a pot. When they take any boys prisoners, they dismember them, and make use of them until they grow up to manhood, and then when they wish to make a feast they kill and eat them, for they say that the flesh of boys and women is not good to eat. Three of these boys came fleeing to us thus mutilated. At the end of four days arrived the captain who had lost

---

Esta gente saltea en las otras islas, que traen las mugeres que pueden haber, en especial mozas y hermosas, las cuales tienen para su servicio, ó para tener por mancebas, é traen tantas que en cincuenta casas ellos no parecieron, y de las cativas se vinieron mas de veinte mozas. Dicen tambien estas mugeres que estos usan de una crueldad que parece cosa increible; que los hijos que en ellas han se los comen, que solamente crian los que han en sus mugeres naturales. Los hombres que pueden haber, los que son vivos llevánselos á sus casas para hacer carnicería dellos, y los que han muertos luego se los comen. Dicen que la carne del hombre es tan buena que no hay tal cosa en el mundo; y bien parece porque los huesos que en estas casas hallamos todo lo que se puede roer todo lo tenian roido, que no habia en ellos sino lo que por su mucha dureza no se podia comer. Allí se halló en una casa cociendo en una olla un pezcuezo de un hombre. Los mochachos que cativan cortanlos el miembro, é sirvense de ellos fasta que son hombres, y despues cuando quieren facer fiesta mátanlos ó cómenselos, porque dicen que

himself with his companions, of whose return we had by this time given up all hope; for other parties had been twice sent out to seek him, one of which came back on the same day that he rejoined us, without having gained any information respecting the wanderers : we rejoiced at their arrival, regarding it as a new accession to our numbers. The captain and the men who accompanied him brought back some women and boys, ten in number. Neither this party, nor those who went out to seek them, had seen any of the men of the island, which must have arisen either from their having fled, or possibly from their being but very few men in that locality; for, as the women informed us, ten canoes had gone away to make an attack upon the neighbouring islands. The wanderers had returned from the mountains in such an emaciated condition, that it was distressing to see them. When we asked them how it was that they lost themselves, they said that the trees were so thick and close that they could not see the sky. Some of them who were mariners had climbed the trees to get a sight of the stars, but could never see them, and if they had not found their way to the sea coast, it would have been im-

---

que la carne de los mochachos é de las mogeres no es buena para comer. Destos mochachos se vinieron para nosotros huyendo tres todos tres cortados sus miembros. E á cabo de cuatro dias vino el Capitan que se habia perdido, de cuya venida estabamos ya bien desesparados, porque ya los habian ido á buscar otras cuadrillas por dos veces, é aquel dia vino la una caudrilla sin saber dellos ciertamente. Holgamos con su venida como si nuevamente se hobieran hallado: trajo este Capitan con los que fueron con él diez cabezas entre mochachos y mugeres. Estos ni los otros que los fueron á buscar, nunca hallaron hombres porque se habien huido, ó por ventura que en aquella comarca habia pocos hombres, porque segun se supo de las mugeres eran idas diez canoas con gentes á saltear á otras islas. Vino él é los que fueron con él tan destrozados del monte, que era lástima de los ver: decian, preguntándoles como se habien perdido, dijeron que era la espesura de los arboles tanta que el cielo no podian ver, ó que algunos de ellos, que eran

D

possible to have returned to the fleet. We left this island eight days after our arrival.[1] The next day at noon we saw another island,[2] not very large, at about twelve leagues distance from the one we were leaving. The greater part of the first day of our departure we were kept close in to the coast of this island by a calm, but as the Indian women whom we brought with us said that it was not inhabited, but had been dispeopled by the Carribees, we made no stay in it. On that evening we saw another island:[3] and in the night finding there were some sandbanks near, we dropped anchor, not venturing to proceed until the morning. On the morrow another island[4] appeared, of considerable size, but we touched at none of these because we were anxious to convey consolation to our people who had been left in Española; but it did not please God to grant us our desire, as will hereafter appear. Another day at the dinner hour we arrived at an island[5] which seemed worth the finding, for judging by the

---

marineros, habian subido por los árboles para mirar el estrella é que nunca la podieron ver, é que si no toparan con el mar fuera imposible tornar á la flota. Partimos desta isla ocho dias despues que allí llegamos. Luego otro dia á medio dia vimos otra isla, no muy grande, que estaria desta otra doce leguas; porque el primero dia que partimos lo mas del dia nos fizo calma, fuimos junto con la costa desta isla, é dijeron las Indias que llevabamos que no era habitada, que los Caribes la habian despoblado, é por esto no paramos en ella. Luego esa tarde vimos otra: á esa noche, cerca desta isla, fallamos unos bajos, por cuyo temor sorgimos, que no osamos andar fasta que fuese de dia. Luego á la mañana paresció otra isla harto grande: á ninguna destas no llegamos por consolar los que habian dejado en la Española, é no plogó á Dios segun que abajo paracerá. Otro dia á hora de comer llegamos á una isla ó pareciónos mucho bien, porque parecia muy pob-

---

[1] Tuesday the 12th of November.
[2] The island Montserrat. See Herrera, Dec. 1. L. 2, c. vii.
[3] The admiral called it Santa Maria la Redonda. See *ibid.*
[4] Santa Maria la Antigua. See *ibid.*
[5] The island of St. Martin. See *ibid.*

extent of cultivation in it, it appeared very populous. / We went thither and put into harbour, when the admiral immediately sent on shore a well manned barge to hold speech with the Indians, in order to ascertain what race they were, and also because it was necessary to gain some information respecting our course; although it afterwards plainly appeared that the admiral, who had never made that passage before, had taken a very correct route. But as matters of doubt should always be brought to as great a certainty as possible by inquiry, he wished the natives to be communicated with, and some of the men who went in the barge landed and went up to a village, whence the inhabitants had already withdrawn and hidden themselves. They took in this island five or six women and some boys, most of whom were captives, like those in the other island; for, as we learned from the women whom we had brought with us, the natives of this place also were Caribbees. / As this barge was about to return to the ships with the capture which they had made, a canoe came along the coast containing four men, two women, and a boy; and when they saw

---

lada, segun las muchas labranzas que en ella habia. Fuimos allá é tomamos puerto en la costa: luego mandó el Almirante ir á tierra una barca guarnecida de gente para si pudiese tomar lengua para saber que gente era, é tambien porque habiamos menester informarnos del camino, caso quel Almirante, aunque nunca habia fecho aquel camino, iba muy bien encaminado segun en cabo pareció. Pero porque las cosas dubdosas se deben siempre buscar con la mayor certinidad que haberse pueda, quiso haber allí lengua, de la cual gente que iba en la barca ciertas personas saltaron en tierra, llegaron en tierra á un poblado de donde la gente ya se habia escondido. Tomaron allí cinco ó seis mugeres y ciertos mochachos, de las cuales las mas eran tambien de las cativas como en la otra isla, porque tambien estos eran de los Caribes, segun ya sabiamos por la relacion de las mugeres que traiamos. Ya que esta barca se queria tornar á los navíos con su presa que habia fecho por parte debajo; por la costa venia una canoa en

the fleet they were so stupified with amazement, that for a good hour they remained motionless at the distance of nearly two gunshots from the ships. In this position they were seen by those who were in the barge and also by all the fleet. Meanwhile those in the barge moved towards the canoe, but so close in shore, that the Indians, in their perplexity and astonishment as to what all this could mean, never saw them, until they were so near that escape was impossible; for our men pressed on them so rapidly that they could not get away, although they made considerable effort to do so.

When the Caribbees saw that all attempt at flight was useless, they most courageously took to their bows, both women and men; I say most courageously, because they were only four men and two women, and our people were twenty-five in number. Two of our men were wounded by the Indians, one with two arrow-shots in his breast, and another with one in his side, and if it had not happened that they carried shields and wooden bucklers, and that they soon got near them with the barge and upset their canoe, most of

---

que venian cuatro hombres ó dos mugeres é un mochacho, é desque vieron la flota maravillados se embebecieron tanto que por una grande hora estovieron que no se movieron de un lugar casi dos tiros de lombarda de los navíos. En esto fueron vistos de los que estaban en la barca ó aun de toda la flota. Luego los de la barca fueron para ellos tan junto con la tierra, que con el embebecimiento que tenian, maravillándose ó pensando que cosa seria, nunca los vieron hasta que estovieron muy cerca dellos, que no les pudieron mucho huir aunque harto trabajaron por ello; pero los nuestros aguijaron con tanta priesa que no se les pudieron ir. Los Caribes desque vieron que el hoir no les aprovechaba, con mucha osadia pusieron mano á los arcos, tambien las mugeres como los hombres; ó digo con mucha osadia porque ellos no eran mas de cuatro hombres y dos mugeres, ó los nuestros mas de veinte é cinco, de los cuales firieron dos, al uno dieron dos frechadas en los pechos ó al otro una por el costado, é sino fuera

them would have been killed with their arrows. After their canoe was upset, they remained in the water swimming and occasionally wading (for there were shallows in that part), still using their bows as much as they could, so that our men had enough to do to take them : and after all there was one of them whom they were unable to secure till he had received a mortal wound with a lance, and whom thus wounded they took to the ships. The difference between these Caribbees and the other Indians, with respect to dress, consists in their wearing their hair very long, while the others have it clipt irregularly and paint their heads with crosses and a hundred thousand different devices, each according to his fancy; which they do with sharpened reeds. All of them, both the Caribbees and the others, are beardless, so that it is a rare thing to find a man with a beard. The Caribbees whom we took had their eyes and eyebrows stained, which I imagine they do from ostentation. It gave them a more formidable appearance. One of these captives said, that in an island belonging to them called Cayre[1] (which is the first that we

---

porque llevaban adargas ó tablachutas, ó porque los invistieron presto con la barca é les trastornaron su canoa, asaetearan con sus frechas los mas dellos. E despues de trastornada su canoa quedaron en el agua nadando, ó á las veces haciendo pie, que allí habia unos bajos, é tovieron harto que hacer en tomarlos, que todavía cuanto podian tiraban, é con todo eso el uno no lo pudieron tomar sino mal herido de una lanzada que murió, el cual trajeron ansi herido fasta les navíos. La diferencia destos á los otros indios en el hábito, es que los de' Caribe tienen el cabello muy largo, los otros son tresquilados ó fechas cien mil diferencias en las cabezas de cruces, é de otras pinturas en diversas maneras, cada uno como se le antoja, lo cual se hacen con cañas agudas. Todos ansi los de Caribe como los otros es gente sin barbas, que por maravilla hallarás hombre que las tenga. Estos Caribes que allí tomaron venian tiznados los ojos é las cejas, lo cual me parece que hacen por gala, ó con aquello parescian mas espantables; el

[1] Dominica, see note, p. 31.

saw, though we did not go to it), there is a great quantity of gold and that if we were to take them nails and tools with which to make their canoes, we might bring away as much gold as we liked. On the same day we left that island, having been there no more than six or seven hours; and, steering for another point of land[1] which appeared to lie in our intended course, we reached it by night. On the morning of the following day we coasted along it, and found it to be a large extent of country, but not continuous, for it was divided into more than forty islets.[2] The land was very high and most of it barren, an appearance which we have never observed in any of the islands visited by us before or since: the surface of the ground seemed to suggest the probability of its containing metals. None of us went on shore here, but a small latteen caravel went up to one of the islets and found in it some fishermen's huts; the Indian women whom we brought with us said they were not inhabited. We pro-

---

uno destos dice que en una isla dellos, llamada Cayre, que es la primera que vimos, á la cual no llegamos, hay mucho oro; que vayan allá con clavos é contezuelas para hacer sus canoas, é que traerán cuanto oro quisieren. Luego aquel dia partimos de esta isla, que no estariamos allí mas de seis ó siete horas, fuemos para otra tierra que pareció á ojo que estaba en el camino que habiamos de facer: llegamos noche cerca della. Otro dia de mañana fuimos por la costa della: era muy gran tierra, aunque no era muy continua, que eran mas de cuarenta y tantos islones, tierra muy alta, ó la mas della pelada, la cual no era ninguna ni es de las que antes ni despues habemos visto. Parescia tierra dispuesta para haber en ella metales: á esta no llegamos para saltar en tierra, salvo una carabela latina llegó á un islon de estos, en el cual hallaron ciertas casas de pescadores. Las Indias que traiamos dijeron que no eran pobladas. Andovimos por esta costa lo

[1] The island of *Santa Cruz*, where they anchored on Thursday the fourteenth of November. See Herrera, Dec. 1. L. 2, cap. vii.

[2] The admiral named the largest of these islands *St. Ursula*, and all the others *The eleven thousand Virgins*. See *ibid.*

ceeded along the coast the greater part of that day, and on the evening of the next we discovered another island called Burenquen,[1] which we judged to be thirty leagues in length, for we were coasting along it the whole of one day. This island is very beautiful and apparently fertile: hither the Caribbees come with the view of subduing the inhabitants, and often carry away many of the people. These islanders have no boats nor any knowledge of navigation; but, as our captives inform us, they use bows as well as the Caribbees, and if by chance when they are attacked they succeed in taking any of their invaders, they will eat them in like manner as the Caribbees themselves in the contrary event would devour them. We remained two days in this island, and a great number of our men went on shore, but could never get speech of the natives, who had all fled, from fear of the Caribbees. All the above-mentioned islands were discovered in this voyage, the admiral having seen nothing of them in his former voyage. They are all very beautiful and possess a most luxuriant soil, but this last island appeared to exceed

---

mas deste dia, hasta otro dia en la tarde que llegamos á vista de otra isla llamada Burenquen, cuya costa corrimos todo un dia: juzgábase que ternia por aquella banda treinta leguas. Esta isla es muy hermosa y muy fértil á parecer: á estu vienon los de Caribe á conquistar, de la cual llevaban mucha gente; estos no tienen fustas ningunas nin saben andar por mar; pero, segun dicen estos Caribes que tomamos, usan arcos como ellos, é si por caso cuando los vienen á saltear los pueden prender tambien se los comen como los de Caribe á ellos. En un puerto desta isla estovimos dos dias, donde saltó mucha gente en tierra; pero jamas podimos haber lengua, que todos se fuyeron como gente temorizadas de los Caribes. Todas estas islas dichas fueron descubiertas deste camino, que fasta aquí ninguna dellas habia visto el Almirante el otro viage, todos son muy hermosas ó de muy buena tierra; pero esta paresció mejor á todos: aquí casi se acabaron las islas que

[1] The island of *Porto Rico*, to which the admiral gave the name of *St. John the Baptist*. See Herrera, Dec. 1. L. 2, cap. vii.

all the others in beauty. Here terminated the islands, which on the side towards Spain had not been seen before by the admiral, although we regard it as a matter of certainty that there is land more than forty leagues beyond the foremost of these newly discovered islands, on the side nearest to Spain. We believe this to be the case, because, two days before we saw land, we observed some birds called rabihorcados (or pelicans), marine birds of prey which do not sit or sleep upon the water, making circumvolutions in the air at the close of evening previous to taking their flight towards land for the night. These birds could not be going to settle at more than twelve or fifteen leagues distance, because it was late in the evening, and this was on our right hand on the side towards Spain; from which we all judged that there was land there still undiscovered; but we did not go in search of it, because it would have taken us round out of our intended route. I hope that in a few voyages it will be discovered. It was at dawn that we left the before-mentioned island of Burenquen,[1] and on that day before nightfall we

---

fácia la parte de España habia dejado de ver el Almirante, aunque tenemos por cosa cierta que hay tierra mas de cuarenta leguas antes de estas primeras hasta España, porque dos dias antes que viesemos tierra vimos unas aves que llaman rabihorcados, que son aves de rapiña marinas é ni sientan ni duermen sobre el agua, sobre tarde rodeando sobir en alto, é despues tiran su via á buscar tierra para dormir, las cuales no podrian ir á caer segun era tarde de doce ó quince leguas arriba, y esto era á la man derecha donde veniamos hasta la parte de España; de donde todos juzgaron allí quedar tierra, lo cual no se buscó porque se nos hacia rodeo para la via que traiamos. Espero que á pocos viages se hallará. Desta isla sobredicha partimos una madrugada, é aquel dia, antes que fuese noche, hobimos vista de tierra, la cual tampoco era conocida de ninguno de los qua habian venido el otro viage; pero por las nuevas de las indias que traiamos sospechamos que era la

[1] Porto Rico.

caught sight of land, which though not recognized by any of those who had come hither in the former voyage, we believed to be Española, from the information given us by the Indian women whom we had with us: and in this island we remain at present.[1] Between it and Burenquen[2] another island appeared at a distance, but of no great size. When we reached Española the land, at the part where we approached it, was low and very flat,[3] on seeing which, a general doubt arose as to its identity; for, neither the admiral nor his companions, on the previous voyage, had seen it on this side.

The island being large, is divided into provinces; the part which we first touched at, is called Hayti; another province adjoining it, they call Xamaná; and the next province is named Bohio, where we now are. These provinces are again subdivided, for they are of great extent. Those who have seen the length of its coast, state that it is two hundred leagues long, and I, myself, should judge it not to be

---

Española, en la cual agora estamos. Entre esta isla ó la otra de Buriquen parecia de lejos otra, aunque no era grande. Desque llegamos á esta Española, por el comienzo de alla era tierra baja y muy llana, del conocimiento de la cual aun estaban todos dubdosos si fuese la que es, porque aquella parte nin el Almirante ni los otros que con él vinieron habian visto, ó aquesta isla como es grande es nombrada por provincias, e á esta parte que primero llegamos llaman Hayti, y luego á la otra provincia junta con esta llaman Xamaná, ó á la otra Bohio; en la cual agora estamos; ansi hay en ellas muchas provincias porque es gran cosa, porque segun afirman los que la han visto por la costa de largo, dicen que habrá doscientas leguas : á mi me parece que á lo menos habrá ciento

---

[1] On Friday, the twenty-second of November, the admiral first caught sight of the island of Española. See Herrera, Dec. 1. L. 2, cap. vii.

[2] Mona Island.

[3] Apparently between Point Macao and Point Engaño, which is flat. The higher land of the north coast commences at Point Macao.

less than a hundred and fifty leagues: as to its breadth, nothing is hitherto known; it is now forty days since a caravel left us with the view of circumnavigating it, and is not yet returned.[1] The country is very remarkable, and contains a vast number of large rivers, and extensive chains of mountains, with broad open valleys, and the mountains are very high: it does not appear that the grass is ever cut throughout the year. I do not think that they have any winter in this part, for at Christmas were found many birds-nests, some containing the young birds, and others containing eggs. No four-footed animal has ever been seen in this or any of the other islands, except some dogs of various colours, as in our own country, but in shape like large house-dogs; and also some little animals, in colour, size, and fur, like a rabbit, with long tails, and feet like those of a rat; these animals climb up the trees, and many who have tasted them, say they are very good to eat:[2] there are not any wild beasts. There are great numbers of small snakes, and some

---

é cincuenta; del ancho della hasta agora no se sabe. Alla es ido cuarenta dias ha á rodearla una carebela, la cual no es venida hasta hoy. Es tierra muy singular, donde hay infinitos rios grandes ó sierras grandes é valles grandes rasos, grandes montañas: sospecho que nunca se secan las yerbas en todo el año. Non creo que hay invierno ninguno en esta nin en las atras, porque por Navidad se fallan muchos nidos de aves, dellas con pájaros, é dellas con huevos. En ella ni en las otras nunca se ha visto animal de cuatro pies, salvo algunos perros de todas colores como en nuestra patria, la hechura como unos gosques grandes; de animales salvages no hay. Otrosí, hay un animal de color de conejo ó de su pelo, el grandor de un conejo nuevo, el rabo largo, los pies ó manos como de raton, suben por los árboles, muchos los han comido, dicen que es muy bueno de comer: hay culebras muchas

---

[1] On the parallel of 18° 25' the island has an extreme length of 400 miles, and its extreme breadth may be taken at 150 on the meridian of 71° 20'.   [2] In all probability a species of *capromys*.

lizards, but not many; for the Indians consider them as great a luxury as we do pheasants: they are of the same size as ours, but different in shape. In a small adjacent island[1] (close by a harbour called Monte Christo, where we stayed several days) our men saw an enormous kind of lizard, which they said was as large round as a calf,[2] with a tail as long as a lance, which they often went out to kill: but bulky as it was, it got into the sea, so that they could not catch it. There are, both in this and the other islands, an infinite number of birds like those in our own country, and many others such as we had never seen. No kind of domestic fowl has been seen here, with the exception of some ducks in the houses in Zuruquia; these ducks were larger than those of Spain, though smaller than geese,— very pretty, with flat crests, most of them as white as snow, but some black.

We ran along the coast of this island nearly a hundred leagues, concluding, that within this range we should find the spot where the admiral had left some of his men, and

---

no grandes; lagartos aunque no muchos, porque los indios hacen tanta fiesta dellos como hariamos allá con faisanes, son del tamaño de los de allá, salvo que en la hechura son diferentes, aunque en una isleta pequeña, que está junto con un puerto que llaman Monte Christo, donde estovimos muchos dias, vieron muchos dias un lagarto muy grande que decian que seria de gordura de un becerro é atan complido como una lanza, é muchas veces salieron por lo matar, ó con la mucha espesura se les metia en la mar, de manera que no se pudo haber dél derecho. Hay en esta isla y en las otras infinitas aves de las de nuestra patria, é otras muchas que allá nunca se vieron: de las aves domésticas nunca se ha visto acá ninguna, salvo en la Zuruquia habia en las casas unas ánades, las mas dellas blancas como la nieve é algunas dellas negras, muy lindas, con crestas rasas, mayores que las de allá, me-

[1] Cabras or Goat Island, close to "el Fraile" in the Bay of Monte Cristi.   [2] An alligator.

which we supposed to be about the middle of the coast. As we passed by the province called Xamaná, we sent on shore one of the Indians, who had been taken in the previous voyage, clothed, and carrying some trifles, which the admiral had ordered to be given him. On that day died one of our sailors, a Biscayan, who had been wounded in the affray with the Caribbees, when they were captured, as I have already described, through their want of caution. As we were proceeding along the coast, an opportunity was afforded for a boat to go on shore to bury him, the boat being accompanied by two caravels to protect it. When they reached the shore, a great number of Indians came out to the boat, some of them wearing necklaces and ear-rings of gold, and expressed a wish to accompany the Spaniards to the ships; but our men refused to take them, because they had not received permission from the admiral. / When the Indians found that they would not take them, two of them got into a small canoe, and went up to one of the caravels that had put in to shore; they were received on board with great kindness, and taken to the admiral's ship, where, through

---

nores que ánsares. Por la costa desta isla corrimos al pie de cien leguas porque hasta donde el Almirante habia dejado la gente, habria en este compás, que será en comedio ó en medio de la isla. Andando por la provincia della llamada Xamaná, en derecho echamos en tierra uno de los indios quel etro viage habian llevado vestido, é con algunas cosillas quel Almirante le habia mandado dar. Aquel dia se nos murió un marinero vizcaino que habia seido herido de los Caribes, que ya dije que se tomaron, por su mala guarda, ó porque ibamos por costa de tierra, diése lugar que saliese una barca á enterrarlo, é fueron en reguarda de la barca dos carabelas cerca con tierra. Salieron á la barca en llegando en tierra muchos indios, de los cuales algunos traian oro al cuello, ó á las orejas; querian venir con los cristianos á los navíos, ó no los quisieron traer, porque no llevaban licencia del Almirante; los cuales desque vieron que no los querian traer se metieron dos dellos en una canoa pequeña, ó se vinieron á una cara-

the medium of an interpreter, they related that a certain king had sent them to ascertain who we were, and to invite us to land, adding that they had plenty of gold, and also of provisions, to which we should be welcome/ The admiral desired that shirts, and caps, and other trifles, should be given to each of them, and said that as he was going to the place where Guacamari dwelt, he would not stop then, but that on a future day they would have an opportunity of seeing him, and with that they departed. We continued our route till we came to an harbour called Monte Cristi, where we remained two days, in order to observe the position of the land; for the admiral had an objection to the spot where his men had been left with the view of forming a station. We went on shore therefore to observe the formation of the land. /There was a large river of excellent water close by;[1] but the ground was inundated, and very ill-calculated for habitation./ As we went on making our observations on the river and the land, some of our men found two dead bodies by the river's side, one with a rope round his neck, and the other with one round his foot: this was on the first day of

---

bela de las que se habian acercado á tierra, en la cual los recibieron con su amor, é trajéronlos á la nao del Almirante, é dijeron, mediante un interprete, que un Rey fulano les enviaba á saber que gente eramos, ó á rogar que quisiesemos llegar á tierra, porque tenian mucho oro é le darian dello, ó de lo que tenian de comer: el Almirante les mandó dar sendas camisas ó bonetes é otras cosillas, é les dijo que porque iba á donde estaba Guacamarí non se podria detener, que otro tiempo habria que le pudiese ver, ó con esto se fueron. No cesamos de andar nuestro camino fasta llegar á un puerto llamado Monte Cristi, donde estuvimos dos dias para ver la disposicion de la tierra, porque no habia parecido bien al Almirante el logar donde habia dejado la gente para hacer asiento. Decendimos en tierra para ver la dispusicion: habia cerca de allí un gran rio de muy buena agua; pero es toda tierra anegada é muy indispuesta para habitar. Andando veyendo el rio é tierra

[1] The river Yaque.

our landing. On the following day they found two other corpses farther on, and one of these was observed to have a great quantity of beard. This was regarded as a very suspicious circumstance by many of our people, because, as I have already said, all the Indians are beardless. This harbour is twelve leagues from the place where the Spaniards had been left under the protection of Guacamari, the king of that province, whom I suppose to be one of the chief men of the island. After two days we set sail for that spot, but as it was late when we arrived,[1] and there were some shoals, where the admiral's ship had been lost, we did not venture to put in close to the shore, but remained that night at a little less than a league from the coast, waiting until the morning, when we might enter securely. On that evening, a canoe, containing five or six Indians, came out at a considerable distance from where we were, and approached us

hallaron algunos de los nuestros en una parte dos hombres muertos junto con el rio, el uno con un lazo al pescuezo y el otro con otro al pie, esto fue el primero dia. Otro dia siguiente hallaron otros dos muertos mas adelante de aquellos, el uno destos estaba en disposicion que se le pudo conocer tener muchas barbas. Algunos de los nuestros sospecharon mas mal que bien, é con razon, porque los indios son todos desbarbados, como dicho he. Este puerto está del lugar donde estaba la gente cristiana doce leguas: pasados dos dias alzamos velas para el lugar donde el Almirante habia dejado la sobredicha gente, en compañía de un Rey destos indios, que se llamaba Guacamarí, que pienso ser de los principales desta isla. Este dia llegamos en derecho de aquel lugar; pero era ya tarde, ó porque allí habia unos bajos donde el otro dia se habia perdido la nao en que habia ido el Almirante, no osamos tomar el puerto cerca de tierra fasta que otro dia de mañana se desfondase ó pudiesen entrar seguramente:

[1] The admiral anchored at the entrance of the harbour of Navidad, on Wednesday, the twenty-seventh of November, towards midnight, and on the following day put into the harbour. See Herrera, Dec. 1. L. 2, cap. viii and ix.

with great celerity. The admiral believing that he insured our safety by keeping the sails set, would not wait for them; they, however, perseveringly rowed up to us within gunshot, and then stopped to look at us; but when they saw that we did not wait for them, they put back and went away. After we had anchored that night at the spot in question,[1] the admiral ordered two guns to be fired, to see if the Spaniards, who had remained with Guacamari, would fire in return, for they also had guns with them; but when we received no reply, and could not perceive any fires, nor the slightest symptom of habitations on the spot, the spirits of our people became much depressed, and they began to entertain the suspicion which the circumstances were naturally calculated to excite. While all were in this desponding mood, and when four or five hours of the night had passed away, the same canoe which we had seen in the evening, came up, and the Indians with a loud voice addressed the captain of the caravel which they first approached, inquiring

---

quedamos aquella noche no una legua de tierra. Esa tarde, viniendo para allí de lejos, salió una canoa en que parescian cinco ó seis indios, los cuales venian á prisa para nosotros. El Almirante creyendo que nos seguraba hasta alzarnos, no quiso que los esperasemos, ó porfiando llegaron hasta un tiro de lombarda de nosotros, ó parabanse á mirar, ó desde allí desque vieron que no los esperabamos dieron vuelta é tornaron su via. Despues que surgimos en aquel lugar sobredicho tarde, el Almirante mandó tirar dos lombardas á ver si respondian los cristianos que habian quedado con el dicho Guacamarí, porque tambien tenian lombardas, los cuales nunca respondieron ni menos parescian huegos ni señal de casas en aquel lugar, de lo qual se desconsoló mucho la gente ó tomaron la sospecha que de tal caso se debia tomar. Estando ansi todos muy tristes, pasadas cuatro ó cinco horas de la noche, vino la misma canoa que esa tarde habiamos visto, é venia dando voces, preguntando por el Almirante un Capitan de

[1] The Bay of Caracol, four leagues west of Fort Dauphin.

for the admiral; they were conducted to the admiral's vessel, but would not go on board till he had spoken to them, and they had asked for a light, in order to assure themselves that it was he who conversed with them. One of them was a cousin of Guacamari, who had been sent by him once before: it appeared, that after they had turned back the previous evening, they had been charged by Guacamari with two masks of gold as a present; one for the admiral, the other for a captain who had accompanied him on the former voyage. They remained on board for three hours, talking with the admiral in the presence of all of us, he showing much pleasure in their conversation, and inquiring respecting the welfare of the Spaniards whom he had left behind. Guacamari's cousin replied, that those who remained were all well, but that some of them had died of disease, and others had been killed in quarrels that had arisen amongst them: he said also that the province had been invaded, by two kings named Caonabó and Mayreni, who had burned the habitations of the people; and that Guacamari was at some distance, lying ill of a wound in his leg, which was the occa-

---

una carabela donde primero llegaron: trajéronlos á la nao del Almirante, los cuales nunca quisieron entrar hasta que el Almirante los hablase; demandaron lumbre para lo conocer, ó despues que lo conocieron entraron. Era uno dellos primo del Guacamarí, el cual los habia enviado otra vez. Despues que se habian tornado aquella tarde traian caratulas de oro que Guacamarí enviaba en presente; la una para el Almirante ó la otra para un Capitan quel otro viage habia ido con él. Estovieron en la nao hablando con el Almirante en presencia de todos por tres horas mostrando mucho placer, preguntándoles por los Cristianos que tales estaban: aquel pariente dijo que estaban todos buenos, aunque entro ellos habia algunos muertos de dolencia é otros de diferencia que habia contecido entre ellos, é que Guacamarí estaba en otro lugar ferido en una pierna é por eso no habia venido, pero que otro dia vernia; porque otros dos Reyes, llamado el uno Caonabó y el otro Mayrení, habian venido á pelear con él é que

sion of his not appearing, but that he would come on the next day. The Indians then departed, saying they would return on the following day with the said Guacamari, and left us consoled for that night. Next morning we looked for Guacamari's arrival; and, meanwhile, some of our men landed by command of the admiral, and went to the spot where the Spaniards had formerly been : they found the building which they had inhabited, and which they had in some degree fortified with a palisade, burnt and levelled with the ground; they found also some rags and stuffs which the Indians had brought to throw upon the house. They observed too that the Indians who were seen near the spot, looked very shy, and dared not approach, but, on the contrary, fled from them. This we thought did not look well; for the admiral had told us that in the former voyage, when he arrived at this place, so many came in canoes to see our people, that there was no keeping them off; and as we now noticed that they were suspicious of us, it gave us a very unfavourable impression. We threw trifles, such as buttons and beads, towards them, in order to conciliate them, but only four, a

---

le habian quemado el logar; é luego esa noche se tornaron diciendo que otra dia vernian con el dicho Guacamarí, é con esto nos dejaron por esa noche consolados. Otro dia en la mañana estovimos esperando que viniese el dicho Guacamarí, é entretanto saltaron en tierra algunos por mandado del Almirante, é fueron al lugar donde solian estar, é halláronle quemado un cortijo algo fuerte con una palizada, donde los Cristianos habitaban, é tenian lo suyo quemado é derribado, é ciertas bernias é ropas que los indios habian traido á echar en la casa. Los dichos indios que por allí parecian andaban muy cahareños, que no se osaban allegar á nosotros, antes huian; lo cual no nos pareció bien porque el Almirante nos habia dicho que en llegando á quel lugar salian tantas canoas dellos á bordo de los navíos á vernos que no nos podriamos defender dellos, é que en el otro viage ansí lo facian; é como agora veiamos que estaban sospechosos de nosotros no nos parecia bien, con todo halagándoles aquel dia é arrojándolos

E

relation of Guacamari's and three others, took courage to
enter the boat, and were rowed on board. When they were
asked concerning the Spaniards, they replied that all of
them were dead: we had been told this already by one of
the Indians whom we had brought from Spain, and who had
conversed with the two Indians that on the former occasion
came on board with their canoe, but we had not believed it.
Guacamari's kinsman was asked who had killed them: he
replied that king Caonabó and king Mayreni had made an
attack upon them, and burnt the buildings on the spot,
that many were wounded in the affray, and among them
Guacamari, who had received a wound in his thigh, and had
retired to some distance: he also stated that he wished to
go and fetch him; upon which some trifles were given to
him, and he took his departure for the place of Guacamari's
abode. All that day we remained in expectation of them,
and when we saw that they did not come, many suspected
that the Indians who had been on board the night before,
had been drowned; for they had had wine given them two
or three times, and they had come in a small canoe that

---

algunas cosas, ansi como cascabeles é cuentas, hobo de asegurarse
un su pariente del dicho Guacamarí é otros tres, los cuales entraron en la barca é trajéronlos á la nao. Despues que le pre-
guntaron por los Cristianos dijeron que todos eran muertos, aunque ya nos lo habia dicho un indio de los que llevabamos de
Castilla que lo habian hablado los dos indios que antes habian
venido á la nao, que se habian quedado á bordo de la nao con su
canao, pero lo ne habiamos creido. Fue preguntado á este pariente do Guacamarí quien los habia muerto: dijo que el Rey de
Canoabó y el Rey Mayrení, é que le quemaron las cosas del lugar,
que estaban dellos muchos heridos, é tambien el dicho Guacamarí estaba pasado un muslo, y él que estaba en otro lugar y que
él queria ir luego allá á lo llamar, al cual dieron algunas cosas, é
luego se partió para donde estaba Guacamarí. Todo aquel dia
los estobimos esperando, é desque vimos que no venian, muchos
tenian sospecha que se habian ahogado los indios que antenoche

might be easily upset. The next morning the admiral went on shore, taking some of us with him; we went to the spot where the settlement had been, and found it utterly destroyed by fire, and the clothes of the Spaniards lying about upon the grass, but on that occasion we saw no dead body. There were many different opinions amongst us; some suspecting that Guacamari himself was concerned in the betrayal and death of the Christians; others thought not, because his own residence was burnt: so that it remained a very doubtful question. The admiral ordered all the ground which had been occupied by the fortifications of the Spaniards to be searched, for he had left orders with them to bury all the gold that they might get. While this was being done, the admiral wished to examine a spot at about a league's distance, which seemed to be suitable for building a town, for there was yet time to do so;—and some of us went thither with him, making our observations of the land as we went along the coast, until we reached a village of seven or eight houses, which the Indians forsook when they

---

habian venido, porque los habian dado á beber dos ó tres veces de vino, é venian en una canoa pequeña que se los podria trastornar. Otro dia de mañana salió á tierra el Almirante é algunos de nosotros, é fuemos donde solia estar la villa, la cual nos vimos toda quemada é los vestidos de los cristianos se hallaban por aquella yerba. Por aquella hora no vimos ningun muerto. Habia entre nosotros muchas razones diferentes, unos sospechando que el mismo Guacamarí fuese en la traicion ó muerte de los Cristianos, otros los parecia que no, pues estaba quemada su villa, ansí que la cosa era mucho para dudar. El Almirante mandó catar todo el sitio donde los Cristianos estaban fortalecidos porquel los habia mandado que desque toviesen alguna cantidad de oro que lo enterrasen. Entretanto que esto se hacia quiso llegar á ver á cerca de una legua do nos parecia que podria haber asiento para poder edificar una villa porque ya era tiempo, adonde fuimos ciertos con él mirando la tierra por la costa, fasta que llegamos á un poblado donde habia siete ú ocho casas; las quales habian

saw us approach, carrying away what they could, and leaving the things which they could not remove, hidden amongst the grass, around the houses. These people are so degraded that they have not even the sense to select a fitting place to live in; those who dwell on the shore, build for themselves the most miserable hovels that can be imagined, and all the houses are so covered with grass and dampness, that I wonder how they can contrive to exist. In these houses we found many things belonging to the Spaniards, which it could not be supposed they would have bartered; such as a very handsome Moorish mantle, which had not been unfolded since it was brought from Spain, stockings and pieces of cloth, also an anchor belonging to the ship which the admiral had lost here on the previous voyage; with other articles, which the more confirmed our suspicions. On examining some things which had been very cautiously sewn up in a small basket, we found a man's head wrapped up with great care; this we judged might be the head of a father, or mother, or of some person whom they much regarded: I have since heard that many were found in the

---

desamparado los indios luego que nos vieron ir, é llevaron lo que pudieron ó lo otro dejaron escondido entre yerbas junto con las casas, que es gente tan bestial que no tienen discrecion para buscar lugar para habitar, que los que viven á la marina es maravilla cuan bestialmente edifican, que las casas enderedor tienen tan cubiertas de yerba ó de humidad, que estoy espantado como viven. En aquellas casas hallamos muchas cosas de los Cristianos, las cuales no se creian que ellos hobiesen rescatado, ansí como una almalafa muy gentil, la cual no se habia descogido de como la llevaron de Castilla, ó calzas ó pedazos de paños, é una ancla de la nao quel Almirante habia allí perdido el otro viage, é otras cosas, de las cuales mas se esforzó nuestra opinion; y de acá hallamos, buscando las cosas que tenian guardadas en una esportilla mucho cosida ó mucho á recabdo, una cabeza de hombre mucho guardada. Allí juzgamos por entonces que seria la cabeza de padre ó madre, ó de persona que mucho querian. Des-

same state, which makes me believe that our first impression was the true one. After this we returned. We went on the same day to the site of the settlement; and when we arrived, we found many Indians, who had regained their courage, bartering gold with our men : they had bartered to the extent of a mark: we also learned that they had shown where the bodies of eleven of the dead Spaniards were laid, which were already covered with the grass that had grown over them; and they all with one voice asserted that Caonabó and Mayreni had killed them; but notwithstanding all this, we began to hear complaints that one of the Spaniards had taken three women to himself, and another four, from whence we drew the inference that jealousy was the cause of the misfortune that had occurred. On the next morning, as no spot in that vicinity appeared suitable for our making a settlement, the admiral ordered a caravel to go in one direction to look for a convenient locality, while some of us went with him another way. In the course of our explorations, we discovered a harbour of great security; the neighbourhood of which, so far as regarded the formation of the

---

pues he oido que hayan hallado muchas desta manera, por donde creo ser verdad lo que allí juzgamos; desde allí nos tornamos. Aquel dia venimos por donde estaba la villa, y cuando llegamos hallamos muchos indios que se habian asegurado y estaban rescatando oro : tenian rescatado fasta un marco: hallamos que habian mostrado donde estaban muertos once cristianos, cubiertos ya de la yerba que habia crecido sobre ellos, ó todos hablaban por una boca que Caonabó ó Mayreni les habian muerto; pero con todo eso asomaban queja que los Cristianos uno tenia tres mugeres, otro cuatro, donde creemos quel mal que les vino fue de zelos. Otro dia de mañana, porque en todo aquello no habia logar dispuesto para nosotros poder hacer asiento, acordó el Almirante fuese una carabela á una parte para mirar lugar conveniente, ó algunos que fuimos con él fuimos á otra parte, á do hallamos un puerto muy seguro ó muy gentil disposicion de tierra para habitar, pero porque estaba lejos de donde nos deseabamos

land, was excellent for habitation; but as it was far from any mine of gold, the proximity of which was very desirable, the admiral decided that we should settle in some spot which would give us greater certainty of attaining that object, provided the position of the land should prove equally convenient. On our return, we found the other caravel arrived, in which Melchior and four or five other trustworthy men had been exploring with a similar object. They reported that as they went along the coast, a canoe came out to them containing two Indians, one of whom was the brother of Guacamari, and was recognised by a pilot who was in the caravel. When he questioned them as to their purpose, they replied that Guacamari sent to beg the Spaniards to come on shore, as he was residing near, with as many as fifty families around him. The chief men of the party then went on shore in the boat, and proceeding to the place where Guacamari was, found him stretched on his bed, complaining of a severe wound. They conferred with him, and inquired respecting the Spaniards; his reply was in accordance with the account already given by the others, viz.— that they had been killed by Caonabó and Mayreni, who

---

que estaba la mina de oro, no acordó el Almirante de poblar sino en otra parte que fuese mas cierta si se hallase conveniente disposicion. Cuando venimos deste lugar hallamos venida la otra carabela que habia ido á la otra parte á buscar el dicho lugar en la cual habio ido Melchior e otros cuatro ó cinco hombres de pro. E yendo costeando por tierra salió á ellos una canoa en que venian dos indios, el uno era hermano de Guacamarí, el cual fue conocido por un piloto que iba en la dicha carabela, ó preguntó quien iba allí, al cual, dijeron los hombres principales, dijeron que Guacamarí les rogaba que se llegasen á tierra, donde él tenia su asiento con fasta cincuenta casas. Los dichos principales saltaron en tierra con la barca é fueron donde él estaba, el cual fallaron en su cama echado faciendo del doliente ferido. Fablaron con él preguntándole por los Cristianos: respondió concertando con la mesma razon de los otros, que era que Caonabó ó Mayreni

also had wounded him in the thigh. In confirmation of his assertion, he showed them the limb bound up, on seeing which, they concluded that his statement was correct. At their departure he gave to each of them a jewel of gold, according to his estimate of their respective merits. The Indians beat the gold into very thin plates, in order to make masks of it, and set it in a cement which they make for that purpose. Other ornaments they make of it, to wear on the head and to hang in the ears and nostrils, and for these also they require it to be thin. It is not the costliness of the gold that they value in their ornaments, but its showy appearance. Guacamari desired them by signs as well as he was able, to tell the admiral that as he was thus wounded, he prayed him to have the goodness to come to see him. The sailors told this to the admiral when he arrived, and he resolved to go the next morning, for the spot could be reached in three hours, being scarcely three leagues distance from the place where we were; but as it would be the dinner-hour when we arrived, we dined before we went on shore. After dinner, the admiral gave

---

los habian muerto, ó que á él habian ferido en un muslo, el cual mostró ligado : los que entonces lo vieron ansí les pareció que era verdad como él lo dijo : al tiempo del despedirse dió á cada uno dellos una joya de oro, á cada uno como le pareció que lo merescia. Este oro facian en fojas muy delgadas, porque lo quieren para facer carátulas ó para poderse asentar en betun que ellos facen, si así no fuese no se asentaria. Otro facen para traer en la cabeza ó para colgar en las orejas é narices, ansí que todavía es menester que sea delgado, pues que ellos nada desto hacen por riqueza salvo por buen parecer. Dijo el dicho Guacamarí por señas e como mejor pudo, que porque él estaba ansí herido que dijesen al Almirante que quisiese venir á verlo. Luego quel Almirante llegó los sobredichos le contaron este caso. Otro dia de mañana acordó partir para allá, al cual lugar llegariamos dentro de tres horas, porque apenas habria dende donde estábamos allá tres leguas; ansí que cuando allí llegamos era hora de comer :

orders that all the captains should come with their barges to proceed to the shore, for already on that morning, previous to our departure, the aforesaid brother of Guacamari had come to speak to the admiral to urge his visit. Then the admiral went on shore accompanied by all the principal officers, so richly dressed that they would have made a distinguished appearance even in any of our chief cities : he took with him some articles as presents, having already received from Guacamari a certain quantity of gold, and it was reasonable that he should make a commensurate response to his acts and expressions of goodwill : Guacamari had also provided himself with a present. When we arrived, we found him stretched upon his bed, which was made of cotton net-work, and, according to their custom, suspended.[1] He did not arise, but from his bed made the best gesture of courtesy of which he was capable. He showed much feeling ; with tears in his eyes lamented the death of the Spaniards, and began by explaining to the best of his power, how some died of disease, others had gone to Caonabó in search of the mine of gold, and had there been killed, and that the rest had

comimos ante de salir en tierra. Luego que hobimos comido mandó el Almirante que todos los Capitanes viniesen con sus barcas para ir en tierra, porque ya esa mañana antes que partiésemos de donde estábamos habia venido el sobredicho su hermano á hablar con el Almirante, é á darle priesa que fuese al lugar donde estaba el dicho Guacamarí. Allí fue el Almirante á tierra é toda la gente de pro con él, tan ataviados que en una cibdad prencipal parecieran bien : llevó algunas cosas para le presentar porque ya habia recibido dél alguna cantidad de oro, é era razon le respondiese con la obra é voluntad quel habia mostrado. El dicho Guacamarí ansí mismo tenia aparejado para hacerle presente. Cuando llegamos hallámosle echado en su cama, como ellos lo usan, colgado en el aire, fecha una cama de algodon como de red ; no se levantó, salvo dende la cama hizo el semblante de cortesia como él mejor sopo, mostró mucho sentimiento con lágrimas en los ojos por la muerte de los Cristianos, é co-

[1] This is the earliest mention of a hammock.

been attacked and slain in their own town. According to the appearance of the dead bodies, it was not two months since this had happened. He then presented the admiral with eight marks and a half of gold, five or six hundred pieces of jewellery of various colours, and a cap with similar jewel-work, which I think they must value very highly, because in it was a jewel which was presented with great reverence. It appears to me that these people put more value upon copper than gold. The surgeon of the fleet and myself being present, the admiral told Guacamari that we were skilled in the treatment of human disorders, and wished that he would shew us his wound. He replied that he was willing; upon which I said it would be necessary that he should, if possible, go out of the house, because we could not see well on account of the place being darkened by the throng of people; to this he consented, I think more from timidity than inclination, and left the house leaning on the arm of the admiral. After he was seated, the surgeon approached him and began to untie his bandage; then he told

---

menzó á hablar en ello mostrando, como mejor podia, como unos murieron de dolencia, é como otros se habian ido á Caonabó á buscar la mina del oro é que allí los habian muerto, é los otros que se los habian venido á matar allí en su villa. A lo que parecian los cuerpos de los muertos no habia dos meses que habia acaecido. Esa hora el presentó al Almirante ocho marcos y medio de oro, é cinco ó seiscientos labrados de pedreria de diversos colores, é un bonete de la misma pedrería, lo cual me parece deben tener ellos en mucho. En el bonete estaba un joyel, lo cual le dió en mucha veneracion. Pareceme que tienen en mas el cobre quel oro. Estábamos presentes yo y un zurugiano de armada; entonces dijo el Almirante al dicho Guacamarí que nosotros eramos sabios de las enfermedades de los hombres que nos quisiese mostrar la herida: él respondió que le placia, para lo cual yo dije que seria necesario, si pudiese, que saliese fuera de casa, porque con la mucha gente estaba escura é no se podria ver bien; lo cual él fizo luego, creo mas de empacho que de gana;

the admiral that the wound was made with a *ciba*, by which he meant with a stone. When the wound was uncovered, we went up to examine it: it is certain that there was no more wound on that leg than on the other, although he cunningly pretended that it pained him much. Ignorant as we were of the facts, it was impossible to come to a definite conclusion. There were certainly many proofs of an invasion by a hostile people, so that the admiral was at a loss what to do. He with many others thought, however, that for the present, and until they could ascertain the truth, they ought to conceal their distrust; for, after ascertaining it, they would be able to claim whatever indemnity they thought proper. That evening Guacamari accompanied the admiral to the ships, and when they showed him the horses and other objects of interest, their novelty struck him with the greatest amazement: he took supper on board, and returned that evening to his house. The admiral told him that he wished to settle there and to build houses; to which he assented, but said that the place was not wholesome, because it was very damp: and so it most certainly was.

---

arrimándose á el salió fuera. Despues de asentado, llego el zurugiano á él é comenzó de desligarle: entonces dijo al Almirante que era ferida fecha con ciba, que quiere decir con piedra. Despues que fue desatada llegamos á tentarle. Es cierto que no tenia mas mal en aquella que en la otra, aunque él hacia del raposo que le dolia mucho. Ciertamente no se podia bien determinar porque las razones eran ignotas, que ciertamente muchas cosas habia que mostraban haber venido á él gente contraria. Ansimesmo el Almirante no sabia que se hacer: paresció1e, ó á otros muchos, que por entonces fasta bien saber la verdad que se debia disimular, porque despues de sabida, cada que quisiesen, se podia dél recibir enmienda. E aquella tarde se vino con el Almirante á las naos, é mostráronle caballos ó cuanto ahí habia, de lo cual quedó muy maravillado como de cosa estraña á él; tomó colacion en la nao, é esa tarde luego se tornó á su casa: el Almirante dijo que queria ir á habitar allí con él ó queria facer

All this passed through the interpretation of two of the Indians who had gone to Spain in the last voyage, and who were the sole survivors of seven that had embarked with us; five died on the voyage, and these but narrowly escaped. The next day we anchored in that port: Guacamari sent to know when the admiral intended leaving, and was told that he should do so on the morrow. The same day Guacamari's brother, and others with him, came on board, bringing gold to barter: on the day of our departure also they bartered a great quantity of gold. There were ten women on board, of those which had been taken in the Caribbee islands, principally from Burenquen, and it was observed that the brother of Guacamari spoke with them ;. we think that he told them to make an effort to escape that night; for certainly during our first sleep they dropped themselves quietly into the water, and went on shore, so that by the time they were missed they had reached such a distance that only four could be taken by the boats which went in pursuit, and these were secured when just leaving

---

casas, y él respondió que le placia, pero que el lugar era mal sano porque era muy humido, é tal era él por cierto. Esto todo pasaba estando por intérpretes dos indios de los que el otro viage habian ido á Castilla, los cuales habian quedado vivos de siete que metimos en el puerto, que los cinco se murieron en el camino, los cuales escaparon á uña de caballo. Otro dia estuvimos surtos en aquel puerto ; é quiso saber cuando se partiria el Almirante : le mandó decir que otro dia. En aquel dia vinieron á la nao el sobredicho hermano suyo é otros con él, é trajeron algun oro para rescatar. Ansí mesmo el dia que allá salimos se rescató buena cantidad de oro. En la nao habia diez mugeres de las que se habian tomado en las islas de Cariby ; eran las mas dellas de Boriquen. Aquel hermano de Guacamarí habló con ellas : creemos que les dijo lo que luego esa noche pusieron por obra y es que al primer sueño muy mansamente se echaron al agua é se fueron á tierra, de manera que cuando fueron falladas menos iban tanto trecho que con las barcas no pudieron tomar mas de las

the water: they had to swim considerably more than half a league. The next morning the admiral sent to desire that Guacamari would cause search to be made for the women who had escaped in the night, and that he would send them back to the ships. When the messengers arrived they found the place forsaken and not a soul there; this made many openly declare their suspicions, but others said they might have removed to another village, as was their custom. That day we remained quiet, because the weather was unfavourable for our departure. On the next morning the admiral resolved that as the wind was adverse, it would be well to go with the boats to inspect a harbour on the coast at two leagues distance further up,[1] to see if the formation of the land was favourable for a settlement; and we went thither with all the ship's boats, leaving the ships in the harbour. As we moved along the coast the people manifested a sense of insecurity, and when we reached the spot to which we were bound all the natives had fled. While we were walking about this place we found an Indian stretched

cuatro, las cuales tomaron al salir del agua; fueron nadando mas de una gran media legua. Otro dia de mañana envió el Almirante á decir á Guacamarí que le enviase aquellas mugeres que la noche antes se habian huido, é que luego las mandase buscar. Cuando fueren hallaron el lugar despoblado, que no estaba persona en el: ahí tornaron muchos fuerte á afirmar su sospecha, otros decian que se habria mudado á otra poblacion quellos ansí lo suelen hacer. Aquel dia estovimos allí quedos por que el tiempo era contrario para salir: otro dia de mañana acordó el Almirante, pues que el tiempo era contrario, que seria bien ir con las barcas á ver un puerto la costa arriba, fasta el cual habria dos leguas, para ver si habria dispusicion de tierra para hacer habitacion; donde fuemos con todas las barcas de los navíos dejando los navíos en el puerto. Fuimos corriendo toda la costa, é tambien estos no se seguraban bien de nosotros; llegamos á un lugar de donde todos eran huidos. Andando por él fallamos junto con las casas, metido en el monte, un indio ferido de una

[1] Port Dauphin.

on the hill-side, close by the houses, with a gaping wound in his shoulder caused by a dart, so that he had been disabled from fleeing any further. The natives of this island fight with sharp darts, which they discharge from cross-bows in the same manner as boys in Spain shoot their small arrows, and which they send with considerable skill to a great distance; and certainly upon an unarmed people these weapons are calculated to do serious injury. The man told us that Caonabó and his people had wounded him and burnt the houses of Guacamari. Thus we are still kept in uncertainty respecting the death of our people, on account of the paucity of information on which to form an opinion, and the conflicting and equivocal character of the evidence we have obtained. We did not find the position of the land in this port favourable for healthy habitation, and the admiral resolved upon returning along the upper coast by which we had come from Spain, because we had had tidings of gold in that direction. But the weather was so adverse that it cost more labour to sail thirty leagues in a backward direction than the whole voyage from Spain; so that, what with

---

vara, de una ferida que resollaba por las espaldas, que no habia podido huir mas lejos. Los desta isla pelean con unas varas agudas, las cuales tiran con unas tiranderas como las que tiran los mochachos las varillas en Castilla, con las cuales tiran muy lejos asaz certero. Es cierto que para gente desarmada que pueden hacer harto daño. Este nos dijo que Caonabó é los suyos lo habian ferido, é habian quemado las casas á Guacamarí. Ansí quel poco entender que los entendemos é las razones equívocas nos han traido á todos tan afuscados que fasta agora no se ha podido saber la verdad de la muerte de nuestra gente, ó no hallamos en aquel puerto dispusicion saludable parer hacer habitacion. Acordó el Almirante nos tornásemos por la costa arriba por do habíamos venido de Castilla, porque la nueva del oro era fasta allá. Fuenos el tiempo contrario, que mayor pena nos fue tornar treinta leguas atrás que venir desde Castilla, que con el tiempo contrario ó la largueza del camino ya eran tres meses pasados cuando

the contrary wind and the length of the passage, three months had elapsed before we set foot on land. It pleased God, however, that through the check upon our progress caused by contrary winds, we succeeded in finding the best and most suitable spot that we could have selected for a settlement, where there was an excellent harbour[1] and abundance of fish, an article of which we stood in great need from the scarcity of meat. The fish caught here are very singular and more wholesome than those of Spain. The climate does not allow the fish to be kept from one day to another, for all animal food speedily becomes unwholesome, on account of the alternate heat and damp.

The land is very rich for all purposes. Near the harbour there are two rivers; one large,[2] and another of moderate breadth somewhat near it: the water is of a very remarkable quality. On the bank of it is being built a city called Marta,[3] one side of which is bounded by the water with a ravine of cleft rock, so that at that part there is no need of fortification; the other half is girt with a plantation of trees

---

decendimos en tierra. Plugó á nuestro Señor que por la contrariedad del tiempo que no nos dejó ir mas adelante, hobimos de tomar tierra en el mejor sitio y dispusicion que pudieramos escoger, donde hay mucho buen puerto é grrn pesquería, de la cual tenemos mucha necesidad por el carecimiento de las carnes. Hay en esta tierra muy singular pescado mas sano quel de España. Verdad sea que la tierra no consiente que se guarde de un dia para ótro porque es caliente é humida, é por ende luego las cosas introfatibles ligeramente se corrompen. La tierra es muy gruesa para todas cosas; tiene junto un rio prencipal é otro razouable, asaz cerca de muy singular agua: edificase sobre la ribera dél una cibdad Marta, junto quel lugar se deslinda con el agua, de manera que la metad de la cibdad queda cercada de agua con una barranca de peña tajada, tal que por allí no ha menester defensa ninguna; la otra metad está cercada de una arbo-

[1] Port Isabelique, or Isabella, ten leagues to the east of Monte Christi.
[2] The river Isabella.   [3] The infant city of Isabella

so thick that a rabbit could scarcely pass through it; and so green that fire will never be able to burn it. A channel has been commenced for a branch of the river, which the managers say they will lead through the middle of the settlement, and will place on it mills of all kinds requiring to be worked by water. Great quantities of vegetables have been planted, which certainly attain a more luxuriant growth here in eight days than they would in Spain in twenty. We were frequently visited by numbers of Indians, among whom were some of their caciques or chiefs, and many women. They all came loaded with *ages*,[1] a sort of turnip, very excellent for food, which we dressed in various ways. This food was so nutritious as to prove a great support to all of us after the privations we endured when at sea, which in truth were more severe than ever were suffered by man; and as we could not tell what weather it would please God to send us on our voyage, we were obliged to limit ourselves most rigorously with regard to food, in order that, at all events, we might at least have the means of

---

leda espesa que apenas podrá un conejo andar por ella; es tan verde que en ningun tiempo del mundo fuego la podrá quemar: hase comenzado á traer un brazo del rio, el cual dicen los maestros qué trairán por medio del lugar, ó asentarán en él moliendas ó sierras de agua, ó cuanto se pudiere hacer con agua. Han sembrado mucha hortaliza, la cual es cierto que crece mas en ocho dias que en España en veinte. Vienen aquí continuamente muchos indios é caciques con ellos, que son como capitanes dellos, ó muchas indias: todos vienen cargados de *ages*, que son como nabos, muy excelente manjar, de los cuales facemos acá muchas maneras de manjares en cualquier manera; es tanto cordial manjar que nos tiene á todos muy consolados, porque de verdad la vida que se trajo por la mar ha seido la mas estrecha que nunca hombres pasaron, ó fue ansí necesario porque no sabiamos que tiempo nos haria, ó cuanto permitiría Dios que estoviesemos en el camino; ansí que fue cordura estrecharnos, porque

[1] Yams.

supporting life: this *age* the Caribbees call *nabi*, and the Indians *hage*. The Indians barter gold, provisions, and every thing they bring with them, for tags of laces, beads, and pins, and pieces of porringers and dishes. They all, as I have said, go naked as they were born, except the women of this island, who some of them wear a covering of cotton, which they bind round their hips, while others use grass and leaves of trees. When they wish to appear fulldressed, both men and women paint themselves, some black, others white and various colours, in so many devices that the effect is very laughable: they shave some parts of their heads, and in others wear long tufts of matted hair, which have an indescribably ridiculous appearance: in short, whatever would be looked upon in our country as characteristic of a madman, is here regarded by the highest of the Indians as a mark of distinction.

In our present position, we are in the neighbourhood of many mines of gold, not one of which, we are told, is more than twenty or twenty-five leagues off: the Indians say that some of them are in Niti, in the possession of Caonabó,

---

cualquier tiempo que viniera pudieramos conservar la vida. Rescatan el oro é mantenimientos é todo lo que traen por cabos de agujetas, por cuentas, por alfileres, por pedasos de escudillas é de plateles. A este *age* llaman los de Caribi *nabi*, é los indios *hage*. Toda esta gente, como dicho tengo, andan como nacieron, salvo las mugeres de esta isla traen cubiertas sus verguenzas, dellos con ropa de algodon que les ciñen las caderas, otras con yerbas é fojas de árboles. Sus galas dellos é dellas es pintarse, unos de negro, otros de blanco é colorado, de tantos visajes que en verlos es bien cosa de reir; las cabezas rapadas en logares, é en logares con vedijas de tantas maneras que no se podria escrebir. En conclusion, que todo lo que allá en nuestra España quieren hacer en la cabeza de un loco; acá el mejor dellos vos lo terná en mucha merced. Aquí estamos en comarca de muchas minas de ora, que segun lo que ellos dicen no hay cada una dellas de veinte ó veinte ó cinco leguas: las unas dicen que son en Niti, en

who killed the Christians; the others are in another place called Cibao, which, if it please God, we shall see with our eyes before many days are over; indeed we should go there at once, but that we have so many things to provide that we are not equal to it at present. One third of our people have fallen sick within the last four or five days, which I think has principally arisen from the toil and privations of the journey; another cause has been the variableness of the climate; but I hope in our Lord that all will be restored to health. My idea of this people is, that if we could converse with them, they would all become converted, for they do whatever they see us do, making genuflections to the altars, and at the Ave Maria and the other parts of the devotional service, and making the sign of the cross. They all say that they wish to be Christians, although in truth they are idolaters, for in their houses they have many kinds of figures: when asked what such a figure was, they would reply it is a thing of *Turey*, by which they meant "of Heaven." I made a pretence of throwing them on the fire, which grieved them so that they began to weep: they

---

poder de Caonabó, aquel que mató los cristianos; otras hay en otra parte que se llama Cibao, las cuales, si place á nuestro Señor, sabremos ó veremos con los ojos antes que pasen muchos dias, porque agora se ficiera sino porque hay tantas cosas de proveer que no bastamos para todo, porque la gente ha adolecido en cuatro ó cinco dias el tercio della, creo la mayor causa dello ha seido el trabajo ó mala pasada del camino: allende de la diversidad de la tierra; pero espero en nuestro Señor que todos se levantarán con salud. Lo que parece desta gente es que si lengua toviesemos que todos se convertirian, porque cuanto nos veen facer tanto facen, en hincar las rodillas á los altares, é al Ave Maria, é á las otras devociones é santiguarse: todos dicen que quieren ser cristianos, puesto que verdaderamente son idólatras, porque en sus casas hay figuras de muchas maneras; yo les he preguntado que es aquello, dicenme que es cosa de *Turey*, que quiere decir del cielo. Yo acometi á querer echarselos en el fuego

F

believe that everything we bring comes from heaven, and therefore call it *Turey*, which, as I have already said, means heaven in their language. The first day that I went on shore to sleep, was the Lord's day. The little time that we have spent on land, has been so much occupied in seeking for a fitting spot for the settlement, and in providing necessaries, that we have had little opportunity of becoming acquainted with the productions of the soil, yet although the time has been so short, many marvellous things have been seen. We have met with trees bearing wool, of a sufficiently fine quality (according to the opinion of those who are acquainted with the art) to be woven into good cloth; there are so many of these trees that we might load the caravels with wool, although it is troublesome to collect, for the trees are very thorny,[1] but some means may be easily found of overcoming this difficulty. There are also cotton trees as large as peach trees, which produce cotton in the greatest abundance. We found trees producing wax as good both in colour and smell as bees-wax and equally

---

é haciaseles de mal que querian llorar: pero ansi piensan que cuanto nosotros traemos que es cosa del cielo, que á todo llaman *Turey*, que quiere decir cielo. El dia que yo salí á dormir en tierra fue el primero dia del Señor: el poco tiempo que habemos gastado en tierra ha seido mas en hacer donde nos metamos, é buscar las cosas necessarias, que en saber las cosas que hay en la tierra, pero aunque ha sido poco se han visto cosas bien de maravillar, que se han visto árboles que llevan lana y harto fina, tal que los que saben del arte dicen que podrán hacer buenos paños dellos. Destos árboles hay tantos que se podrán cargar las carabelas de la lana, aunque es trabajosa de coger, porque los árboles son muy espinosos; pero bien se puede hallar ingenio para la coger. Hay infinito algodon de árboles perpetuos tan grandes como duraznos. Hay árboles que llevan cera en color y en sabor, é en arder tan buena como la de abejas, tal que no hay diferencia mucha de la una á la otra. Hay infinitos árboles de trementina muy singular é muy

[1] A species of the natural order *Bombaceæ*; perhaps the *Eriodendron anfractuosum*.

useful for burning, indeed there is no great difference between them. There are vast numbers of trees which yield surprisingly fine turpentine, and a great abundance of tragacanth, also very good. We found other trees which I think bear nutmegs, because the bark tastes and smells like that spice, but at present there is no fruit on them;[1] I saw one root of ginger, which an Indian wore hanging round his neck. There were also aloes; not like those which we have hitherto seen in Spain, but no doubt they are of the same kind as those used by our doctors.[2] A sort of cinnamon also has been found; but, to speak the truth, it is not so fine as that with which we are already acquainted in Spain. I do not know whether this arises from ignorance of the proper season to gather it, or whether the soil does not produce better. We have also seen some yellow mirabolans; at this season they are all lying under the trees, and have a bitter flavour, arising, I think, from the rottenness occasioned

---

fina. Hay mucho alquitira, tambien muy buena. Hay árboles que pienso que llevan nueces moscadas, salvo que agora estan sin fruto, é digo que lo pienso porque el sabor y olor de la corteza es como de nueces moscadas. Vi una raiz de gengibre que la traia un indio colgada al cuello. Hay tambien linaloe, aunque no es de la manera del que fasta agora se ha visto en nuestras partes; pero no es de dudar que sea una de las especias de linaloes que los dotores ponemos. Tambien se ha hallado una manera de canela, verdad es que no es tan fina como la que allá se ha visto, no sabemos si por veutura lo hace el defeto de saberla coger en sus tiempos como se ha de coger, ó si por ventura la tierra no la lleva mejor. Tambien se ha hallado mirabolanos cetrinos, salvo que agora no estan sino debajo del árbol, como la tierra es muy humida

[1] These were probably trees of the laurel tribe, the bark of which is generally spicy like cinnamon. The cinnamon mentioned below was probably also one of these and not true cinnamon.

[2] Barbadoes aloes, still considered as of inferior quality to those of Socotra.

by the moisture of the ground; but the taste of such parts as have remained sound, is that of the genuine mirabolan. There is also very good mastic. None of the natives of these islands, as far as we have yet seen, possess any iron; they have, however, many tools, such as hatchets and axes, made of stone, which are so handsome and well finished, that it is wonderful how they contrive to make them without the use of iron. Their food consists of bread, made of the roots of a vegetable which is between a tree and a vegetable, and the *age*, which I have already described as being like the turnip, and very good food; they use, to season it, a spice called *agi*, which they also eat with fish and such birds as they can catch of the many kinds which abound in the island. They have, besides, a kind of grain like hazel-nuts, very good to eat. They eat all the snakes, and lizards, and spiders, and worms, that they find upon the ground; so that, to my fancy, their bestiality is greater than that of any beast upon the face of the earth. The admiral had at one time determined to leave the search for the mines until he had first

---

estan podridos, tienen el sabor mucho amargo, yo creo sea del podrimiento; pero todo lo otro, salvo el sabor que está corrompido, es de mirabolanos verdaderos. Hay tambien almástica muy buena. Todas estas gentes destas islas, que fasta agora se han visto, no poseen fierro ninguno. Tienen muchas ferramientas, ansi como hachas ó azuelas hechas de piedra tan gentiles é tan labradas que es maravilla como sin fierro se pueden hacer. El mantenimiento suyo es pan hecho de raices de una yerba que es entre árbol ó yerba, é el age, de que ya tengo dicho que es como nabos, que es muy buen mantenimiento: tienen por especia, por lo adobar, una especia que se llama *agi*, con la cual comen tambien el pescado, como aves cuando las pueden haber, que hay infinitas de muchas maneras. Tienen otrosí unos granos como avellanas, muy buenos de comer. Comen cuantas culebras ó lagartos ó arañas é cuantos gusanos se hallan por el suelo; ansi que me

dispatched the ships which were to return to Spain[1] on
account of the great sickness which had prevailed among the
men, but afterwards he resolved upon sending two bands
under the command of two captains, the one to Cibao,[2] and
the other to Niti, where, as I have already said, Caonabó
lived. These parties went, one of them returning on the
twentieth, and the other on the twenty-first of January.
The party that went to Cibao saw gold in so many places that
one scarcely dares state the fact, for in truth they found it in
more than fifty streamlets and rivers, as well as upon their
banks; so that, the captain said they had only to seek throughout that province, and they would find as much as they wished.
He brought specimens from the different parts, that is, from
the sand of the rivers and small springs. It is thought, that
by digging as we know how, it will be found in greater pieces,
for the Indians neither know how to dig nor have the means

parece es mayor su bestialidad que de ninguna bestia del mundo.
Despues de una vez haber determinado el Almirante de dejar el
descobrir las minas fasta primero enviar los navíos que se habian
de partir á Castilla, por la mucha enfermedad que habia seido en
la gente, acordó de enviar dos cuadrillas con dos Capitanes, el uno
á Cibao y el otro á Niti, donde está Caonobó, de que ya he dicho,
las cuales fueron é vinieron el uno á veinte dias de Enero, é el otro
á veinte é uno : el que fue á Cibao halló oro en tantas partes que
no lo osa hombre decir, que de verdad en mas de cincuenta arroyos
é rios hallaban oro, é fuera de los rios por tierra ; de manera que
en toda aquella provincia dice que do quiera que lo quieran buscar

[1] In fact he sent twelve vessels under the command of Antonio de
Torres, who set sail from the port of Navidad, on the second of February, 1494, charged with an account of all that had occurred. (Navarrete.)

[2] This was Alonzo de Ojeda, who went out with fifteen men, in the
month of January 1494, to seek the mines of Cibao, and returned a few
days after with good news, having been well received everywhere by the
natives. (Navarrete.)

of digging more than a hand's depth. The other captain who went to Niti, returned also with news of a great quantity of gold in three or four places; of which he likewise brought specimens.

Thus, surely, their Highnesses the King and Queen may henceforth regard themselves as the most prosperous and wealthy Sovereigns in the world; never yet, since the creation, has such a thing been seen or read of; for on the return of the ships from their next voyage, they will be able to carry back such a quantity of gold as will fill with amazement all who hear of it. Here I think I shall do well to break off my narrative. I think those who do not know me who hear these things may consider me prolix, and somewhat an exaggerator, but God is my witness, that I have not exceeded, by one tittle, the bounds of truth.

The preceding is the translation of that part of Doctor Chanca's letter, which refers to intelligence respecting the

---

lo hallarán. Trajo muestra de muchas partes como en la arena de los rios é en las hontizuelas, que estan sobre tierra, creese que cabando, como sabemos hacer, se hallará en mayores pedazos, porque los indios no saben cabar ni tienen con que puedan cabar de un palmo arriba. El otro que fue á Niti trajo tambien nueva de mucho oro en tres ó cuatro partes; ansi mesmo trajo la muestra dello. Ansi que de cierto los Reyes nuestros Señores desde agora se pueden tener por los mas prósperos é mas ricos Príncipes del mundo, porque tal cosa hasta agora no se ha visto ni leido de ninguno en el mundo, porque verdaderamente á otro camino que los navíos vuelvan pueden llevar tanta cantidad de oro que se puedan maravillar cualesquiera que lo supieren. Aquí me parece será bien cesar el cuento : creo los que no me conocen que oyeren éstas cosas, me ternán por prolijo é por hombre que ha alargado algo; pero Dios es testigo que yo no he traspasado una jota los términos de la verdad.

Hasta aquí es el treslado de lo que conviene á nuevas de aquellas

Indies.[1] The remainder of the letter does not bear upon the subject, but treats of private matters, in which Doctor Chanca requests the interference and support of the Chapter of Seville (of which city he was a native), in behalf of his family and property, which he had left in the said city. This letter reached Seville in the month of[2]   in the year fourteen hundred and ninety-three.

---

partes é Indias. Lo demas que venia en la carta no hace al caso, porque son cosas particulares que el dicho Dotor Chanca, como natural de Sevilla, suplicaba y encomendaba á los del Cabildo de Sevilla que tocaba á su hacienda y á los suyos, que en la dicha cibdad habia dejado, y llegó esta á Sevilla en el mes de
        año de mil é cuatrocientos énoventa y tres años.

[1] It is to be regretted, Navarrete here justly remarks, that Dr. Chanca should not have described the subsequent occurrences in Hispaniola, which are very important, and which have been related by cotemporary historians.

[2] A similar gap in the original. The date of the year is a mistake. This letter might have been brought by the ships commanded by Torres, and consequently must have been written at the end of January, 1494, after the expedition of Ojeda. (Navarrete.)

MEMORIAL.

Memorial of the results of the Second Voyage of the Admiral, Christopher Columbus, to the Indies, drawn up by him for their Highnesses King Ferdinand and Queen Isabella; and addressed to Antonio de Torres, from the City of Isabella, the 30th of January, 1494. The reply of their Highnesses is affixed at the end of each chapter.[1]

THE report which you, Antonio de Torres, captain of the ship *Marigalante*, and Governor of the city of Isabella, have to make, on my behalf, to the King and Queen our sovereigns, is as follows:

Imprimis: after having delivered the credentials which you bear from me to their Highnesses, you will do homage in my name, and commend me to them as to my natural

MEMORIAL

Que para los Reyes Católicos dió el Almirante D. Cristobal Colon, en la ciudad Isabela, á 30 de Enero de 1494 á Antonio de Torres, sobre el suceso de su segundo viage á las Indias; y al final de cada capítulo la respuesta de sus Altezas.

Lo que vos Antonio de Torres, capitan de la nao *Marigalante*, é Alcaide de la ciudad Isabela, habeis de decir ó suplicar de mi parte al Rey ó la Reina nuestros Señores es lo siguiente:

Primeramente, dadas las cartas ¡de creencia que llevais de mí para sus Altezas, besareis por mi sus reales pies ó manos, é me encomendareis en sus Altezas como á Rey é Reina mis Señores naturales, en cuyo servicio yo deseo fenecer mis dias, como esto mas

[1] In the original, the replies are affixed in the margin of each chapter. (Navarrete).

sovereigns, in whose service I desire to continue till death ; and you will furthermore be able to lay before them all that you have yourself seen and known respecting me.

Their Highnesses accept and acknowledge the service.

Item : Although, by the letters which I have written to their Highnesses, as well as to Father Buil and to the Treasurer, a clear and comprehensive idea may be formed of all that has transpired since our arrival ; you will, notwithstanding, inform their Highnesses, on my behalf, that God has been pleased to manifest such favour towards their service, that not only has nothing hitherto occurred to diminish the importance of what I have formerly written or said to their Highnesses; but on the contrary I hope, by God's grace, shortly to prove it more clearly by facts ; because we have found upon the sea shore, without penetrating into the interior of the country, some spots showing so many indications of various spices, as naturally to suggest the hope of the best results for the future. The same holds good with respect to the gold mines ; for two parties only, who were sent out in different directions to discover them, and who, because they had

---

largamente vos podreis decir á sus Altezas, segun lo que en mi vistes é supistes.

Sus Altezas se lo tienen en servicio.

Item : Como quiera que por las cartas que á sus altezas escribo y aun el Padre Fray Buil y el Tesorero, podrán comprender todo lo que acá despues de nuestra llegada se fizo, y esto harto por menudo y extensamente ; con todo direis á sus Altezas de mi parte, que á Dios ha placido darme tal gracia para en su servicio, que hasta aquí no hallo yo menos ni se ha hallado en cosa alguna de lo que yo escribí y dije, y afirmé á sus Altezas en los dias pasados, antes por gracia de Dios espero que aun muy mas claramente y muy presto por la obra parecerá, porque las cosas de especería en solas las orillas de la mar, sin haber entrado dentro en la tierra, se halla tal rastro é principios della, que es razon que se esperen muy mejores fines, y esto mismo en las minas del oro, porque con solos dos que fueron á descubrir cada uno por su parte, sin detenerse

few people with them, remained out but a short time, found, nevertheless, a great number of rivers whose sands contained this precious metal in such quantity, that each man took up a sample of it in his hand; so that our two messengers returned so joyous, and boasted so much of the abundance of gold, that I feel a hesitation in speaking and writing of it to their Highnesses. But as Gorbalan, who was one of the persons who went on the discovery, is returning to Spain, he will be able to relate all that he has seen and observed; although there remains here another individual,—named Hojeda, formerly servant of the Duke of Medinaceli, and a very discreet and pains-taking youth,— who without doubt discovered, beyond all comparison, more than the other, judging by the account which he gave of the rivers he had seen; for he reported, that each of them contained things that appeared incredible. It results from all this, that their Highnesses ought to return thanks to God, for the favour which He thus accords to all their Highnesses' enterprises.

Their Highnesses return thanks to God for all that is recorded, and regard as a very signal service all that the Admiral has

allá porque era poca gente, se han descubierto tantos rios tan poblados de oro, que cualquier de los que lo vieron é cogieron, solamente con las manos por muestra, vinieron tan alegres, y dicen tantas cosas de la abundancia dello, que yo tengo empacho de las decir y escribir á sus altezas; pero porque allá vá Gorbalan, que fue uno de los descubridores, el dirá lo que vió, aunque acá queda otro que llaman Hojeda, criado del Duque de Medinaceli, muy discreto mozo y de muy gran recabdo, que sin duda y aun sin comparacion, descubrió mucho mas, segun el memorial de los rios que él trajo, diciendo que en cada uno de ellos hay cosa de no creella; por lo cual sus Altezas pueden dar gracias á Dios, pues tan favorablemente se ha en todas sus cosas.

Sus Altezas dan muchas gracias a Dios por esto, y tienen en muy senalado servicio al Almirante todo lo que en esto ha fecho y hace, porque conocen que despues de Dios á él son en cargo de todo lo que

already done, and is yet doing; for they are sensible that, under God, it is he who has procured for them their present and future possessions in these countries; and as they are about to write to him on this subject more at length, they refer to their letter.

Item. You will repeat to their Highnesses what I have already written to them, that I should have ardently desired to have been able to send them, by this occasion, a larger quantity of gold than what they have any hope of our being able to collect, but that the greater part of the people we employed fell suddenly ill. Moreover, the departure of this present expedition could not be delayed any longer, for two reasons: namely, on account of the heavy expense which their stay here occasioned; and because the weather was favourable for their departure, and for the return of those who should bring back the articles of which we stand in the most pressing need. If the former were to put off the time of their starting, and the latter were to delay their departure, they would not be able to reach here by the month of May. Besides, if I wished now to undertake a journey to the rivers with those who are well,—whether with those who

en esto han habido y hobieren; y porque cerca desto le escriben mas largo, á su carta se remiten.

Item: Dieris á sus Altezas, como quier que ya se les escribe, que yo deseaba mucho en esta armada poderles enviar mayor cuantidad de oro del que acá se espera poder coger, si la gente que acá está nuestra, la mayor parte subitamente no cayera doliente; pero porque ya esta armada non so podia detener acá mas, siquiera por la costa grande que hace, siquiera porque el tiempo es este propio para ir y poder volver los que han de traer acá las cosas que aquí hacen mucha mengua, porque si tardasen de irse de aquí non podrian volverse para Mayo los que han de volver, y allende desto si con los sanos que acá se hallan, así en mar como en tierra en la poblacion, yo quisiera emprender de ir á las minas ó rios agora, habia muchas dificultades é aun peligros, porque de aquí á veinte y tres ó veinte y cuatro leguas, en donde hay puertos ó rios para

are at sea, or those who are on land in the huts,—I should experience great difficulties, and even dangers; because, in traversing three or four-and-twenty leagues, where there are bays and rivers to pass, we should be obliged to carry, as provision for so long a journey, and for the time necessary for collecting the gold, many articles of food, etc., which could not be carried on our backs, and there are no beasts of burden to be found, to afford the necessary assistance. Moreover, the roads and passes are not in such a condition as I should wish for travelling over; but they have already begun to make them passable. It would be also extremely inconvenient to leave the sick men here in the open air, or in huts, with such food and defences as they have on shore; although these Indians appear every day to be more simple and harmless to those who land for the purpose of making investigations. In short, although they come every day to visit us, it would nevertheless be imprudent to risk the loss of our men and our provisions, which might very easily happen, if an Indian were only, with a lighted coal, to set fire to the huts, for they ramble about both night and day;

---

pasar y para tan largo camino, y para estar allá al tiempo que seria menester para coger el oro, habia menester llevar muchos mantenimientos, los cuales non podrian llevar á cuestas, ni hay bestias acá que á esto pudiesen suplir, ni los caminos ó pasos non estan tan aparejados, como quier que se han comenzado á adobar para que se podiesen pasar; y tambien era grande inconveniente dejar acá los dolientes en lugar abierto y chozas, y las provisiones y mantenimientos que estan en tierra, que como quier que estos indios se hayan mostrado á los descubridores, y se muestran cada dia muy simples y sin malicia; con todo, porque cada dia vienen acá entre nosotros non pareció que fuera buen consejo meter á riesgo y á ventura de perderse esta gente y los mantenimientos, lo que un indio con un tizon podria hacer poniendo huego á las chozas, porque de noche y de dia siempre van y vienen; á causa

for this reason, we keep sentinels constantly on the watch while the dwellings are exposed and undefended.

He has done well.

Further, as we have remarked that the greatest part of those who have gone out to make discoveries, have fallen sick on their return, and that some have even been obliged to abandon the undertaking in the middle of their journey, and return, it was equally to be feared that the same would occur to those who were at the time enjoying good health, if they were also to go. There were two evils to fear:—one, the chance of falling ill in undertaking the same work, in a place where there were no houses nor any kind of protection, and of being exposed to the attacks of the cacique called Caonabo, who, by all accounts, is a badly-disposed man, and extremely daring; who, if he were to find us in a dispirited condition and sick, might venture upon what he would not dare to do if we were well. The other evil consisted in the difficulty of carrying the gold; for, either we should have to carry it in small quantities, and go and return every day, and thus daily expose ourselves to the chance of sickness;

---

dellos tenemos guardas en el campo mientras la poblacion está abierta y sin defension.

Que lo hizo bien.

Otrosí: Como habemos visto en los que fueron por tierra á descobrir que los mas cayeron dolientes despues de vueltos, y aun algunos se hobieron de volver del camino, era tambien razon de temer que otro tal conteciese a los que agora irian destos sanos que se hallan, y seguirse hian dos peligros de allí, el uno de adolecer allá en la misma obra dó no hay casa ni reparo alguno de aquel Cacique que llaman Caonabó que es hombre, segun relacion de todos, muy malo y muy mas atrevido, el cual viéndonos allá así desbaratados y dolientes, podria emprender lo que non osaria si fuesemos sanos: y con esto mismo se allega otra dificultad de traer acá lo que llegasemos de oro, porque ó habiamos de traer poco y ir y venir cada dia, y meterse en el riesgo de las dolencias,

or we should have to send it under the escort of a party of our people, and equally run the risk of losing them.

He has done well.

These are the reasons, you will tell their Highnesses, why the departure of the expedition has not been delayed, and why only a sample of the gold is sent to them; but I trust in the mercy of God, who in all things and in every place has guided us hitherto, that all our men will be soon restored to health, as, indeed, they are already beginning to be; for they have but to try this country for a little time and they speedily recover their health. One thing is certain, that if they could have fresh meat, they would very quickly, by the help of God, be up and doing; and those who are most sickly, would speedily recover. I hope that they may be restored. The small number of those who continue well, are employed every day in barricading our dwelling, so as to put it in a state of defence, and in taking necessary measures for the safety of our ammunition; which will be finished now in a few days, for all our fortifications will con-

---

ó se habia de enviar con alguna parte de la gente con el mismo peligro de perderlo.

Lo hizo bien.

Así que, direis á sus Altezas, que estas son las cabsas porque de presente non se ha detenido el armada, ni se les envia oro mas de las muestras; pero confiando en la misericordia de Dios, que en todo y por todo nos ha guiado hasta aquí, esta gente convalescerá presto, como ya lo hace, porque solamente les prueba la tierra de algunas ceciones, y luego se levantan; y es cierto que si toviesen algunas carnes frescas para convalescer muy presto serian todos en pie con ayuda de Dios, ó aun los mas estarian ya convalescidos en este tiempo, espero que ellos convalescerán: con estos pocos sanos que acá quedan, cada dia se entiende en cerrar la poblacion y meterla en alguna defensa, y los mantenimientos en seguro, que será fecho en breves dias, porque non ha de ser sino albarradas que non son gente los indios, que si dormiendo non nos fallasen

sist simply of stone walls.[1] These precautions will be sufficient, as the Indians are not a people to be much afraid of; and, unless they should find us asleep, they would not dare to undertake any hostile movement against us, even if they should entertain the idea of so doing. The misfortune which happened to those who remained here, must be attributed to their want of vigilance; for however few they were in number, and however favourable the opportunities that the Indians may have had for doing what they did, they would never have ventured to do them any injury, if they had only seen that they took proper precautions against an attack. As soon as this object is gained, I will undertake to go in search of these rivers; either proceeding hence by land, and looking out for the best expedients that may offer, or else by sea, rounding the island until we come to the place which is described as being only six or seven leagues from where these rivers that I speak of are situated; so that we may collect the gold in safety, and put it in security against all attacks in some stronghold or tower, which may be quickly built for that purpose: and thus, when the two caravels shall return thither, the gold may be taken away and finally sent

---

para emprender cosa ninguna, aunque la toviesen pensada, que así hicieron á los otros que acá quedaron por su mal recabdo, los cuales por pocos que fuesen, y por mayores ocasiones que dieran á los indios de haber ó de hacer lo que hicieron, nunca ellos ósaran emprender de dañarles si los vieran á buen recabdo: y esto fecho luego se entenderá en ir á los dichos rios, ó desde acquí tomando el camino, y buscando los mejores expedientes que se puedan, ó por la mar rodeando la isla fasta aquella parte de donde se dice que no debe haber mas de seis ó siete leguas hasta los dichos rios; por forma que con seguridad se pueda cojer el oro y ponerlo en recabdo de alguna fortaleza ó torre que allí se haga luego, para tenerlo cogido al tiempo que las dos carabelas volverán acá, é para

[1] *Albarrada*—an Arabic word implying a stone wall without mortar.

home in safety at the first favourable season for making the voyage.

This is well and exactly as he should do.

Item. You will inform their Highnesses (as indeed has been already said), that the cause of the sickness so general among us, is the change of air and water, for we find that all of us are affected, though few dangerously; consequently, the preservation of the health of the people will depend, under God, on their being provided with the same food that they are accustomed to in Spain: neither those who are here now, nor those that shall come, will be in a position to be of service to their Highnesses, unless they enjoy good health. We ought to have fresh supplies of provisions until the time that we may be able to gather a sufficient crop from what we shall have sown or planted here : I speak of wheat, barley, and grapes, towards the cultivation of which not much has been done this year, from our being unable earlier to choose a convenient settlement. When we had chosen it, the small number of labourers that were with us fell sick; and, even when they recovered, we had so few cattle, and those so lean and weak, that the utmost they

---

que luego con el primer tiempo que sea para navegar este camino se envie á buen recabdo.

Que está bien, y así lo debe hacer.

Item: Direis á sus Altezas, como dicho es, que las causas de las dolencias tan general de todos es de mudamiento de aguas y aires, porque vemos que á todos arreo se extiende y peligran pocos; por consiguiente la conservacion de la sanidad, despues de Dios, está que esta gente sea proveida de los mantenimientos que en España acostumbraba, porque dellos, ni de otros que viniesen de nuevo sus Altezas se podrán servir si no estan sanos; y esta provision ha de durar hasta que acá se haya fecho cimiento de lo que acá se sembrare é plantare, digo de trigos y cebadas, ó viñas, de lo cual para este año se ho fecho poco, porque no se pudo de antes tomar asiento, y luego que se tomó adolescieron aquellos poquitos labradores que acá estaban, los cuales aunque estovieran sanos

could do was very little; however, they have sown a few plots of ground, for the sake of trying the soil, which seems excellent, in the hope of thereby obtaining some relief in our necessities. We are very confident, from what we can see, that wheat and grapes will grow very well in this country. We must, however, wait for the fruit; and if it grows as quickly and well as the corn, in proportion to the number of vines that have been planted, we shall certainly not stand in need of Andalusia and Sicily here. There are also sugar-canes, of which the small quantity that we have planted has taken root. The beauty of the country in these islands,— the mountains, the valleys, the streams, the fields watered by broad rivers,—is such that there is no country on which the sun sheds his beams that can present a more charming appearance.

Since the land is so fertile, it is desirable to sow of all kinds as much as possible; and Don Juan de Fonseca is instructed to send over immediately everything requisite for that purpose.

---

tenian tan pocas bestias y tan magras y flacas, que poco es lo que pudieran hacer: con todo, alguna cosa han sembrado, mas para probar la tierra, que parece muy maravillosa, para que de alli se puede esperar remedio alguno en nuestras necesidades. Somos bien ciertos, como la obra lo muestra, que en esta tierra asi el trigo como el vino nacerá muy bien; pero hase de esperar el fruto, el cual si tal será como muestra la presteza del nacer del trigo, y de algunos poquitos de sarmientos que se pusieron, es cierto que non fará mengua el Andalucía ni Secilia aquí, ni en las cañas de azucar, segun unas poquitas que se pusieron han prendido; porque es cierto que la hermosura de la tierra de estas islas, así de montes ó sierras y aguas, como de vegas donde hay rios cabdales, es tal la vista que ninguna otra tierra que sol escaliente puede ser mejor al parecer ni tan fermosa.

Pues la tierra es tal, que debe procurar que se siembre lo mas que ser pudiere de todas cosas, y á D. Juan de Fonseca se escribe que envie de contino todo lo que fuere menester para esto.

Item. You will say, that as a large portion of the wine that we brought with us has run away, in consequence, as most of the men say, of the bad cooperage of the butts made at Seville, the article that we stand most in need of now, and shall stand in need of, is wine; and although we have biscuit and corn for some time longer, it is nevertheless necessary that a reasonable quantity of these be sent to us, for the voyage is a long one, and it is impossible to make a calculation for every day; the same holds good with respect to pork and salt beef, which should be better than what we brought out with us on this voyage. Sheep, and still better, lambs and lambkins, more females than males, young calves and heifers, also are wanted, and should be sent by every caravel that may be dispatched hither; and at the same time some asses, both male and female, and mares for labour and tillage; for here there are no beasts that a man can turn to any use. As I fear that their Highnesses may not be at Seville, and that their officers or ministers will not, without their express instructions, make any movement towards the

Item: Direis que á cabsa de haberse derramado mucho vino en este camino del que la flota traia, y esto, segun dicen los mas, á culpa de la mala obra que los toneleros ficieron en Sevilla, la mayor mengua que agora tenemos, aquí, ó esperamos por esto tener, es de vinos, y como quier que tengamos para mas tiempo así vizcocho como trigo, con todo es necesario que tambien se envie alguna cuantidad razonable, porque el camino es largo y cada dia no se puede proveer, ó asimismo algunas canales, digo tocinos, y otra cecina que sea mejor que la que habemos traido este camino. De carneros vivos y aun antes corderos y cordericas, mas fembras que machos, y algunos becerros y becerras pequeños son menester, que cada vez vengan en cualquier carabela que acá se enviare, y algunas asnas y asnos, y yeguas para trabajo y simiente, que acá ninguna de estas animalias hay de que hombre se pueda ayudar ni valer. Y porque recelo que sus Altezas no se fallarán en Sevilla, ni los Oficiales ó Ministros suyos sin expreso mandamiento non pro-

carrying out of the necessary arrangements for the return voyage; and that, in the interval between the report and the reply, the favourable moment for the departure of the vessels which are to return hither (and which should be in all the month of May) may elapse, you will tell their Highnesses, as I charged and ordered you, that I have given strict orders that the gold that you carry with you be placed in the hands of some merchant in Seville, in order that he may therefrom disburse the sums necessary for loading the two caravels with wine, corn, and other articles detailed in this memorial; and this merchant shall convey or send the said gold to their Highnesses, that they may see it, receive it, and from it cause to be defrayed the expenses that may arise from the fitting-up and loading of the said two caravels. It is necessary, for the encouragement of the men who remain here, and for the support of their spirits, that an effort should be made to let the expedition arrive in the course of the month of May, so that before summer they may have the fresh provisions, and other necessaries, especially against sickness. We particularly stand in need of raisins, sugar, almonds, honey, and rice, of which we ought

---

veerían en lo porque agora con este primero camino es necesario que venga, porque en la consulta y en la respuesta se pasaria la sazon del partir los navíos que acá por todo Mayo es necesario quo sean; direis á sus Altezas, como yo vos dí cargo y mandé, que del oro que allá llevais empeñándolo, ó poniêndolo en poder de algun mercader en Sevilla, el cual distraya y ponga los maravedis que serán menester para cargar dos carabelas de víno y de trigo, y de las otras cosas que llevais por memorial, el cual mercader lleve ó envie el dicho oro para sus Altezas, que le vean, resciban y hagan pagar lo que hobiere distraido é puesto para el despacho y cargazon de las dichas dos carabelas, las cuales por consolar y esforzar esta gente que acá queda, cumple que fagan mas de poder de ser acá vueltas por todo el mes de Mayo, porque la gente antes de entrar en el verano vea é tengan algun refrescamiento destas

to have had a great quantity, but brought very little with us, and what we had is now consumed. The greater part of the medicines, also, that we brought from Spain are used up, so many of our number having been sick. For all these articles, both for those who are in good health and for the sick, you carry, as I have already said, memorials signed by my hand; you will execute my orders to the full, if there be sufficient money wherewith to do so, or you will at least procure what is more immediately necessary, and which ought, consequently, to come as speedily as possible by the two vessels. As to the remainder, you will obtain their Highnesses' permission for their being sent by other vessels without loss of time.

Their Highnesses will give instructions to Don Juan de Fonseca to make immediate inquiry respecting the imposition in the matter of the casks, in order that those who supplied them shall at their own expense make good the loss occasioned by the waste of the wine, together with the costs. He will have to see that sugar-canes of good quality be sent, and will imme-

---

cosas, en especial para las dolencias; de las cuales cosas acá ya tenemos gran mengua, como son pasas, azucar, almendras, miel é arroz, que debiera venir en gran cuantidad y vino muy poca, é aquello que vino es ya consumido é gastado, y aun la mayor parte de las medecinas que de allá trojieron, por la muchedumbre de los muchos dolientes; de las cuales cosas, como dicho es, vos llevais memoriales así para sanos, como para dolientes, firmados de mi mano, los cuales cumplidamente si el dinero bastare, ó á lo menos lo que mas necesario sea para agora despachar, es para que lo puedan luego traer los dichos dos navíos, y lo que quedare procurareis con sus Altezas que con otros navíos venga lo mas presto que ser pudiere.

Sus Altezas enviaron á mandar á D. Juan de Fonseca que luego haya informacion de los que hicieron ese engaño en los toneles, y de sus bienes haga que se cobre todo el daño que vino en el vino, con las costas; y en lo de las cañas vea como las que se enviaren sean buenas, y en las otras cosas que aquí dice que las provea luego.

diately look to the despatch of the other articles herein required.

Item. You will tell their Highnesses, that as we have no interpreter through whom we can make these people acquainted with our holy faith, as their Highnesses and we ourselves desire, and as we will do so soon as we are able, we send by these two vessels some of these cannibal men and women, as well as some children, both male and female, whom their Highnesses might order to be placed under the care of the most competent persons to teach them the language. At the same time they might be employed in useful occupations, and by degrees through somewhat more care being bestowed upon them than upon other slaves, they would learn one from the other. By not seeing or speaking to each other for a long time, they will learn much sooner in Spain than they will here, and become much better interpreters. We will, however, not fail to do what we can; it is true, that as there is but little communication between one of these islands and another, there is some difference in their mode of expressing themselves, which mainly depends on the distance between them. But as amongst all

---

Item : Direis á sus Altezas que á cabsa que acá no hay lengua por medio de la cual á esta gente se pueda dar á entender nuestra santa Fé, como sus Altezas desean, y aun los que acá estamos, como quier que se trabajará cuanto pudieren, se envian de presente con estos navíos así de los canibales, hombres y mugeres y niños y niñas, los cuales sus Altezas pueden mandar poner en poder de personas con quien puedan mejor aprender la lengua, ejercitándolos en cosas de servicio, y poco á poco mandando poner en ellos algun mas cuidado que en otros esclavos para que deprendan unos de otros, que no se hablen ni se vean sino muy tarde, que mas presto deprenderán allá que no acá, y serán mejores intérpretes, como quier que acá non se dejará de hacer lo que se pueda; es verdad que como esta gente platican poco los de la una isla con los de la otra, en las lenguas hay alguna diferencia entre ellos, segun como estan mas cerca ó mas lejos: y porque entre las otras

these islands, those inhabited by the cannibals are the largest and the most populous, it must be evident that nothing but good can come from sending to Spain men and women who may thus one day be led to abandon their barbarous custom of eating their fellow-creatures. By learning the Spanish language in Spain, they will much earlier receive baptism and advance the welfare of their souls; moreover, we shall gain great credit with the Indians who do not practise the above-mentioned cruel custom, when they see that we have seized and led captive those who injure them, and whose very name alone fills them with horror. You will assure their Highnesses, that our arrival in this country, and the sight of so fine a fleet, have produced the most imposing effect for the present, and promise great security hereafter; for all the inhabitants of this great island, and of the others, when they see the good treatment that we shall shew to those who do well, and the punishment that we shall inflict on those who do wrong, will hasten to submit, so that we shall be able to lay our commands on them as vassals of their Highnesses. And as even now they not only

---

islas las de los canibales son mucho grandes, y mucho bien pobladas, parecerá acá que tomar dellos y dellas y enviarlos allá á Castilla non seria sino bien, porque quitarse hian una vez de aquella inhumana costumbre que tienen de comer hombres, y allá en Castilla entendiendo la lengua muy mas presto rescibirian el Bautismo, y farian el provecho de sus animas: aun entre estos pueblos que non son de esas costumbres, se ganaria gran crédito por nosotros viendo que aquellos prendiesemos y cativasemos, de quien ellos suelen rescibir daños, y tienen tamaño miedo que del nombre solo se espantan; certificando á sus Altezas que la venida é vista de esta flota acá en esta tierra así junta y hermosa, ha dado muy grande autoridad á esto y muy grande seguridad para las cosas venideras, por que toda esta gente de esta grande isla y de las otras, viendo el buen tratamiento que á los buenos se fará, y el castigo que á los malos se dará, verná á obediencia prestament para poderlos mandar como vasallos de sus Altezas.

readily comply with every wish that we express, but also of their own accord endeavour to do what they think will please us, I think that their Highnesses may feel assured that, on the other side also, the arrival of this fleet has, in many respects, secured for them, both for the present and the future, a wide renown amongst all Christian Princes ; but they themselves will be able to form a much better judgment on this subject than it is in my power to give expression to.

Let him be informed of what has transpired respecting the cannibals that came over to Spain. He has done well and let him do as he says; but let him endeavour by all possible means to convert them to our holy Catholic religion, and do the same with respect to the inhabitants of all the islands to which he may go.

Item. You will tell their Highnesses, that the welfare of the souls of the said cannibals, and of the inhabitants of this island also, has suggested the thought that the greater the number that are sent over to Spain the better, and thus good service may result to their Highnesses

---

Y como quier que ellos agora donde quier que hombre se halle non solo hacen de grado lo que hombre quiere que fagan, mas ellos de su voluntad se ponen á todo lo que entienden que nos puede placer, y tambien pueden ser ciertos sus Altezas que non menos allá, entre los cristianos Príncipes haber dado gran reputacion la venida desta armada por muchos respetos, así presentes como venideros, los cuales sus Altezas podrán mejor pensar y entender que non sabria decir.

Decirle heis lo que acá ha habido en lo de dos canibales que acá vinieron.

Que está muy bien, y así lo debe hacer; pero que procure allá, como si ser pudiere, se reduzgan á nuestra santa Fé católica, y asimismo lo procure con los de las islas donde está.

Item : Direis á sus Altezas, que el provecho de las almas de los dichos canibales, y aun destos de acá, ha traido el pensamiento que cuantos mas allá se llevasen seria mejor, y en ello podrian sus

in the following manner. Considering what great need we have of cattle and of beasts of burthen, both for food and to assist the settlers in this and all these islands, both for peopling the land and cultivating the soil, their Highnesses might authorize a suitable number of caravels to come here every year to bring over the said cattle, and provisions, and other articles; these cattle, etc., might be sold at moderate prices for account of the bearers, and the latter might be paid with slaves, taken from among the Caribbees, who are a wild people, fit for any work, well proportioned and very intelligent, and who, when they have got rid of the cruel habits to which they have become accustomed, will be better than any other kind of slaves. When they are out of their country, they will forget their cruel customs; and it will be easy to obtain plenty of these savages by means of row-boats that we propose to build. It is taken for granted, that each of the caravels sent by their Highnesses, will have on board a confidential man, who will take care that the vessels do not stop anywhere else than here, where they are to unload and reload their vessels. Their Highnesses might

---

Altezas ser servidos desta manera: que visto cuanto son acá menester los ganados y bestias de trabajo para el sostenimiento de la gente que acá ha de estar, y bien de todas estas islas, sus Altezas podrán dar licencia é permiso á un número de carabelas suficiente que vengan acá cada año, y trayan de los dichos ganados y otros mantenimientos y cosas para poblar el campo y aprovechar la tierra, y esto en precios razonables á sus costas de los que las trugieren, las cuales cosas se les podrian pagar en esclavos de estos canibales, gente tan fiera y dispuesta, y bien proporcionada y de muy buen entendimiento, los cuales quitados de aquella inhumanidad creemos que serán mejores que otros ningunos esclavos, la cual luego perderán que sean fuera de su tierra, y de estos podrán haber muchos con las fustas de remos que acá se entienden de hacer, fecho empero presupuesto que cada una de las carabelas que viniesen de sus Altezas pusiesen una persona fiable, la cual defendiese las dichas carabelas que non descendiesen

fix duties on the slaves that may be taken over, upon their arrival in Spain. You will ask for a reply upon this point, and bring it to me, in order that I may be able to take the necessary measures, should the proposition merit the approbation of their Highnesses.

The consideration of this subject has been suspended for a time, until fresh advices arrive from the other side: let the Admiral write what he thinks upon the subject.

Item. You will also tell their Highnesses, that freighting the ships by the ton, as the Flemish merchants do, will be more advantageous and less expensive than any other mode, and it is for this reason that I have given you instructions to freight in this manner the caravels that you have now to send off, and it will be well to adopt this plan with all the others that their Highnesses may send provided it meets their approbation; but I do not mean to say that this measure should be applied to the vessels that shall come over licensed for the traffic of slaves.

Their Highnesses have given directions to Don Juan de

á ninguna otra parte ni isla salvo aquí, donde ha de estar la carga y descarga de toda la mercaduría; y aun destos esclavos que se llevaren, sus Altezas podrian haber sus derechos allá; y desto traeréis ó enviareis respuesta, porque acá se hagan los aparejos que son menester con mas confianza, si á sus Altezas pareciere bien.

En esto se ha suspendido por agora hasta que venga otro camino de allá, y escriba el Almirante lo que en esto le paresciere.

Item: Tambien direis á sus Altezas que mas provechoso es, y menos costa, fletar los navíos como los fletan los mercaderes para Flandes por toneladas que non de otra manera; por ende que yo vos dí cargo de fletar á este respecto las dos carabelas que habeis luego de enviar: y así se podrá hacer de todas las otras que sus Altezas enviaren, si de aquella forma se ternán por servidos; pero non entiendo decir esto de las que han de venir con su licencia por la mercaduria de los esclavos.

Sus Altezas mandan á D. Juan de Fonseca que en el fletar de las carabelas tenga esta forma si ser pudiere.

Fonseca, to have the caravels freighted in the manner described, if it can be done.

Item. You will tell their Highnesses, that in order to save any extra expense, I have purchased the caravels mentioned in the memorial of which you are the bearer, in order to keep them here with the two vessels, the *Gallega* and the *Capitana*, of which, by advice of the pilot its commander, I purchased the three-eighths for the price declared in the said memorial, signed by my hand. These vessels will not only give authority and great security to those who will have to remain on shore and whose duty it will be to make arrangements with the Indians for collecting the gold; but they will be also very useful to ward off any attack that may be made upon them by strangers; moreover, the caravels will be required for the task of making the discovery of terra firma, and of the islands which lie scattered about in this vicinity. You will therefore beg their Highnesses to pay, at the term of credit arranged with the sellers, the sums which these vessels shall cost, for without doubt their Highnesses will be very soon reimbursed for what they may expend; at least, such is my belief and hope in the mercy of God.

Item: Direis á sus Altezas que á causa de escusar alguna mas costa, yo merqué estas carabelas que llevais por memorial para retenerlas acá con estos dos naos, conviene á saber, la Gallega y esa otra Capitana, de la cual merqué por semejante del Maestre della los tres ochavos por el precio que en el dicho memorial destas copias llevais firmado de mi mano, los cuales navíos non solo darán autoridad y gran seguridad á la gente que ha de estar dentro y conversar con los indios para cojer el oro, mas aun para otra cualquier cosa de peligro que de gente estraña pudiese acontescer, allende que las carabelas son necesarias para el descubrir de la tierra firme y otras islas que entre aquí ó allá estan; y suplicareis á sus Altezas que los maravedis que estos navíos cuestan manden pagar en los tiempos que se les ha prometido, porque sin dubda ellos ganarán bien su costa, segun yo creo y espero en la misericordia de Dios.

The Admiral has done well. You will tell him that the sum mentioned has been paid to the seller of the vessels, and that Don Juan de Fonseca has been ordered to pay the cost of the caravels purchased by the Admiral.

Item. You will speak to their Highnesses, and beseech them on my behalf, in the most humble manner possible, to be pleased to give mature reflection to the observations I may make, in letters or more detailed statements, with reference to the peacefulness, harmony, and good feeling of those who come hither; in order that for their Highnesses service persons may be selected who will hold in view the purpose for which these men are sent, rather than their own interest; and since you yourself have seen and are acquainted with these matters, you will speak to their Highnesses upon this subject, and will tell them the truth on every point exactly as you have understood it; you will also take care that the orders which their Highnesses shall give on this point be put into effect, if possible, by the first vessels, in order that no further injury occur here in the matters that affect their service.

El Almirante lo hizo bien, y decirle heis como acá se pagó al que vendió la nao, y mandaron á D. Juan de Fonseca que pague lo de las carabelas que el Almirante compró.

Item: Direis á sus Altezas y suplicareis de mi parte cuanto mas humilmente pueda, que les plega mucho mirar en lo que por las cartas y otras escripturas verán mas largamente tocante á la paz é sosiego e concordia de los que acá estan, y que para las cosas del servicio de sus Altezas escojan tales personas que non se tenga recelo dellas y que miren mas á lo por que se envian que non á sus propios intereses; y en esto, pues que todas las cosas vistes ó supistes, hablareis ó direis á sus Altezas la verdad de todas las cosas como las comprendistes, y que la provision de sus Altezas que sobre ello mandaren facer venga con los primeros navíos si posible fuere, á fin que acá non se hagan escándalos en cosa que tanto va en el servicio de sus Altezas.

Their Highnesses are well informed of all that takes place, and will see to it that everything is done as it should be.

Item. You will describe to their Highnesses the position of this city, the beauty of the province in which it is situated, as you have seen it, and as you can honestly speak of it; and you can inform them, that in virtue of the powers which I have received from them, I have made you governor of the said city; and you will tell them also that I humbly beseech them, out of consideration for your services, to receive your nomination favourably, which I sincerely hope they may do.

Their Highnesses are pleased to sanction your appointment as governor.

Item. As Messire Pedro Margarite, an officer of the household to their Highnesses, has done good service, and will, I hope, continue to do so for the future in all matters which may be entrusted to him, I have felt great pleasure in his continuing his stay in this country; and I have been much pleased to find that Gaspar and Beltran also remain: and as they are all three well known to their Highnesses as faithful servants, I shall place them in posts or employments of trust. You will beg their Highnesses especially to have regard to the situation of the said Messire Pedro Margarite, who is

---

Sus Altezas estan bien informados desto, y en todo se proveerá como conviene.

Item: Direis á sus Altezas el asiento de esta ciudad, ó la fermosura de la provincia alderedor como lo vistes y compreendistes, y como yo vos hice Alcayde della por los poderes que de sus Altezas tengo para ello, á las cuales humilmente suplico que en alguna parte de satisfaccion de vuestros servicios tengan por bien la dicha provision, como de sus Altezas yo espero.

A sus Altezas plaze que vos seais Alcayde.

Item: Porque Mosen Pedro Margarité, criado de sus Altezas, há bien servido, y espero que así lo hara adelante en las cosas que le fueren encomendadas, he habido placer de su quedada aqui, y tambien de Gaspar y de Beltran por ser conocidos criados de sus Altezas para los poner en cosas de confianza: suplicareis á sus

married and the father of a family, and beseech them to give him some vacant command in the order of Santiago, of which he is a knight, in order that his wife and children may thus have a competence to live upon. You will also make mention of Juan Aguado, a servant of their Highnesses; you will inform them of the zeal and activity with which he has served them in all matters that have been entrusted to him; and also that I beseech their Highnesses on his behalf, as well as on behalf of those above mentioned, not to forget my recommendation, but to give it full consideration.

Their Highnesses grant an annual pension of thirty thousand maravedis to Messire Pedro Margarite, and pensions of fifteen thousand maravedis to Gaspard and Beltram, which will be reckoned from this day, the 15th of August 1494. They give orders that the said pensions be paid by the Admiral out of the sums to be paid in the Indies, and by Don Juan de Fonseca out of the sums to be paid in Spain. With respect to the matter of Juan Aguado, their Highnesses will not be forgetful.

Item. You will inform their Highnesses of the continual labour that Doctor Chanca has undergone, from the pro-

---

Altezas que especial al dicho Mosen Pedro, que es casado y tiene hijos le provean de alguna encomienda en la Orden de Santiago, de la cual él tiene el hábito, porque su muger é hijos tengan en que vivir. Asimismo hareis relacion de Juan Aguado, criado de sus Altezas, cuan bien é diligentemente ha servido en todo lo que le ha seido mandado; que suplico á sus Altezas á él é á los sobredichos los hayan por encomendados é por presentes.

Sus Altezas mandan asentar á Mosen Pedro 30000 maravedis cada ano, y á Gaspar y Beltran á cada uno 15000 maravedis cada año desde hoy 15 de Agosto de 94 en adelante, y así les haga pagar el Almirante en lo que allá se hobiere de pagar, y D. Juan de Fonseca en lo que acá se hobiere de pagar: y en lo de Juan Aguado sus Altezas habrán memoria de él.

Item: Direis á sus Altezas el trabajo que el Doctor Chanca tiene con el afruenta de tantos dolientes, y aun la estrechura de los man-

digious number of sick and the scarcity of provisions : and
that, in spite of all this, he exhibits the greatest zeal and
kindness in everything that relates to his profession. As
their highnesses have entrusted me with the charge of fixing
the salary that is to be paid to him while out here (although
it is certain that he neither receives, nor can receive anything
from any one, and does not receive anything from his position, equal to what he did, and could still do in Spain,
where he lived peaceably and at ease, in a very different style
from what he does here; and, although he declares that he
earned more in Spain, exclusive of the pay which he received
from their Highnesses), I have, nevertheless, not ventured
to place to the credit of his account more than fifty thousand
maravedis per annum, as the sum which he is to receive for
his yearly labour during the time of his stay in this country.
I beg their Highnesses to give their sanction to this salary,
exclusive of his maintenance while here; and I do so, because
he asserts that all the medical men who attend their Highnesses in the royal yachts, or in any of their expeditions, are
accustomed to receive by right the day's pay out of the
annual salary of each individual. Let this be as it may, I

---

tenimientos, é aun con todo ello se dispone con gran diligencia y
caridad en todo lo que cumple á su oficio, y porque sus Altezas remitieron á mí el salario que acá se le habia de dar, porque estando
acá es cierto quel non toma ni puede haber nada de ninguno, ni
ganar de su oficio como en Castilla ganaba, ó podria ganar estando
á su reposo ó viviendo de otra manera que acá no vive; y así que
como quiera que él jura que es mas lo que allá ganaba allende el
salario que sus Altezas le dan, y non me quise estender mas de
cincuenta mil maravedis por el trabajo que acá pasa cada un año
mientras acá estoviere ; los cuales suplico á sus Altezas le manden
librar con el sueldo de acá y eso mismo, porque él dice y afirma
que todos los fisicos de vuestras Altezas, que andan en reales ó
semejantes cosas que estas, suelen haber de derecho un dia de
sueldo en todo el año de toda la gente : con todo he seido informado, y dicenme, que como quier que esto sea, la costumbre es

am informed for certain, that on whatever service they are engaged, it is the custom to give them a certain fixed sum, settled at the will and by order of their Highnesses, as compensation for the said day's pay. You will, therefore, beg their Highnesses to decide this matter, as well with respect to the annual pay as to the above-mentioned usage, so that the said doctor may be reasonably satisfied.

Their Highnesses acknowledge the justice of Doctor Chanca's observations, and it is their wish that the Admiral shall pay him the sum which he has allowed him, exclusive of his fixed annual salary. With respect to the day's pay allowed to medical men, it is not the custom to authorize them to receive it, except when they are in personal attendance upon our Lord the King.

Item. You will tell their Highnesses what great devotion Coronel has shown to the service in many respects, and what great proofs he has given of it in every important matter that has been trusted to him, and how much we feel his loss now that he is sick. You will represent to them how just it is that he should receive the recompense of such good and loyal services, not only in the favours which may

---

de darles cierta suma tasada á voluntad y mandamiento de sus Altezas en compensa de aquel dia de sueldo. Suplicareis á sus Altezas que en ello manden proveer, así en lo del salario como de esta costumbre, por forma que el dicho Doctor tenga razon de ser contento.

A sus Altezas place desto del Doctor Chanca, y que se le pague esto desde quel Almirante gelo asentó, y que gelos pague con lo del sueldo.

En esto del dia del sueldo de los físicos, non lo acostumbran haber sino donde el Rey nuestro Senor esté en persona.

Item: Direis á sus Altezas de Coronel cuanto es hombre para servir á sus Altezas en muchas cosas, y cuanto ha servido hasta aquí en todo lo mas necesario, y la mengua que dél sentimos agora que está doliente, y que sirviendo de tal manera es razon quel sienta el fruto de su servicio, non solo en las mercedes para

hereafter be shown to him, but also in his present pay, in order that he, and all those that are with us, may see what profit will accrue to them from their zeal in the service; for the importance and difficulty of exploring the mines should call for great consideration towards those to whom such extensive interests are entrusted; and, as the talents of the said Coronel have made me determine upon appointing him principal constable of this portion of the Indies, and, as his salary is left open, I beg their Highnesses to make it as liberal as may be in consideration of his services, and to confirm his nomination to the service which I have allotted to him, by giving him an official appointment thereto.

Their Highnesses grant him, besides his salary, an annual pension of fifteen thousand maravedis; the same to be paid him at the same time as the said salary.

Item. You will, at the same time, tell their Highnesses that the bachelor, Gil Garcia, came out here in quality of principal alcalde, without having any salary fixed or allowed to him: that he is a good man, well-informed, correct in his conduct, and very necessary to us; and that I beg their Highnesses to be pleased to appoint him a salary sufficient

---

despues mas en lo de su salario en lo presente, en manera quél é los que acá están sientan que les aprovecha el servicio, porque segun el ejercicio que acá se ha de tener en cojer este oro, no son de tener en poco las personas en quien tanta diligencia hay: y porque por su habilidad se proveyó acá por mí del oficio de Alguacil mayor destas Indias, y en la provision va el salario en blanco, que suplico á sus Altezas gelo manden henchir como mas sea su servicio, mirando sus servicios, confirmándole la provision que acá se le dió, o proveyéndole de él de juro.

Sus Altezas mandan que le asienten quince mil maravedis cada año mas de su sueldo, é que se le paguen cuando le pagaren su sueldo.

Asimismo direis á sus Altezas como aquí vino el Bachiller Gil García por Alcalde mayor é non se le ha consignado ni nombrado salario, y es persona de bien y de buenas letras, é diligente, é es acá bien necesario; que suplico á sus Altezas lo manden nombrar

for his support; and that it be remitted to him together with his pay from the other side.

Their Highnesses grant him an annual pension of twenty thousand maravedis during his stay in the Indies, and that over and above his fixed appointments; and it is their order that this pension be paid to him at the same time as his salary.

Item. You will tell their Highnesses, as I have already told them in writing, that I think it will be impossible to go this year to make discoveries until arrangements have been made to work the two rivers in which the gold has been found in the most profitable manner for their Highnesses' interest; and this may be done more effectively hereafter, because it is not a thing that every one can do to my satisfaction, or with advantage to their Highnesses' service, unless I be present; for whatever is to be done always turns out best under the eye of the party interested.

It is the most necessary thing possible that he should strive to find the way to this gold.

Item. You will tell their Highnesses, that the horse-soldiers that came from Grenada to the review which took place

---

é consignar su salario, por manera que él so pueda sostener, é lo sea librado con el dinero del sueldo de acá.

Sus Altezas le mandan asentar cada año viente mil maravedis en tanto que allá estoviere y mas su sueldo, y que gelo paguen cuando pagaren el sueldo.

Item : Direis á sus Altezas como quier que ya so lo escribo por las cartas, que para este año non entiendo que sea posible ir á descobrir hasta que esto destos rios que se hallaron de oro sea puesto en el asiento debido á servicio de sus Altezas, que despues mucho mejor se podrá facer, porque no es cosa que nadie la podiese facer sin mi presencia á mi grado, ni á servicio de sus Altezas, por muy bien que lo ficiese, como es en dubda segun lo que hombre veo por su presencia.

Trabaje como lo mas preciso que ser pueda se sepa lo utito de ese oro.

Item : Direis á sus Altezas como los escuderos de caballo que vinieron de Granada, en el alarde que ficieron en Sevilla mostraron

at Seville, offered good horses, but that at the time of their being sent on board, they took advantage of my absence (for I was somewhat indisposed), and changed them for others, the best of which does not seem worth two thousand maravedis, for they sold the first and bought these; and this deception on the part of the horse-soldiers, is very like what I have known to occur to many gentlemen in Seville of my acquaintance. It seems that Juan de Soria, after the price was paid, for some private interest of his own, put other horses in the place of those that I expected to find, and when I came to see them, there were horses there that had never been offered to me for sale. In all this the greatest dishonesty has been shown, so that I do not know whether I ought to complain of him alone, since these horse-soldiers have been paid their expenses up to the present day, besides their salary and the hire of their horses, and when they are ill, they will not allow their horses to be used, because they are not present. It is not their Highnesses' wish that these horses should be purchased for anything but their Highnesses' service, but these men think they are only to be employed on

---

buenos caballos, é despues al embarcar, yo no lo ví porque estaba un poco doliente, y metiéronlos tales quel mejor dellos non parece que vale dos mil maravedis, porque vendieron los otros y compraron estos, y esto fue de la suerte que se hizo lo de mucha gente que allá en los alardes de Sevilla yo vi muy buena; parece que Juan de Soria, despues dea dado el dinero del sueldo, por algun interese suyo puso otros en lugar de aquellos que yo acá pensaba fallar, y fallo gente que yo nunca habia visto: en esto ha habido gran maldad, de tal manera que yo no sé si me queje dél solo: por esto, visto que á estos escuderos se ha fecho la costa hasta aquí, allende de sus sueldos y tambien á sus caballos, y se hace de presente y son personas que cuando ellos estan dolientes, ó non se les antoja, non quieren que sus caballos sirvan sin ellos mismos; sus Altezas no quieren que se les compren estos caballos sino que sirvan á sus Altezas, y esto mismo no les paresce que deban servir ni cosa

work which requires them to ride on horse-back, which is not the case at present. All these considerations lead me to think, that it would be more convenient to buy their horses, which are worth but little, and thus avoid being exposed daily to new disputes; finally, their Highnesses will decide on what plan is best for their own interests.

Their Highnesses order Don Juan de Fonseca to make inquiries respecting the matter of the horses, and if it be true that such a deception has been practised, to send up the culprits to be punished as they deserve; also to gain information respecting the other people that the admiral speaks of, and to send the result of the information to their Highnesses. With respect to the horse soldiers, it is their Highnesses' wish and command that they continue where they are, and remain in service, because they belong to the guards and to the class of their Highnesses' servants. Their Highnesses also command the said horse soldiers to give up their horses into the charge of the Admiral on all occasions when they shall be required, and if the use of the horses should occasion any loss, their Highnesses direct that compensation shall be made for the amount of the injury, through the medium of the Admiral.

---

ninguna sino á caballo; lo cual agora de presente non face mucho al caso, ó por esto parece que seria mejor comprarles los caballos, pues que tan poco valen, y non estar cada dia con ellos en estas pendencias; por ende que sus Altezas determinen esto como fuere su servicio.

Sus Altezas mandan á D. Juan de Fonseca, que se informe de esto de estos caballos, y si se hallare que es verdad que hicieron ese engaño, lo envien á sus Altezas porque lo mandarán castigar; y tambien se informe desto que dice de la otra gente, y envie la pesquisa á sus Altezas: y en lo destos escuderos sus Altezas mandan que esten allá y sirvan, pues son de las guardas y criados de sus Altezas; y á los escuderos mandan sus Altezas que den los caballos cada vez que fueren menester y el Almirante lo mandare, y si algun daño recibieren los caballos yendo otros en ellos, por medio del Almirante mandan sus Altezas que gelo paguen.

Item. You will mention to their Highnesses, that more than two hundred persons have come here without fixed salaries, and that some of them are very useful to the service; and in order to preserve system and uniformity, the others have been ordered to imitate them. For the first three years, it is desirable that we should have here a thousand men, in order to keep a safeguard upon the island and upon the rivers that supply the gold: and even if we were able to mount a hundred men on horse-back, so far from being an evil, it will be a very necessary thing for us; but their Highnesses might pass by the question of the horse-men until gold shall be sent. In short, their Highnesses should give instructions as to whether the two hundred people who have come over without pay, should receive pay like the others, if they do their work well; for we certainly have great need of them to commence our labours, as I have already shown.

It is their Highnesses' wish and command, that the two hundred persons without pay shall replace such of those who are paid as have failed, or as shall hereafter fail, in their duty, provided they are fit for the service and please the Admiral; and their Highnesses order the Accomptant to enter their names

Item: Direis á sus Altezas como aquí han venido mas de doscientas personas sin sueldo, y hay algunos dellos que sirven bien, y aun los otros por semejante se mandan que lo hagan así y porque para estos primeros tres años será gran bien que aqui esten mil hombres para asentar y poner en muy gran seguridad esta Isla y rios de oro, y aunque hobiese ciento de caballo non se perderia nada, antes parece necesario, aunque en estos de caballo fasta que oro se envie sus Altezas podrán sobreceer: con todo á estas doscientas personas, que vienen sin sueldo, sus Altezas deben enviar á decir si se les pagará sueldo como á los otros sirviendo bien, porque cierto son necesarios como dicho tengo para este comienzo.

De estas doscientas personas que aquí dice que fueron sin sueldo, mandan sus Altezas que entren en lugar de los que han faltado y faltaren de los que iban á sueldo, seyendo habiles y á contentamiento del

in the place of those who shall fail in their duty, as the Admiral shall determine.

Item. As there are means of diminishing the expenses that these people occasion, by employing them, as other Princes do, in industrial occupations, I think it would be well that all ships that come here should be ordered to bring, besides the ordinary stores and medicines, shoes, and leather for making shoes, shirts, both of common and superior quality, doublets, laces, some peasants' clothing, breeches, and cloth for making clothes, all at moderate prices; they might also bring other articles, such as conserves, which do not enter into the daily ration, yet are good for preserving health. The Spaniards that are here would always be happy to receive such articles as these in lieu of part of their pay; and if they were purchased by men who were selected for their known loyalty, and who take an interest in the service of their Highnesses, considerable economy would result from this arrangement. Ascertain their Highnesses' pleasure on this head, and if the plan be deemed expedient for the service, it should be put in practice at once.

Almirante, y sus Altezas mandan al Contador que los asiente en lugar de los que faltaren como el Almirante lo dijere.

Item: Porque en algo la costa de esta gente se puede aliviar con industria y formas que otros Principes suelen tener en otras, lo gastado mejor que acá se podria escusar, paresce que seria bien mandar traer en los navíos que vinieren allende de las otras cosas que son para los mantenimientos comunes, y de la botica, zapatos y cueras para los mandar facer; camisas comunes y de otras, jubones, lienzo, sayos, calzas, paños para vestir en razonables precios; y otras cosas, como son conservas, que son fuera de racion, y para conservacion de la salud, las cuales cosas todas la gente de acá rescibiria de grado en descuento de su sueldo, y si ullá esto se mercase por Ministros leales y que mirasen el servicio de sus Altezas, se ahorraria algo: por ende sabreis la voluntad de sus Altezas cerca desto, y si les pareciere ser su servicio luego se debe poner en obra.

This matter may rest for the present until the Admiral shall write more fully on the subject; meanwhile, Don Juan de Fonseca shall be ordered to instruct Don Ximenes de Bribiesca to make the necessary arrangements for the execution of the proposed plans.

Item. You will tell their Highnesses that, in a review that was holden yesterday, it was remarked that a great number of the people were without arms, which I think must be attributed partly to the exchange made at Seville, or in the harbour, when those who presented themselves armed were left for a while, and for a trifle exchanged their arms for others of an inferior quality. I think it would be desirable that two hundred cuirasses, a hundred arquebuses, a hundred arblasts, and many other articles of defensive armour, should be sent over to us; for we have great need of them to arm those who are at present without them.

Don Juan de Fonseca has already been written to, to provide them.

Item. Inasmuch as many married persons have come over here, and are engaged in regular duties, such as masons and other tradesmen, who have left their wives in Spain,

---

Por este camino se solia ser fasta que mas escriba el Almirante, y ya enviarán á mandar á D. Juan de Fonseca con Jimeno de Bribiesca que provea en esto.

Item: Tambien direis á sus Altezas, que por cuanto ayer en el alarde que se tomó se falló la gente muy desarmada lo cual pienso que en parte contesció por aquel trocar que allá se fizo en Sevilla ó en el puerto cuando se dejaron los que se mostraron armados, y tomaron otros que daban algo á quien los trocaba, paresce que seria bien que se mandasen traer doscientas corazas, y cien espingardas y cien ballestas, y mucho almacen, que es la cosa que mas menester habemos, y de todas estas armas se podrán dar á los desarmados.

Ya se escribe á D. Juan de Fonseca que provea en esto.

Item: Por cuanto algunos oficiales que acá vinieron como son albañies y de otros oficios, que son casados y tienen sus mugeres

and wish that the pay that falls due to them may be paid to their wives, or whomsoever they may appoint, in order that they may purchase for them such articles as they may need, I therefore beseech their Highnesses to take such measures as they may deem expedient on this subject; for it is of importance to their interests that these people be well provided for.

Their Highnesses have already ordered Don Juan de Fonseca to attend to this matter.

Item. Besides the other articles which I have begged from their Highnesses in the memorial which you bear, signed by my hand, and which articles consist of provisions and other stores, both for those who are well and for those who are sick, it would be very serviceable that fifty pipes of molasses should be sent hither from the island of Madeira; for it is the most nutritious food in the world, and the most wholesome. A pipe of it does not ordinarily cost more than two ducats, exclusive of the casks; and if their Highnesses would order one of the caravels to call at the said island on the return voyage, the purchase might be made, and they might, at the

---

allá, y querrian que allá lo que se les debe de su sueldo se diese á sus mugeres ó á las personas á quien ellos enviaren sus recabdos, para que les compren las cosas que acá han menester; que á sus Altezas suplico les mande librar, porque su servicio es que estos esten proveidos acá.

Ya enviaron á mandar sus Altezas á D. Juan de Fonseca que provea en esto.

Item: Porque allende las otras cosas que allá se envian á pedir por los memoriales que llevais de mi mano firmados, así para mantenimiento de los sanos como para los dolientes, seria muy bien que se hobiesen de la isla de la Madera cincuenta pipas de miel de azúcar, porque es el mejor mantenimiento del mundo y mas sano, y non suele costar cada pipa sino á dos ducados sin el casco, y si sus Altezas mandan que á la vuelta pase por allí alguna carabela las podrá mercar, y tambien diez cajas de azúcar que es mucho menester, que esta es la mejor sazon del año, digo entre

same time, buy ten casks of sugar, of which we stand greatly in need. It is the most favourable season of the year to obtain it at a cheap rate, that is to say, between this and the month of April. The necessary orders might be given, if their Highnesses think proper, and yet the place of destination be carefully concealed.

Don Juan de Fonseca will see to it.

Item. You will tell their Highnesses that, although the rivers contain in their beds the quantity of gold described by those who have seen it, there is no doubt that the gold is produced not in the rivers but the earth; and that the water happening to come in contact with the mines, washes it away mingled with the sand. And as among the great number of rivers that have been already discovered there are some of considerable magnitude, there are also some so small that they might rather be called brooks than rivers, only two fingers' breadth deep, and very short in their course; there will, therefore, be some men wanted to wash the gold from the sand, and others to dig it out of the earth. This latter operation will be the principal and the most productive; it will be expedient, therefore, that their Highnesses send

---

aquí é el mes de Abril para fallarlo, é haber dello buena razon y podriase dar orden mandándolo sus Altezas, ó que non supiesen allá para donde lo quieren.

D. Juan de Fonseca que provea en esto.

Item: Direis á sus Altezas, por cuanto aunque los rios tengan en la cuantidad que se dice por los que lo han visto, pero que lo cierto dello es quel oro non se engendra en los rios mas en la tierra, quel agua topando con las minas lo trae envuelto en las arenas, y porque en estos tantos rios se han descubierto, como quiera que hay algunos grandecitos hay otros tan pequeños que son mas fuentes que no rios, que non llevan de dos dedos de agua, y se falla luego el cabo doede nasce; para lo cual non solo serán provechosos los lavadores para cogerlo en el arena, mas los otros para cavarlo en la tierra, que será lo mas especial ó de mayor cuantidad; é por esto será bien que sus Altezas envien lavadores,

men both for the washing and for the mining, from among those who are employed in Spain in the mines at Almaden[1], so that the work may be done in both manners. We shall not, however, wait for the arrival of these workmen, but hope, with the aid of God and with the washers that we have here with us, when they shall be restored to health, to send a good quantity of gold by the first caravels that shall leave for Spain.

This shall be completely provided for in the next voyage out; meanwhile, Don Juan de Fonseca has their Highnesses' orders to send as many miners as he can find. Their Highnesses write also to Almaden, with instructions to select the greatest number that can be procured, and to send them up.

Item. You will beseech their Highnesses very humbly in my name, to be pleased to pay regard to my strong recommendation of Villacorta, who, as their Highnesses are aware, has been extremely useful, and has shown the greatest possible zeal in this affair. As I know him to be a zealous man and well disposed to their Highnesses' service, I shall take it as a favour if they will deign to grant him some

---

ó de los que andan en las minas allá en Almaden, porque en la una manera y en la otra se faga el ejercicio, como quier que acá non esperaremos á ellos, que con los lavadores que aquí tenemos, esperamos con la ayuda de Dios, si una vez la gente está sana, allegar un buen golpe de oro para las primeras carabelas que fueron.

A otro camino se proveerá en esto cumplidamente; en tanto mandan sus Altezas á D. Juan de Fonseca que envie luego los mas minadores que pudiere haber, y escriben al Almaden, que de allí tomen los que mas pudieren y los envien.

Item: Suplicareis á sus Altezas de mi parte muy humildemente, que quieran tener por muy encomendado á Villacorta, el cual, como sus Altezas saben, ha mucho servido en esta negociacion, y con muy buena voluntad, y segun le conozco persona diligente y afeci-

[1] In La Mancha, New Castile, famous for mines of quicksilver.

post of trust adapted to his qualifications, and in which he might give proof of his industry and warm desire to serve their Highnesses: and you will manage that Villacorta shall have practical evidence that the work which he has done for me, and in which I found him needful to me, has been of some profit to him.

This shall be done as he wishes.

Item. That the said Messire Pedro, Gaspar, Beltran, and others remaining here, came out in command of caravels which have now gone back, and are in receipt of no salary whatever; but as these are people who should be employed in the most important and confidential positions, their pay has not been fixed, because it ought to be different from that of the rest; you will beg their Highnesses, therefore, on my behalf, to settle what ought to be given them either yearly or monthly, for the advantage of their Highnesses' service.

Given in the City of Isabella, the thirtieth of January, in the year fourteen hundred and ninety-four.

This point has been already replied to above; but as in the said clause he says that they should receive their pay,

---

onada á su servicio; rescebiré merced que se le dé algun cargo de confianza, para lo cual él ser sufficiente, y pueda mostrar su deseo de servir y diligencia, y esto procurareis por forma que el Villacorta conozca por la obra que lo que ha trabajado por mi en lo que yo le hobe menester le aprovecha en esto.

Así se hará.

Item: Que los dichos Mosen Pedro y Gaspar y Beltran, y otros que han quedado acá, trajieron capítanias de carabelas, que son agora vueltas, y non gozan del sueldo; pero porque son tales personas, que se han de poner en cosas principales y de confianza, non se les ha determinado el sueldo que sea diferenciado de los otros: suplicareis de mi parte á sus Altezas determinen lo que se les ha de dar en cada un año, ó por meses, como mas fueren servidos. Fecho en la ciudad Isabela á treinta dias de Enero de mil cuatrocientos y noventa y cuatro años.

Ya está respondido arriba, pero porque en el dicho capítulo que en

it is now their Highnesses' command that their salary shall be paid to them from the time that they gave up their command.

---

esto habia dice que gozan del salario, desde agora mandan sus Altezas que se les cuenten á todos sus salarios desde que dejaron las capitanías.

THIRD VOYAGE OF COLUMBUS.

Narrative of the Voyage which Don Christopher Columbus made the third time that he came to the Indies, when he discovered terra firma, as he sent it to their Majesties from the Island of Hispaniola.

MOST serene and most exalted and powerful Princes, the King and Queen, our Sovereigns: The Blessed Trinity moved your Highnesses to this enterprise of the Indies; and of His Infinite goodness has chosen me to proclaim it to you; wherefore as His ambassador I approached your royal presence, moved by the consideration that I was appealing to the most exalted monarchs in Christendom, who exercised so great an influence over the Christian faith, and its advancement in the world. Those who heard of it looked upon it as impossible, for they fixed all their hopes on the favours

TERCER VIAGE DE COLON.

La historia del viage quel Almirante D. Cristobal Colon hizo la tercera vez que vino á las Indias cuando descubrió la tierra firme, comò lo envió á los Reyes desde la Isla Española.

SERENÍSIMOS é muy altos é muy poderosos Príncipes Rey é Reina nuestros Señores: La Santa Trinidad movió á vuestras Altezas á esta empresa de las Indias, y por su infinita bondad hizo á mí mensagero dello, al cual vine con el embajada á su Real conspetu, movido como á los mas altos Príncipes de cristianos y que tanto se ejercisaban en la fé y acrecentamiento della; las personas que entendieron en ello lo tuvieron por imposible, y el caudal hacian sobre bienes de fortuna, y allí echaron el clavo. Puse en esto seis

of fortune, and pinned their faith solely upon chance. I gave to the subject six or seven years of great anxiety, explaining, to the best of my ability, how great service might be done to our Lord, by this undertaking, in promulgating His sacred name and our holy faith among so many nations;—an enterprise so exalted in itself, and so calculated to enhance the glory and immortalise the renown of great sovereigns. It was also requisite to refer to the temporal prosperity which was foretold in the writings of so many trustworthy and wise historians, who related that great riches were to be found in these parts. At the same time I thought it desirable to bring to bear upon the subject the sayings and opinions of those who have written upon the geography of the world, and finally, your Highnesses came to the determination that the undertaking should be entered upon. In this your Highnesses exhibited the noble spirit which has been always manifested by you on every great subject; for all others who had thought of the matter or heard it spoken of, unanimously treated it with contempt, with the exception of two friars,[1] who always re-

---

ó siete años de grave pena, amostrando lo mejor que yo sabia cuanto servicio se podia hacer á nuestro Señor en esto en divulgar su santo nombre y Fé á tantos pueblos; lo cual todo era cosa de tanta excelencia y buena fama y gran memoria para grandes Príncipes: fue tambien necesario de hablar del temporal adonde se les amostró el escrebir de tantos sabios dignos de fé, los cuales escribieron historias. Los cuales contaban que en estas partes habia muchas riquezas, y asimismo fue necesario traer á esto el decir é epinion de aquellos que escribieron é situaron el mundo: en fin vuestras Altezas determinaron questo se pusiese en obra. Aquí mostraron el grande corazon que siempre ficieron en toda cosa grande, porque todos los que habian entendido en ello y oido esta platica todos á una mano lo tenian á burla, salvo dos frailes

[1] These were Fray Juan Perez de Marchena, a Franciscan, keeper of the Convent de la Rabida, and Fray Diejo de Deza, a Dominican, afterwards Archbishop of Seville.

mained constant in their belief of its practicabilty. I, myself, in spite of fatiguing opposition, felt sure that the enterprise would nevertheless prosper, and continue equally confident of it to this day, because it is a truth, that though everything will pass away, the Word of God will not, and everything that he has said will be fulfilled; who so clearly spoke of these lands, by the mouth of the prophet Isaiah, in so many places in Scripture, that from Spain the holy name of God was to be spread abroad. Thus I departed in the name of the Holy Trinity, and returned very soon, bringing with me an account of the practical fulfilment of everything I had said. Your Highnesses again sent me out, and in a short space of time, by God's mercy, not by[1]
I discovered three hundred and thirty-three leagues of terra firma on the eastern side, and seven hundred islands,[2] besides those which I discovered on the first voyage;

---

que siempre fueron constantes. Yo, bien que llevase fatiga, estaba bien seguro que esto no vernia á menos, y estoy de contino, porque es verdad que todo pasará, y no la palabra de Dios, y se complirá todo lo que dijó; el cual tan claro habló de estas tierras por la boca de Isaías en tantos lugares de su Escriptura, afirmando que de España les seria divulgado su santo nombre. E partí en nombre de la Santa Trinidad, y volví muy presto con la experiencia de todo cuanto yo habia dicho en la mano: tornáronme á enviar vuestras Altezas, y en poco espacio digo, no de   le descubri por virtud divinal trescientas y treinta y tres leguas de la tierra firme, fin de Oriente, y setcentas [sic] islas de nombre, allende de

[1] A similar gap in the original.
[2] He did not discover terra firma in the second voyage as he here says, but imagined the island of Cuba to be terra firma, because he was unable to explore it fully; nor was it ascertained to be an island till two years after his death, when, by order of the king, the Comendador Mayor Nicolas Ovando gave Sebastian de Ocampo a commission to circumnavigate the island, and he explored the whole coast in the year 1508. (See Herrera, Dec. i, lib. 7, cap. i.) Amongst the number of these islands, Columbus doubtless included many of those to the south of Cuba, lying in the part which he called the *Queen's Gardens.*

I also succeeded in circumnavigating the island of Española, which is larger in circumference than all Spain, the inhabitants of which are countless, and all of whom may be laid under tribute. It was then that complaints arose, disparaging the enterprise that I had undertaken, because, forsooth, I had not immediately sent the ships home laden with gold,—no allowance being made for the shortness of the time, and all the other impediments of which I have already spoken. On this account (either as a punishment for my sins, or, as I trust, for my salvation), I was held in detestation, and had obstacles placed in the way of every thing I said, or for which I petitioned. I therefore resolved to apply to your Highnesses, to inform you of all the wonderful events that I had experienced, and to explain the reason of every proposition that I made, making reference to the nations that I had seen, among whom, and by whose instrumentality, many souls may be saved. I related how the natives of Española had been laid under tribute to your Highnesses, and regarded you as their sovereigns. And I laid before your Highnesses abundant samples of gold and copper,— proving the existence of extensive mines of those metals. I

---

lo descubierto en el primero víage, y le allané la Isla Española que boja mas que España, en que la gente della es sin cuento, y que todos le pagasen tributo. Nació allí mal decir y menosprecio de la empresa comenzada en ello, porque no habia yo enviado luego los navíos cargados de oro, sin considerar le brevedad del tiempo, y lo otro que yo dije de tantos inconvenientes; y en esto por mis pecados ó por mi salvacion creo que será, fue puesto en aborrecimiento y dado impedimento á cuanto yo decia y demandaba; por lo cual acordé de venir á vuestras Altezas, y maravillarme de todo, y mostrarles la razon que en todo habia, y les dige de los pneblos que yo habia visto, en qué ó de qué se podrian salvar muchas animas, y les truje las obligaciones de la gente de la Isla Española, de como se obligaban á pagar tributo ó les tenian por sos Reyes y Señores, y les truje abastante muestra de oro, y que hay mineros y granos muy grandes, y asimismo de cobre; y les truje de muchas

also laid before your Highnesses many sorts of spices, too numerous to detail; and I spoke of the great quantity of brazil-wood, and numberless other articles found in those lands. All this was of no avail with some persons, who began, with determined hatred, to speak ill of the enterprise, not taking into account the service done to our Lord in the salvation of so many souls, nor the enhancement of your Highnesses' greatness to a higher pitch than any earthly prince has yet enjoyed; nor considering, that from the exercise of your Highnesses' goodness, and the expense incurred, both spiritual and temporal advantage was to be expected, and that Spain must in the process of time derive from thence, beyond all doubt, an unspeakable increase of wealth. This might be manifestly seen by the proofs given in the written descriptions of the voyages already made, showing that the fulfilment of every other hope may be reasonably expected. Nor were they affected by the consideration of what great princes throughout the world have done to increase their fame: as, for example, Solomon, who sent from Jerusalem, to the uttermost parts of the east, to see Mount Sopora [Σωφίρ, Ophir], in which expedition his ships were detained three years; and which mountain your High-

---

maneras de especerias, de que seria largo de escrebir, y les dije de la gran cantidad de brasil, y otras infinitas cosas. Todo no aprovechó para con algunas personas que tenian gana y dado comienzo á mal decir del negocio, ni entrar con fabla del servicio de nuestro Señor con se salvar tantas animas, ni á decir questo era grandeza de vuestras Altezas, de la mejor calidad que hasta hoy haya usado Príncipe, por quel ejercicio é gasto era para el espiritual y temporal, y que no podia ser que andando el tiempo no hobiese la España de aquí grandes provechos, pues que se veian las señales que escribieron de lo de estas partidas tan manifiestas; que tambien se llegaria á ver todo el otro complimiento, ni á decir cosas que usaron grandes Principes en el mundo para crecer su fama, así como de Salomon que envió desde Hierusalem en fin de Oriente á ver el monte Sopora, en que se detovieron los

nesses now possess in the island of Española. Nor, as in the case of Alexander, who sent to observe the mode of government in the island of Taprobana,[1] in India; and Cæsar Nero, to explore the sources of the Nile,[2] and to learn the causes of its increase in the summer, when water is needed; and many other mighty deeds that princes have done, and which it is allotted to princes to achieve. Nor was it of any avail that no prince of Spain, as far as I have read, has ever hitherto gained possession of land out of Spain; and that the world of which I speak is different from that of which the Romans, and Alexander, and the Greeks made mighty efforts with great armies to gain possession. Nor have they been affected by the recent noble example of the kings of Portugal, who have had the courage to explore as far as Guinea, and to make the discovery of it, expending so much gold and so many lives in the undertaking, that a calculation of the population of the kingdom would show that one half of them have died in Guinea: and though it is now a long

---

navíos tres años, el cual tienen vuestras Altezas agora en la Isla Española; ni de Alejandre, que envió á ver el regimiento de la Isla de Trapobana en India, y Nero Cesar á ver las fuentes del Nilo, y la razon porque crecian en el verano, cuando las aguas son pocas, y otras muchas grandezas que hicieron Príncipes, y que á Príncipes son estas cosas dadas de hacer; ni valia decir que yo nunca habia leido que Príncipes de Castilla jamas hobiesen ganado tierra fuera della, y que esta de acáes otro mundo en que se trabajaron Romanos y Alejandre y Griegos, para la haber con grandes ejercicios, ni decir del presente de los Reyes de Portugal, que tovieron corazon para sostener á Guinea, y del descobrir della, y que gastaron oro y gente á tanta, que quien contase toda la del Reino se hallaria que otra tanta como la mitad son muertos en Guinea, y todavia la continuaron hasta que les salió dello lo que

[1] Ceylon.
[2] These examples quoted by the admiral from ancient history, are commented upon very learnedly, and at considerable length, by his historian, Las Casas, in chapters 128 and 129 of his unpublished history. (Navarrete.)

time since they commenced these great exertions, the return for their labour and expense has hitherto been but trifling; this people has also dared to make conquests in Africa, and to carry on their exploits to Ceuta, Tangier, Argilla, and Alcazar, repeatedly giving battle to the Moors; and all this at great expense; simply because it was an exploit worthy of a prince, undertaken for the service of God, and to advance the enlargement of His kingdom. The more I said on the subject, the more two-fold was reproach cast upon it, even to the expression of abhorrence, no consideration being given to the honour and fame that accrued to your Highnesses throughout all Christendom from your Highnesses having undertaken this enterprise; so that there was neither great nor small who did not desire to hear tidings of it. Your Highnesses replied to me encouragingly, and desired that I should pay no regard to those who spoke ill of the undertaking, inasmuch as they had received no authority or countenance whatever from your Highnesses.

I started from San Lucar, in the name of the most Holy Trinity, on Wednesday the 30th of May,[1] much fatigued with

---

parece, lo cual todo comenzaron de largo tiempo, y hay muy poco que les da renta; los cuales tambien osaron conquistar en Africa, y sostener la empresa á Cepta, Tanjar y Arcilla, é Alcazar, y de contino dar guerra á los moros, y todo esto con grande gasto, solo por hacer cosa de Príncipe servir á Dios y acrecentar su Señorío.

Cuanto yo mas decia tanto mas se doblaba á poner esto á vituperio, amostrando en ello aborrecimiento, sin considerar cuánto bien pareció en todo el mundo, y cuánto bien se dijo en todos los cristianos de vuestras Altezas por haber tomado esta empresa, que no hobo grande ni pequeño que no quisiese dello carta. Respondiéronme vuestras Altezas riéndose y diciendo que yo no curase de nada porque no daban autoridad ni creencia á quien les mal decia de esta empresa.

Partí en nombre de la Santísima Trinidad, Miercoles 30 de

[1] Of the year 1498.

my voyage, for I had hoped, when I left the Indies, to find repose in Spain; whereas, on the contrary, I experienced nothing but opposition and vexation. I sailed to the island of Madeira by a circuitous route, in order to avoid any encounter with an armed fleet from France,[1] which was on the look out for me off Cape St. Vincent. Thence I went to the Canaries,[2] from which islands I sailed with but one ship and two caravels, having dispatched the other ships to Española by the direct road to the Indies;[3] while I myself moved southward, with the view of reaching the equinoctial line, and of then proceeding westward, so as to leave the island of Española to the north. But having reached the Cape Verde islands[4] (an incorrect name[5], for they are so barren that nothing

Mayo de la villa de S. Lúcar, bien fatigado de mi viage, que adonde esperaba descanso, cuando yo partí de estas Indias, se me dobló la pena, y navegué á la Isla de la Madera por camino no acostumbrado, por evitar escándalo que pudiera tener con un armada de Francia, que me aguardaba al Cabo de S. Vicente, y de allí á las Islas de Canaria, de adonde me partí con una nao y dos carabelas, y envié los otros navíos á derecho camino á las Indias á la Isla Española, y yo navegué al Austro con propósito de llegar á la línea equinocial, y de allí seguir al Poniente hasta

[1] Herrera says (Dec. i, lib. 3, cap. 9) that it was a Portuguese squadron; but Las Casas (cap. 30) distinctly states it to have been French.

[2] Herrera and Don Ferdinand Columbus say that he reached the island of Puerto Santo on the seventh of June, from which island he sailed directly for Madeira, and thence to Gomera, which he reached on the nineteenth, and put to sea again on the twenty-first.

[3] The commanders of the three ships which the admiral despatched to Española, were Pedro de Arana, native of Cordova, brother to the mother of Ferdinand Columbus; Alonzo Sanchez de Carabajal, magistrate of Baeza; and Juan Antonio Columbus, a relative of the admiral; all of whom were known to and are spoken of by F. Bartolomé de Las Casas, in chapter 130 of his unpublished history. (Navarrete.)

[4] This was on the twenty-seventh of June. He anchored in the island of Sal, and on the thirtieth proceeded to the island of Santiago, from whence he put to sea again on the fourth of July.

[5] The islands took the name from the Cape itself, not from the verdure which had caused that name to be given to the Cape. The Cape

green was to be seen there, and the people so sickly that I
did not venture to remain among them), I sailed away four
hundred and eighty miles, which is equivalent to a hundred
and twenty leagues, towards the south-west, where, when it
grew dark, I found the north star to be in the fifth degree.
The wind then failed me, and I entered a climate where the
intensity of the heat was such, that I thought both ships and
men would have been burnt up, and everything suddenly got
into such a state of confusion, that no man dared go below
deck to attend to the securing of the water-cask and the provisions. This heat lasted eight days; on the first day the
weather was fine, but on the seven other days it rained and
was cloudy, yet we found no alleviation of our distress; so
that I certainly believe, that if the sun had shone as on the
first day, we should not have been able to escape in any way.

I recollect, that in sailing towards the Indies, as soon as I
passed a hundred leagues to the westward of the Azores, I
found the temperature change: and this is so all along from

---

que la Isla Española me quedase al Septentrion, y llegado á las
Islas de Cabo Verde, falso nombre, porque son atan secas que no
ví cosa verde en ellas, y toda la gente enferma, que no osé detenerme en ellas, y navegué al Sudueste cuatrocientas y ochenta
millas, que son ciento y veinte leguas, adonde en anocheciendo
tenia la estrella del norte en cinco grados ; allí me desamparó el
viento y entré en tanto ardor y tan grande que creí que se me
quemasen los navíos y gente, que todo de un golpe vino á tan
desordenado, que no habia persona que osase descender debajo
de cubierta á remediar la vasija y mantenimientos ; duró este
ardor ocho dias; al primer dia fue claro, y los siete dias siguientes
llovió ó hizo ñumblado, y con todo no fallamos remedio, que cierto
si así fuera de sol como el primero, yo creo que no pudiera escapar
en ninguna manera.

Verde was discovered by Diniz Dias about 1445: the Cape Verde
Islands were discovered in 1460 by Diogo Gomez, as shown for the first
time in my *Prince Henry the Navigator*, pp. 297-298, and not by Antonio de Nolle in 1457, as incorrectly stated by Cadamosto.

north to south. I determined, therefore, if it should please
the Lord to give me a favourable wind and good weather, so
that I might leave the part where I then was, that I would
give up pursuing the southward course, yet not turn backwards, but sail towards the west, moving in that direction in
the hope of finding the same temperature that I had experienced when I sailed in the parallel of the Canaries,—and
then, if it proved so, I should still be able to proceed more
to the south. At the end of these eight days it pleased our
Lord to give me a favourable east wind, and I steered to the
west, but did not venture to move lower down towards the
south, because I discovered a very great change in the sky
and the stars, although I found no alteration in the temperature. I resolved, therefore, to keep on the direct westward course, in a line from Sierra Leone, and not to change
it until I reached the point where I had thought I should
find land, where I would repair the vessels, and renew, if
possible, our stock of provisions, and take in what water
we wanted. At the end of seventeen days, during which
our Lord gave me a propitious wind, we saw land at noon of

Acórdome que navegando á las Indias siempre que yo paso al
Poniente de las Islas de los Azores cien leguas, allí fallo mudar la
temperanza, y esto es todo de Septentrion en Austro, y determiné
que si á nuestro Señor le pluguiese de me dar viento y buen
tiempo que pudiese salir de adonde estaba, de dejar de ir mas al
Austro, ni volver tampoco atrás, salvo de navegar al Poniente, á
tanto que ya llegase á estar con esta raya con esperanza que yo
fallaria allí así temperamiento, como habia fallado cuando yo
navegaba en el paralelo de Canaria. E que si así fuese que entonces yo podria ir mas al Austro, y plugó á nuestro Señor que al
cabo de estos ocho dias de me dar buen viento Levante, y yo
seguí al Poniente, mas no osé declinar abajo al Austro porque
fallé grandísimo mudamiento en el cielo y en las estrellas, mas
non fallé mudamiento en la temperancia; así acordé de proseguir
delante'siempre justo al Poniente, en aquel derecho de la Sierra
Lioa, con propósito de non mudar derrota fasta adonde yo habia

Tuesday the 31st of July.¹ This I had expected on the Monday before, and held that route up to this point; but as the sun's strength increased, and our supply of water was failing, I resolved to make for the Caribee Islands, and set sail in that direction; when, by the mercy of God, which He has always extended to me, one of the sailors went up to the main-top and saw to the westward a range of three mountains. Upon this we repeated the "Salve Regina," and other prayers, and all of us gave many thanks to our Lord. I then gave up our northward course, and put in for the land: at the hour of complines we reached a cape, which I called Cape Galea,² having already given to the island the name of Trinidad, and here we found a harbour, which would have been excellent but there was no good anchorage. We saw houses and people on the spot, and the country around was very beautiful, and as fresh and green as the gardens of Valencia in the month of March. I was disappointed at

pensado que fallaria tierra, y allí adobar los navíos, y remediar si pudiese los mantenimientos y tomar agua que no tenia; y al cabo de diez y siete dias, los cuales nuestro Señor me dió de próspero viento, Martes 31 de Julio á medio dia nos amostró tierra é yo la esperaba el Lunes antes, y tuve aquel camino fasta entonces, que en saliendo el sol, por defecto del agua que no tenia, determiné de andar á las Islas de los Caribales, y tomé esa vuelta; y como su alta Magestad haya siempre usado de misericordia conmigo, por acertamiento subió un marinero á la gavia, y vido al Poniente tres moñtanas juntas: dijimos la Salve Regina y otras prosas, y dimos todos muchas gracias á nuestro Señor, y despues dejé el camino de Septentrion, y volví hácia la tierra, adonde yo llegué á hora de completas á un Cabo á que dije de la Galea despues de haber nombrado á la Isla de la Trinidad, y allí hobiera muy buen puerto si fuera fondo, y habia casas y gente, y muy lindas tierras,

¹ It was first seen by a mariner of Huelva, a servant of the admiral, named Alonzo Perez. (Navarrete.)

² It is now called Cape Galeota, and is the most south-eastern point of the island of Trinidad.

not being able to put into the harbour, and ran along the
coast to the westward. After sailing five leagues I found
very good bottom and anchored. The next day I set sail
in the same direction, in search of a harbour where I might
repair the vessels and take in water, as well as improve the
stock of provisions which I had brought out with me. When
we had taken in a pipe of water, we proceeded onwards till
we reached the cape, and there finding good anchorage and
protection from the east wind, I ordered the anchors to be
dropped, the water-cask to be repaired, a supply of water
and wood to be taken in, and the people to rest themselves
from the fatigues which they had endured for so long a time.
I gave to this point the name of Sandy Point (Punta del
Arenal). All the ground in the neighbourhood was filled
with foot-marks of animals, like the impression of the foot
of a goat;[1] but although it would have appeared from this
circumstance that they were very numerous, only one was
seen, and that was dead. On the following day a large
canoe came from the eastward, containing twenty-four men,
all in the prime of life, and well provided with arms, such
as bows, arrows, and wooden shields; they were all, as I

---

atan fermosas y verdes come las huertas de Valencia en Marzo.
Pesóme cuando no pude entrar en el puerto, y corri la costa de
esta tierra del luengo fasta el poniente, y andadas cinco leguas
fallé muy buen fondo y surgí, y en el otro dia dí la vela á este
camino buscando puerto para adobar los navíos y tomar agua, y
remediar el trigo y los bastimentos que llevaba solamente. Allí
tomé una pipa de agua, y con ella anduve ansi hasta llegar al
cabo, y allí fallé abrigo de Levante y buen fondo, y así mandé
surgir y adobar la vasija y tomar agua y leña, y descendir la
gente á descansar de tanto tiempo que andaban penando.

A esta punta llamó del Arenal, y allí se falló toda la tierra fol-
lada de unas animalías que tenian la pata como de cabra, y bien
que segun parece ser allí haya muchas, no se vido sino una
muerta. El dia siguiente vino de hácia oriente una grande canoa
con veinte y cuatro hombres, todos mancebos é muy ataviados

[1] In all probability deer.

have said, young, well-proportioned, and not dark black, but whiter than any other Indians that I had seen,—of very graceful gesture and handsome forms, wearing their hair long and straight, and cut in the Spanish style. Their heads were bound round with cotton scarfs elaborately worked in colours, which resembled the Moorish head-dresses. Some of these scarfs were worn round the body and used as a covering in lieu of trousers. The natives spoke to us from the canoe while it was yet at a considerable distance, but none of us could understand them; I made signs to them, however, to come nearer to us, and more than two hours were spent in this manner,—but if by any chance they moved a little nearer, they soon pushed off again. I caused basins and other shining objects to be shown to them to tempt them to come near; and after a long time, they came somewhat nearer than they had hitherto done,—upon which, as I was very anxious to speak with them and had nothing else to show them to induce them to approach, I ordered a drum to be played upon the quarter-deck, and some of our young men to dance, believing the Indians would come to see the amusement. No sooner, however, did they per-

---

de armas, arcos y flechas y tablachinas, y ellos, como dije, todos, mancebos, de buena disposicion y no negros, salvo mas blancos que otros que haya visto en las Indias, y de muy lindo gesto, y fermosos cuerpos, y los cabellos largos y llanos, cortados á la guisa Castilla, y traian la cabeza atada con un pañuelo de algodon tejido á labores y colores, el cual creia yo que era almaizar. Otro de estos pañuelos traían ceñido é se cobijaban con él en lugar de pañetes. Cuando llegó esta canoa habló de muy lejos, ó yo ni otro ninguno no los entendiamos, salvo que yo les mandaba hacer señas que se allegasen, y en esto se pasó mas de dos horas, y si se llegaban un poco luego se desviaban. Yo les hacia mostrar bacines y otras cosas que lucian por enamorarlos porque viniesen, y á cabo de buen rato se allegaron mas que hasta entonces no habian, y yo deseaba mucho haber lengua, y no tenia ya cosa que me pareciese que era de mostrarles para que viniesen; salvo que

ceive the beating of the drum and the dancing, than they all left their oars, and strung their bows, and each man laying hold of his shield, they commenced discharging their arrows at us; upon this, the music and dancing soon ceased, and I ordered a charge to be made from some of our crossbows; they then left us, and went rapidly to the other caravel, and placed themselves under its poop. The pilot of that vessel received them courteously, and gave to the man who appeared to be their chief, a coat and hat; and it was then arranged between them, that he should go to speak with him on shore. Upon this the Indians immediately went thither and waited for him; but as he would not go without my permission, he came to my ship in a boat, whereupon the Indians got into their canoe again and went away, and I never saw any more of them or of any of the other inhabitants of the island. When I reached the point of Arenal, I found that the island of Trinidad formed with the land of Gracia[1] a strait of two leagues' width from west to east, and as we had to pass through it to go to the north, we found

hice sobir un tamborin en el castillo de popa que tañesen, ó unos mancebos que danzasen, creyendo que se allegarian á ver la fiesta; y luego que vieron tañer y danzar todos dejaron los remos y echaron mano á los arcos y los encordaron, y embrazo cada uno su tablachina, y comenzaron á tirarnos flechas: cesó luego el tañer y danzar, y mandé luego sacar unas ballestas, y ellos dejáronme y fueren á mas andar á otra carabela y de golpe se fueron debajo la popa della, y el piloto entró con ellos, y dió un sayo é un bonete á un hombre principal que le pareció dellos, y quedó concertado que le iria hablar allí en la playa, adonde ellos luego fueron con la canoa esperándole, y él como no quiso ir sin mi licencia, como ellos le vieron venir á la nao con la barca, tornaron á entrar en la canoa é se fueron, é nunca mas los vide ni á otros de esta isla.

Cuando yo llegué á esta punta del Arenal, allí se hace una boca grande do dos leguas de Poniente á Levante, la Isla de la Trinidad

[1] Coast of Paria.

some strong currents which crossed the strait, and which made a great roaring, so that I concluded there must be a reef of sand or rocks, which would preclude our entrance; and behind this current was another and another, all making a roaring noise like the sound of breakers against the rocks. I anchored there, under the said point of Arenal, outside of the strait, and found the water rush from east to west with as much impetuosity as that of the Guadalquivir at its conflux with the sea; and this continued constantly day and night, so that it appeared to be impossible to move backwards for the current or forwards for the shoals. In the dead of night, while I was on deck, I heard an awful roaring that came from the south towards the ship; I stopped to observe what it might be, and I saw the sea rolling from west to east like a mountain as high as the ship, and approaching by little and little; on the top of this rolling sea came a mighty wave roaring with a frightful noise and the same terrific uproar as the other currents, producing, as I have already said,

---

con la tierra de Gracia y que para haber de entrar dentro para pasar al Septentrion habia unos hileros de corrientes que atravesaban aquella boca y traian un rugir muy grande, y creí yo que seria un arrecife de bajos é peñas, por el cual no se pouria entrar dentro en ella, y detras de este hilero habia otro y otro que todos traian un rugir grande como ola de la mar que va á romper y dar en peñas. Surgí allí á la dicha punta del Arenal, fuera de la dicha boca, y fallé que venia el agua del Oriente fasta el Poniente con tanta furia como hace Guadalquivir en tiempo de avenida, y esto de contino noche y dia, que creí quo no podria volver atrás por la corriente, ni ir adelante por los bajos; y en la noche ya muy tarde, estando al bordo de la nao, oí un rugir muy terrible que venia de la parte del Austro hácia la nao, y me paré á mirar, y ví levantando la mar de Poniente á Levante, en manera de una loma tan alta como la nao, y todavia venia hácia mi poco á poco, y encima della venia un filero de corriente que venia rugiendo con muy grande estrépito con aquella furia de aquel rugir que de los otros hileros que yo dije que me parecian ondas de mar que daban en

a sound as of breakers upon the rocks.[1] To this day I
have a vivid recollection of the dread I then felt, lest the
ship might founder under the force of that tremendous sea;
but it passed by, and reached the mouth of the before-
mentioned passage, where the uproar lasted for a considerable
time. On the following day I sent out boats to take soundings, and found that in the strait, at the deepest part of the
embouchure, there were six or seven fathoms of water, and
that there were constant contrary currents, one running inwards, and the other outwards. It pleased the Lord, however,
to give us a favourable wind, and I passed inwards through
that strait, and soon came to still water. In fact some water
which was drawn up from the sea, proved to be fresh. I
then sailed northwards till I came to a very high mountain,
at about twenty-six leagues from the Punta del Arenal; here
two lofty headlands appeared, one towards the east, and
forming part of the island of Trinidad,[2] and the other, on
the west, being part of the land which I have already called
Gracia;[3] we found here a channel still narrower than that of
Arenal,[4] with similar currents, and a tremendous roaring of

peñas, que hoy en dia tengo el miedo en el cuerpo que no me
trabucasen la nao cuando llegasen debajo della, y passó y llegó
fasta la boca adonde allí se detuvo grande espacio. Y el otro dia
siguiente envié las barcas á sondar y fallé en el mas bajo de la
boca, que habia seis ó siete brazas de fondo, y de contino andaban
aquellos hileros unos por entrar y otros por salir, y plugo á
nuestro Señor de me dar buen viento, y atravesé por esa boca
adentro, y luego hallé tranquilidad, y por acertamiento se sacó del
agua de la mar y la hallé dulce. Navegué al Septentrion fasta
una sierra muy alta, adonde serian veinte y seis leguas de esta
punta del Arenal, y allí habia dos cabos de tierra muy alta, el uno
de la parte del Oriente, y era de la misma Isla de la Trinidad, y
el otro del Occidente de la tierra que dije de Gracia, y allí hacia

[1] Produced by the confluence of the Oronoco with the sea. See
Rapin, *Hist. Phil.*, vol. iv, p. 272.
[2] Point Peña Blanca.   [3] Point Peña.   [4] Serpent's Mouth.

water; the water here also was fresh. Hitherto I had held no communication with any of the people of this country, although I very earnestly desired it; I therefore sailed along the coast westwards, and the further I advanced, the fresher and more wholesome I found the water; and when I had proceeded a considerable distance, I reached a spot where the land appeared to be cultivated. There I anchored, and sent the boats ashore, and the men who went in them found the natives had recently left the place; they also observed that the mountain was covered with monkeys. They came back, and as the coast at that part presented nothing but a chain of mountains, I concluded that further west we should find the land flatter, and consequently in all probability inhabited. Actuated by this thought I weighed anchor, and ran along the coast until we came to the end of the cordillera; I then anchored at the mouth of a river, and we were soon visited by a great number of the inhabitants, who informed us, that the country was called Paria, and that further westward it was more fully peopled. I took four of these

---

una boca muy angosta mas que aquella de la punta del Arenal, y allí habia los mismos hileros y aquel rugir fuerte del agua como era en la punta del Arenal, y asimismo allí la mar era agua dulce; y fasta entonces yo no habia habido lengua con ninguna gente de estas tierras, y lo deseaba en gran manera, y por esto navegué al luengo de la costa de esta tierra hácia el Poniente, y cuanto mas andaba hallaba el agua de la mar mas dulce y mas sabrosa, y andando una gran parte llegué á un lugar donde me parecian las tierras labradas y surgí y envió las barcas á tierra, y fallaron que de fresco se habia ido de allí gente, y fallaron todo el monte cubierto de gatos paules: volviéronse, y como esta fuese sierra me pareció que mas allá al Poniente las tierras eran mas llanas, y que allí seria poblado, y por esto seria poblado, y mandé levantar las anclas y corrí esta costa fasta el cabo de esta sierra, y allí á un rio surgi, y luego vino mucha gente, y me dijeron como llamaron á esta tierra Paria y que de allí mas al Poniente era mas poblada; tomé dellos cuatro, y despues navegué al Poniente, y

natives, and proceeded on my westward voyage; and when I had gone eight leagues further, I found on the other side of a point which I called Punta de la Aguja (Needle Point)[1] one of the most lovely countries in the world, and very thickly peopled: it was three o'clock in the morning when I reached it, and seeing its verdure and beauty, I resolved to anchor there and communicate with the inhabitants. Some of the natives soon came out to the ship, in canoes, to beg me, in the name of their king, to go on shore; and when they saw that I paid no attention to them, they came to the ship in their canoes in countless numbers, many of them wearing pieces of gold on their breasts, and some with bracelets of pearls on their arms; on seeing which I was much delighted, and made many inquiries with the view of learning where they found them. They informed me, that they were to be procured in their own neighbourhood, and also northward of that country. I would have remained here, but the provisions of corn, and wine, and meats, which I had brought out with so much care for the people whom I had left behind, were nearly wasted, so that all my anxiety

andadas ocho leguas mas al Poniente allende una punta á que yo llamé del Aguja: hallé unas tierras las mas hermosas del mundo, y muy pobladas: llegué allí una mañana á hora de tercia, y por ver esta verdura y esta hermosura acordé surgir y ver esta gente, de los cuales luego vinieron en canoas á la nao á rogarme, de partes de su Rey, què descendiose en tierra; é cuando vieron que no curé dellos vinieron á la nao infinitísimos en canoas, y muchos traían piezas de oro al pescuezo, y algunos atados á los brazos algunas perlas: holgué mucho cuando las ví é procuró mucho de saber donde las hallaban, y me dijeron que allí, y de la parte del Norte de aquella tierra.

Quisiera detenerme, mas estos bastimentos, que yo traía, trigo y vino é carne para esta gente que acá esta se me acababan de perder, los cuales hobe allá con tanta fatiga, y por esto yo no buscaba sino á mas andar á venir á poner en ellos cobro, y no me

[1] It is now called Point Alcatraz, or Point Pelican.

was to get them into a place of safety, and not to stop for any thing. I wished, however, to get some of the pearls that I had seen, and with that view sent the boats on shore. The natives are very numerous, and all handsome in person, and of the same colour as the Indians we had already seen; they are, moreover, very affable, and received our men who went on shore most courteously, seeming very well disposed towards us. These men relate, that when the boats reached the shore, two of the chiefs, whom they took to be father and son, came forward in advance of the mass of the people, and conducted them to a very large house with façades, and not round and tent-shaped as the other houses were; in this house were many seats, on which they made our men sit down, they themselves sitting with them. They then caused bread to be brought, with many kinds of fruits, and various sorts of wine, both white and red, not made of grapes, but apparently produced from different fruits. The most reasonable inference is, that they use maize, which is a plant that bears an ear like that of wheat, some of which I took with me to Spain, where it now grows abundantly; the best of this they seemed to regard as most excellent, and set a

---

detener para cosa alguna: procuré de haber de aquellas perlas, y envié las barcas á tierra: esta gente es muy mucha, y toda de muy buen parecer, de la misma color que los otros de antes, y muy tratables: la gente nuestra que fue á tierra los hallaron tan convenibles, y los recibieron muy honradamente: dicen que luego que llegaron las barcas á tierra que vinieron dos personas principales cón todo el pueblo, creen que el uno el padre y el otro era su hijo, y los llevaron á una casa muy grande hecha á dos aguas, y no redonda, como tienda de campo, como son estas otras, y allí tenian muchas sillas á donde los ficieron asentar, y otras donde ellos se asentaron; y hicieron traer pan, y de muchas maneras frutas ó vino de muchas maneras blanco ó tinto, mas no de uvas: debe él de ser de diversas maneras uno de una fruta y otro de otra; y asimismo debe de ser dello de maiz, que es una simiente que hace una espiga como una mazorca de que llevé yo allá, y hay

great value upon it. The men remained together at one
end of the house, and the women at the other. Great vexation was felt by both parties that they could not understand
each other, for they were mutually anxious to make inquiries
respecting each other's country. After our men had been
entertained at the house of the elder Indian, the younger
took them to his house, and gave them an equally cordial
reception; after which they returned to their boats and
came on board. I weighed anchor forthwith, for I was
hastened by my anxiety to save the provisions which were
becoming spoiled, and which I had procured and preserved
with so much care and trouble, as well as to attend to my
own health, which had been affected by long watching;
and although on my former voyage, when I went out to
discover terra firma, I passed thirty-three days without natural rest, and was all that time without seeing it, yet
never were my eyes so much affected with bleeding or so
painful as at this period. These people, as I have already
said, are very graceful in form,—tall, and lithe in their
movements, and wear their hair very long and smooth. They

---

ya mucho en Castilla, y parece que aquel que lo tenia mejor lo
traía por mayor excelencia, y lo daba en gran precio : los hombres
todos estaban juntos á un cabo de la casa, y las mugeres en otro.
Recibieron ambas las partes gran pena porque no se entendian,
ellos para preguntar á los otros de nuestra patria, y los nuestros
por saber de la suya. E despues que hobieron rescebido colacion
allí en casa del mas viejo, los llevó el mozo á la suya, e fizo otro
tanto, é despues se pusieron en las barcas é se vinieron á la nao,
é yo luego levanté las anclas porque andaba mucho de priesa por
remediar los mantenimientos que se me perdian que yo habia
habido con tanta fatiga, y tambien por remediarme á mí que
habia adolescido por el desvelar de los ojos, que bien quel viage
que yo fuí á descubrir la tierra firme estuviese teinta y tres dias
sin concebir sueño, y estoviese tanto tiempo sin vista, non se me
deñaron los ojos, ni se me rompieron de sangre y con tantos
dolores como agora.

also bind their heads with handsome worked handkerchiefs, which from a distance look like silk or gauze; others use the same material in a longer form, wound round them so as to cover them like trousers, and this is done by both the men and the women. These people are of a whiter skin than any I have seen in the Indies. It is the fashion among all classes to wear something at the breast, and on the arms, and many wear pieces of gold hanging low on the bosom. Their canoes are larger, lighter, and of better build than those of the islands which I have hitherto seen, and in the middle of each they have a cabin or room, which I found was occupied by the chiefs and their wives. I called this place "Jardines," that is "the Gardens," for it corresponded to that appellation. I made many inquiries as to where they found the gold, in reply to which, all of them directed me to an elevated tract of land at no great distance, on the confines of their country, lying to the westward; but they all advised me not to go there, for fear of being eaten, and at the time, I imagined that by their description they wished to imply, that they were cannibals who dwelt there,

---

Esta gente, como ya dije, son todos de muy linda estatura, altos de cuerpos, é de muy lindos gestos, los cabellos muy largos ó llanos, y traen las cabezas atadas con unos pañuelos labrados, como ya dije, hermosos, que parecen de lejos de seda y almaizares: otro traen ceñido mas largo que se cobijan con él en lugar de pañetes, ansi hombres como mugeres. La color de esta gente es mas blanca que otra que haya visto en las Indias; todos traían al pescuezo y á los brazos algo á la guisa de estas tierras, y muchos traían piezas de oro bajo colgado al pescuezo. Las canoas de ellos son muy grandes y de mejor hechura que no son estas otras, y mas livianas, y en el medio de cada una tienen un apartamiento como cámara en que ví que andaban los principales con sus mugeres. Llamó allí á este lugar Jardines, porque así conforman por el nombre. Procuré mucho de saber donde cogian aquel oro, y todos me aseñalaban una tierra frontera dellos al Poniente, que

but I have since thought it possible, that they meant merely to express, that the country was filled with beasts of prey. I also inquired of them where they obtained the pearls, and in reply to this question likewise, they directed me to the westward, and also to the north, behind the country they occupied. I did not put this information to the test, on account of the provisions, and the weakness of my eyes, and because the large ship that I had with me was not calculated for such an undertaking. The short time that I spent with them was all passed in putting questions; and at the hour of vespers [six P.M.], as I have already said, we returned to the ships, upon which I weighed anchor and sailed to the westward. I proceeded onwards on the following day, until I found that we were only in three fathoms water; at this time I was still under the idea that it was but an island, and that I should be able to make my exit by the north. With this view I sent a light caravel in advance of us, to see whether there was any exit, or whether the passage was closed. The caravel proceeded a great distance, until it reached a very large gulf, in which

---

era muy alta, mas no lejos ; mas todos me decian que no fuese allá porque allí comian los hombres, y entendí entonces que decian que eran hombres caribales, ó que serian como los otros, y despues he pensado que podria ser que lo decian porque allí habria animalias. Tambien les pregunté adonde cogian las perlas, y me señalaron tambien que al Poniente, y al Norte detrás de esta tierra donde estaban. Dejélo de probar por esto de los mantenimientos, y del mal de mis ojos, y por una nao grande que traigo que no es para semejante hecho.

Y como el tiempo fue breve se pasó todo en preguntas, y se volvieron á los navíos, que seria hora de visperas, como ya dije, y luego levanté las anclas y navegué al Poniente ; y asimesmo el dia siguiente fasta que me fallé que no habia si non tres brazas de fondo, con creencia que todavía esta seria isla, y que yo podria salir al Norte; y así visto envié una carabela sotil adelante á ver si habia salida ó si estaba cerrado, y ansi anduvo mucho camino fasta un golfo muy grande en el cual parecia que habia otros

there appeared to be four smaller gulfs, from one of which debouched a large river. They invariably found ground at five fathoms, and a great quantity of very fresh water, indeed, I never tasted any equal to it. I was very disappointed when I found that I could make no exit, either by the north, south, or west, but that I was enclosed on all three sides by land. I therefore weighed anchor, and sailed in a backward direction, with the hope of finding a passage to the north by the strait, which I have already described; but I could not return along the inhabited part where I had already been, on account of the currents, which drove me entirely out of my course. But constantly, at every headland, I found the water sweet and clear, and we were carried eastwards very powerfully towards the two straits already mentioned. I then conjectured, that the currents and the overwhelming mountains of water which rushed into these straits with such an awful roaring, arose from the contest between the fresh water and the sea. The fresh water struggled with the salt to oppose its entrance, and the salt contended against the fresh in its efforts to gain a passage outwards. I also formed the conjecture, that at one time there was a continuous neck of land from the island of

---

cuatro medianos, y del uno salia un rio grandísimo: fallaron siempre cinco brazas de fondo y el agua muy dulce, en tanta cantidad que yo jamas bebíla pareja della. Fuí yo muy descontento della cuando ví que no podia salir al Norte ni podia andar ya al Austro ni al Poniente porque yo estaba cercado por todas partes de la tierra, y así levanté las anclas, y torne atrás para salir al Norte por la boca que yo arriba dije, y no pude volver por la poblacion adonde yo habia estado, por causa de las corrientes que me habian desviado della, y siempre en todo cabo hallaba el agua dulce y clara, y que me llevaba al Oriente muy recio fácia las dos bocas que arriba dije, y entonces conjeturé que los hilos de la corriente, y aquellas lomas que salian y entraban en estas bocas con aquel rugir tan fuerte que era pelea del agua dulce con la salada. La dulce empujaba á la otra porque no entrase, y la salada porque la otra no saliese; y conjeturé que allí donde son

Trinidad to the land of Gracia, where the two straits now are, as your Highnesses will see, by the drawing which accompanies this letter. I passed out by this northern strait, and found the fresh water come even there; and when, by the force of the wind, I was enabled to effect a passage, I remarked, while on one of the watery billows which I have described, that the water on the inner side of the current was fresh, and on the outside salt.

When I sailed from Spain to the Indies, I found, that as soon as I had passed a hundred leagues westward of the Azores, there was a very great change in the sky and the stars, in the temperature of the air, and in the water of the sea; and I have been very diligent in observing these things. I remarked, that from north to south, in traversing these hundred leagues from the said islands, the needle of the compass, which hitherto had turned towards the north-east, turned a full quarter of the wind to the north-west, and this took place from the time when we reached that line. At the same time an appearance was presented, as if the sea shore had been transplanted thither, for we found the sea covered

---

estas dos bocas que algun tiempo seria tierra continua á la Isla de la Trinidad con la tierra de Gracia, como podrán ver vuestras Altezas por la pintura de lo que con esta les envio. Salí yo por esta boca del Norte y hallé quel agua dulce siempre vencia, y cuando pasé, que fue con fuerza de viento, estando en una de aquellas lomas, hallé en aquellos hilos de la parte de dentro el agua dulce, y de fuera salada.

Cuando yo navegué de España á las Indias fallo luego en pasando cien leguas á Poniente de los Azores grandísimo mudamiento en el cielo é en las estrellas, y en la temperancia del aire, y en las aguas de la mar, y en esto he tenido mucha diligencia en la experiencia.

Fallo que de Septentrion en Austro, pasando las dichas cien leguas de las dichas islas, que luego en las agujas de marear, que fasta entonces nordesteaban, noruestean una cuarta de viento todo entero, y esto es en allegando allí á aquella línea, como quien

all over with a sort of weed, resembling pine branches, and with fruits like that of the mastic tree, so thick, that on my first voyage I thought it was a reef, and that the ships could not avoid running aground; whereas until I reached this line, I did not meet with a single bough. I also observed, that at this point the sea was very smooth, and that though the wind was rough, the ships never rolled. I likewise found, that within the same line, towards the west, the temperature was always mild, and that it did not vary summer or winter. While there, I observed that the north star described a circle five degrees in diameter; that when its satellites[1] are on the right side, then the star was at its lowest point, and from this point it continues rising until it reaches the left side, where it is also at five degrees, and then again it sinks until it at length returns to the right side. In this voyage I proceeded immediately from Spain to the island of Madeira, thence to the Canaries, and then to the Cape Verde islands, and from the Cape Verde islands I sailed southwards, even

---

traspone una cuesta, asimesmo fallo la mar toda llena de yerba de una calidad que parece ramitos de pino y muy cargada de fruta como de lantisco, y es tan espesa que al primer viage pensé que era bajo, y que daria en seco con los navíos, y hasta llegar con esta raya no se falla un solo ramito : fallo tambien en llegando allí la mar muy suave y llana, y bien que vento recio nunca se levanta. Asimismo hallo dentro de la dicha raya hácia Poniente la temperancia del cielo muy suave, y no discrepa de la cantidad quier sea invierno, quier sea en verano. Cuando allí estoy hallo que la estrella del Norte escribe un círculo el cualo tiene en el diámetro cinco grados, y estando las guardas en el brazo derecho estonces está la estrella en el mas bajo, y se vá alzando fasta que llega al brazo izquierdo, y estonces está cinco grados, y de allí se vá abajando fasta llegar á volver otra vez al brazo derecho.

Yo allegué agora de España á la Isla de la Madera, y de allí á Canaria, y dende á las Islas de Cabo Verde, de adonde cometí el viage para navegar al Austro fasta debajo la linea equinocial, como

[1] The stars composing the constellation of Ursa Minor.

below the equinoctial line, as I have already described. When I reached the parallel of Sierra Leone, in Guinea, I found the heat so intense, and the rays of the sun so fierce, that I thought that we should have been burnt; and although it rained and the sky was heavy with clouds, I still suffered the same oppression, until our Lord was pleased to grant me a favourable wind, giving me an opportunity of sailing to the west, so that I reached a latitude where I experienced, as I have already said, a change in the temperature. Immediately upon my reaching this line, the temperature became very mild, and the more I advanced, the more this mildness increased; but I did not find the positions of the stars correspond with these effects. I remarked at this place, that when night came on, the polar star was five degrees high, and then the satellites were over head; afterwards, at midnight, I found that star elevated ten degrees, and when morning approached, the satellites were fifteen degrees below. I found the smoothness of the sea continue, but not so the weeds; as to the polar star, I watched it with great wonder, and devoted

---

ya dije : allegado á estar en derecho con el paralelo que pasa por la Sierra Leoa en Guinea, fallo tan grande ardor, y los rayos del sol tan calientes que pensaba de quemar, y bien que lloviese y el cielo fuese muy turbado siempre yo estaba en esta fatiga, fasta que nuestro Señor proveyó de buen viento y á mi puso en voluntad que yo navegase al Occidente con este esfuerzo, que en llegando á la raya de que yo dije que allí fallaria mudamiento en la temperancia. Despues que yo emparejé á estar en derecho de esta raya luego fallé la temperancia del cielo muy suave, y cuanto mas andaba adelante mas multiplicaba; mas no hallé conforme á esto las estrellas.

Fallé allí que en anocheciendo tenia yo la estrella del Norte alta cinco grados, y estonces las guardas estaban encima de la cabeza, y despues á la media noche fallaba la estrella alta diez grados, y en amaneciendo que las guardas estaban en los pies quince.

La suavelidad de la mar fallé conforme, mas no en la yerba : en esto de la estrella del Norte tomé grande admiracion, y por esto

many nights to a careful examination of it with the quadrant, and I always found that the lead and line fell to the same point. I look upon this as something new, and it will probably be admitted, that it is a short distance for so great a change to take place in the temperature. I have always read, that the world comprising the land and the water was spherical, and the recorded experiences of Ptolemy and all others, have proved this by the eclipses of the moon, and other observations made from east to west, as well as by the elevation of the pole from north to south. But as I have already described, I have now seen so much irregularity, that I have come to another conclusion respecting the earth, namely, that it is not round as they describe, but of the form of a pear, which is very round except where the stalk grows, at which part it is most prominent; or like a round ball, upon one part of which is a prominence like a woman's nipple, this protrusion being the highest and nearest the sky, situated under the equinoctial line, and at the eastern extremity of this sea,—I call that the

---

muchas noches con mucha diligencia tornaba yo á repricar la vista della con el cuadrante, y siempre fallé que caía el plomo y hilo á un punto.

Por cosa nueva tengo yo esto, y podrá ser que será tenida que en poco espacio haga tanta diferencia el cielo.

Yo siempre lei que el mundo, tierra ó agua era esférico ó las autoridades y esperiencias que Tolomeo y todos los otros escribieron de este sitio, daban ó amostraban para ello así por eclipses de la luna y otras demostraciones que hacen de Oriente fasta Occidente, como de la elevacion del polo de Septentrion en Austro. Agora ví tanta disformidad, como ya dije, y por esto me puse á tener esto del mundo, y fallé que no era redondo en la forma que escriben; salvo que es de la forma de una pera que sea toda muy redonda, salvo allí donde tiene el pezon que allí tiene mas alto, ó como quien tiene una pelota muy redonda, y en un lugar della fuese como una teta de muger allí puesta, y que esta parte deste pezon sea la mas alta ó mas propincua al cielo, y sea debajo la líuea equinocial, y en esta mar Océana en fin del Oriente : llamo yo fin

eastern extremity, where the land and the islands end. In confirmation of my opinion, I revert to the arguments which I have above detailed respecting the line, which passes from north to south, a hundred leagues westward of the Azores; for in sailing thence westward, the ships went on rising smoothly towards the sky, and then the weather was felt to be milder, on account of which mildness, the needle shifted one point of the compass; the further we went, the more the needle moved to the north-west, this elevation producing the variation of the circle, which the north star describes with its satellites; and the nearer I approached the equinoctial line, the more they rose, and the greater was the difference in these stars and in their circles. Ptolemy and the other philosophers, who have written upon the globe, thought that it was spherical, believing that this hemisphere was round as well as that in which they themselves dwelt, the centre of which was in the island of Arin,[1] which is under the equinoc-

---

de Oriente, adonde acaba toda la tierra é islas, é para esto allego todas las razones sobre-escriptas de la raya que pasa al Occidente delas islas de los Azores cien leguas de Septentrion en Austro, que en pasando de allí al Poniente ya van los navíos alzándose hácia el cielo suavemente, y entonces se goza de mas suave temperancia y se muda el aguja del marear por causa de la suavidad desa cuarta de viento, y cuanto mas va adelante é alzándose mas noruestea, y esta altura causa el desvariar del circulo que escribe la estrella del Norte con las guardas, y cuanto mas pasare junto con la línea equinocial, mas se subirán en alto, y mas diferencia habrá en las dichas estrellas, y en los circulos dellas. Y Tolomeo y los otros sabios que escribieron de este mundo, creyeron que era esférico, creyendo queste hemisferio que fuese redondo como aquel de allá donde ellos estaban, el cual tiene el centro en la Isla de

[1] A misspelling, not infrequent in those days, for the sacred city (not island) of Odjein or Ougein in Malwa, whence the Indians reckoned their first meridian. The change of the name to Arin in Arabic is thus explained by M. Reinaud in his *Mémoire sur l'Inde*, p. 373. The dj of the Indians was sometimes rendered z by the Arabs, and thus

tial line between the Arabian Gulf and the Gulf of Persia; and the circle passes over Cape St. Vincent, in Portugal, westward, and eastward, by Cangara and the Seras,[1] in which hemisphere I make no difficulty as to its being a perfect sphere as they describe; but this western half of the world, I maintain, is like the half of a very round pear, having a raised projection for the stalk, as I have already described, or like a woman's nipple on a round ball. Ptolemy and the others who have written upon the globe, had no information respecting this part of the world, which was then unexplored; they only established their arguments with respect to their own hemisphere, which, as I have already said, is half of a perfect sphere. And now that your Highnesses have commissioned me to make this voyage of discovery, the truths which I have stated are evidently proved, because in this voyage, when I was off the island of Hargin,[2] and its vicinity, which is twenty degrees to the north of the equinoctial line,

---

Arin, qués debajo la linea equinocial entre el sino Arabico y aquel de Persia, y el círculo pasa sobre el Cabo de S. Vicente en Portugal por el Poniente, y pasa en Oriente por Cangara y por las Seras, en el cual hemisferio no hago yo que hay ninguna dificultad, salvo que sea esférico redondo como ellos dicen: mas este otro digo que es como sería la mitad de la pera bien redonda, la cual toviese el pezon alto como y dije, ó como una teta de muger en una pelota redonda, así que desta media parte non hobo noticia Tolomeo ni los otros que escribieron del mundo por ser muy ignoto; solamente hicieron raiz sobre el hemisferio, adonde ellos estaban ques redondo esférico, como arriba dije. Y agora que vuestras Altezas lo han mandado navegar y buscar y descobrir, se amuestra evidentísimo, porque estando yo en este viage al Septentrion veinte grados de la línea equinocial, allí era en derecho de

the Arab translators wrote the word Ozein; but as in manuscripts the vowels were often omitted, the mass of readers to whom the name of Odjein was indifferent, would pronounce it Azin, and as the copyist would sometimes forget to insert the point which distinguisned a z from an r, Azin would be read Arin.

[1] Japan and China. [2] Arguin, off the west coast of Africa.

I found the people are black, and the land very much burnt;
and when after that I went to the Cape Verde islands, I
found the people there much darker still, and the more
southward we went, the more they approach the extreme of
blackness; so that when I reached the parallel of Sierra
Leone, where, as night came on, the north star rose five
degrees, the people there were excessively black; and as I
sailed westward, the heat became extreme. But after I had
passed the meridian, or line which I have already described,
I found the climate become gradually more temperate; so
that when I reached the island of Trinidad, where the north
star rose five degrees as night came on, there, and in the
land of Gracia, I found the temperature exceedingly mild;
the fields and the foliage likewise were remarkably fresh and
green, and as beautiful as the gardens of Valencia in April.
The people there are very graceful in form, less dark than
those whom I had before seen in the Indies, and wear their
hair long and smooth; they are also more shrewd, intelligent,
and courageous. The sun was then in the sign of Virgo,

Hargin, ó de aquellas tierras : é allí es la gente negra é la tierra
muy quemada, y despues que fuí á las Islas de Cabo Verde, allí en
aquellas tierras es la gente mucho mas negra, y cuanto mas bajo
se van al Austro tanto mas llegan al extremo, en manera que allí
en derecho donde yo estaba, qués la Sierra Leoa, adonde se me
alzaba la estrella del Norte en anocheciendo cinco grados, allí es
la gente negra en extrema cantidad, y despues que de allí navegué
al Occidente tan extremos calores; y pasada la raya de que yo
dije fallé multiplicar la temperancia, andando en tanta cantidad
que cuando yo llegué á la isla de la Trinidad, adonde la estrella
del Norte en anocheciendo tambien se me alzaba cinco grados, allí
y en la tierra de Gracia hallé temperancia suavísima, y las tierras
y árboles muy verdes, y tan hermosos como en Abril en las huertas
de Valencia; y la gente de allí de muy linda estatura, y blancos
mas que otros que haya visto en las Indias, ó los cabellos muy lar
gos ó llanos, é gente mas astuta é de mayor ingenio, ó no cobardes.
Entonces era el sol en Virgen encima de nuestras cabezas é suyas,

over our heads and theirs; therefore, all this must proceed from the extreme blandness of the temperature, which arises, as I have said, from this country being the most elevated in the world, and the nearest to the sky. On these grounds, therefore, I affirm, that the globe is not spherical, but that there is the difference in its form which I have described; the which is to be found in this hemisphere, at the point where the Indies meet the ocean, the extremity of the hemisphere being below the equinoctial line. And a great confirmation of this is, that when our Lord made the sun, the first light appeared in the first point of the east, where the most elevated point of the globe is; and although it was the opinion of Aristotle, that the antarctic pole, or the land under it, was the highest part of the world, and the nearest to the heavens, other philosophers oppose him, and say, that the highest part was below the arctic pole, by which reasoning it appears, that they understood, that one part of the world must be loftier, and nearer the sky, than the other; but it never struck them that it might be under the equinoctial, in the way that I have said, which is not to be won-

---

ansí que todo esto procede por la suavísima temperancia que allí es, la cual procede por estar mas alto en el mundo mas cerca del aire que cuento; y así me afirmo quel mundo no es esférico, salvo que tiene esta diferencia que ya dije : la cual es en este hemisferio adonde caen las Indias ó la mar Oceana, y el extremo dello es debajo la línea equinocial, y ayuda mucho á esto que sea ansí, porque el sol cuando nuestro Señor lo hizo fue en el primer punto de Oriente, ó la primera luz fue aquí en Oriente, allí donde es el extremo de la altura deste mundo; y bien quel parecer de Aristotel fuese que el Polo antártico ó la tierra ques debajo dél sea la mas alta parte en el mundo, y mas propincua al cielo, otros sabios le impugnan diciendo que es esta ques debajo del ártico, por las cuales razones parece que entendian que una parte deste mundo debia de ser mas propincua y noble al cielo que otra, y no cayeron en esto que sea debajo del equinocial por la forma que yo dije, y no es maravilla porque deste hemisferio non se hobiese noticia

dered at, because they had no certain knowledge respecting this hemisphere, but merely vague suppositions, for no one has ever gone or been sent to investigate the matter, until now that your Highnesses have sent me to explore both the sea and the land. I found that between the two straits, which, as I have said, face each other in a line from north to south, is a distance of twenty-six leagues; and there can be no mistake in this calculation, because it was made with the quadrant. I also find, that from these two straits on the west up to the above-mentioned gulf, to which I gave the name of the Gulf of Pearls,[1] there are sixty-eight leagues of four miles to the league, which is the reckoning we are accustomed to make at sea; from this gulf the water runs constantly with great impetuosity towards the east, and this is the cause why, in these two straits, there is so fierce a turmoil from the fresh water encountering the water of the sea. In the southern strait, which I named the Serpent's Mouth, I found that towards evening the polar star was nearly at five degrees elevation; and in the northern, which I called the Dragon's Mouth, it was at an elevation of nearly seven degrees. The before-mentioned Gulf of Pearls is to the west

cierta, salvo muy liviana y por argumento, porque nadie nunca lo ha andado ni enviado á buscar, hasta agora que vuestras Altezas le mandaron explorar é descubrir la mar y la tierra.

Fallo que de allí de estas dos bocas, las cuales como yo dije estan frontero por línea de Septentrion en Austro, que haya de la una á la otra veinte y seis leguas, y no pudo haber en ello yerro porque se midieron con cuadrante, y destas dos bocas de accidente fasta el golfo que yo dije, al cual llamé de las Perlas, que son sesenta é ocho leguas de cuatro millas dada una como acostumbramos en la mar, y que de allá de este golfo corre de contino el agua muy fuerte hácia el oriente; y que por esto tienen aquel combate estas dos bocas con la salada. En esta boca de Austro á que yo llamé de la Sierpe, fallé en anocheciendo que yo tenia la estrella del Norte alta cuasi cinco grados, y en aquella del otra Sep-

[1] The innermost gulf within the Gulf of Paria.

of the¹   of Ptolemy, nearly three thousand nine hundred miles, which make nearly seventy equinoctial degrees, reckoning fifty-six miles and two-thirds to a degree. The Holy Scriptures record, that our Lord made the earthly paradise, and planted in it the tree of life, and thence springs a fountain from which the four principal rivers in the world take their source; namely, the Ganges in India, the Tigris, and Euphrates in²   which rivers divide a chain of mountains, and forming Mesopotamia, flow thence into Persia,—and the Nile, which rises in Ethiopia, and falls into the sea at Alexandria.

I do not find, nor have ever found, any account by the Romans or Greeks, which fixes in a positive manner the site of the terrestrial paradise, neither have I seen it given in any mappe-monde, laid down from authentic sources. Some placed it in Ethiopia, at the sources of the Nile, but

---

tentrion, á que yo llamé del Drago, eran cuasi siete, y fallo quel dicho Golfo de las Perlas está occidentalal Occidente de el   de Tolomeo cuasi tres mil ó novecientas millas, que son cuasi setenta grados equinociales, contando por cada uno cincuenta y seis millas é dos tercios.

La Sacra Escriptura testifica que nuestro Señor hizo al Paraiso terrenal, y en él puso el Arbol de la vida, y del sale una fuente de donde resultan en este mundo cuatro rios principales: Ganges en India, Tigris y Eufrates en   los cuales apartan la sierra y hacen la Mesopotamia y van à tener en Persia, y el Nilo que nace en Etiopia y va en la mar en Alejandría.

Yo no hallo ni jamas he hallado escriptura de Latinos ni de Griegos que certificadamente diga el sitio en este mundo del Paraiso terrenal, ni visto en ningun mapamundo, salvo, situado con autoridad de argumento. Algunos le ponian allí donde son las fuentes del Nilo en Etiopia; mas otros anduvieron todas estas

---

[1] A similar gap in the original. In all probability "first meridian" or some such words, are omitted.

[2] A similar gap in the original, which would seem to want the words "Asiatic Turkey."

others, traversing all these countries, found neither the temperature nor the altitude of the sun correspond with their ideas respecting it; nor did it appear that the overwhelming waters of the deluge had been there. Some pagans pretended to adduce arguments to establish that it was in the Fortunate Islands, now called the Canaries, etc.

St. Isidore, Bede, Strabo,[1] and the Master of scholastic history,[2] with St. Ambrose, and Scotus, and all the learned theologians, agree that the earthly paradise is in the east, etc.

I have already described my ideas concerning this hemisphere and its form, and I have no doubt, that if I could pass below the equinoctial line, after reaching the highest point of which I have spoken, I should find a much milder temperature, and a variation in the stars and in the water; not that I suppose that elevated point to be navigable, nor even that there is water there; indeed, I believe it is impossible to ascend thither, because I am convinced that it is the spot of the earthly paradise, whither no one can go but by God's permission; but this land which your Highnesses

---

tierras y no hallaron conformidad dello en la temperancia del cielo, en la altura hácia el cielo, porque se pudiese comprehender que el era allí, ni que las aguas del diluvio hobiesen llegado allí, las cuales subieron encima, &c. Algunos gentiles quisieron decir por argumentos, que el era en las islas Fortunatas que son las Canarias, &c.

S. Isidro y Beda y Strabo, y el Maestro de la historia escolástica, y San Ambrosio, y Scoto, y todos los sanos teólogos conciertan quel Paraiso terrenal es en el Oriente, &c.

Ya dije lo que yo hallaba deste hemisferio y de la hechura, y creo que si yo pasara por debajo de la línea equinocial que en llegando allí en esto mas alto que fallara muy mayor temperancia, y diversidad en las estrellas y en las aguas; no porque yo crea que allí donde es el altura del extremo sea navegable ni agua, ni que se pueda subir allá, porque creo que allí es el Paraiso terrenal adonde no puede llegar nadie, salvo por voluntad Divina; y creo

---

[1] Walafried Strabus, Abbé of Reichenau in Baden.
[2] Petrus Comestor, who wrote the "Historica Scholastica."

have now sent me to explore, is very extensive, and I think there are many other countries in the south, of which the world has never had any knowledge.

I do not suppose that the earthly paradise is in the form of a rugged mountain, as the descriptions of it have made it appear, but that it is on the summit of the spot, which I have described as being in the form of the stalk of a pear; the approach to it from a distance must be by a constant and gradual ascent; but I believe that, as I have already said, no one could ever reach the top; I think also, that the water I have described may proceed from it, though it be far off, and that stopping at the place which I have just left, it forms this lake. There are great indications of this being the terrestrial paradise, for its site coincides with the opinion of the holy and wise theologians whom I have mentioned; and moreover, the other evidences agree with the supposition, for I have never either read or heard of fresh water coming in so large a quantity, in close conjunction with the water of the sea; the idea is also corroborated by the blandness of the temperature; and if the water of which I speak, does not proceed from the earthly paradise, it seems to be a still

---

que esta tierra que agora mandaron descubrir vuestras Altezas sea grandísima y haya otras muchas en el Austro de que jamas se hobo noticia.

Yo no tomo quel Paraise terrenal sea en forma de montaña aspera como el escrebir dello nos amuestra, salvo quel sea en el colmo allí donde dije la figura del pezon de la pera, y que poco á poco andando hácia allí desde muy lejos se va subiendo á él; y creo que nadie no podria llegar al colmo como yo dije, y creo que pueda salir de allí esa agua, bien que sea lejos y venga á parar allí donde yo vengo, y faga este lago. Grandes indicios son estos del Paraiso terrenal, porquel sitio es conforme á la opinion de estos santos é sanos teólogos, y asimismo las señales son muy conformes, que yo jamas leí ni oí que tanta cantidad de agua dulce fuese así adentro ó vecina con la salada; y en ello ayuda asimismo la suavísima temperancia, y si de allí del Paraiso no sale, parece aun

greater wonder, for I do not believe that there is any river in the world so large or so deep.

When I left the Dragon's Mouth, which is the northernmost of the two straits which I have described, and which I so named on the day of our Lady of August,[1] I found that the sea ran so strongly to the westward, that between the hour of mass,[2] when I weighed anchor, and the hour of complines,[3] I made sixty-five leagues of four miles each; and not only was the wind not violent, but on the contrary very gentle, which confirmed me in the conclusion, that in sailing southward, there is a continuous ascent, while there is a corresponding descent towards the north.

I hold it for certain, that the waters of the sea move from east to west with the sky, and that in passing this track, they hold a more rapid course, and have thus eaten away large tracts of land, and hence has resulted this great number of islands; indeed, these islands themselves afford an additional proof of it, for on the one hand all those which lie west and

---

mayor maravilla, porque no creo que se sepa en el mundo de rio tan grande y tan fondo.

Despues que yo salí de la boca del Dragon, ques la una de las dos aquella del Septentrion, á la cual así puse nombre, el dia siguiente, que fue dia de Nuestra Señora de Agosto, fallé que corria tanto la mar al Poniente, que despues de hora de misa que entré en camino, anduve fasta hora de completas sesenta y cinco leguas de cuatro millas cada una, y el viento no era demasiado, salvo muy suave; y esto ayuda el cognoscimiento que de allí yendo al Austro se va mas alto, y andando hácia el Septentrion, como entonces se va descendiendo.

Muy conoscido tengo que las aguas de la mar llevan su curso de Oriente á Occidente con los cielos, y que allí en esta comarca cuando pasan llevan mas veloce camino, y por esto han comido tanta parte de la tierra, porque por eso son acá tantas islas, y ellas mismas hacen desto testimonio, porque todas á una mano

[1] The feast of the Assumption.
[2] Probably six A.M.   [3] Nine P.M.

east, or a little more obliquely north-west and south-east, are broad; while those which lie north and south, or north-east and south-west, that is, in a directly contrary direction to the said winds, are narrow; furthermore, that these islands should possess the most costly productions, is to be accounted for by the mild temperature, which comes to them from heaven, since these are the most elevated parts of the world. It is true, that in some parts, the waters do not appear to take this course, but this only occurs in certain spots, where they are obstructed by land, and hence they appear to take different directions.

Pliny writes that the sea and land together form a sphere, but that the ocean forms the greatest mass, and lies uppermost, while the earth is below and supports the ocean, and that the two afford a mutual support to each other, as the kernel of a nut is confined by its shell. The Master of scholastic history, in commenting upon Genesis, says, that the waters are not very extensive; and that although when they were first created they covered the earth, they were yet

---

son largas de Poniente á Levante, y Norueste é Sueste ques un poco mas alto ó bajo, y angostas de Norte á Sur, y Nordeste Sudueste, que son en contrario de los otros dichos vientos, y aquí en ellas todas nascen cosas preciosas por la suave temperancia que les procede del cielo por estar hácia el mas alto del mundo. Verdad es que parece en algunos lugares que las aguas no hagan este curso; mas esto no es, salvo particularmente en algunos lugares donde alguna tierra le está al encuentro, y hace parecer que andan diversos caminos.

Plinio escribe que la mar ó la tierra hace todo una esfera, y pone questa mar Oceana sea la mayor cantidad del agua, y está hácia el cielo, y que la tierra sea debajo y que le sostenga, y mezclado es uno con otro como el amago de la nuez con una tela gorda que va abrazado en ello. El Maestro de la Historia escolástica sobre el Genesis dice que las aguas son muy pocas, que bien que cuando fueron criadas que cobijasen toda la tierra que entonces eran vaporables en manera de niebla, y que despues que

vaporous like a cloud, and that afterwards they became condensed, and occupied but small space, and in this notion Nicolas de Lira agrees. Aristotle says that the world is small, and the water very limited in extent, and that it is easy to pass from Spain to the Indies; and this is confirmed by Avenruyz,[1] and by the Cardinal Pedro de Aliaco, who, in supporting this opinion, shows that it agrees with that of Seneca, and says that Aristotle had been enabled to gain information respecting the world by means of Alexander the Great, and Seneca by means of the Emperor Nero, and Pliny through the Romans; all of them having expended large sums of money, and employed a vast number of people, in diligent inquiry concerning the secrets of the world, and in spreading abroad the knowledge thus obtained. The said cardinal allows to these writers greater authority than to Ptolemy, and other Greeks and Arabs; and in confirmation of their opinion concerning the small quantity of water on the surface of the globe, and the limited amount of land covered by that water, in comparison of what had been re-

---

fueron sólidas ó juntadas que ocuparon muy poco lugar, y en esto concierta Nicolao de Lira. El Aristotel dice que este mundo es pequeño y es el agua muy poca, y que facilmente se puede pasar de España á las Indias, y esto confirma el Avenruyz y le alega el Cardenal Pedro de Aliaco, autorizando este decir y aquel de Séneca, el cual conforma con estos diciendo que Aristoteles pudo saber muchos secretos del mundo á causa de Alejandro Magno, y Séneca á causa de Cesar Nero y Plinio por respecto de los Romanos, los cuales todos gastaron dineros ó gente, y pusieron mucha diligencia en saber los secretos del mundo y darlos á entender á los pueblos; el cual Cardenal da á estos grande autoridad mas que á Tolomeo ni á otros Griegos ni Arabes, y á confirmacion de decir quel agua sea poca y quel cubierto del mundo della sea poco, al respecto de lo que se decia por autoridad de Tolomeo y de sus secuaces: á esto trae una autoridad de Esdras

[1] Averrhóes, an Arabian philosopher of the twelfth century.

lated on the authority of Ptolemy and his disciples, he finds a passage in the third book of Esdras, where that sacred writer says, that of seven parts of the world six are discovered, and the other is covered with water. The authority of the third and fourth books of Esdras is also confirmed by holy persons, such as St. Augustin, and St. Ambrose in his *Exameron,* where he says,—"Here my son Jesus shall first come, and here my son Christ shall die!" These holy men say that Esdras was a prophet as well as Zacharias, the father of St. John, and *El Braso*[1] Simon; authorities which are also quoted by Francis de Maïrones.[2] With respect to the dryness of the land, experience has shown that it is greater than is commonly believed; and this is no wonder, for the further one goes the more one learns.

I now return to my subject of the land of Gracia, and of the river and lake found there, which latter might more properly be called a sea; for a lake is but a small expanse of water, which, when it becomes great, deserves the name of a sea, just as we speak of the Sea of Galilee and the Dead

---

del 3°. libro suyo, adonde dice que de siete partes del mundo las seis son descubiertas y la una es cubierta de agua, la cual autoridad es aprobada por Santos, los cuales dan autoridad al 3°. ó 4°. libro de Esdras, ansí como es S. Agustin é S. Ambrosio en su *examaron,* adonde alega allí vendrá mi hijo Jesus é morira mi hijo Cristo, y dicen que Esdrás fue Profeta, y asimismo Zacarías, padre de S. Juan, y el braso Simon; las cuales autoridades tambien alega Francisco de Maïrones: en cuanto en esto del enjuto de la tierra mucho se ha experimentado ques mucho mas de lo quel vulgo crea; y no es maravilla, porque andando mas mas se sabe.

Torno á mi propósito de la tierra de Gracia y rio y lago que allí fallé, atan grande que mas se le puede llamar mar que lago, porque *lago* es lugar de agua, y en seyendo grande se dice *mar,* como se dijo á la mar de Galilea y al mar Muerto, y digo que sino

[1] This expression is described by the ancient copyist of the letter as being "badly written"; probably miscopied for "El beato", "The blessed."

[2] A Scotist of the fourteenth century, surnamed "Doctor illuminatus et acutus."

Sea; and I think that if the river mentioned does not proceed from the terrestrial paradise, it comes from an immense tract of land situated in the south, of which no knowledge has been hitherto obtained. But the more I reason on the subject, the more satisfied I become that the terrestrial paradise is situated in the spot I have described; and I ground my opinion upon the arguments and authorities already quoted. May it please the Lord to grant your Highnesses a long life, and health and peace to follow out so noble an investigation; in which I think our Lord will receive great service, Spain considerable increase of its greatness, and all Christians much consolation and pleasure, because by this means the name of our Lord will be published abroad.

In all the countries visited by your Highnesses' ships, I have caused a high cross to be fixed upon every headland, and have proclaimed, to every nation that I have discovered, the lofty estate of your Highnesses, and of your court in Spain. I also tell them all I can respecting our holy faith and of the belief in the holy mother Church, which has its members in all the world; and I speak to them also of the

---

procede del Paraiso terrenal que viene este rio y procede de tierra infinita, pues al Austro, de la cual fasta agora no se ha habido noticia, mas yo muy asentado tengo en el anima que allí adonde dije es el Paraiso terrenal, y descanso sobre las razones y autoridades sobre-escriptas.

Plega á nuestro Señor de dar mucha vida y salud y descanso á vuestras Altezas para que puedan proseguir esta tan noble empresa, en la cual me parece que rescibe nuestro Señor mucho servicio, y la España crece de mucha grandeza, y todos los Cristianos mucha consolacion y placer, porque aquí se divulgará el nombre de nuestro Señor; y en todas las tierras adonde los navíos de vuestras Altezas van, y en todo cabo mando plantar una alta cruz, y á toda la gente que hallo notifico el estado de vuestras Altezas y como su asiento es en España, y les digo de nuestra santa fe todo lo que yo puedo, y de la creencia de la Santa Madre Iglesia, la cual tiene sus miembros en todo el mundo, y les digo la policía

courtesy and nobleness of all Christians, and of the faith they have in the Holy Trinity. May it please the Lord to forgive those who have calumniated and still calumniate this excellent enterprise, and oppose and have opposed its advancement, without considering how much glory and greatness will accrue from it to your Highnesses throughout all the world. They cannot state anything in disparagement of it, except its expense, and that I have not immediately sent back the ships loaded with gold. They speak this without considering the shortness of the time, and how many difficulties there are to contend with; and that every year there are individuals who singly earn by their deserts out of your Majesties' own household, more revenue than would cover the whole of this expense. Nor do they take into consideration that the princes of Spain have never gained possession of any land out of their own country, until now that your Highnesses have become the masters of another world, where our holy faith may become so much increased, and whence such stores of wealth may be derived; for although we have not sent home ships laden with gold, we have,

y nobleza de todos los Cristianos, y la fe que en la Santa Trinidad tienen; y plega á nuestro Señor de tirar de memoria á las personas que han impugnado y impugnan tan excelente empresa, y impiden y impidieron porque no vaya adelante, sin considerar cuanta honra y grandeza es del Real Estado da vuestras Altezas en todo el mundo; no saben que entreponer á maldecir de esto, salvo que se hace gasto en ello, y porque luego no enviaron los navíos cargados de oro sin considerar la brevedad del tiempo y tantos inconvenientes como acá se han habido, y no considerar que en Castilla en casa de vuestras Altezas salen cada año personas que por su merecimiento ganaron en ella mas de renta cada uno dellos mas de lo ques necesario que se gaste en esto; ansimesmo sin considerar que ningunos Príncipes de España jamas ganaron tierra alguna fuera della, salvo agora que vuestras Altezas tienen acá otro mundo, de adonde puede ser tan acrescentada nuestra santa fe, y de donde se podrán sacar tantos provechos, que bien que no

nevertheless, sent satisfactory samples, both of gold and of other valuable commodities, by which it may be judged that in a short time large profit may be derived. Neither do they take into consideration the noble spirit of the princes of Portugal, who so long ago carried into execution the exploration of Guinea, and still follow it up along the coast of Africa, in which one-half of the population of the country has been employed, and yet the King is more determined on the enterprise than ever. The Lord grant all that I have said, and lead them to think deeply upon what I have written; which is not the thousandth part of what might be written of the deeds of princes who have set their minds upon gaining knowledge, and upon obtaining territory and keeping it.

I say all this, not because I doubt the inclination of your Highnesses to pursue the enterprise while you live,—for I rely confidently on the answers your Highnesses once gave me by word of mouth,—nor because I have seen any change in your Highnesses, but from the fear of what I have heard from those of whom I have been speaking; for I know that

se hayan enviado los navíos cargados de oro, se han enviado suficientes muestras dello y de otras cosas de valor, por donde se puede juzgar que en breve tiempo se podrá haber mucho provecho, y sin mirar el gran corazon de los Príncipes de Portugal que há tanto tiempo que prosiguen la impresa de Guinea, y prosiguen aquella de Africa, adonde han gastado la mitad de la gente de su Reino, y agora está el Rey mas determinado á ello que nunca. Nuestro Señor provea en esto como yo dije, y les ponga en memoria de considerar de todo esto que va escripto, que no es de mil partes la una de lo que yo podria escrebir de cosas de Príncipes que se ocuparon á saber y conquistar y sostener.

Todo esto dije, y no porque crea que la voluntad de vuestras Altezas sea salvo proseguir en ello en cuanto vivan, y tengo por muy firme lo que me respondió vuestras Altezas una vez que por palabra le decir desto, no porque yo hobiese visto mudamiento ninguno en vuestras Altezas salvo por temor de lo que yo oia

water dropping on a stone will at length make a hole. Your Highnesses responded to me with that nobleness of feeling which all the world knows you to possess, and told me to pay no attention to these calumniations; for that your intention was to follow up and support the undertaking, even if nothing were gained by it but stones and sand. Your Highnesses also desired me to be in no way anxious about the expense, for that much greater cost had been incurred on much more trifling matters, and that you considered all the past and future expense as well laid out; for that your Highnesses believed that our holy faith would be increased, and your royal dignity enhanced, and that they were no friends of the royal estate who spoke ill of the enterprise.

And now, during the despatch of the information respecting these lands which I have recently discovered, and where I believe in my soul that the earthly paradise is situated, the "Adelantado" will proceed with three ships, well stocked with provisions, on a further investigation, and will make all the discoveries he can about these parts. Meanwhile, I shall send your Highnesses this letter, accompanied by a map of

---

destos que yo digo, y tanto da una gotera de agua en una piedra que le hace un agujero; y vuestras Altezas me respondió con aquel corazon que se sabe en todo el mundo que tienen, y me dijo que no curase de nada de eso, porque su voluntad era de proseguir esta empresa y sostenerla, aunque no fuese sino piedras y peñas, y quel gasto que en ello se hacia que lo tenia en nada, que en otras cosas no tan grandes gastaban mucho mas, y que lo tenian todo por muy bien gastado lo del pasado y lo que se gastase en adelante, porque creian que nuestra santa fe sería acrecentada y su Real Señorío ensanchado, y que no eran amigos de su Real Estado aquellos que les maldecian de esta empresa: y agora entre tanto que vengan á noticia desto destas tierras que agora nuevamente he descubierto, en que tengo asentado en el ánima que allí es el Paraiso terrenal, irá el Adelantado con tres navíos bien ataviados para ello á ver mas adelante, y descubrirán todo lo que pudieren haciá aquellas partes. Entretanto yo enviaré á vuestras Altezas esta escriptura y la pin-

the country, and your Majesties will determine on what is to
be done, and give your orders as to how it is your pleasure
that I should proceed: the which, by the aid of the Holy
Trinity, shall be carried into execution with all possible diligence, in the faithful service and to the entire satisfaction of
your Majesties. Thanks be to God.

tura de la tierra, y acordarán lo que en ello se deba facer, y me
enviarán á mandar, y se cumplirá con ayuda de la Santa Trinidad
con toda diligencia en manera que vuestras Altezas sean servidos
y hayan placer. Deo gracias.

LETTER

Of the Admiral to the (quondam) nurse[1] of the Prince John, written near the end of the year 1500.

MOST virtuous lady: Although it is a novelty for me to complain of the ill-usage of the world, it is, nevertheless, no novelty for the world to practise ill-usage. Innumerable are the contests which I have had with it, and I have resisted all its attacks until now, when I find, that neither strength nor prudence is of any avail to me: it has cruelly reduced me to the lowest ebb. Hope in Him who created us all is my support: His assistance I have always found near at hand. On one occasion, not long since, when I was extremely depressed, He raised me with His Divine arm, saying:

CARTA

Del Almirante al ama (que habia sido) del Principe D. Juan, escrita hacia fines del año 1500.

MUY virtuosa Señora: Si mi queja del mundo es nueva, su uso de maltratar es de muy antiguo. Mil combates me ha dado y á todos resistí fasta agora que no me aprovechó armas ni avisos. Con crueldad me tiene echado al fondo. La esperanza de aquel que crió á todos me sostiene: su socorro fue siempre muy presto. Otra vez, y no de lejos estando yo mas bajo, me levantó con su brazo divino, diciendo: *ó hombre de poca fe, levantate que yo soy, no hayas miedo.* Yo vine con amor tan entrañable á servir á estos Principes, y hé

[1] Although Zuñiga says that Doña Maria de Guzman was appointed nurse by Queen Isabella at the birth of Prince John, it is nevertheless certain that this letter was addressed by Columbus to Doña Juana de la Torres, a great favourite of the queen, sister of Antonio de Torres, who was with the admiral in the second voyage, and who bore the memorial to their Highnesses.

"O man of little faith, arise, it is I, be not afraid."[1] I offered myself with such earnest devotion to the service of these princes, and I have served them with a fidelity hitherto unequalled and unheard of. God made me the messenger of the new heaven and the new earth, of which He spoke in the Apocalypse by St. John, after having spoken of it by the mouth of Isaiah; and He showed me the spot where to find it. All proved incredulous; except the Queen my mistress, to whom the Lord gave the spirit of intelligence and great courage, and made her the heiress of all, as a dear and well beloved daughter. I went to take possession of it in her royal name. All sought to cover the ignorance in which they were sunk, by dwelling on the inconveniences and expense of the proposed enterprise. Her Highness held the contrary opinion, and supported it with all her power. Seven years passed away in deliberations, and nine have been spent in accomplishing things truly memorable, and worthy of being preserved in the history of man. Never had such a thing been conceived.

I have now reached that point, that there is no man so vile

---

servido de servicio de que jamas se oyó ni vido. Del nuevo cielo y tierra que decia nuestro Señor por S. Juan en el Apocalipse, despues de dicho por boca de Isaías, me hizo dello mensagero, y amostró en cual parte. En todos hobo incredulidad, y á la Reina mi Señor dió dello el espíritu de inteligencia y esfuerzo grande, y lo hizo de todo heredera como á cara y muy amada hija. La posesion de todo esto fuí yo á tomar en su Real nombre. La ignorancia en que habian estado todos quisieron enmendallo traspasando el poco saber á fablar en inconvenientes y gastos. Su Alteza lo aprobaba al contrario, y lo sostuvo fasta que pudo. Siete años se pasaron en la platica y nueve ejecutando cosas muy señaladas y dignas de memoria se pasaron en este tiempo: de todo no se fizo

[1] This is related by his son Don Ferdinand, in cap. 84 of his history, and is more amply described in the letter addressed by Columbus to the sovereigns, describing his fourth voyage. It took place the day after Christmas day, 1499.

but thinks it his right to insult me. The day will come when the world will reckon it a virtue to him who has not given his consent to their abuse. If I had plundered the Indies, even to the country where is the fabled altar of St. Peter's, and had given them all to the Moors, they could not have shown towards me more bitter enmity than they have done in Spain. Who would believe such things of a country where there has always been so much nobility? I should much like to clear myself of this affair, if only it were consistent with etiquette to do so, face to face with my queen. The support which I have found in our Lord, and in her Highness, made me persevere, and, in order to relieve somewhat the griefs which death had occasioned her,[1] I undertook another voyage to the new heavens and new earth, which had been hitherto concealed; and if these are not appreciated in Spain, like the other parts of the Indies, it is not at all wonderful, since it is to my labours that they are indebted for them. The Holy Spirit encompassed St.

---

concepto. Llegué yo y estoy que non ha nadie tan vil que no piense de ultrajarme. Por virtud se contará en el mundo á quien puede no consentillo. Si yo robara las Indias ó tierra que san face[2] en ello de que agora es la fabla del altar de S. Pedro, y las diera á los moros, no pudieran en España amostrarme mayor enemiga. Quién creyera tal adonde hobo siempre tanta nobleza? Yo mucho quisiera despedir del negocio si fuera honesto para con mi Reina: el esfuerzo de nuestro Señor y de su Alteza fizo que yo continuase, y por aliviarle algo de los enojos en que á causa de la muerte estabo, cometí viaje nuevo al nuevo cielo é mundo, que fasta entonces estaba en oculto, y sino es tenido allí en estima, así como los otros de las Indias, no es maravilla porque salió á parecer de mi industria. A S. Pedro abrasó el Espíritu Santo y

[1] He refers to the death of Prince John, which occurred in Salamanca, on the fourth of October 1497.

[2] There is no sense in this expression, nor as it is given in the "Codice Colombo Americano", where it stands thus: "que jaz hase ellas de que", etc. Perhaps "hase" is miscopied for "hacia" "towards."

Peter, and the rest of the twelve, who all had conflicts here below; they wrought many works, they suffered great fatigues, but at last they obtained the victory. I believed that this voyage to Paria would produce a certain amount of contentment, because of the pearls and the discovery of gold in the island of Española. I left orders for the people to fish for pearls, and collect them together, and made an agreement with them that I should return for them; and I was given to understand that the supply would be abundant.

If I have not written respecting this to their Highnesses, it is because I wished first to render an equally favourable account of the gold; but it has happened with this as with many other things; I should not have lost them, and with them my honour, if I had been only occupied about my own private interests, and had suffered Española to be lost, or even if they had respected my privileges and the treaties. I say the same with regard to the gold which I had then collected, and which I have brought in safety, by Divine grace, after so much loss of life and such excessive fatigues.

In the voyage which I made by way of Paria, I found nearly half the colonists of Española in a state of revolt, and they have made war upon me until now as if I had been a

---

con él otros doce, y todos combatieron acá, y los trabajos y fatigas fueron muchas; en fin de todo llevaron la victoria. Este viaje de Paria creí que apaciguara algo por las perlas y la fallada del oro en la Española. Las perlas mandé yo ayuntar y pescar á la gente con quien quedó el concierto de mi vuelta por ellas, y á mi comprender á medida de fanega : si yo non lo escribí a SS. AA. fue porque así quisiera haber fecho del oro antes. Esto me salió como otras cosas muchas; no las perdiera ni mi honra si buscara yo mi bien propio y dejara perder la Española, ó se guardaran mis previlegios é asientos. Y otro tanto digo del oro que yo tenia agora junto, que con tantas muertes y trabajos, por virtud divinal, he llegado á perfecto. Cuando yo fuí á Paria fallé cuasi la mitad de la gente en la Española alzados, y me han guerreado fasta agora

Moor;[1] while on the other side, I had to contend with the no less cruel Indians. Then arrived Hojeda,[2] and he attempted to put the seal to all these disorders; he said that their Highnesses had sent him, with promises of presents, of immunities, and treaties; he collected a numerous band, for in the whole island of Española, there were few men who were not vagabonds, and there were none who had either wife or children. This Hojeda troubled me much, but he was obliged to retreat, and at his departure he said, that he would return with more ships and men, and reported also, that he had left the queen at the point of death.[3] In the meanwhile, Vincent Yañez came with four caravels; and there were some tumults and suspicions, but no further evil. The Indians reported many other caravels to the cannibals, and in Paria; and afterwards spread the news of the arrival of six other caravels, commanded by a brother of the alcalde;

como á moro, y los indios por otro cabo gravemente. En esto vino Hojeda y probó á echar el sello, y dijo que sus Altezas lo enviaban con promesas de dádivas y franquezas y paga: allegó gran cuadrilla, que en toda la Española muy pocos hay, salvo vagabundos y ninguno con muger y fijos. Este Hojeda me trabajó harto y fuele necesario de se ir, y dejó dicho que luego seria de vuelta con mas navíos y gente, y que dejaba la Real persona de la Reina á la muerte. En esto llegó Viceinte Yañez con cuatro carabelas: hobo alboroto y sospechas, mas no daño. Los indios dijeron de otras muchas á los canibales y en Paria, y despues una nueva de seis otras carabelas que traía un hermano

[1] After the admiral had discovered the island of Trinidad, he sailed along the coast of Paria, discovered the island of Margarita, and entered the harbour of San Domingo the thirtieth of August 1498, where he found the colony in rebellion, and the Spaniards embroiled in quarrels, both with each other and with the Indians.

[2] Alonzo de Hojeda reached Española on the fifth of September 1498.

[3] Roldan was by this time reconciled to the Admiral, and the rebellion was allayed, when Hojeda arrived, making great boast of his favour with bishop Fonseca, Columbus' enemy, and endeavoured to excite fresh animosity against him; but he had to leave Española completely.

but this was from pure malice, and at a time when at length there remained but little hope that their Highnesses would send any more ships to the Indies, and we no longer expected them, and when it was said openly that her Highness (the queen) was dead. At this time, one Adrian attempted a new revolt, as he had done before;[1] but our Lord did not permit his evil designs to succeed. I had determined not to inflict punishment on any person, but his ingratitude obliged me, however regretfully, to abandon this resolution. I should not have acted otherwise with my own brother, if he had sought to assassinate me, and to rob me of the lordship which my sovereigns had given to my keeping. This Adrian, as is now evident, had sent Don Ferdinand to Xaragua, to assemble some of his partisans, and had some discussions with the alcalde, which ended in violence, but all without any good. The alcalde seized him and a part of his band; and in fact, executed justice without my having ordered it. While they were in prison, they were expecting a caravel, in which they hoped to embark; but the news which I told them of what had

---

del Alcalde, mas fue con malicia, y esto fue ya á la postre cuando ya estaba muy rota la esperanza que sus Altezas hobiesen jamas de enviar navíos á las Indias, ni nos esperarlos, y que vulgarmente decian que su Alteza era muerta. Un Adrian en este tiempo probó alzarse otra vez como de antes, mas nuestro Señor no quiso que llegase á efecto su mal propósito. Yo tenia propuesto en mi de no tocar el cabello á nadie, y á este por su ingratitud con lágrimas no se pudo guardar, así como yo lo tenia pensado. A mi hermano no hiciera menos si me quisiera matar y robar el señorío que mi Rey é Reina me tenian dado en guarda. Este Adrian, segun se muestra, tenia enviado á D. Fernando á Jaragua á allegar á algunos sus secuaces, y allá hobo debate con el Alcalde, adonde nació discordia de muerte; mas no llegó á efecto. El Alcalde le prendió y á parte de su cuadrilla: y el caso era que él los justiciaba sin que yo lo proveyere: estovieren presos esperando carabela en que se fuesen: las nuevas de Hojeda que yo dije

[1] Adrian Mogica, who had been one of the rebels with Roldan.

happened to Hojeda, deprived them of the hope that he would arrive in this ship. It is now six months that I have been ready to leave, to bring to their Highnesses the good news of the gold, and to give up the government of these dissolute people, who fear neither God nor their king nor queen, but are full of imbecility and malice. I should have been able to pay every one with six hundred thousand maravedis, and for this purpose there were four millions and more of the tithes, without reckoning the third part of the gold.

Before my departure (from Spain) I have often entreated their Highnesses to send to these parts, at my expense, some one charged to administer justice; and since, when I found the alcalde in a state of revolt, I have besought them afresh to send at least one of their servants with letters, because I myself have had so strange a character given to me, that if I were to build churches or hospitals, they would call them caves for robbers. Their Highnesses provided for this at last, but in a manner quite unequal to the urgency of the circumstances; however, let that point rest, since such is their good pleasure. I remained two years in Spain without being able to obtain anything for myself, or those who came

---

ficieron perder la esperanza que ya no venia. Seis meses habia que yo estaba despachado para venir á sus Altezas con las buenas nuevas del oro y fuir de gobernar gente disoluta que no teme á Dios ni á su Rey ni Reina, llena de achaques y de malicias. A la gente acabara yo de pagar con seiscientos mil maravedises: y para ello habia cuatro cuentos de diezmos ó alguno sin el tercio del oro. Antes de mi partida supliqué tantas veces á sus Altezas que enviasen allá á mi costa á quien tuviese cargo de la justicia, y despues que fallé alzado al Alcalde se lo supliqué de nuevo ó por alguna gente, ó al menos algun criado con cartas, porque mi fama es tal que aunque yo faga iglesias y hospitales siempre serán dichas espeluncas para latrones. Proveyeron ya al fin, y fue muy al contrario de lo que la negociacion demandaba: vaya en buena hora, pues que es á su grado. Yo estuve allá dos años sin poder

with me,[1] but this man has gained for himself a full purse: God knows if all will be employed for his service. Already, to begin with, there is a revenue for twenty years, which is, according to man's calculation, an age; and they gather gold in such abundance, that there are people who, in four hours, have found the equivalent of five marks; but I will speak on this subject more fully hereafter. If their Highnesses would condescend to silence the popular rumours, which have gained credence among those who know what fatigues I have sustained, it would be a real charity; for calumny has done me more injury than the services which I have rendered to their Highnesses, and the care with which I have preserved their property and their government, have done me good. By their so doing, I should be re-established in reputation, and spoken of throughout the universe: for the matter is of a kind which must every day be more talked of and appreciated.

In the meanwhile, the commander Bobadilla arrived at St. Domingo,[2] at which time I was at La Vega, and the Ade-

---

ganar una provision de favor para mí ni por los que allá fuesen, y este llevó una arca llena: si pararán todas á su servicio Dios lo sabe. Ya por comienzos hay franquezas por veinte años, que es la edad de un hombre, y se coge el oro, que hobo persona de cinco marcos en cuatro horas, de que diré despues mas largo. Si pluguiese á sus Altezas de desfacer un vulgo de los que saben mis fatigas, que mayor daño me ha hecho el mal decir de las gentes que no me ha aprovechado el mucho servir y guardar su facienda y senorío, seria limosna, é yo restituido en mi honra, é se fablaria dello en todo el mundo, porquel negocio es de calidad que cada dia ha de ser mas sonada y en alta estima. En esto vino el Comendador Bobadilla á Santo Domingo, yo estaba en la Vega y

[1] Columbus returned to Cadiz from his second voyage, on the 11th of June, 1496. He was well received by the sovereigns, and they gave orders for preparing the requisites for a third voyage; but the fulfilment of these orders was delayed by Bishop Fonseca until the 30th of May, 1498.

[2] Francesco de Bobadilla, commander of the order of Calatrava, reached San Domingo on the 23rd of August, 1500.

lantado at Xaragua, where this Adrian had made his attempt; but by that time everything was quiet, the land was thriving, and the people at peace. The day after his arrival he declared himself governor, created magistrates, ordered executions, published immunities from the collection of gold and from the paying of tithes; and, in fine, announced a general franchise for twenty years, which is, as I have said, the calculation of an age. He also gave out that he was going to pay everyone, although they had not even done the service which was due up to that day; and he further proclaimed that he had to send me back loaded with chains, and my brother also (this he has done) ;[1] and that neither I, nor any of my family, should ever return to these lands : and, in addition, he made innumerable unjust and disgraceful charges against me. All this took place, as I have said, on the very day after his arrival, at which time I was absent at a distance, thinking neither of him nor of his coming. Some letters of their Highnesses, of which he brought a considerable number signed in blank, he filled up with exaggerated language, and sent round to the alcalde and his myrmidons, accompanying them with compliments and flattery. To me

---

el Adelantado en Jaragua, donde este Adrian habia hecho cabeza, mas ya todo era llano y la tierra rica, y en paz toda. El segundo dia que llegó se crió Gobernador y fizo oficiales y ejecuciones, y apregonó franquezas del oro y diezmos, y generalmente de toda otra cosa por veinte años, que como digo es la edad de un hombre, y que venia para pagar á todos, bien que no habian servido llenamente hasta ese dia, y publicó que á mi me habia de enviar en fierros, y á mis hermanos, así como lo ha fecho, y que nunca yo volveria mas allí ni otro de mi linage, diciendo de mi mil deshonestidades y descorteses cosas. Esto todo fue el segundo dia quel llegó, como dije, y estando yo lejos absente sin saber dello ni de su venida. Unas cartas de sus Altezas firmadas en blanco, de

[1] This expression of the Admiral's, makes it appear that he wrote this letter when he was near reaching Cadiz, on the 25th of November, 1500.

he never sent either a letter or a messenger, nor has he done so to this day. Reflect upon this, madam ! what could any man in my situation think ? Could it be that honour and favour were to be conferred on him who had lent himself to plundering their Highnesses of their sovereignty, and who had done so much injury and mischief ?—Could it be that he who had defended and preserved their cause through so many dangers, was to be dragged through the mire ? When I heard this, I thought he must be like Hojeda, or one of the other rebels ; but I held my peace, when I learned for certain, from the friars, that he had been sent by their Highnesses. I wrote to him, to salute him on his arrival, to let him know that I was ready to set out to go to court, and that I had put up to sale all that I possessed. I entreated him not to be in haste on the subject of the grants ; and I assured him that I would shortly yield this, and everything else connected with the government, implicitly into his charge. I wrote the same thing to the ecclesiastics, but I received no answer either from the one or the other. On the contrary, he took a hostile position, and obliged those

---

que el llevaba una cantidad, hinchó y envió al Alcalde y á su compañía con favores y encomiendas. A mi nunca me envió carta ni mensagero, ni me ha dado fasta hoy. Piense vuestra merced qué pensaria quien tuviera mi cargo ? honrar y favorecer á quien probó á robar á sus Altezas el señorío, y ha fecho tanto mal y daño! y arrastrar á quien con tantos peligros se lo sostuvo ? Cuando supe esto, creí que esto seria como lo de Hojeda, ó uno de los otros: templóme que supe de los frailes de cierto que sus Altezas lo enviaban. Escrebile yo que su venida fuese en buena hora, y que yo estaba despachado para ir á la corte, y fecho almoneda de cuanto yo tenia, y que en esto de las franquezas que no se acelerase, que esto y el gobierno yo se lo daria luego tan llano como la palma, y así lo escribía a los religiosos. Ni él ni ellos me dieron respuesta, antes se puso él en son de guerra, y apremiaba á cuantos allí iban que le jurasen por Gobernador, dijeronme que por veinte años. Luego que yo supe de estas franquezas pensé

M

who went to his residence to acknowledge him for governor, as I have been told, for twenty years. As soon as I knew what he had done with regard to the immunities, I proposed to repair this great mistake, and I thought he would himself be glad of it; for, without any reason or necessity, he had bestowed upon vagabonds privileges of such importance, that they would have been excessive even for men with wives and children. I published verbally, and in writing, that he could not make use of his credentials, because mine were of higher authority, and I showed the grants brought by Juan Aguado. All this I did for the purpose of gaining time, that their Highnesses might be informed as to the state of the country, and that they might have opportunity to give fresh orders upon everything touching their interests. It is useless to publish such grants in the Indies,—all is in favour of the settlers who have taken up their abode there, because the best lands are given up to them; and, at a low estimate, they are worth two hundred thousand maravedis a head for the four years, at which they are taken, without a single stroke of the mattock. I should not say so much if these people were married men; but there are not six among them

---

de adobar un yerro tan grande, y que él seria contento, las cuales dió sin necesidad y causa de cosa tan gruesa y á gente vagabunda, que fuera demasiado para quien trujera muger y hijos. Publiqué por palabra y por cartas que él no podia usar de sus provisiones, porque las mias eran las mas fuertes, y les mostré las franquezas que llevó Juan Aguado. Todo esto que yo fice era por dilatar, porque sus Altezas fuesen sabidores del estado de la tierra, y hobiesen lugar de tornar á mandar en ello lo que fuese su servicio. Tales franquezas escusado es de las apregonar en las Indias. Los vecinos que han tomado vecindad es logro, porque se les dan las mejores tierras y á poco valer valerán docientos mil maravedis al cabo de los cuatro años que la vecindad se acaba, sin que den una azadonada en ellas. No diria yo así si los vecinos fuesen casados, mas no hay seis entre todos que no esten sobre el aviso de ayuntar lo que pudieren y se ir en buena hora. De Castilla seria bien que

all, whose purpose is not to amass all they can, and then decamp with it. It would be well that people should come from Spain, but that only such should be sent as are well known, so that the country may be peopled with honest men. I had agreed with these settlers that they should pay the third of the gold and of the tithes ; and this they not only assented to, but were very grateful to their Highnesses. I reproached them when I heard they had afterwards refused it ; they expected, however, to deal with me on the same terms as with the commander, but I would not consent to it. He meanwhile irritated them against me, saying, that I wished to deprive them of that which their Highnesses had given them ; and strove to make me appear their enemy, in which he succeeded to the full. He induced them to write to their Highnesses, that they should send me no more commissioned as governor (truly I do not desire it any more for myself, or for any who belong to me, while the people remain unchanged) ; and to conciliate them, he ordered inquiries to be made respecting me with reference to imputed misdeeds, such as were never invented in hell. But God is above, who with so much wisdom and power rescued Daniel and the three children,

fuesen, y aun saber quién y cómo, y se poblase de gente honrada. Yo tenia asentado con estos vecinos que pagarian el tercio del oro y los diezmos, y esto á su ruego, y lo recibieron en grande merced de sus Altezas. Reprendiles cuando yo oí que se dejaban dello, y esperaban quél conmigo faria otro tanto, mas fue el contrario. Indignólos contra mí diciendo, que yo les queria quitar lo que sus Altezas les daban, y trabajo de me los echar acuestas, y lo hizo, y que escribiesen á sus Altezas que no me enviasen mas al cargo, y así se lo suplico yo por mí y por toda cosa mia, en cuanto no haya otro pueblo, y me ordenó él con ellos pesquisas de maldades que al infierno nunca se supo de las semejantes. Allí está nuestro Señor que escapó á Daniel y á los tres muchachos con tanto saber y fuerza como tenia, y con tanto aparejo si le pluguiere como con su gana. Supiera yo remediar todo esto y lo otro que está dicho

and who, if he please, can rescue me with a similar manifestation of his power, and to the advancement of his own cause. I should have known well enough how to find a remedy for the evils which I now describe and have been describing as having happened to me since I came to the Indies, if I had had the wish or had thought it decent, to busy myself about my personal interest; but now I find myself undone, because I have hitherto maintained the justice and augmented the territorial dominions of their Highnesses. Now that so much gold is found, these people stop to consider whether they can obtain the greatest quantity of it by theft, or by going to the mines. For one woman they give a hundred castellanos,[1] as for a farm; and this sort of trading is very common, and there are already a great number of merchants who go in search of girls; there are at this moment from nine or ten on sale; they fetch a good price, let their age be what it will. I assert that when I said that the commander could not confer immunities, I did what he desired, although I told him that it was to gain time until their Highnesses had received information respecting the country, and had given their orders as to the regulations best calculated to

---

y ha pasado despues que estoy en las Indias, si me consintiera la voluntad á procurar por mi bien propio y me fuera honesto. Mas el sostener de la justicia y acrecentar el señorío de sus Altezas fasta agora, me tiene al fondo. Hoy en dia que se falla tanto oro hay division en que haya mas ganancia, ir robando ó ir á las minas. Por una muger tambien se fallan cien castellanos como por una labranza, y es mucho en uso, y ha ya fartos mercaderes que andan buscando muchachas: de nueve á diez son agora en precio: de todas edades ha de tener un bueno. Digo que en decir yo que el Comendador no podia dar franquezas que hice yo lo que él deseaba; bien que yo á él dijese que era para dilatar fasta que sus Altezas toviesen el aviso de la tierra y tornasen á ver y mandar lo que fuese su servicio. Digo que la fuerza del maldecir de desconcertados me ha hecho mas daño que mis servicios fecho

[1] An ancient gold coin, varying in value under different kings.

advance their interest. I assert that the calumnies of injurious men have done me more harm, than my services have done me good : which is a bad example for the present as well as for the future. I declare solemnly that a great number of men have been to the Indies, who did not deserve baptism in the eyes of God or men, and who are now returning thither. The governor has made every one hostile to me ; and it appears, from the manner of his acting, and the plans that he has adopted, that he was already my enemy, and very virulent against me when he arrived ; and it is said, that he has been at great expense to obtain this office : but I know nothing about the matter except what I have heard. I never before heard of any one who was commissioned to make an inquiry, assembling the rebels, and taking, as evidence against their governor, wretches without faith, and who are unworthy of unbelief. If their Highnesses would cause a general inquiry to be made throughout the land, I assure you they would be astonished, that the island has not been swallowed up. I believe that you will recollect, that when I was driven by a tempest into the port of Lisbon (having lost my sails), 1 was falsely accused of having put in thither with the intention of giving the Indies to the sovereign of

---

provecho : mal ejemplo es por lo presente y por lo futuro. Fago juramento que cantidad de hombres han ido á las Indias que no merescian el agua para con Dios y con el mundo, y agora vuelven allá. Enemistólos á ellos todos conmigo, y él parece, segun se hobo y segun sus formas, que ya lo venia y bien encendido, ó es que se dice que ha gastado mucho por venir á este negocio ; no se dello mas de lo que oyo. Yo nunca oí que el pesquisidor allegase los rebeldes y los tomase por testigos contra aquel que gobierna á ellos y á otros sin fe, ni dignos della. Si sus Altezas mandasen hacer una pesquisa general allí vos digo yo que verian por gran maravilla como la isla no sé funde. Yo creo que se acordará vuestra merced cuando lo tormenta sin velas me echó en Lisbona, que fuí acusado falsamente que habia ido ya allá al Rey para darle las Indias. Despues supieron sus Altezas al contrario, y que todo

that country. Since then, their Highnesses have learned the contrary, and that it was all malice. Although I am an ignorant man, I do not imagine that any one supposed me so stupid as not to be aware, that even if the Indies had belonged to me, I could not support myself without the assistance of some prince. In such case where should I find better support, or more security against expulsion, than in the king and queen our sovereigns? who, from nothing, have raised me to so great an elevation, and who are the greatest princes of the world, on the land and on the sea. These princes know how I have served them, and they uphold my privileges and rewards; and if any one violates them, their Highnesses augment them by ordering great favour to be shown me, and ordain me many honours, as was shown in the affair of Juan Aguado. Yes, as I have said, their Highnesses have received some services from me, and have taken my sons into their household, which would not have happened with another prince, because where there is no attachment, all other considerations prove of little weight. If I have now spoken severely of a malicious slander, it is against my will,

---

fue con malicia. Bien que yo sepa poco: no sé quien me tenga por tan torpe que yo no conozca que aunque las Indias fuesen mias, que yo no me pudiera sostener sin ayuda de Príncipe. Si esto es así, adónde pudiera yo tener mejor arrimo y seguridad de no ser echado dellas del todo que en el Rey é Reina nuestros Señores, que de nada me han puesto en tanta honra y son los mas altos Príncipes por la mar y por la tierra del mundo? los cuales tienen que yo les haya servido, ó me guardan mis privilegios y mercedes, y si alguien me los quebranta sus Altezas me los acrescientan con aventaja, como se vido en lo de Juan Aguado, y me mandar hacer mucha honra, y como dije ya sus Altezas rescibieron de mí servicios y tienen mis hijos sus criados, lo que eu ninguna manera pudiera esto llegar con otro Príncipe, porque adonde no hay amor todo lo otro cesa. Dije yo agora ansi contra un maldecir con malicia y contra mi voluntad, porque es cosa que ni en sueños debiera allegar á memoria, porque las formas y fechos

for it is a subject I would not willingly recall even in my dreams. The governor Bobadilla has maliciously exhibited in open day his character and conduct in this affair; but I will prove without difficulty, that his ignorance, his cowardice, and his inordinate cupidity, have frustrated all his undertakings. I have already said that I wrote to him, as well as to the monks, and I set out almost alone, all our people being with the Adelantado and elsewhere, to remove suspicion; when he heard this he seized Don Diego, and sent him on board a caravel, loaded with irons; on my arrival he did the same to me; and afterwards to the Adelantado when he came. I have never spoken with him, and to this day he has not permitted any one to hold converse with me, and I solemnly declare that I cannot think for what reason I was made prisoner. His first care was to take the gold that I had, and that without measuring or weighing it, although I was absent; he said he would pay those to whom it was owing, and if I am to believe what has been reported to me, he reserved to himself the greater part, and sent for strangers to make the bargains. I had put aside some samples of this gold, some as large as a goose's or a hen's egg, and of various sizes, which a few persons had collected

del Comendador Bobadilla, con malicia las quiere alumbrar en esto: mas yo lo faré ver con el brazo izquierdo que su poco saber y gran cobardiá con desordenada cudicia le ha fecho caer en ello. Ya dije como yo le escrebí y á los frailes, y luego partí así como le dije muy solo, porque toda la gente estaba con el Adelantado, y tambien por le quitar de sospecha: él cuando lo supo echó á D. Diego preso en una carabela cargado de fierros, y á mi en llegando fizo otro tanto, y despues al Adelantado, cuando vino. Ni le fablé mas á él ni consintió que hasta hoy nadie me haya fablado, y fago juramento que no puedo pensar por qué sea yo preso. La primera diligencia que fizo fue á tomar el oro, el cual hobo sin medida ni peso, ó yo absente dijo que queria él pagar dello á la gente, y segun oí para sí fizo la primera parte, y enviar por resgate resgatadores nuevos. Desto oro tenia yo apartado ciertas muestras,

in a short space of time, that their Highnesses might be
gratified and impressed with the importance of the affair,
when they saw a quantity of large stones full of gold. This
gold was the first that, after he had feathered his own nest
(which he was in great haste to do), his malice suggested to
give away, in order that their Highnesses might have a low
opinion of the whole affair: the gold which required melting,
diminished at the fire, and a chain weighing nearly twenty
marks disappeared altogether. I have been yet more concerned respecting this matter of the gold than even about
the affair of the pearls, that I have not been able to bring
them to their Highnesses. In every thing that he thought
could add to my annoyance, the governor has always shown
himself ready to bestir himself. Thus, as I have said, with
six hundred thousand maravedis, I should have paid every
one, without injustice to any; and I had more than four
millions of tithes and constabulary dues, without touching
the gold. He made the most absurd gifts, although I believe he began with himself first; their Highnesses will be
able to ascertain the truth on this subject when they demand
the account to be rendered them, especially if I may assist

---

granos muy gruesos como huevos como de ánsar, de gallina y de
pollas, y de otras muchas fechuras, que algunas personas tenian
cogido en breve espacio, con que se alegrasen sus Altezas, y por
ello comprendiesen el negocio con una cantidad de piedras grandes
llenas de oro. Este fue el primero á se dar con malicia, porque
sus Altezas no tuviesen este negocio en algo fasta quel tenga fecho
el nido de que se dá buena priesa. El oro que está por fundir
mengua al fuego: una cadena que pesaria fasta veinte marcos
nunca se ha visto. Yo he sido muy agraviado en esto del oro mas
aun que de las perlas, porque no las he traido á sus Altezas. El
Comendador en todo lo que le pareció que me dañaria luego fue
puesto en obra. Ya dije, con seiscientos mil maravedises pagara
á todos sin robar á nadie y habia mas de cuatro cuentos de diezmos y alguacilazgo sin tocar en el oro. Hizo unas larguezas que
son de risa, bien que creo que encomenzó en sí la primera parte:

at the examination. He is continually saying, that there is a considerable sum owing, while it is only what I have already reported, and even less. I have been wounded extremely by the thought, that a man should have been sent out to make inquiry into my conduct, who knew, that if he sent home a very aggravated account of the result of his investigation, he would remain at the head of the government. Would to God, their Highnesses had sent either him or some other person two years ago, for then I know that I should have had no cause to fear either scandal or disgrace; they could not then have taken away my honour, and I could not have been in the position to have lost it. God is just, and He will in due time make known by whom and how it has been done. Let them judge me, as a governor who had been sent to Sicily or some province or city under regular government, and where the laws could be executed without fear of danger to the public weal or subjection to any enormous wrong. I ought to be judged as a captain sent from Spain to the Indies, to conquer a nation numerous and warlike, with customs and religion altogether different to ours; a people who dwell in the mountains, without regular habi-

---

allá lo sabran sus Altezas cuando le mandaren tomar cuenta, en especial si yo estuviese á ella. El no face sino decir que se debe gran suma, y es la que yo dije y no tanto. Yo he sido muy mucho agraviado en que se haya enviado pesquisidor sobre mí, que sepa que si la pesquisa que él enviare fuere muy grave que él quedará en el gobierno.—Pluguiera á nuestro Señor que sus Altezas le enviaran á él ó á otro dos años há, porque sé que yo fuera ya libre de escándalo y de infamia, y no se me quitara mi honra ni la perdiera: Dios es justo, y ha de hacer que se sepa por que y cómo. Allí me juzgan como Gobernador que fue á Cecilia ó ciudad ó villa puesta en regimiento y adonde las leyes se pueden guardar por entero sin temor de que se pierda todo, y rescibo grande agravio. Yo debo ser juzgado como Capitan que fue de España á conquistar fasta las Indias á gente belicosa y mucha, y de costumbres y seta á nos muy contraria: los cuales viven por sierras y montes,

tations for themselves or for us; and where, by the Divine will, I have subdued another world to the dominion of the King and Queen, our sovereigns; in consequence of which, Spain, that used to be called poor, is now the most wealthy of kingdoms. I ought to be judged as a captain, who for so many years has borne arms, never quitting them for an instant. I ought to be judged by cavaliers who have themselves won the meed of victory;[1] by knights of the sword and not of title deeds; as least, so it would have been among the Greeks and Romans, or any modern nation in which exists so much nobility as in Spain; for under any other judgment I receive great injury, because in the Indies there is neither civil right nor judgment seat.

Already the road is opened to the gold and pearls, and it may surely be hoped that precious stones, spices, and a thousand other things, will also be found. Would to God that it were as certain that I should suffer no greater wrongs than I have already experienced, as it is that I would, in the name of our Lord, again undertake my first voyage; and that I would undertake to go to Arabia Felix as far as Mecca, as I

---

sin pueblo asentado ni nosotros; y adonde por voluntad Divina he puesto só el señorio del Rey é de la Reina nuestros Señores otro mundo; y por donde la España, que era dicha pobre, es la mas rica. Yo dobo ser juzgado como Capitan que de tanto tiempo fasta hoy trae las armas á cuestas sin las dejar una hora, y de Caballeros de conquistas y del uso, y no de letras, salvo si fuesen de Griegos ó de Romanos, ó de otros modernos de que hay tantos y tan nobles en España, ca de otra guisa rescibo grande agravio porque en las Indias no hay pueblo ni asiento. Del oro y perlas ya está abierta la puerta y cantidad de todo, piedras preciosas y especería, y de otras mil cosas se pueden esperar firmemente; y nunca mas mal me viniese como con el nombre de Nuestro Señor le daria el primer viage, así como diera la negociacion del Arabia

[1] The old Spaniards used to give the name of "*caballero de conquista,*" to each of the conquerors, among whom the conquered lands were divided.

have said in the letter that I sent to their Highnesses by
Antonio de Torres, in answer to the division of the sea and
land between Spain and the Portuguese; and I would go
afterwards to the North Pole, as I have said and given in
writing to the monastery of the Mejorada.

The tidings of the gold which I said I would give, are,
that on Christmas-day, being greatly afflicted and tormented
by the wicked Spaniards and the Indians, when I was at
the point of leaving all to save my life if possible, our Lord
comforted me miraculously, saying to me, "*Take courage,
be not dismayed nor fear, I will provide for all; the seven
years, the term of the gold, are not yet passed; and in this,
as in the rest, I will redress thee.*" I learned that same day,
that there were twenty-four leagues of land where they found
mines at every step, which appear now to form but one.
Some of the people collected a hundred and twenty castellanos' worth in one day, others ninety; and there have been
those who have gathered the equivalent of nearly two hundred and fifty castellanos. They consider it a good day's
work when they collect from fifty to seventy, or even from
twenty to fifty, and many continue searching; the mean day's
work is from six to twelve, and those who get less are very

---

feliz fasta la Meca, como yo escribí á sus Altezas con Antonio de
Torres en la respuesta de la reparticion del mar é tierra con los
Portugueses: y despues viniera á lo de polo artico, así coma lo
dije y dí por escripto en el monesterio de la Mejorada. Las nuevas
del oro que yo dije que daria son que dia de Navidad, estando yo
muy afligido guerreado de los malos Cristianos y de Indios, en
términos de dejar todo y escapar si pudiese la vida; me consoló
nuestro Señor milagrosamente y dijo: "*Esfuerza, no desmayes
ni temas : yo proveeré en todo ; los siete años del término del oro
no son pasados, y en ello y en lo otro te daré remedio.*" Ese dia
supe que habia ochenta leguas de tierra, y en todo cabo dellas minas ; el parecer agora es que sea toda una. Algunos han cogido
ciento y veinte castellanos en un dia, otros noventa, y se ha llegado
fasta docientos y cincuenta. De cincuenta fasta setenta, y otros

dissatisfied. It appears that these mines, like all others, do not yield equally every day; the mines are new, and those who collect their produce inexperienced. According to the judgment of everybody here, it seems that, if all Spain were to come over, every individual, however inexpert he might be, would gain the equivalent of at least one or two castellanos in a day; and so it is up to the present time. It is certain that any man who has an Indian to work for him, collects as much, but the management depends upon the Spaniard. See, now, what discernment was shown by Bobadilla when he gave up everything for nothing, and four millions of tithes without any reason, and even without being asked to do so, and without first giving notice to their Highnesses of his intention; and this is not the only evil which he has caused. I know, assuredly, that the errors which I may have fallen into, have been committed without any intention of doing wrong, and I think that their Highnesses will believe me when I say so; but I know and see that they show mercy towards those who intentionally do injury to their service. I, however, feel very certain that the day will come when they will treat me much better;

---

muchos de veinte fasta cincuenta, es tenido por buen jornal y muchos lo continuaban : el comun es seis fasta doce, y quien de aquí abaja no es contento. Parece tambien que estas minas son como las otras que responden en los dias no igualmente : las minas son nuevas y los cogedores. El parecer de todos es que aunque vaya allá toda Castilla, que por torpe que sea la persona, que no abajará de un castellano ó dos cada dia, y agora es esto así en fresco. Es verdad que el que tiene algun indio coge esto, mas el negocio con siste en el Cristiano. Ved que discrecion fue de Bobadilla dar todo por ninguno y cuatro cuentos de diezmos sin causa ni ser requerido, sin primero lo notificar á sus Altezas; y el daño no es este solo. Yo sé que mis yerros no han sido con fin de facer mal, y creo que sus Altezas lo creen así como yo lo digo; y sé y veo que usan de misericordia con quien maliciosamente los desirve. Yo creo y tengo por muy cierto que muy mejor y mas piedad

since, if I have been in error, it has been innocently and under the force of circumstances, as they will shortly understand beyond all doubt: I, who am their creature, and whose services and usefulness they will every day be more willing to acknowledge. They will weigh all in the balance, even as, according to the Holy Scripture, it will be with the evil and the good at the day of judgment. If, nevertheless, their Highnesses ordain me another judge, which I do not expect, and if my examination is to be holden in the Indies, I humbly beseech them to send over two conscientious and respectable persons at my expense, and they would readily acknowledge that, at this time, five marks of gold may be found in four hours: be it however as it may, it is highly necessary that their Highnesses should have this matter inquired into. The governor, on his arrival at St. Domingo, took up his abode in my house, and appropriated to himself all that was therein. Well and good; perhaps he was in want of it: but even a pirate does not behave in this manner towards the merchants that he plunders. That which grieves me most is the seizure of my papers, of which I have never been able to recover one; and those that would have been most use-

---

harán conmigo que caí en ello con inocencia y forzosamente, como sabran despues por entero, y el cual soy su fechura, y mirirán á mis servicíos, y cognoscerán de cada dia que son muy aventajados. Todo pornan en una balanza, así como nos cuenta la Santa Escritura que será el bien con el mal en el dia del juicio. Si todavía mandan que otro me juzgue, lo cual no espero, y que sea por pesquisa de las Indias, humilmente les suplico que envien allá dos personas de consciencia y honrados á mi costa, los cuales fallaran de ligero agora que se halla el oro cinco marcos en cuatro horas, con esto ó sin ello es muy necesario que lo provean. El Comendador, en llegando á Santo Domingo se aposentó en mi casa; así como la falló así dió todo por suyo: vaya en buena hora, quizá lo habia menester: cosario nunca tal usó con mercader. De mis escripturas tengo yo mayor queja que así me las haya tomado, que jamas se le pudo sacar una, y aquellas que mas me habian de

ful to me in proving my innocence, are precisely those which he has kept most carefully concealed. Behold the just and honest inquisitor! But whatever he may have done, they tell me that he has now bidden good bye to justice and is simply a despot. Our Lord God retains His power and wisdom as of old; and, above all things, He punishes injustice and ingratitude.

---

aprovechar en mi disculpa esas tenia mas ocultas. Ved que justo y honesto pesquisidor. Cosa de cuantas él haya hecho me dicen que haya seido con término de justicia, salvo absolutamente. Dios nuestro Señor está con sus fuerzas y saber, como solia, y castiga en todo cabo, en especial la ingratitud de injurias.

FOURTH VOYAGE OF COLUMBUS.

A Letter written by Don Christopher Columbus, Viceroy and Admiral of the Indies, to the most Christian and mighty Sovereigns, the King and Queen of Spain, in which are described the events of his voyage, and the countries, provinces, cities, rivers, and other marvellous matters therein discovered, as well as the places where gold and other substances of great richness and value are to be found.

MOST Serene, and very high and mighty Princes, the King and Queen our Sovereigns:—My passage from Cadiz to the Canary occupied four days, and thence to the Indies, from which I wrote, sixteen days. My intention was to expedite my voyage as much as possible while I had good vessels, good crews and stores, and because Jamaica was the place to which I was bound. I wrote this in Dominica.

Up to the period of my reaching these shores I expe-

CUARTO VIAGE DE COLON.

Carta que escribió D. Cristóbal Colon, Virey y Almirante de las Indias, á los Cristianísimos y muy poderosos Rey y Reina de España, nuestros Señores, en que les notifica cuanto le ha acontecido en su viage; y las tierras, provincias, ciudades, rios y otras cosas maravillosas, y donde hay minas de oro en mucha cantidad, y otras cosas de gran riqueza y valor.

SERENÍSIMOS y muy altos y poderosos Príncipes Rey é Reina, nuestros Señores: De Caliz pasé á Canaria en cuatro dias, y dende á las Indias en diez y seis dias, donde escribia. Mi intencion era dar prisa á mi viage en cuanto yo tenia los navíos buenos, la gente y los bastimentos, y que mi derrota era en el Isla Jamaica; y en la Isla Dominica escribí esto: fasta allí truje el tiempo á

rienced most excellent weather, but the night of my arrival came in with a dreadful tempest, and the same bad weather has continued ever since. On reaching the island of Española I despatched a packet of letters, by which I begged as a favour that a ship should be supplied me at my own cost in lieu of one of those that I had brought with me, and which had become unseaworthy, and could no longer carry sail. The letters were taken, and your Highnesses will know if a reply has been given to them. For my part I was forbidden to go on shore; the hearts of my people failed them lest I should take them further, and they said that if any danger were to befall them, they should receive no succour, but, on the contrary, in all probability have some great affront offered them. Moreover every man had it in his power to tell me that the new Governor would have the superintendence of the countries that I might acquire.

The tempest was terrible throughout the night, all the ships were separated, and each one driven to the last extremity, without hope of anything but death; each of them also looked upon the loss of the rest as a matter of certainty.

---

pedir por la boca. Esa noche que alli entré fué con tormenta y grande, y me persiguió despues siempre. Cuando llegué sobre la Española invié el envoltorio de cartas, y á pedir por merced un navío por mis dineros, porque otro que yo llevaba era inavegable y no sufria velas. Las cartas tomaron, y sabrán si se las dieron la respuesta. Para mí fué mandarme de parte de ahí, que yo no pasase ni llegase á la tierra: cayó el corazon á la gente que iba conmigo, por temor de los llevar yo lejos, diciendo que si algun caso de peligro les viniese que no serian remediados allí, antes les sería fecha alguna grande afrenta. Tambien á quien plugo dijo que el Comendador habia de proveer las tierras que yo ganase. La tormenta era terrible, y en aquella noche me desmembró los navíos : á cada uno llevó por su cabo sin esperanzas, salvo de muerte : cada uno de ellos tenia por cierto que los otros eran perdidos. ¿ Quién nasció, sin quitar á Job, que no muriera deses-

What man was ever born, not even excepting Job, who would not have been ready to die of despair at finding himself as I then was, in anxious fear for my own safety, and that of my son, my brother, and my friends, and yet refused permission either to land or to put into harbour on the shores which by God's mercy I had gained for Spain with so much toil and danger?

But to return to the ships: although the tempest had so completely separated them from me as to leave me single, yet the Lord restored them to me in his own good time. The ship which we had the greatest fear for, had put out to sea for safety, and reached the island of Gallega, having lost her boat and a great part of her provisions, which latter loss indeed all the ships suffered. The vessel in which I was, though dreadfully buffeted, was saved by our Lord's mercy from any injury whatever; my brother went in the ship that was unsound, and he under God was the cause of its being saved. With this tempest I struggled on till I reached Jamaica, and there the sea became calm, but there was a strong current which carried me as far as the Queen's Garden without seeing land. Hence as opportunity afforded I pushed on for terra firma, in spite of the wind and a fear-

---

perado? que por mi salvacion y de mi fijo, hermano y amigos me fuese en tal tiempo defendida la tierra y los puertos que yo, por la voluntad de Dios, gané á España sudando sangre? E torno á los navíos que así me habia llevado la tormenta y dejado á mí solo. Deparómelos nuestro Señor cuando le plugo. El navío Sospechoso habia echado à la mar, por escapar, fasta la isola la Gallega; perdió la barca, y todos gran parte de los bastimentos: en el que yo iba, abalumado á maravilla, nuestro Señor le salvó que no hubo daño de una paja. En el Sospechoso iba mi hermano; y él, despues de Dios, fue su remedio. E con esta tormenta, así a gatas, me llegué á Jamaica: allí se mudó de mar alta en calmería y grande corriente, y me llevó fasta el Jardin de la Reina sin ver tierra. De allí, cuando pude, navegué á la tierra firme; adonde

ful contrary current, against which I contended for sixty days, and after all only made seventy leagues. All this time I was unable to get into harbour, nor was there any cessation of the tempest, which was one continuation of rain, thunder, and lightning; indeed it seemed as if it were the end of the world. I at length reached the Cape of Gracias a Dios, and after that the Lord granted me fair wind and tide ; this was on the twelfth of September. Eighty-eight days did this fearful tempest continue, during which I was at sea, and saw neither sun nor stars; my ships lay exposed, with sails torn, and anchors, rigging, cables, boats, and a great quantity of provisions lost; my people were very weak and humbled in spirit, many of them promising to lead a religious life, and all making vows and promising to perform pilgrimages, while some of them would frequently go to their messmates to make confession. Other tempests have been experienced, but never of so long a duration or so fearful as this : many whom we looked upon as brave men, on several occasions showed considerable trepidation ; but the distress of my son who was with me grieved me to the soul, and the more when I considered his tender age, for

---

me salió el viento y corriente terrible al opósito : combati con ellos sesenta dias, y en fin no le pude ganar mas de setenta leguas. En todo este tiempo no entré puerto, ni pude, ni me dejó tormenta del cielo, agua y trombones y relámpagos de continuo, que parecia el fin del mundo. Llegué al cabo de Gracias á Dios, y de allí me dió nuestro Señor próspero el viento y corriente. Esto fue á doce de Setiembre. Ochenta y ocho dias habia que no me habia dejado espantable tormenta, á tanto que no vide el sol ni estrellas por mar; que á los navíos tenia yo abiertos, á las velas rotas, y perdidas anclas y jarcia, cables, con las barcas y muchos bastimentos, la gente muy enferma, y todos contritos, y muchos con promesa de religion, y no ninguno sin otros votos y romerías. Muchas veces habian llegado á se confesar los unos á los otros. Otras tormentas se han visto, mas no durar tanto ni con tanto espanto. Muchos esmorecieron, harto y hartas veces, que teniamos por

he was but thirteen years old, and he enduring so much toil for so long a time. Our Lord, however, gave him strength even to enable him to encourage the rest, and he worked as if he had been eighty years at sea, and all this was a consolation to me. I myself had fallen sick, and was many times at the point of death, but from a little cabin that I had caused to be constructed on deck, I directed our course. My brother was in the ship that was in the worst condition and the most exposed to danger; and my grief on this account was the greater that I brought him with me against his will.

Such is my fate, that the twenty years of service through which I have passed with so much toil and danger, have profited me nothing, and at this very day I do not possess a roof in Spain that I can call my own; if I wish to eat or sleep, I have nowhere to go but to the inn or tavern, and most times lack wherewith to pay the bill. Another anxiety wrung my very heartstrings, which was the thought of my son Diego, whom I had left an orphan in Spain, and stripped of the honour and property which were due to him on my account, although I had looked upon it as a certainty, that

---

esforzados. El dolor del fijo que yo tenia allí me arrancaba el ánima, y mas por verle de tan nueva edad de trece años en tanta fatiga, y durar en ello tanto : nuestro Señor le dió tal esfuerzo que él avivaba á los otros, y en las obras hacia el como si hubiera navegado ochenta años, y él me consolaba. Yo habia adolescido y llegado fartas veces á la muerte. De una camarilla, que yo mandé facer sobre cubierta, mandaba la via. Mi hermano estaba en el peor navío y mas peligroso. Gran dolor era mio, y mayor porque lo truje contra su grado ; porque por mi dicha, poco me han aprovechado veinte años de servicio que yo he servido con tantos trabajos y peligros, que hoy dia no tengo en Castilla una teja ; si quiero comer ó dormir no tengo, salvo al meson ó taberna, y las mas de las veces falta parar pagar el escote. Otra lastima me arrancaba el corazon por las espaldas, y era D. Diego mi hijo, que yo dejé en España tan huérfano y desposesionado de mi honra é hacienda; bien que tenia por cierto que allá como justos y

your Majesties, as just and grateful Princes, would restore it to him in all respects with increase. I reached the land of Cariay, where I stopped to repair my vessels and take in provisions, as well as to afford relaxation to the men, who had become very weak. I myself (who, as I said before, had been several times at the point of death) gained information respecting the gold mines of which I was in search, in the province of Ciamba; and two Indians conducted me to Carambaru, where the people (who go naked) wear golden mirrors round their necks, which they will neither sell, give, nor part with for any consideration. They named to me many places on the sea-coast where there were both gold and mines. The last that they mentioned was Veragua, which was about five-and-twenty leagues distant from the place where we then were. I started with the intention of visiting all of them, but when I had reached the middle of my journey I learned that there were other mines at so short a distance that they might be reached in two days. I determined on sending to see them. It was on the eve of St. Simon and St. Jude, which was the day fixed for our departure; but that night there arose so violent a storm, that we

---

agradecidos Principes le restituirian con acrescentamiento en todo. Llegué á tierra de Cariay, adonde me detuve á remediar los navíos y bastimentos, y dar aliento á la gente, que venia muy enferma. Yo que, como dije, habia llegado muchas veces á la muerte, allí supe de las minas del oro de la provincia de Ciamba, que yo buscaba. Dos indios me llevaron á Carambaru, adonde la gente anda desnuda y al cuello un espejo de oro, mas no le querian vender ni dar á trueque. Nombraronme muchos lugares en la costa de la mar, adonde decian que habia oro y minas; el postrero era Veragua, y lejos de allí obra de veinte y cinco leguas: partí con intencion de los tentar á todos, y llegado ya el medio supe que habia minas á dos jornadas de andadura: acorde de inviarlas á ver vispera de San Simon y Judas, que habia de ser la partida: en esa noche se levantó tanta mar y viento, que fue necesario de correr hácia adonde él quiso; é el indio adalid

were forced to go wherever it drove us, and the Indian who was to conduct us to the mines was with us all the time. As I had found every thing true that had been told me in the different places which I had visited, I felt satisfied it would be the same with respect to Ciguare, which according to their account, is nine days' journey across the country westward: they tell me there is a great quantity of gold there, and that the inhabitants wear coral ornaments on their heads, and very large coral bracelets and anklets, with which article also they adorn and inlay their seats, boxes, and tables. They also said that the women there wore necklaces hanging down to their shoulders. All the people agree in the report I now repeat, and their account is so favourable that I should be content with the tithe of the advantages that their description holds out. They are all likewise acquainted with the pepper-plant. According to the account of these people, the inhabitants of Ciguare are accustomed to hold fairs and markets for carrying on their commerce, and they showed me also the mode and form in which they transact their various exchanges. Others assert that their ships carry guns, and that the men go clothed and use bows and arrows,

---

de las minas siempre conmigo. En todos estos lugares, adonde yo habia estado, fallé verdad todo lo que yo habia oido : esto me certifico que es así de la provincia de Ciguare, que segun ellos, es descrita nueve jornadas de andadura por tierra al Poniente : allí dicen que hay infinito oro, y que traen corales en las cabezas, manillas á los pies y á los brazos dello, y bien gordas ; y dél, sillas, arcas, y mesas las guarnecen y enforran. Tambien dijeron que las mugeres de allí traian collares colgados de la cabeza á las espaldas. En esto que yo dijo, la gente toda de estos lugares conciertan en ello, y dicen tanto que yo seria contento con el diezmo. Tambien todos conocieron la pimienta. En Ciguare usan tratar en ferias y mercaderías : esta gente así lo cuentan, y me amostraban el modo y forma que tienen en la barata. Otrosi dicen que las naos traen bombardas, arcos y flechas, espadas y corazas, y andan vestidos, y en la tierra hay caballos, y usan la

swords, and cuirasses, and that on shore they have horses which they use in battle, and that they wear rich clothes and have most excellent houses.[1] They also say that the sea surrounds Ciguare, and that at ten days' journey from thence is the river Ganges. These lands appear to have the same bearings with respect to Veragua, as Tortosa has to Fontarabia, or Pisa to Venice. When I left Carambaru and reached the places in its neighbourhood, which I have above-mentioned as being spoken of by the Indians, I found the customs of the people correspond with the accounts that had been given of them, except as regarded the golden mirrors: any man who had one of them would willingly part with it for three hawks'-bells, although they were equivalent in weight to ten or fifteen ducats. These people resemble the natives of Española in all their habits. They have various modes of collecting the gold, none of which will bear comparison with the plans adopted by the Christians.

All that I have here stated is from hearsay. This, however, I know, that in the year ninety-four I sailed twenty-four degrees to the westward in nine hours, and there can

---

guerra, y traen ricas vestiduras, y tienen buenas cosas. Tambien dicen que la mar boxa á Ciguare, y de allí á diez jornadas es el rio de Gangues. Parece que estas tierras estan con Veragua, como Tortosa con Fuenterabía, ó Pisa con Venecia. Cuando yo partí de Carambaru y llegué á esos lugares que dije, fallé la gente en aquel mismo uso, salvo que los espejos del oro : quien los tenia los daba por tres cascabeles de gabilan por el uno, bien que pesasan diez ó quince ducados de peso. En todos sus usos son como los de la Española. El oro cogen con otras artes, bien que todos son nada con los de los Cristianos. Esto que yo he dicho es lo que oyo. Lo que yo sé es que el año de noventa y cuatro navegué en veinte y cuatro grados al Poniente en término de

[1] The word "cosas" has been replaced on conjecture by "casas," such being the idea entertained in the Italian translation, republished by Morelli.

be no mistake upon the subject, because there was an eclipse; the sun was in Libra and the moon in Aries. What I had learned by the mouth of these people I already knew in detail from books. Ptolemy thought that he had satisfactorily corrected Marinus, and yet this latter appears to have come very near to the truth. Ptolemy places Catigara at a distance of twelve lines to the west of his meridian,[1] which he fixes at two degrees and a third above Cape St. Vincent, in Portugal. Marinus comprises the earth and its limits in fifteen lines, and the same author describes the Indus in Ethiopia as being more than four-and-twenty degrees from the equinoctial line, and now that the Portuguese have sailed there they find it correct. Ptolemy says also that the most southern land is the first boundary, and that it does not go lower down than fifteen degrees and a third. The world is but small; out of seven divisions of it the dry part occupies six, and the seventh only is covered by water.[2] Experience has shown

---

nueve horas, y no pudo haber yerro porque hubo eclipses : el sol estaba en Libra y la luna en Ariete. Tambien esto que yo supe por palabra habialo yo sabido largo por escrito. Tolomeo creyó de haber bien remedado á Marino, y ahora se falla su escritura bien propincua al cierto. Tolomeo asienta Catigara á doce lineas lejos de su Occidente, que él asentó sobre el cabo de San Vicente en Portugal dos grados y un tercio. Marino en quince líneas constituyó la tierra ó términos. Marino en Etiopia escribe al Indo la línea equinocial mas de veinte y cuatro grados, y ahora que los Portugueses le navegan le fallan cierto. Tolomeo diz que la tierra mas austral es el plazo primero, y que no abaja mas de quince grados y un tercio. E el mundo es poco : el enjuto de ello es seis partes, la séptima solamente cubierta de agua : la experi-

[1] The "line" of Columbus implies fifteen degrees, or one hour of longitude ; and the twelve lines which describe the distance of Catigara from the meridian of Ptolemy, equal one hundred and eighty degrees. Marinus of Tyre, reckoned two hundred and twenty-five degrees to the same space, which is equivalent to the fifteen lines stated by Columbus.

[2] Every one will immediately see the incorrectness of this notion, arising from the belief of Columbus that the country he had discovered

it, and I have written it with quotations from the Holy
Scripture, in other letters, where I have treated of the
situation of the terrestrial paradise, as approved by Holy
Church; and I say that the world is not so large as vulgar
opinion makes it, and that one degree from the equinoctial
line measures fifty-six miles and two-thirds; and this may
be proved to a nicety. But I leave this subject, which it is
not my intention now to treat upon, but simply to give a
narrative of my laborious and painful voyage, although of all
my voyages it is the most honourable and advantageous. I
have said that on the eve of St. Simon and St. Jude I ran
before the wind wherever it took me, without power to resist
it; at length I found shelter for ten days from the rough-
ness of the sea and the tempest overhead, and resolved not
to attempt to go back to the mines, which I regarded as
already in our possession. When I started in pursuance of
my voyage it was under a heavy rain, and reaching the
harbour of Bastimentos I put in, though much against my
will. The storm and a rapid current kept me in for fourteen

encia ya está vista, y la escribí por otras letras y con adornamiento
de la Sacra Escriptura con el sitio del Paraiso terrenal, que la
santa Iglesia aprueba : digo que el mundo no es tan grande como
dice el vulgo, y que un grado de la equinoccial está cincuenta y
seis millas y dos tercios : pero esto se tocará con el dedo. Dejo
esto, por cuanto no es mi propósito de fablar en aquella materia,
salvo de dar cuenta de mi duro y trabajoso viage, bien que él sea
el mas noble y provechoso. Digo que víspera de San Simon y
Judas corrí donde el viento me llevaba, sin poder resistirle. En
un puerto excusé diez dias de gran fortuna de la mar y del cielo :
allí acordé de no volver atras á las minas, y dejelas ya por
ganadas. Partí, por seguir mi viage, lloviendo : llegué á puerto
de Bastimentos, adonde entró y no de grado : la tormenta y gran
corriente me entró allí catorce dias; y despues partí, y no con

was the east coast of Asia. Instead of the land bearing a proportion of
six-sevenths to the water, the water bears a proportion of about two-
thirds to the land.

days, when I again set sail, but not with favourable weather. After I had made fifteen leagues with great exertions, the wind and the current drove me back again with great fury, but in again making for the port which I had quitted, I found on the way another port, which I named Retrete, where I put in for shelter with as much risk as regret, the ships being in sad condition, and my crews and myself exceedingly fatigued. I remained there fifteen days, kept in by stress of weather, and when I fancied my troubles were at an end, I found them only begun. It was then that I changed my resolution with respect to proceeding to the mines, and proposed doing something in the interim, until the weather should prove more favourable for my voyage. I had already made four leagues when the storm recommenced, and wearied me to such a degree that I absolutely knew not what to do; my wound reopened, and for nine days my life was despaired of. Never was the sea seen so high, so terrific, and so covered with foam; not only did the wind oppose our proceeding onward, but it also rendered it highly dangerous to run in for any headland, and kept me in that sea which seemed to me as a sea of blood, seething like a cauldron on a mighty fire. Never did the sky look

---

buen tiempo. Cuando yo hube andado quince leguas forzosamente, me reposó atras el viento y corriente con furia: volviendo yo al puerto de donde habia salido fallé en el camino al Retrete, adonde me retruje con harto peligro y enojo y bien fatigado yo y los navíos y la gente: detúveme allí quince dias, que así lo quiso el cruel tiempo; y cuando creí de haber acabado me fallé de comienzo: allí mudé de sentencia de volver á las minas, y hacer algo fasta que me viniese tiempo para mi viage y marear; y llegado con cuatro leguas revino la tormenta, y̑ me fatigó tanto á tanto que ya no sabia de mi parte. Allí se me refrescó del mal la llaga: nueve dias anduve perdido sin esperanza de vida: ojos nunca vieron la mar tan alta, fea y hecha espuma. El viento no era para ir adelante, ni daba lugar para correr hácia algun cabo. Allí me detenia en aquella mar fecha sangre, herbiendo como

more fearful; during one day and one night it burned like a furnace, and emitted flashes in such fashion that each time I looked to see if my masts and my sails were not destroyed; these flashes came with such alarming fury that we all thought the ship must have been consumed. All this time the waters from heaven never ceased, not to say that it rained, for it was like a repetition of the deluge. The men were at this time so crushed in spirit, that they longed for death as a deliverance from so many martyrdoms. Twice already had the ships suffered loss in boats, anchors, and rigging, and were now lying bare without sails.

When it pleased our Lord, I returned to Puerto Gordo, where I recruited my condition as well as I could. I then once more attempted the voyage towards Veragua, although I was by no means in a fit state to undertake it. The wind and currents were still contrary. I arrived at nearly the same spot as before, and there again the wind and currents still opposed my progress; once more I was compelled to put into harbour, not daring to encounter the opposition of Saturn[1] with such a boisterous sea, and on so formidable a

---

caldera por gran fuego. El cielo jamas fue visto tan espantoso: un dia con la noche ardió como forno : y así echaba la llama con los rayos, que cada vez miraba yo si me habia llevado los masteles y velas; venian con tanta furia espantables que todos creiamos que me habian de fundir los navíos. En todo este tiempo jamas cesó agua del cielo, y no para decir que llovia, salvo que resegundaba otro diluvio. La gente estaba ya tan molida que deseaban la muerte para salir de tantos martirios. Los navíos ya habian perdido dos veces las barcas, anclas, cuerdas, y estaban abiertos, sin velas.

Cuando plugo á nuestro Señor volví á Puerto Gordo, adonde reparé lo mejor que pude. Volví otra vez hácia Veragua para mi viage, aunque yo no estuviera para ello. Todavía era el viento y corrientes contrarios. Llegué casi adonde antes, y allí me salió otra vez el viento y corrientes al encuentro, y volví otra vez al puerto, que no osé esparar la oposicion de Saturno con mares tan

[1] Morelli has given this passage thus: "la opposizion de Saturno con

coast; for it almost always brings on a tempest or severe weather. This was on Christmas-day, about the hour of mass. Thus, after all these fatigues, I had once more to return to the spot from whence I started; and when the new year had set in, I returned again to my task: but although I had fine weather for my voyage, the ships were no longer in a sailing condition, and my people were either dying or very sick. On the day of the Epiphany, I reached Veragua in a state of exhaustion; there, by our Lord's goodness, I found a river and a safe harbour, although at the entrance there were only ten spans of water. I succeeded in making an entry, but with great difficulty; and on the following day the storm recommenced, and had I been still on the outside at that time, I should have been unable to enter on account of the bar. It rained without ceasing until the fourteenth of February, so that I could find no opportunity of penetrating into the interior, nor of recruiting my condition in any respect whatever; and on the twenty-fourth of January, when I considered myself in perfect safety,

---

desbaratados en costa brava, porque las mas de las veces trae tempestad ó fuerte tiempo. Esto fue dia de Navidad en horas de misa. Volví otra vez adonde yo habia salido con harta fatiga; y pasado año nuevo torné á la porfia, que aunque me hiciera buen tiempo para mi viage, ya tenia los navíos innavegables, y la gente muerta y enferma. Dia de la Epifania llegué á Veragua, ya sin aliento : allí me deparó nuestro Señor un rio y seguro puerto, bien que á la entrada no tenia salvo diez palmos de fondo : metíme en él con pena, y el dia siguiente recordó la fortuna : si me falla fuera, no pudiera entrar á causa del banco. Llovió sin cesar fasta catorce de Febrero, que nunca hubo lugar de entrar en la tierra, ni de me remediar en nada : y estando ya seguro á veinte y cuatro de Enero, de improviso vino el rio muy alto y fuerte;

Marte." The adjective " desbarados," however, sufficiently proves this reading to be incorrect. It would seem that Columbus meant the opposition of Saturn with the Sun.

the river suddenly rose with great violence to a considerable height, breaking my cables and the supports[1] to which they were fastened, and nearly carrying away my ships altogether, which certainly appeared to me to be in greater danger than ever. Our Lord, however, brought a remedy as He has always done. I do not know if any one else ever suffered greater trials.

On the sixth of February, while it was still raining, I sent seventy men on shore to go into the interior, and, at five leagues' distance they found several mines. The Indians who went with them, conducted them to a very lofty mountain, and thence showing them the country all round, as far as the eye could reach, told them there was gold in every part, and that, towards the west, the mines extended twenty days' journey; they also recounted the names of the towns and villages where there was more or less of it. I afterwards learned that the cacique Quibian, who had lent these Indians, had ordered them to show the distant mines, and which belonged to an enemy of his; but that in his own territory,

---

quebróme las amarras y proeses, y hubo de llevar los navíos, y cierto los ví en mayor peligro que nunca. Remedió nuestro Señor, como siempre hizo. No sé si hubo otro con mas martirios.

A seis de Febrero, lloviendo, invió setenta hombres la tierra adentro; y á las cinco leguas fallaron muchas minas: los Indios que iban con ellos los llevaron á un cerro muy alto, y de allí les mostraron hácia toda parte cuanto los ojos alcanzaban, diciendo que en toda parte habia oro, y que hácia el Poniente llegaban las minas veinte jornadas, y nombraban las villas y lugares, y adonde habia de ello mas ó menos. Despues supe yo que el Quibian que habia dado estos Indios, les habia mandado que fuesen á mostrar las minas lejos y de otro su contrario; y que adentro de su pueblo cogian, cuando el queria, un hombre en diez dias una mozada de

[1] The word *proeses* or *proizes*, answers to our English word bollards —or the posts to which cables are fastened.

one man might, if he would, collect in ten days as much as
a child could carry. I bring with me some Indians, his servants, who can bear witness to this fact. The boats went
up to the spot where the dwellings of these people are
situated; and, after four hours, my brother returned with
the guides, all of them bringing back gold which they had
collected at that place. The gold must therefore be abundant,
and of good quality, for none of these men had ever seen
mines before; very many of them had never seen pure gold,
and most of them were seamen and lads. Having building
materials in abundance, I established a settlement, and made
many presents to Quibian, which is the name they gave to
the lord of the country. I plainly saw that harmony would
not last long, for the natives are of a very rough disposition,
and the Spaniards very encroaching; and, moreover, I had
taken possession of land belonging to Quibian. When he
saw what we did, and found the traffic increasing, he resolved
upon burning the houses, and putting us all to death; but
his project did not succeed, for we took him prisoner, together with his wives, his children, and his servants. His
captivity, it is true, lasted but a short time, for he eluded the

---

oro : los indios sus criados y testigos de esto traigo conmigo.
Adonde él tiene el pueblo llegan las barcas. Volvió mi hermano
con esa gente, y todos con que habian cogido en cuatro horas
qué fué allá á la estada. La calidad es grande, porque ninguno de
estos jamas habia visto minas, y los mas oro. Los mas eran gente
de la mar, y casí todos grumetes. Yo tenia mucho aparejo para
edificar y muchos bastimentos. Asenté pueblo, y dí muchas
dádivas al Quibian, que así llaman al Señor de la tierra; y bien
sabia que no habia de durar la concordia : ellos muy rústicos y
nuestra gente muy importunos, y me aposesionaba en su término :
despues que él vido las cosas fechas y el tráfago tan vivo acordó
de las quemar y matarnos á todos: muy al reves salió su
propósito : quedó preso él, mugeres y fijos y criados; bien que
su prision duró poco : el Quibian se fuyo á un hombre honrado, á

custody of a trustworthy man, into whose charge he had been given, with a guard of men; and his sons escaped from a ship, in which they had been placed under the special charge of the master.

In the month of January the mouth of the river was entirely closed up, and in April the vessels were so eaten with the teredo, that they could scarcely be kept above water. At this time the river forced a channel for itself, by which I managed, with great difficulty, to extricate three of them after I had unloaded them. The boats were then sent back into the river for water and salt, but the sea became so high and furious, that it afforded them no chance of exit; upon which the Indians collected themselves together in great numbers, and made an attack upon the boats, and at length massacred the men. My brother, and all the rest of our people, were in a ship which remained inside; I was alone, outside, upon that dangerous coast, suffering from a severe fever and worn with fatigue. All hope of escape was gone. I toiled up to the highest part of the ship, and, with a quivering voice and fast-falling tears, I called upon your Highnesses' war-captains from each point of the compass to come to my succour, but there was no reply. At length,

---

quien se habia entregado con guarda de hombres; é los hijos se fueron á un Maestre de navío, a quien se dieron en él á buen recaudo.

En Enero se habia cerrado la boca del rio. En Abril los navíos estaban todos comidos de broma, y no los podia sostener sobre agua. En este tiempo hizo el rio una canal, por donde saqué tres dellos vacios con gran pena. Las barcas volvieron adentro por la sal y agua. La mar se puso alta y fea, y no les dejó salir fuera: los Indios fueron muchos y juntos y las combatieron, y en fin los mataron. Mi hermano y la otra gente toda estaban en un navío que quedo adentro : yo muy solo de fuera en tan brava costa, con fuerte fiebre, en tanta fatiga : la esperanza de escapar era muerta : subi así trabajando lo mas alto, llamando á voz temerosa, llorando y muy aprisa, los maestros de la guerra de vuestras Altezas, á to-

groaning with exhaustion, I fell asleep, and heard a compassionate voice address me thus :—" *O fool, and slow to believe and to serve thy God, the God of all! what did He do more for Moses, or for David his servant, than He has done for thee? From thine infancy He has kept thee under His constant and watchful care. When He saw thee arrived at an age which suited His designs respecting thee, He brought wonderful renown to thy name throughout all the land. He gave thee for thine own the Indies, which form so rich a portion of the world, and thou hast divided them as it pleased thee, for He gave thee power to do so. He gave thee also the keys of those barriers of the ocean sea which were closed with such mighty chains; and thou wast obeyed through many lands, and gained an honourable fame throughout Christendom. What did the Most High do for the people of Israel, when He brought them out of Egypt? or for David, whom from a shepherd He made to be king in Judæa? Turn to Him, and acknowledge thine error—His mercy is infinite. Thine old age shall not prevent thee from accomplishing any great undertaking. He holds under His sway the greatest possessions. Abraham had exceeded a*

---

dos cuatro los vientos, por socorro ; mas nunca me respondieron. Cansado, me dormecí gimiendo: una voz muy piadosa oí, diciendo: "¡ O estulto y tardo á creer y servir á tu Dios, Dios de todos! ¿ Que hizo él mas por Moysés ó por David su siervo? Desque nasciste, siempre él tuvo de tí muy grande cargo. Cuando te vido en edad de que él fue contento, maravillosamente hizo sonar tu nombre en la tierra. Las Indias, que son parte del mundo tan ricas, te las dió por tuyas : tu las repartiste adonde te plugo, y te dió poder para ello. De los atamientos de la mar océana, que estaban cerrados con cadenas tan fuertes, te dió las llaves; y fuiste obedescido en tantas tierras, y de los cristianos cobraste tan honrada fama. ¿ Qué hizo el mas Alto [por el] pueblo de Israel cuando le sacó de Egipto ? ¿ Ni por David, que de pastor hizo Rey en Judea ? Tórnate á el, y conoce ya tu yerro : su misericordia es infinita : tu vejez no impedirá á toda cosa grande : muchas heredades tiene él grandísimas. Abrahan

*hundred years of age when he begat Isaac; nor was Sarah
young. Thou criest out for uncertain help: answer, who
has afflicted thee so much and so often, God or the world?
The privileges promised by God, He never fails in bestowing;
nor does He ever declare, after a service has been rendered
Him, that such was not agreeable with His intention, or that
He had regarded the matter in another light; nor does He
inflict suffering, in order to make a show of His power. His
acts answer to His words; and He performs all His promises
with interest. Is this the usual course? Thus I have told
you what the Creator has done for thee, and what He does
for all men. Even now He partially shows thee the reward
of so many toils and dangers incurred by thee in the service
of others."*

I heard all this, as it were, in a trance; but I had no
answer to give in definite words, and could but weep for my
errors. He who spoke to me, whoever he was, concluded by
saying,—*"Fear not, but trust; all these tribulations are recorded on marble, and not without cause."* I arose as soon
as I could; and at the end of nine days there came fine

---

*pasaba de cien años cuando engendró á Isaac, ¿ ni Sara era moza ?
Tú llamas por socorro incierto : responde, ¿ quién te ha afligido tanto
y tantas veces, Dios ó el mundo ? Los privilegios y promesas que dá
Dios, no las quebranta, ni dice despues de haber recibido el servicio,
que su intencion no era este, y que se entiende de otra manera, ni dá
martirios por dar color á la fuerza : él vá al pie de la letra : todo lo
que él promete cumple con acrescentamiento : ¿ esto es uso ? Dicho
tengo lo que tu Criador ha fecho por tí y hace con todos. Ahora
medio muestra el galardon de estos afanes y peligros que has pasado
sirviendo á otros."*

Yo así amortecido oí todo ; mas no tuve yo respuesta á palabras
tan ciertas, salvo llorar por mis yerros. Acabó él de fablar, quien
quiera que fuese, diciendo : *"No temas, confia : todas estas tribu-
laciones estan escritas en piedra mármol, y no sin causa."*

Levantéme cuando pude : y al cabo de nueve dias hizo bonanza,

weather, but not sufficiently so to allow of drawing the vessels out of the river. I collected the men who were on land, and, in fact, all of them that I could, because there were not enough to admit of one party remaining on shore while another stayed on board to work the vessels. I myself should have remained with my men to defend the buildings I had constructed, had your Highnesses been cognizant of all the facts; but the doubt whether any ships would ever reach the spot where we were, as well as the thought, that while I was asking for succour I might bring succour to myself, made me decide upon leaving. I departed, in the name of the Holy Trinity, on Easter night, with the ships rotten, worm-eaten, and full of holes. One of them I left at Belem, with a supply of necessaries; I did the same at Belpuerto. I then had only two left, and they in the same state as the others. I was without boats or provisions, and in this condition I had to cross seven thousand miles of sea; or, as an alternative, to die on the passage with my son, my brother, and so many of my people. Let those who are in the habit of finding fault and censuring, ask, while they sit in security at home, " Why did you not do so and so under such circumstances?" I wish they now had this voyage to make.

---

mas no para sacar navíos del rio. Recogí la gente que estaba en tierra, y todo el resto que puede, porque no bastaban para quedar y para navegar los navíos. Quedara yo á sostener el pueblo contodos, si vuestras Altezas supieran de ello. El temor que nunca aportarian allí navíos me determinó á esto, y la cuenta que cuando se haya de proveer de socorro se proveera de todo. Partí en nombre de la Santísima Trinidad, la noche de Pascua, con los navíos podridos, abrumados, todos fechos agujeros. Allí en Belen dejé uno, y hartas cosas. En Belpuerto hice otro tanto. No me quedaron salvo dos en el estado de los otros, y sin barcas y bastimentos, por haber de pasar siete mil millas de mar y de agua, ó morir en la via con fijo y hermano y tanta gente. Respondan ahora los que suelen tachar y reprender, diciendo allá de en salvo : ¿ por qué no haciades esto allí? Los quisiera yo en esta jornada. Yo bien

I verily believe that another journey of another kind awaits them, if there is any reliance to be placed upon our holy faith.

On the thirteenth of May I reached the province of Mago,[1] which is contiguous to that of Cathay, and thence I started for the island of Española. I sailed two days with a good wind, after which it became contrary. The route that I followed called forth all my care to avoid the numerous islands, that I might not be stranded on the shoals that lie in their neighbourhood. The sea was very tempestuous, and I was driven backward under bare poles. I anchored at an island, where I lost, at one stroke, three anchors; and, at midnight, when the weather was such that the world appeared to be coming to an end, the cables of the other ship broke, and it came down upon my vessel with such force that it was a wonder we were not dashed to pieces; the single anchor that remained to me, was, next to the Lord, our only preservation. After six days, when the weather became calm, I resumed my journey having already lost all my tackle; my ships were pierced with worm-holes, like a bee-hive, and the

---

creo que otra de otro saber los aguarda: á nuestra fe es ninguna. Llegué á trece de Mayo en la provincia de Mago, que parte con aquella del Catayo, y de allí partí para la Española: navegué dos dias con buen tiempo, y despues fue contrario. El camino que yo llevaba era para desechar tanto número de islas, por no me embarazar en los bajos de ellas. La mar brava me hizo fuerza, y hube volver atras sin velas: surgí á una isla adonde de golpe perdí tres anclas, y á la media noche, que parecia que el mundo se ensolvia, se rompieron las amarras al otro navío, y vino sobre mí, que fue maravilla como no nos acabamos de se hacer rajas: el ancla, de forma que me quedó, fue ella despues de nuestro Señor, quien me sostuvo. Al cabo de seis dias que ya era bonanza, volví á mi camino: asi ya perdido del todo de aparejos y con los navíos hora-

[1] Columbus, who now fancies himself in China, by this word "Mago," means Mangi, the name given by Marco Polo, whose travels he had read, to Southern China, while Northern China was Cathay.

crew entirely paralysed with fear and in despair. I reached the island a little beyond the point at which I first arrived at it, and there I stayed to recover myself from the effects of the storm; but I afterwards put into a much safer port in the same island. After eight days I put to sea again, and reached Jamaica by the end of June; but always beating against contrary winds, and with the ships in the worst possible condition. With three pumps, and the use of pots and kettles, we could scarcely with all hands clear the water that came into the ship, there being no remedy but this for the mischief done by the ship-worm. I steered in such a manner as to come as near as possible to Española, from which we were twenty-eight leagues distant, but I afterwards wished I had not done so, for the other ship which was half under water was obliged to run in for a port. I determined on keeping the sea in spite of the weather, and my vessel was on the very point of sinking when our Lord miraculously brought us upon land. Who will believe what I now write? I assert that in this letter I have not related one hundredth part of the wonderful events that occurred in this voyage; those who were with the Admiral[1] can bear witness to it.

dados de gusanos mas que un panal de abejas, y la gente tan acobardada y perdida, pasé algo adelante de donde yo habia llegado denantes: allí me torné á reposar atras la fortuna: paré en la misma isla en mas seguro puerto: al cabo de ocho dias torné á la via y llegué á Jamaica en fin de Junio siempre con vientos punteros, y los navíos en peor estado: con tres bombas, tinas y calderas no podian con toda la gente vencer el agua que entraba en el navío, ni para este mal de broma hay otra cura. Cometíel camino para me acercar á lo mas cercar de la Española, que son veinte y ocho leguas, y no quisiera haber comenzado. El otro navío corrió á buscar puerto casi anegado. Yo porfié la vuelta de la mar con tormenta. El navio se me anegó, que milagrosamente me trujo nuestro Señor á tierra. ¿Quién creyera lo que yo aquí escribo? Digo que de cien partes no he dicho la una en esta letra.

[1] Of course he here speaks of himself.

If your Highnesses would be graciously pleased to send to my help a ship of above sixty-four tons, with two hundred quintals of biscuits and other provisions, there would then be sufficient to carry me and my crew from Española to Spain. I have already said that there are not twenty-eight leagues between Jamaica and Española; and I should not have gone there, even if the ships had been in a fit condition for so doing, because your Highnesses ordered me not to land there.. God knows if this command has proved of any service. I send this letter by means of and by the hands of Indians; it will be a miracle if it reaches its destination.

This is the account I have to give of my voyage. The men who accompanied me were a hundred and fifty in number, among whom were many calculated for pilots and good sailors, but none of them can explain whither I went nor whence I came. The reason is very simple. I started from a point above the port of Brazil, and while I was in Española, the storm prevented me from following my intended route, for I was obliged to go wherever the wind drove me; at the same time I fell very sick, and there was no one who had

---

Los que fueron con el Almirante lo atestigüen. Si place á vuestras Altezas de me hacer merced de socorro un navío que pase de sesenta y cuatro, con ducientos quintales de bizcocho y algun otro bastimento, abastará para me llevar á mí y á esta gente á España de la Española. En Jamaica ya dije que no hay veinte y ocho leguas á la Española. No fuera yo, bien que los navíos estuvieran para ello. Ya dije que me fue mandado de parte de vuestras Altezas que no llegase á alla. Si este mandar ha aprovechado, Dios lo sabe. Esta carta invio por via y mano de Indios : grande maravilla será si allá llega. De mi viage digo : que fueron ciento y cincuenta personas conmigo, en que hay hartos suficientes para pilotos y grandes marineros : ninguno puede dar razon cierta por donde fuí yo ni vine : la razon es muy presta. Yo partí de sobre el puerto del Brasil : en la Española no me dejó la tormenta ir al camino que yo queria : fue por fuerza correr adonde el viento quiso. En ese dia caí yo muy enfermo : ninguno habia navegado

navigated in these parts before. However, after some days, the wind and sea became tranquil, and the storm was succeeded by a calm, but accompanied with rapid currents. I put into harbour at an island called Isla de las Bocas, and then steered for terra firma; but it is impossible to give a correct account of all our movements, because I was carried away by the current so many days without seeing land. I ascertained, however, by the compass and by observation, that I moved parallel with the coast of terra firma. No one could tell under what part of the heavens we were, nor at what period I bent my course for the island of Española. The pilots thought we had come to the island of St. John, whereas it was the land of Mango, four hundred leagues to the westward of where they said. Let them answer and say if they know where Veragua is situated. I assert that they can give no other account than that they went to lands, where there was an abundance of gold, and this they can certify surely enough; but they do not know the way to return thither for such a purpose; they would be obliged to go on a voyage of discovery as much as if they had never been there before. There is a mode of reckoning derived

---

hácia aquella parte: cesó el viento y mar dende á ciertos dias, y se mudó la tormenta en calmería y grandes corrientes. Fuí á aportar á una isla que se dijo de las Bocas, y de allí a Tierra firme. Ninguno puede dar cuenta verdadera de esto, porque no hay razon que abaste; porque fue ir con corriente sin ver tierra tanto número de dias. Seguí la costa de la Tierra firme: esta se asentó con compás y arte. Ninguno hay que diga debajo cuál parte del cielo ó cuándo yo partí de ella para venir á la Española. Los pilotos creian venir á parar á la isla de Sanct-Joan; y fue en tierra de Mango, cuatrocientas leguas mas al Poniente de adonde decian. Respondan, si saben, adónde es el sitio de Veragua. Digo que no pueden dar otra razon ni cuenta, salvo que fueron á unas tierras adonde hay mucho oro, y certificarle; mas para volver á ella el camino tienen ignoto: seria necesario para ir á ella descubrirla como de primero. Una cuenta hay y razon de astrología y cierta:

from astronomy which is sure and safe, and a sufficient guide to anyone who understands it. This resembles a prophetic vision. The Indian vessels do not sail except with the wind abaft, but this is not because they are badly built or clumsy, but because the strong currents in those parts, together with the wind, render it impossible to sail with the bowline,[1] for in one day they would lose as much way as they might have made in seven; for the same reason I could make no use of caravels, even though they were Portuguese latteens. This is the cause that they do not sail unless with a regular breeze, and they will sometimes stay in harbour waiting for this seven or eight months at a time; nor is this anything wonderful, for the same very often occurs in Spain. The nation of which Pope Pius writes[2] has now been found,

---

quien la entiende esto le abasta. A vision profética se asemeja esto. Las naos de las Indias, si no navegan salvo á popa, no es por la mala fechura, ni por ser fuertes; las grandes corrientes que allí vienen; juntamente con el viento hacen que nadie porfie con bolina, porque en un dia perderian lo que hubiesen ganado en siete; ni saco carabela aunque sea latina portuguesa. Esta razon hace que no naveguen, salvo con colla, y por esperarle se detienen á las veces seis y ocho meses en puerto; ni es maravilla, pues que en España muchas veces acaece otro tanto. La gente de que escribe Papa Pio, segun el sitio y señas, se ha hallado, mas no los

[1] Bow-lines are ropes employed to keep the windward edges of the principal sails steady, and are only used when the wind is so unfavourable that the sails must be all braced sideways, or close hauled to the wind.

[2] In this remarkable notion, Columbus refers to a work of the learned Æneas Sylvius Piccolomini, entitled *Cosmographia Pape Pii*, printed in Venice in 1503. It is not paginated, but if the reader will count to the nineteenth and twentieth pages he will find the following passages: "Post Sacas ad septentrionem Messagetæ reperiuntur:......Fæda gens et brutis simillima apud quam genus mortis optimum judicabatur ut senio confecti in frusta cœderentur et cum carnibus ovilis promiscue ederentur: eos qui morbo decederent ut impios abjicientes tamque dignos qui a feris devorarentur, Equites ac pedites inter eos optimi fuere

judging at least by the situation and other evidences, excepting the horses with the saddles and poitrels and bridles of gold; but this is not to be wondered at, for the lands on the sea-coast are only inhabited by fishermen, and moreover I made no stay there, because I was in haste to proceed on my voyage. In Cariay and the neighbouring country there are great enchanters of a very fearful character. They would have given the world to prevent my remaining there an hour. When I arrived they sent me immediately two girls very showily dressed; the eldest could not be more than eleven years of age and the other seven, and both exhibited so much immodesty, that more could not be expected from public women; they carried concealed about them a magic powder; when they came I gave them some articles to dress themselves out with, and directly sent them back to the shore. I saw here, built on a mountain, a sepulchre as large as a house, and elaborately sculptured, the body lay

---

caballos, pretales y frenos de oro, ni es maravilla, porque allí las tierras de la costa de la mar no reuieren, salvo pescadores, ni yo me detuve porque andaba á prisa. En Cariay y en essas tierras de su comarca, son grandes fechiceros y muy medrosos. Dieran el mundo porque no me detuviera allí una hora. Cuando llegué allí luego me inviaron dos muchachas muy ataviadas: la mas vieja no seria de once años y la otra de siete; ambas con tanta desenvoltura que no serian mas unas putas: traian polvos de hechizos escondidos: en llegando las mandé adornar de nuestras cosas y las invié luego á tierra: allí vide una sepultura en el monte, grande como

arcu; gladio; thorace; ac securi æneâ utentes; aureas zonas; aurea equorum frena ac pectoralia habentes. Ferri parum apud eos fuit: argento carebant; ære et auro abundabant: insularum cultores herbarum radices edebant, et agrestes fructus: ex quibus pocula exprimebant. Vestis erat arborum cortex: qui paludes inhabitabant piscibus vescebantur: focarum coria e mari prodeuntium induebant," etc. From Herodotus we gather an accurate idea of the situation of the Massagetæ, viz., in the immense plain to the east of the Caspian and on the east bank of the Jaxaretes. Strabo corroborates the account of Herodotus as to the repulsive habits of these old Mongolians.

uncovered and with the face downwards; they also spoke to me of other very excellent works of art. There are many species of animals both small and large, and very different from those of our country. I had at the time two boars, that an Irish dog would not dare to face. An archer had wounded an animal like an ape, except that it was larger, and had a face like a man's; the arrow had pierced it from the neck to the tail, which made it so fierce that they were obliged to disable it by cutting off one of its arms and a leg; one of the boars grew wild on seeing this and fled; upon which I ordered the *begare* (as the inhabitants called him) to be thrown to the boar, and though the animal was nearly dead, and the arrow had passed quite through his body, yet he threw his tail round the snout of the boar, and then holding him firmly, seized him by the nape of the neck with his remaining hand, as if he were engaged with an enemy. This action was so novel and so extraordinary, that I have thought it worth while to describe it here. There is a great variety of animals here, but they all die of the barra.[1] I saw some very large fowls (the

---

una casa y labrada, y el cuerpo descubierto y mirando en ella. De otras artes me dijeron y mas excelentes. Animalias menudas y grandes hay hartas y muy diversas de las nuestras. Dos puercos hube yo en presente, y un perro de Irlanda no osaba esperarlos. Un ballestero habia herido una animalia, que se parece á gato paul, salvo que es mucho mas grande, y el rostro de hombre: teníale atravesado con una saeta desde los pechos á la cola, y porque era feroz le hubo de cortar un brazo y una pierna: el puerco en viéndole se le encrespó y se fue huyendo: yo cuando esto ví mandé echarle *begare*, que así se llama adonde estaba: en llegando á él, así estando á la muerte y la saeta siempre en el cuerpo, le echó la cola por el hocico y se la amarró muy fuerte, y con la mano que le quedaba le arrebató por el copete como á enemigo. El auto tan nuevo y hermosa montería me hizo escribir esto. De muchas maneras de animalias se hubo, mas todas mueren de barra. Gallinas

[1] This is a malady undefined in any dictionary.

feathers of which resemble wool), lions, stags, fallow-deer, and birds.

When we were so harassed with our troubles at sea, some of our men imagined that we were under the influence of sorcery, and even to this day entertain the same notion. Some of the people whom I discovered were cannibals, as was evidenced by the brutality of their countenances. They say that there are great mines of copper in the country, of which they make hatchets and other elaborate articles, both cast and soldered; they also make of it forges, with all the apparatus of the goldsmith, and crucibles. The inhabitants go clothed; and in that province I saw some large sheets of cotton very elaborately and cleverly worked, and others very delicately pencilled in colours. They told me that more inland towards Cathay they have them interwoven with gold. For want of an interpreter we were able to learn but very little respecting these countries, or what they contain. Although the country is very thickly peopled, yet each nation has a very different language; indeed so much so, that they can no more understand each other than we understand the Arabs.

---

muy grandes y la pluma como lana vide hartas. Leones, ciervos, corzos otro tanto, y así aves.

Cuando yo andaba por aquella mar en fatiga en algunos se puso heregía que estabamos enfechizados, que hoy dia estan en ello. Otra gente fallé que comian hombres: la desformidad de su gesto lo dice. Allí dicen qué hay grandes mineros de cobre: hachas de ello, otras cosas labradas, fundidas, soladas hube, y fraguas con todo su aparejo de platero y los crisoles. Allí van vestidos; y en aquella provincia vide sábanas grandes de algodon, labradas de muy sotiles labores; otras píntadas muy sútilmente á colores con pinceles. Dicen que en la tierra adentro hácia el Catayo las hay tejidas de oro. De todas estas tierras y de lo que hay en ellas, falta de lengua, no se saben tan presto. Los pueblos, bien que sean espesos, cada uno tiene difcrenciada lengua, y es en tanto que no se entienden los unos con los otros, mas que nos con los de Arabia. Yo creo que esto sea en esta gente salvage de la costa

I think, however, that this applies to the barbarians on the sea-coast, and not to the people who live more inland. When I discovered the Indies, I said that they composed the richest lordship in the world; I spoke of gold and pearls and precious stones, of spices, and the traffic that might be carried on in them; and because all these things were not forthcoming at once I was abused. This punishment causes me to refrain from relating anything but what the natives tell me. One thing I can venture upon stating, because there are so many witnesses of it, viz., that in this land of Veragua I saw more signs of gold in the two first days than I saw in Española during four years, and that there is not a more fertile or better cultivated country in all the world, nor one whose inhabitants are more timid; added to which there is a good harbour, a beautiful river, and the whole place is capable of being easily put into a state of defence. All this tends to the security of the Christians, and the permanency of their sovereignty, while it affords the hope of great increase and honour to the Christian religion; moreover the road hither will be as short as that to Española, because there is a certainty of a fair wind for the passage. Your Highnesses are

de la mar, mas no en la tierra dentro. Cuando yo descubrí las Indias dije que eran el mayor señorío rico que hay en el mundo. Yo dije del oro, perlas, piedras preciosas, especerías, con los tratos y ferias, y porque no pareció todo tan presto fuí escandalizado. Este castigo me hace agora que no diga salvo lo que yo oigo de los naturales de la tierra. De una oso decir, porque hay tantos testigos, y es que yo vide en esta tierra de Veragua mayor señal de oro en dos dias primeros que en la Española en cuatro años, y que las tierras de la comarca no pueden ser mas fermosas, ni mas labradas, ni la gente mas cobarde, y buen puerto, y fermoso rio, y defensible al mundo. Todo esto es seguridad de los cristianos y certeza de señorío, con grande esperanza de la honra y acrescentamiento de la religion cristiana; y el camino, allí será tan breve como á la Española, porque ha de ser con viento. Tan señores son vuestras Altezas de esto como de Jerez ó Toledo: sus

as much lords of this country as of Xeres or Toledo, and your ships that may come here will do so with the same freedom as if they were going to your own royal palace. From hence they will obtain gold, and whereas if they should wish to become masters of the products of other lands, they will have to take them by force, or retire empty-handed, in this country they will simply have to trust their persons in the hands of a savage.

I have already explained my reason for refraining to treat of other subjects respecting which I might speak. I do not state as certain, nor do I confirm even the sixth part of all that I have said or written, nor do I pretend to be at the fountain-head of the information. The Genoese, Venetians, and all other nations that possess pearls, precious stones, and other articles of value, take them to the ends of the world to exchange them for gold. Gold is the most precious of all commodities; gold constitutes treasure, and he who possesses it has all he needs in this world, as also the means of rescuing souls from purgatory, and restoring them to the enjoyment of paradise. They say that when one of the lords of the country of Veragua dies, they bury all the gold he possessed with his body. There were brought to Solomon at one jour-

navíos que fueren allí van á su casa. De allí sacarán oro: en otras tierras, para haber de lo que hay en ellas, conviene que se lo lleven, ó se volverán vacíos; y en la tierra es necesario que fien sus personas de un salvage. Del otro que yo dejo de decir, ya dije por qué me encerré: no digo así, ni que yo me afirme en el tres doble en todo lo que yo haya jamas dicho ni escrito, y que yo estó á la fuente. Genoveses, Venecianos y toda gente que tenga perlas, piedras preciosas y otras cosas de valor, todos las llevan hasta el cabo del mundo para las trocar, convertir en oro: el oro es excelentísimo: del oro se hace tesoro, y con él, quien lo tiene, hace cuanto quiere en el mundo, y llega á que echa las animas al paraiso. Los señores de aquellas tierras de la comarca Veragua cuando mueren entierran el oro que tienen con el cuerpo, así lo dicen: á Salomon llevaron de un camino seiscientos y sesenta y

ney six hundred and sixty-six quintals of gold, besides what the merchants and sailors brought, and that which was paid in Arabia. Of this gold he made two hundred lances and three hundred shields, and the entablature which was above them was also of gold, and ornamented with precious stones: many other things he made likewise of gold, and a great number of vessels of great size, which he enriched with precious stones. This is related by Josephus in his Chronicle "de Antiquitatibus"; mention is also made of it in the Chronicles and in the Book of Kings. Josephus thinks that this gold was found in the Aurea; if it were so, I contend that these mines of the Aurea are identical with those of Veragua, which, as I have said before, extends westward twenty days' journey, at an equal distance from the Pole and the Line. Solomon bought all of it,—gold, precious stones, and silver,—but your Majesties need only send to seek them to have them at your pleasure. David, in his will, left three thousand quintals of Indian gold to Solomon, to assist in building the Temple; and, according to Josephus, it came from these lands. Jerusalem and Mount Sion are to be rebuilt by the hands of

---

seis quintales de oro, allende lo que llevaron los mercaderes y marineros, y allende lo que se pagó en Arabia. De este oro fizo doscientas lanzas y trescientos escudos, y fizo el tablado que habia de estar arriba dellas de oro y adornado de piedras preciosas, y fizo otras muchas cosas de oro, y vasos muchos y muy grandes y ricos de piedras preciosas. Josefo en su corónica de Antiquitatibus lo escribe. En el Paralipomenon y en el libro de los Reyes se cuenta de esto. Josefo quiere que este oro se hobiese en la Aurea: si así fuese digo que aquellas minas de la Aurea son unas y se convienen con estas de Veragua, que como yo dije arriba se alarga al Poniente veinte jornadas, y son en una distancia lejos del polo y de la línea. Salomon compró todo aquello, oro, piedras y plata, ó allí le pueden mandar á coger si les aplace. David en su testamento dejó tres mil quintales de oro de las Indías á Salomon para ayuda de edificar el templo, y segun Josefo era el destas mismas tierras. Hierusalem y el monte Sion ha de ser reedificado por

Christians, as God has declared by the mouth of His prophet in the fourteenth Psalm. The Abbé Joaquim said that he who should do this was to come from Spain; Saint Jeromo showed the holy woman the way to accomplish it; and the emperor of Cathay has, some time since, sent for wise men to instruct him in the faith of Christ. Who will offer himself for this work? Should any one do so, I pledge myself, in the name of God, to convey him safely thither, provided the Lord permits me to return to Spain. The people who have sailed with me have passed through incredible toil and danger, and I beseech your Highnesses, since they are poor, to pay them promptly, and to be gracious to each of them according to their respective merits; for I can safely assert, that to my belief they are the bearers of the best news that ever were carried to Spain. With respect to the gold which belongs to Quibian, the cacique of Veragua, and other chiefs in the neighbouring country, although it appears by the accounts we have received of it to be very abundant, I do not think it would be well or desirable, on the part of your Highnesses, to take possession of it in the way of plunder; by fair dealing, scandal and disrepute will be avoided, and all the gold will

---

mano de cristianos: quien ha de ser, Dios por boca del Profeta en el décimo cuarto salmo lo dice. El Abad Joaquin dijo que este habia de salir de España. San Gerónimo á la santa muger le mostró el camino para ello. El Emperador del Catayo ha dias que mandó sabios que le enseñen en la fé de Cristo. ¿ Quién será que se ofrezca á esto? Si nuestro Señor me lleva á España, yo me obligo de llevarle, con el nombre de Dios, en salvo. Esta gente que vino conmigo han pasado increibles peligros y trabajos. Suplico á V. A., porque son pobres, que les mande pagar luego, y les haga mercedes á cada uno segun la calidad de la persona, que les certifico que á mi creer les traen las mejores nuevas que nunca fueron á España. El oro que tiene el Quibian de Veragua y los otros de la comarca, bien que segun informacion él sea mucho, no me paresció bien ni servicio de vuestras Altezas de se le tomar por via de robo: lo buena orden evitará escándalo y mala fama,

thus reach your Highnesses' treasury without the loss of a grain. With one month of fair weather I shall complete my voyage. As I was deficient in ships, I did not persist in delaying my course; but in everything that concerns your Highnesses' service, I trust in Him who made me, and I hope also that my health will be re-established. I think your Highnesses will remember that I had intended to build some ships in a new manner, but the shortness of the time did not permit it. I had certainly foreseen how things would be. I think more of this opening for commerce, and of the lordship over such extensive mines, than of all that has been done in the Indies. This is not a child to be left to the care of a step-mother.

I never think of Española, and Paria, and the other countries, without shedding tears. I thought that what had occurred there would have been an example for others; on the contrary, these settlements are now in a languid state, although not dead, and the malady is incurable, or at least very extensive: let him who brought the evil come now and cure it, if he knows the remedy, or how to apply it; but when a disturbance is on foot, every one is ready to take

---

y hará que todo ello venga al tesoro, que no quede un grano. Con un mes de buen tiempo yo acabára todo mi viage: por falta de los navíos no porfié á esperarle para tornar á ello, y para toda cosa de su servicio espero en aquel que me hizo, y estaré bueno. Yo creo que V. A. se acordará que yo queria mandar hacer los navíos de nueva manera: la brevedad del tiempo no dió lugar á ello, y cierto yo habio caido en lo que cumplia. Yo tengo en mas esta negociacion y minas con esta escala y señorio, que todo lo otro que está hecho en las Indias. No es este hijo para dar á criar á madrastra. De la Española, de Paria y de las otras tierras no me acuerdo de ellas, que yo no llore: creia yo que el ejemplo dellas hobiese de ser por estotras al contrario: ellas estan boca á yuso, bien que no mueren: la enfermedad es incurable, ó muy larga: quien las llegó á esto venga agora con el remedio si puede ó sabe: al descomponer cada uno es maestro. Las gracias y acrescenta-

the lead. It used to be the custom to give thanks and promotion to him who placed his person in jeopardy; but there is no justice in allowing the man who opposed this underdertaking, to enjoy the fruits of it with his children. Those who left the Indies, avoiding the toils consequent upon the enterprise, and speaking evil of it and me, have since returned with official appointments,—such is the case now in Veragua: it is an evil example, and profitless both as regards the business in which we are embarked, and as respects the general maintenance of justice. The fear of this, with other sufficient considerations, which I clearly foresaw, caused me to beg your Highnesses, previously to my coming to discover these islands and terra firma, to grant me permission to govern in your royal name. Your Highnesses granted my request; and it was a privilege and treaty granted under the royal seal and oath, by which I was nominated viceroy, and admiral, and governor-general of all: and your Highnesses limited the extent of my government to a hundred leagues beyond the Azores and Cape Verde islands, by a line passing from one pole to the other, and gave me ample power over all that I might discover beyond

---

miento siempre fue uso de las dar á quien puso su cuerpo á peligro. No es razon que quien ha sido tan contrario á esta negociacion le goce ni sus fijos. Lós que se fueron de las Indias fuyendo los trabajos y diciendo mal dellas y de mí, volvieron con cargos: así se ordenaba agora en Veragua: malo ejemplo, y sin provecho del negocio y para la justicia del mundo: este temor con otros casos hartos que yo veia claro, me hizo suplicar á V. A. antes que yo viniese á descubrir esas islas y tierra firme, que me las dejasen gobernar en su Real nombre: plúgoles: fue por privilegio y asiento, y con sello y juramento, y me intitularon de Viso-Rey y Almirante y Gobernador general de todo; y aseñalaron el término sobre las islas de los Azores cien leguas, y aquellas del Cabo Verde por línea que pasa de polo á polo, y desto y de todo que mas se descubriese, y me dieron poder largo: la escritura á mas larga-

this line; all which is more fully described in the official document.

But the most important affair of all, and that which cries most loudly for redress, remains inexplicable to this moment. For seven years was I at your royal court, where every one to whom the enterprise was mentioned, treated it as ridiculous; but now there is not a man, down to the very tailors, who does not beg to be allowed to become a discoverer. There is reason to believe, that they make the voyage only for plunder, and that they are permitted to do so, to the great disparagement of my honour, and the detriment of the undertaking itself. It is right to give God His due,—and to receive that which belongs to one's self. This is a just sentiment, and proceeds from just feelings. The lands in this part of the world, which are now under your Highnesses' sway, are richer and more extensive than those of any other Christian power, and yet, after that I had, by the Divine will, placed them under your high and royal sovereignty, and was on the point of bringing your majesties into the receipt of a very great and unexpected revenue; and while I was waiting for ships, to convey me in safety, and with a heart full of joy, to your royal presence, victo-

---

mente lo dice. El otro negocio famosísimo está con los brazos abiertos llamando: extrangero ha sido fasta ahora. Siete años estuve yo en su Real corte, que á cuantos se fabló de esta empresa todos á una dijeron que era burla: agora fasta los sastres suplican por descubrir. Es de creer que van á saltear, y se les otorga, que cobran con mucho perjuicio de mi honra y tanto daño del negocio. Bueno es de dar á Dios lo suyo y acetar lo que le pertenece. Esta es justa sentencia, y de justo. Las tierras que acá obedecen á V. A. son mas que todas las otras de cristianos y ricas. Despues que yo, por voluntad divina, las hube puestas debajo de su Real y alto señorío, y en filo para haber grandísima rénta, de improviso, esperando navíos para venir á su alto conspecto con victoria y grandes nuevas del oro, muy seguro y alegre, fuí preso y echado

riously to announce the news of the gold that I had discovered, I was arrested and thrown, with my two brothers, loaded with irons, into a ship, stripped, and very ill-treated, without being allowed any appeal to justice. Who could believe, that a poor foreigner would have risen against your Highnesses, in such a place, without any motive or argument on his side; without even the assistance of any other prince upon which to rely; but on the contrary, amongst your own vassals and natural subjects, and with my sons staying at your royal court? I was twenty-eight years old[1] when I came into your Highnesses' service, and now I have not a hair upon me that is not grey; my body is infirm, and all that was left to me, as well as to my brothers, has been taken away and sold, even to the frock that I wore, to my great dishonour. I cannot but believe that this was done without your royal permission. The restitution of my honour, the reparation of my losses, and the punishment of those who have inflicted them, will redound to the honour of your royal character; a similar punishment also is due to

---

con dos hermanos en un navío, cargados de fierros, desnudo en cuerpo, con muy mal tratamiento, sin ser llamado ni vencido por justicia: ¿ quién creerá que un pobre extrangero se hobiese de alzar en tal lugar contra V. A. sin causa, ni sin brazo de otro Príncipe, y estando solo entre sus vasallos y naturales, y teniendo todos mis fijos en su Real corte? Yo vine á servir de veinte y ocho años, y agora no tengo cabello en mi persona que no sea cano y el cuerpo enfermo, y gastado cuanto me quedó de aquellos, y me fue tomado y vendido, y á mis hermanos fasta el sayo, sin ser oido ni visto, con gran deshonor mio. Es de creer que esto no se hizo por su Real mandado. La restitucion de mi honra y daños, y el castigo en quien lo fizo, fará sonar su Real nobleza; y otro tanto en quien me robó las perlas, y de quien ha fecho daño en ese

[1] This is most certainly a mistake; probably thirty-eight was originally written, which, supposing Columbus to have been born in 1446-7, would bring the date referred to to 1484, when Columbus really did escape from Portugal into Spain.

those who plundered me of my pearls, and who have brought a disparagement upon the privileges of my admiralty. Great and unexampled will be the glory and fame of your Highnesses, if you do this, and the memory of your Highnesses, as just and grateful sovereigns, will survive as a bright example to Spain in future ages. The honest devotedness I have always shown to your majesties' service, and the so unmerited outrage with which it has been repaid, will not allow my soul to keep silence, however much I may wish it: I implore your Highnesses to forgive my complaints. I am indeed in as ruined a condition as I have related; hitherto I have wept over others;—may Heaven now have mercy upon me, and may the earth weep for me. With regard to temporal things, I have not even a blanca for an offering; and in spiritual things, I have ceased here in the Indies from observing the prescribed forms of religion. Solitary in my trouble, sick, and in daily expectation of death, surrounded by millions of hostile savages full of cruelty, and thus separated from the blessed sacraments of our holy Church, how will my soul be forgotten if it be separated from the body in this foreign land? Weep for me, whoever

---

almirantado. Grandísima virtud, fama con ejemplo será si hacen esto, y quedará á la España gloriosa memoria con la de vuestras Altezas de agradecidos y justos Príncipes. La intencion tan sana que yo siempre tuve al servicio de vuestras Altezas, y la afrenta tan desigual, no da lugar al anima que calle, bíen que yo quiera: suplico á vuestras Altezas me perdonen. Yo estoy tan perdido como dije: yo he llorado fasta aquí á otros: haya misericordia agora el Cielo, y llore por mi la tierra. En el temporal no tengo solamente una blanca para el oferta: en el espiritual he parado aquí en las Indias de la forma que está dicho: aislado en esta pena, enfermo, aguardando cada dia por la muerte, y cercado de un cuento de salvages y llenos de cruelidad y enemigos nuestros, y tan apartado de los Santos Sacramentos de la Santa Iglesia, que se olvidará desta anima si se aparta acá del cuerpo. Llore por mí quien tiene caridad, verdad y justicia. Yo no vine este viage

has charity, truth, and justice! I did not come out on this voyage to gain to myself honour or wealth; this is a certain fact, for at that time all hope of such a thing was dead. I do not lie when I say that I went to your Highnesses with honest purpose of heart, and sincere zeal in your cause. I humbly beseech your Highnesses, that if it please God to rescue me from this place, you will graciously sanction my pilgrimage to Rome and other holy places. May the Holy Trinity protect your Highnesses' lives, and add to the prosperity of your exalted position.

Done in the Indies, in the island of Jamaica, on the seventh of July, in the year one thousand five hundred and three.

á navegar por ganar honra ni hacienda: esto es cierto, porque estaba ya la esperanza de todo en ella muerta. Yo vine á V. A. con sana intencion y buen zelo, y no miento. Suplico humildemente á V. A. que si á Dios place de me sacar de aquí, que haya por bien mi ida á Roma y otras romerías. Cuya vida y alto estado la Santa Trinidad guarde y acresciente. Fecha en las Indias en la Isla de Jamaica á siete de Julio de mil quinientos y tres años.

A NARRATIVE

Given by Diego Mendez [in his will] of some events that occurred in the last voyage of the Admiral Don Christopher Columbus.

DIEGO MENDEZ, citizen of St. Domingo, in the island of Española, being in the city of Valladolid, where the Court of their Majesties was at the time staying, made his will on the sixth day of June, of the year one thousand five hundred and thirty-six, before Fernando Perez, their Majesties' scrivener, and notary public in that their Court, and in all their Kingdoms and Lordships, the witnesses to the same being Diego de Arana, Juan Diez Miranda de la Cuadra, Martin de Orduña, Lucas Fernandez, Alonzo de Angulo, Francisco de Hinojosa and Diego de Aguilar, all servants of my Lady the Vicequeen of the Indies.[1] And among other chapters of the said will there is one which runs literally as follows:—

RELACION

Hecha por Diego Mendez, de algunos acontecimientos del último viage del Almirante Don Cristóbal Colon.

DIEGO MENDEZ, vecino de la ciudad de Santo Domingo de la Isla Española, hallándose en la villa de Valladolid, donde á la sazon estaba la Corte de SS. MM., otorgó testamento en seis dias del mes de Junio del año de mil quinientos treinta y seis, por testimonio de Fernan Perez, escribano de SS. MM., y su notario público en la su Corte y en todos los sus Reinos y Señoríos; siendo testigos al otorgamiento Diego de Arana, Juan Diez Miranda de la Cuadra, Martin de Orduña, Lucas Fernandez, Alonso de Angulo, Francísco de Hinojosa y Diego de Aguilar, todos criados de la Señora Vireina de las Indias. Y entre otros capítulos del mencionado testamento hay uno que á la letra dice así.

[1] Donna Maria de Toledo, widow of Diego Columbus.

Clause of the will, Item : The very illustrious gentlemen, the admiral Don Christopher Columbus, of glorious memory, and his son the admiral Don Diego Columbus, and his grandson the admiral Don Louis, (whom may God long preserve), and through them my Lady the Vicequeen, as tutress and guardian of the latter, are in debt to me, for many and great services that I have rendered them, in as much as I have spent and worn out the best part of my life even to its close in their service; especially did I serve the admiral Don Christopher, going with his Lordship to the discovery of the islands and terra firma, and often putting myself in danger of death in order to save his life and the lives of those who were with him, more particularly when we were shut in at the mouth of the river Belen or Yebra, through the violence of the sea and the winds which drove up the sand, and raised such a mountain of it as to close up the entrance of the port. His Lordship being there greatly afflicted, a multitude of Indians collected together on shore to burn the ships, and kill us all, pretending that they were going to make war

---

Cláusula del testamento. Item: Los muy ilustres Señores, el Almirante D. Cristobal Colon, de gloriosa memoria, y su hijo el Almirante D. Diego Colon, y su nieto el Almirante D. Luis, á quien Dios dé largos dias de vida, y por ellos la Vireina mi Señora, como su tutriz y curadora, me son en cargo de muchos y grandes servicios que yo les hice, en que consumí y gasté todo lo mejor de mi vida hasta acaballa en su servicio; especialmente serví al gran Almirante D. Cristóbal andando con su Señoria descubriendo Islas y Tierra firme, en que puse muchas veces mi persona á peligro de muerte por salvar su vida y de los que con él iban y estaban ; mayormente cuando se nos cerró el puerto del rio de Belen ó Yebra donde estábamos con la fuerza de las tempestades de la mar y de los vientos que acarrearon y amontonaron la arena en cantidad con que cegaron la entrada del puerto. Y estando su Señoria allí muy congojado, juntóse gran multitud de Indios de la tierra para venir á quemarnos los navios y matarnos á todos, con color que decian que iban á hacer guerra a otros

against other Indians of the province of Cabrava Aurira, with whom they were at enmity. Though many of them passed by that part where our ships were lying, none of the fleet took notice of the matter except myself, who went to the admiral and said to him, " Sir, these people who have passed by in order of battle, say that they go to unite themselves with the people of Veragua, to attack the people of Cobrava Aurira: I do not believe it, but, on the contrary, I think that they are collected together to burn our ships and kill all of us,"—as in fact was the case. The admiral then asked me what were the best means of preventing this, and I proposed to his Lordship that I should go with a boat along the coast towards Veragua, to see where the royal court sat. I had not proceeded on my errand half a league when I found nearly a thousand men of war with great stores of provisions of all kinds, and I went on shore alone amongst them, leaving my boat afloat; I then spoke with them, making them understand me as well as I could, and offered to go with them to the battle with that armed boat; but this they strongly refused, saying there was no

---

Indios de las provincias de Cobrava Aurira con quien tenian guerra: y como pasaron muchos dellos por aquel puerto en que teniamos nosotros las naos, ninguno de la armada caia en el negocio sino yo, que fuí al Almirante y le dije: "Señor, estas gentes que por aquí han pasado en orden de guerra dicen que se han de juntar con los de Veragoa para ir contra los de Cobrava Aurira: yo no lo creo sino el contrario, y es que se juntan para quemarnos los navíos y matarnos á todos," como de hecho lo era. Y diciéndome el Almirante cómo se remediaria, yo dije á su Señoría que saldria con una barca é iría por la costa hácia Veragoa, para ver donde asentaban el real. Y no hube andado media legua cuando halle al pie de mil hombres de guerra con muchas vituallas y brevages, y salté en tierra solo entre ellos, dejando mi barca puesta en flota: y hablé con ellos segun pude entender, y ofrecíme que queria ir con ellos á la guerra con aquella barca armada, y ellos se escusaron reciamente diciendo que no lo habian

need of such a thing. After that I returned to the boat, and remained there in sight of them all that night, so that they could not go to the ships to burn or destroy them, according to their previous arrangements, without my seeing them, upon which they changed their plan, and on that same night they all returned to Veragua. I then went back to the ships, and related all this to his Lordship, who thought no little of what I had done, and upon his consulting me as to the best manner of proceeding so as clearly to ascertain what was the intention of the people, I offered to go to them with one single companion; and this task I undertook, though more certain of death than of life in the result.

After journeying along the beach up to the river of Veragua, I found two canoes of strange Indians, who related to me more in detail, that these people were indeed collected together to burn our ships and kill us all, and that they had forsaken their purpose in consequence of the boat coming up to the spot, but that they intended to return after two days to make the attempt once more. I then asked them to carry me in their canoes to the upper

menester: y como yo me volviese á la barca y estuviese allí á vista dellos toda la noche, vieron que no podian ir á las naos para quemallas y destruillas, segun tenian acordado, sin que yo lo viese, y mudaron propósito: y aquella noche se volvieron todos á Veragoa, y yo me volví á las naos y hice relacion de todo á su Señoría, é no lo tuvo en poco. Y platicando conmigo sobrello sobre que manera se ternia para saber claramente el intento de aquella gente, yo me ofrecí de ir allá con un solo compañero, y lo puse por obra, yendo mas cierto de la muerte que de la vida: y habiendo caminado por la playa hasta el rio de Veragoa hallé dos canoas de Indios extrangeros que me contaron muy á la clara como aquellas gentes iban para quemar las naos y matarnos á todos, y que lo dejaron de hacer por la barca que allí sobrevino, y questaban todavia de propósito de volver á hacello dende á dos dias, é yo les rogué que me llevasen en sus canoas el rio arriba, y que gelo pagaria; y ellos se escusaban aconsejándome que en

part of the river, offering to remunerate them if they would do so; but they excused themselves, and advised me by no means to go, for that both myself and my companion would certainly be killed. At length, in spite of their advice, I prevailed upon them to take me in their canoes to the upper part of the river, until I reached the villages of the Indians, whom I found in order of battle. They, however, would not, at first, allow me to go to the principal residence of the cacique, till I pretended that I was come as a surgeon to cure him of a wound that he had in his leg; then, after I had made them some presents, they suffered me to proceed to the seat of royalty, which was situated on the top of a hillock, surmounted by a plain, with a large square surrounded by three hundred heads of the enemies he had slain in battle. When I had passed through the square, and reached the royal house, there was a great clamour of women and children at the gate, who ran into the palace screaming. Upon this, one of the chief's sons came out in a high passion, uttering angry words in his own language; and, laying hands upon me, with one push he thrust me far

---

ninguna manera fuese, porque fuese cierto que en llegando me matarian á mí y al compañero que llevaba. E sin embargo de sus consejos hice que me llevasen en sus canaos el rio arriba hasta llegar á los pueblos de los Indios, los cuales hallé todos puestos en orden de guerra, que no me querian dejar ir al asiento principal del Cacique; y yo fingiendo que le iba á curar como cirujano de una llaga que tenia en una pierna, y con dádivas que les dí me dejaron ir hasta el asiento Real, que estaba encima de un cerro llano con una plaza grande, rodeada de trescientas cabezas de muertos que habian ellos muerto en una batalla: y como yo hubiese pasado toda la plaza y llegado á la Casa Real hubo grande alboroto de mugeres y muchachos que estaban á la puerta, que entraron gritando dentro en el palacio. Y salió de él un hijo del Señor muy enojado diciendo palabras recias en su lenguage, ó puso las manos en mí y de un empellon me desvió muy lejos de sí: diciéndole yo por amansarle como iba á curar á

away from him. In order to appease him, I told him that
I was come to cure the wound in his father's leg, and
showed him an ointment that I had brought for that purpose; but he replied, that on no account whatever should I
go in to the place where his father was. When I saw that
I had no chance of appeasing him in that way, I took out a
comb, a pair of scissors, and a mirror, and caused Escobar,
my companion, to comb my hair and then cut it off. When
the Indian, and those who were with him, saw this, they
stood in astonishment; upon which I prevailed on him to
suffer his own hair to be combed and cut by Escobar; I
then made him a present of the scissors, with the comb and
the mirror, and thus he became appeased. After this, I
begged him to allow some food to be brought, which was
soon done, and we ate and drank in love and good fellow-
ship, like very good friends. I then left him and returned
to the ships, and related all this to my lord the Admiral,
who was not a little pleased when he heard all these circumstances, and the things that had happened to me. He
ordered a large stock of provisions to be put into the ships,
and into certain straw houses that we had built there, with
a view that I should remain, with some of the men, to exa-

---

su padre de la pierna, y mostrándole cierto unguento que para
ello llevaba, dijo que en ninguna manera habia de entrar donde
estaba su padre. Y visto por mí que por aquella via no podia
amansarle, saqué un peine y unas tijeras y un espejo, y hice que
Escobar mi compañero me peinase y cortase el cabello. Lo cual
visto por él y por los que allí estaban quedaban espantados; y yo
entonces hice que Escobar le peinase á él y le cortase el cabello
con las tijeras, y díselas y el peine y el espejo, y con esto se
amansó; y yo pedí que trajesen algo de comer, y luego lo trajeron,
y comimos y bebimos en amor y compaña, y quedamos amigos; y
despedime dél y vine á las naos, y hice relacion de todo esto al
Almirante mi Señor, el cual no poco holgó en saber todas estas
circumstancias y cosas acaecidas por mi; y mandó poner gran
recabdo en las naos y en ciertas casas de paja, que teniamos hechas

mine and ascertain the secrets of the country. The next morning his lordship called me to take counsel with me as to what was to be done. My opinion was that we ought to seize that chief and all his captains; because, when they were taken, the common people would submit. His lordship was of the same opinion. I then submitted the stratagem and plan by which this might be accomplished; and his lordship ordered that the Adelantado, his brother, and I, accompanied by eighty men, should go to put it into execution. We went, and our Lord gave us such good fortune, that we took the cacique and most of his captains, his wives, sons, and grandsons, with all the princes of his race; but in sending them to the ships, thus captured, the cacique extricated himself from the too slight grasp of the man who held him, a circumstance which afterwards caused us much injury. At this moment it pleased God to cause it to rain very heavily, occasioning a great flood, by which the mouth of the harbour was opened and the Admiral enabled to draw out the ships to sea, in order to proceed to

---

allí en la playa con intencion que habia yo de quedar allí con cierta gente para calar y saber los secretos de la tierra.

Otro dia de mañana su Señoría me llamó para tomar parecer conmigo de lo que sobre ello se debia hacer, y fue mi parecer que debiamos prender aquel Señor y todos sus Capitanes, porque presos aquellos se sojuzgaria la gente menuda; y su Señoria fue del mismo parecer: é yo di el ardid y la manera con que se debia hacer, y su Señoría mandó que el Señor Adelantado, su hermano, y yo con él fuesemos á poner en efecto lo sobredicho con ochenta hombres. Y fuimos, y diónos Nuestro Señor tan buena dicha que prendimos el Cacique y los mas de sus Capitanes y mugeres y hijos y nietos con todos los principales de su generacion; y enviándolos á las naos ansí presos, soltóse el Cacique al que le llevaba por su mal recabdo, el cual despues nos hizo mucho daño. En este instante plugó á Dios que llovió mucho, y con la gran avenida abriósenos el puerto, y el Almirante sacó los navíos á la mar para venirse á Castilla, quedando yo en tierra para haber de

Spain; I, meanwhile, remaining on land as Accountant of his Highness, with seventy men, and the greater part of the provisions of biscuit, wine, oil, and vinegar being left with me.

The Admiral had scarcely got to sea (while I stayed on shore with about twenty men, for the others had gone to assist the Admiral), when suddenly more than four hundred natives, armed with cross-bows and arrows, came down upon me, extending themselves along the face of the mountain; they then gave a shriek, then another, and another, and these repeated cries, by the goodness of God, gave me opportunity to prepare for the engagement. While I was on the shore among the huts which we had built, and they were collected on the mountain at about the distance of an arrow's flight, they began to shoot their arrows and hurl their darts, as if they had been attacking a bull. The arrows and cross-bow shots came down thick as hail, and some of the Indians then separated themselves from the rest, for the purpose of attacking us with clubs; none of them, however, returned, for with our swords we cut off their arms and legs, and killed them on the spot; upon

---

quedar en ella por Contador de su Alteza con setenta hombres, y quedábame allí la mayor parte de los mantenimientos de bizcocho y vino y aceite y vinagre.

Acabado de salir el Almirante á la mar, y quedando yo en tierra con obra de veinte hombres porque los otros se habian salido con el Almirante á despedir, subitamente sobrevino sobre mi mucha gente de la tierra, que serian mas de cuatrocientos hombres armados con sus varas y flechas y tiraderos, y tendiéronse por el monte en haz y dieron una grita y otra y luego otra, con las cuales plugo á Dios me apercibieron á la pelea y defensa de ellos: y estando yo en la playa entre los bohios que tenia hechos, y ellos en el monte á trecho de tíro de dardo, comenzaron á flechar y á garrochar como quien agarrocha toro, y eran las flechas y tiraderas tantas y tan continuas como granizo; y algunos dellos se desmandaban para venirnos á dar con las machi-

which the rest took such fright, that they fled, after having
killed in the contest seven out of twenty of our men; while,
on their side, they lost nine or ten of those who advanced
the most boldly towards us. This contest lasted three long
hours, and our Lord gave us the victory in a marvellous
manner, we being so few and they so numerous. After
this fight was over, the captain, Diego Tristan, came with
the boats from the ships to ascend the river, in order to
take in water for the voyage; and, notwithstanding I advised and warned him not to go, he would not trust me,
but, against my wish, went up the river with two boats and
twelve men; upon which the natives attacked him, and
killed him and all the men that he took with him, except
one who escaped by swimming, and from whom we heard
the news. The Indians then took the boats and broke
them to pieces, which caused us great vexation; for the
Admiral was at sea with his ships without boats, while we
were on shore deprived of the means of going to him.
Besides this, the Indians came continually to assail us;

dasnas; pero ninguno dellos volvian porque quedaban allí cortados brazos y piernas y muertos á espada: de lo cual cobraron
tanto miedo que se retiraron atras, habiéndonos muerto siete
hombres en la pelea de veinte que eramos, y de ellos murieron
diez ó nueve de los que se venian á nosotros mas arriscados.
Duró esta pelea tres horas grandes, y Nuestro Soñor nos dio la
vitoria milagrosamente, siendo nosotros tan poquitos y ellos
tanta muchedumbre.
Acabada esta pelea vino de las naos el Capitan Diego Tristan
con las barcas para subir el rio arriba á tomar agua para su viage;
y no embargante que yo le aconsejé y amonesté que no subiese el
rio arriba no me quiso creer, y contra mi grado subió con las dos
barcas y doce hombres el rio arriba, donde le toparon aquella gente
y pelearon con él, y le mataron á él y todos los que llavaba, que
no escapó sino uno á nado que trujo la nueva; y tomaron las
barcas y hiciéronlas pedazos, de que quedamos en gran fatiga, ansí
el Almrante en la mar con sus naos sin barcas como nosotros en

every instant playing trumpets and kettle-drums, and uttering loud cries in the belief that they had conquered us. The only means of defending ourselves against these people, were two very good brass falconets and plenty of powder and ball, with which we frightened them so much that they did not dare approach us. This lasted for the space of four days, during which time I caused several bags to be made out of the sails of one of the vessels which we had remaining on shore, and into them I put all our biscuit. I then took two canoes, and secured them together with sticks across the tops, and, after loading them with the biscuit, the pipes of wine, and the oil and vinegar, I fastened them together with a rope, and had them towed along the sea while it was calm, so that in the seven trips we contrived to get all of it to the ships, and the people were also carried over by few at a time. Meanwhile I remained with five men to the last, and at night I put to sea with the last boatful. The Admiral thought very highly of this conduct of mine, and did not content himself with embracing me and kissing me

---

tierra sin tener con que poder ir á él. Y á todo esto no cesaban los Indios de venirnos á cometer cada rato tañiendo bocinas y atabales, y dando alaridos pensando que nos tenian vencidos. El remedio contra esta gente que teniamos eran dos tiros falconetes de fruslera, muy buenos, y mucha pólvora y pelotas con que los ojeábamos que no osaban llegar á nosotros. Y esto duró por espacio de cuatro dias, en los cuales yo hice cosar muchos costales de las velas de una nao que nos quedaba, y en aquellos puse todo el bizcocho que teniamos, y tomé dos canoas y até la una con la otra parejas, con unos palos atravesados por encima, y en estos cargué el bizcocho todo en viages, y las pipas de vino y azeite y vinagre atadas en una guindaleja y á jorno [*sic*, jorro] por la mar, tirando por ellas las canoas, abonanzando la mar, en siete caminos que hicieron lo llevaron todo á las naos, y la gente que conmigo estaba poco á poco la llevaron, é yo quedé con cinco hombres á la postre siendo de noche, y en la postrera barcada me embarqué: lo cual el Almirante tuvo á mucho, y no se hartaba de me abrazar y besar

on the cheeks for having performed so great a service, but asked me to take the captaincy of the ship *Capitana*, with the government of all the crew, and, in fact, of the entire voyage; which I accepted in order to oblige him, as it was a service of great responsibility.

On the last day of April, in the year fifteen hundred and three, we left Veragua, with three ships, intending to make our passage homeward to Spain, but as the ships were all pierced and eaten by the teredo, we could not keep them above water; we abandoned one of them after we had proceeded thirty leagues; the two which remained were even in a worse condition than that,[1] so that all the hands were not sufficient with the use of pumps and kettles and pans to draw off the water that came through the holes made by the worms. In this state, with the utmost toil and danger, we sailed for thirty-five days, thinking to reach Spain, and at the end of this time we arrived at the lowest point of the island of Cuba, at the province of Homo, where the city of Trinidad now stands, so that we were three hundred leagues

---

en los carrillos por tan gran servicio como allí le hice, y me rogó tomase la capitanía de la nao Capitana y el regimiento de toda la gente y del viage, lo cual yo acepté por le hacer servicio en ello por ser, como era, cosa de gran trabajo.

Postrero de Abril de mil quinientos y tres partimos de Veragoa con tres navíos, pensando venir la vuelta de Castilla: y comō los navíos estaban todos abujerados y comidos de gusanos no los podiamos tener sobre agua; y andadas treinta leguas dejamos el uno, quedándonos otros dos peor acondicionados que aquel, que toda la gente no bastaba con las bombas y calderas y vasijas á sacar el agua que se nos entraba por los abujeros de la broma: y de esta manera, no sin grandísimo trabajo y peligro, pensando venir á Castilla navegamos treinta y cinco dias, y en cabo dellos llegamos á la isla de Cuba á lo mas bajo della, á la provincia de Homo, allá donde agora está el pueblo de la Trinidad; de manera

[1] Possibly the ship they abandoned was inferior in size, or in some other respect.

further from Spain than when we left Veragua for the purpose of proceeding thither; and this, as I have said, with the vessels in very bad condition, unfit to encounter the sea, and our provisions nearly gone. It pleased God that we were enabled to reach the island of Jamaica, where we drove the two ships on shore, and made of them two cabins thatched with straw, in which we took up our dwelling, not however without considerable danger from the natives, who were not yet subdued, and who might easily set fire to our habitation in the night, in spite of the greatest watchfulness. It was there that I gave out the last ration of biscuit and wine; I then took a sword in my hand, three men only accompanying me, and advanced into the island; for no one else dared go to seek food for the Admiral and those who were with him. It pleased God that I found some people who were very gentle and did us no harm, but received us cheerfully, and gave us food with hearty good will. I then made a stipulation with the Indians, who lived in a village called Aguacadiba, and with their cacique, that they should make cassava bread, and that they should

---

que estábamos mas lejos de Castilla trescientas leguas que cuando partimos de Veragoa para ir á ella; y como digo los navíos mal acondicionados, innavegables, y las vituallas que se nos acababan. Plugo á Dios Nuestro Señor que pudimos llegar á la isla de Jamaica, donde zabordamos los dos navíos en tierra, y hicimos de ellos dos casas pajizas, en que estabamos no sin gran peligro de la gente de aquella isla, que no estaba domada ni conquistada, nos pusiesen fuego de noche, que fácilmente lo podian hacer por mas que nosotros velabamos.

Aquí acabé de dar la postrera racion de bizcocho y vino, y tomé una espada en la mano y tres hombres conmigo, y fuíme por esa isla adelante, porque ninguno osaba ir á buscar de comer para el Almirante y los que con él estaban: y plugo á Dios que hallaba la gente tan mansa que no me hacian mal, antes se holgaban conmigo y me daban de comer de buena voluntad. Y en un pueblo que se llama Aguacadiba, concerté con los Indios y Ca-

hunt and fish to supply the Admiral every day with a sufficient quantity of provisions, which they were to bring to the ships, where I promised there should be a person ready to pay them in blue beads, combs and knives, hawks'-bells and fish-hooks, and other such articles which we had with us for that purpose. With this understanding, I despatched one of the Spaniards whom I had brought with me to the admiral, in order that he might send a person to pay for the provisions, and secure their being sent. From thence I went to another village, at three leagues distance from the former, and made a similar agreement with the natives and their cacique, and then despatched another Spaniard to the admiral, begging him to send another person with a similar object to this village. After this I went further on, and came to a great cacique named Huareo, living in a place which is now called Melilla, thirteen leagues from where the ships lay. I was very well received by him; he gave me plenty to eat, and ordered all his subjects to bring together in the course of three days a great quantity of provisions, which they did, and laid them

---

cique que harian pan cazabe, y que cazarian y pescarian, y que darian de todas las vituallas al Almirante cierta cuantía cada dia, y lo llevarian á las naos, con que estuviese allí persona que ge lo pagase en cuentas azules y peines y cuchillos y cascabeles, y anzuelos y otros rescates que para ello llevabamos: y con esto concierto despaché uno de los dos cristianos que conmigo traía al Almirante, para que enviase persona que tuviese cargo de pagar aquellas vituallas y enviarlas.

Y de allí fuí á otro pueblo que estaba tres leguas de este y hice el mismo concierto con el Cacique y Indios, de él, y envié otro cristiano al Almirante para que enviase allí otra persona al mismo cargo.

Y de allí pasé adelante y llegué á un gran Cacique que se llamaba Huareo, donde agora dicen Melilla, que es trece leguas de las naos, del cual fuí muy bien recebido, que me dió muy bien de comer, y mandó que todos sus vasallos trajiesen dende á tres dias

before him, whereupon I paid him for them to his full
satisfaction. I stipulated with him that they should furnish
a constant supply, and engaged that there should be a person appointed to pay them; having made this arrangement,
I sent the other Spaniard to the admiral with the provisions
they had given me, and then begged the cacique to allow
me two Indians to go with me to the extremity of the
island, one to carry the hammock in which I slept, and the
other carrying the food.

In this manner I journeyed eastward to the end of the
island, and came to a cacique who was named Ameyro,
with whom I entered into close friendship. I gave him my
name and took his, which amongst these people is regarded
as a pledge of brotherly attachment. I bought of him
a very good canoe, and gave him in exchange an excellent
brass helmet that I carried in a bag, a frock, and one of
the two shirts that I had with me; I then put out to sea in
this canoe, in search of the place that I had left, the cacique
having given me six Indians to assist in guiding the canoe.
When I reached the spot to which I had dispatched the

---

muchas vituallas, que le presentaron, é yo ge las pagué de manera que fueron contentos: y concerté que ordinariamente las
traerian, habiendo allí persona que ge las pagase, y con este concierto envié el otro cristiano con los mantenimientos que allá me
dieron al Almirante, y pedí al Cacique que me diese dos Indios
que fuesen conmigo fasta el cabo de la isla, que el uno me llevaba
la hamaca en que dormia é el otro la comida. Y desta manera
caminé hasta el cabo de la isla, á la parte del Oriente, y llegué á
un Cacique que se llamaba Ameyro, é hice con él amistades de
hermandad, y díle mi nombre y tomé el suyo, que entre ellos se
tiene por grande hermandad. Y compréle una canoa muy buena
que él tenia, y díle por ella una bacineta de laton muy buena que
llevaba en la manga y el sayo y una camisa de dos que llevaba, y
embarquéme en aquella canoa, y vine por la mar requiriendo las
estancias que habia dejado con seis Indios que el Cacique me dió
para que me la ayudasen á navegar, y venido á los lugares donde

provisions, I found there the Spaniards whom the admiral had sent, and I loaded them with the victuals that I had brought with me, and went myself to the admiral, who gave me a very cordial reception. He was not satisfied with seeing and embracing me, but asked me respecting everything that had occurred in the voyage, and offered up thanks to God for having delivered me in safety from so barbarous a people. The men rejoiced greatly at my arrival, for there was not a loaf left in the ships when I returned to them with the means of allaying their hunger; this, and every day after that, the Indians came to the ships loaded with provisions from the places where I had made the agreements; so that there was enough for the two hundred and thirty people who were with the admiral. Ten days after this, the admiral called me aside, and spoke to me of the great peril he was in, addressing me as follows:—
" Diego Mendez, my son, not one of those whom I have here with me has any idea of the great danger in which we stand except myself and you; for we are but few in number, and these wild Indians are numerous and very fickle and

---

yo habia proveido, hallé en ellos los cristianos que el Almirante habia enviado, y cargué de todas las vituallas que les hallé, y fuime al Almirante, del cual fuí muy bien recebido, que no se hartaba de verme y abrazarme, y preguntar lo que me habia sucedido en el viage, dando gracias á Dios que me habia llevado y traido á salvamiento libre de tanta gente salvage. Y como el tiempo que yo llegué á las naos no habia en ellas un pan que comer, fueron todos muy alegres con mi venida, porque les maté la hambre en tiempo de tanta necesidad, y de allí adelante cada dia venian los Indios cargados de vituallas á las naos de aquellos lugares que yo habia concertado, que bastaban para doscientas y treinta personas que estaban con el Almirante. Dende á diez dias el Almirante me llamó á parte y me dijo el gran peligro en que estaba, diciéndome ansi : " Diego Mendez, hijo : ninguno de cuantos aquí yo tengo siente el gran peligro en que estamos sino yo y vos, porque somos muy poquitos, y estos indios salvages son

capricious : and whenever they may take it into their heads to come and burn us in our two ships, which we have made into straw-thatched cabins, they may easily do so by setting fire to them on the land side, and so destroy us all. The arrangement that you have made with them for the supply of food, to which they agreed with such good-will, may soon prove disagreeable to them ; and it would not be surprising if, on the morrow, they were not to bring us anything at all : in such case we are not in a position to take it by main force, but shall be compelled to accede to their terms. I have thought of a remedy, if you consider it advisable ; which is, that some one should go out in the canoe that you have purchased, and make his way in it to Española, to purchase a vessel with which we may escape from the extremely dangerous position in which we now are. Tell me your opinion." To which I answered:—"My lord, I distinctly see the danger in which we stand, which is much greater than would be readily imagined. With respect to the passage from this island to Española in so small a vessel as a canoe, I look upon it not merely as difficult, but impossible; for I know not who would venture

---

muchos y muy mudables y antojadizos, y en la hora que se les antojare de venir y quemarnos aquí donde estamos en estos dos navios hechos casas pajizas fácilmente pueden echar fuego dende tierra y abrasarnos aquí á todos : y el concierto que vos habeis hecho con ellos del traer los mantenimientos que traen de tan buena gana, mañana se les antojará otra cosa y no nos traerán nada, y nosotros no somos parte para tomargelo per fuerza si no estar á lo que ellos quisieren. Yo he pensado un remedio si á vos os parece : que en esta canoa que comprastes se aventurase alguno á pasar á la Isla Española á comprar una nao en que pudiesen salir de tan gran peligro como este en que estamos. Decidme vuestro parecer." Yo le respondí : " Señor: el peligro en que estamos bien lo veo, que es muy mayor de lo que se puede pensar. El pasar desta Isla á la Isla Española en tan poca vasija como es la canoa, no solamente lo tengo por dificultoso, sino por imposible:

to encounter so terrific a danger as to cross a gulf of forty leagues of sea, and amongst islands where the sea is most impetuous, and scarcely ever at rest." His lordship did not agree with the opinion that I expressed, but adduced strong arguments to show that I was the person to undertake the enterprise. To which I replied:—"My lord, I have many times put my life in danger to save yours, and the lives of all those who are with you, and God has marvellously preserved me: in consequence of this, there have not been wanting murmurers who have said that your lordship entrusts every honourable undertaking to me, while there are others amongst them who would perform them as well as I. My opinion is, therefore, that your lordship would do well to summon all the men, and lay this business before them, to see if, amongst them all, there is one who will volunteer to undertake it, which I certainly doubt; and if all refuse, I will risk my life in your service, as I have done many times already."

On the following day his lordship caused all the men to appear together before him, and then opened the matter to

---

porque haber de atravesar un golfo de cuarenta leguas de mar y entre islas donde la mar es mas impetuosa y de menos reposo, no sé quien se ose aventurar á peligro tan notorio. Su Señoría no me replicó, persuadiendome reciamente que yo era el que lo habia de hacer, á lo cual yo respondí: "Señor: muchas veces he puesto mi vida á peligro de muerte por salvar la vuestra y de todos estos que aqui estan, y nuestro Señor milagrosamente me ha guardado y la vida; y con todo no han faltado murmuradores que dicen que vuestra Señoria me acomete á mí todas las cosas de honra, habiendo en la compañía otros que las harian tan bien como yo: y por tanto paréceme á mí que vuestra Señoría los haga llamar á todos y los proponga este negocio, para ver si entre todos ellos habrá alguno que lo quiera emprender, lo cual yo dudo; y cuando todos se echen de fuera, yo pondré mi vida á muerte por vuestro servicio, como muchas veces lo he hecho.

Luego el dia siguiente su Señoría los hizo juntar á todos delante

them in the same manner as he had done to me. When they heard it they were all silent, until some said that it was out of the question to speak of such a thing; for it was impossible, in so small a craft, to cross a boisterous and perilous gulf of forty leagues' breadth, and to pass between those two islands, where very strong vessels had been lost in going to make discoveries, not being able to encounter the force and fury of the currents. I then arose, and said:—
"My lord, I have but one life, and I am willing to hazard it in the service of your lordship, and for the welfare of all those who are here with us; for I trust in God, that in consideration of the motive which actuates me, he will give me deliverance, as he has already done on many other occasions." When the admiral heard my determination, he arose and embraced me, and, kissing me on the cheek, said,—"Well did I know that there was no one here but yourself who would dare to undertake this enterprise: I trust in God, our Lord, that you will come out of it victoriously, as you have done in the others which you have undertaken." On the following day I drew my canoe on to the shore; fixed a

---

sí, y les propuso el negocio de la manera que á mí: é oido, todos enmudecieron, y algunos dijeron que era por demas platicarse en semejante cosa, porque era imposible en tan pequeña vasija pasar tan impetuoso y peligroso golfo de cuarenta leguas como este, entre estas dos islas donde muy recias naos se habian perdido andando á descubrir, sin poder romper ni forzar el ímpetu y furia de las corrientes. Entonces yo me levanté y dije: "Señor: una vida tengo no mas, yo la quiero aventurar por servicio de vuestra Señoría y por el bien de todos los que aquí estan, porque tengo esperanza en Dios nuestro Señor que vista la intencion con que yo lo hago me librará, como otras muchas veces lo ha hecho." Oida por el Almirante mi determinacion levantóse y abrazóme y besóme en el carrillo, diciendo: "Bien sabia yo que no habia aquí ninguno que osase tomar esta empresa sino vos: esperanza tengo en Dios nuestro Señor saldreis della con vitoria como de las otras que habeis emprendido."

false keel on it, and pitched and greased it; I then nailed some boards upon the poop and prow, to prevent the sea from coming in, as it was liable to do from the lowness of the gunwales; I also fixed a mast in it, set up a sail, and laid in the necessary provisions for myself, one Spaniard, and six Indians, making eight in all, which was as many as the canoe would hold. I then bade farewell to his lordship, and all the others, and proceeded along the coast of Jamaica, up to the extremity of the island,[1] which was thirty-five leagues from the point whence we started. Even this distance was not traversed without considerable toil and danger; for on the passage I was taken prisoner by some Indian pirates, from whom God delivered me in a marvellous manner. When we had reached the end of the island, and were remaining there in the hope of the sea becoming sufficiently calm to allow us to continue our voyage across it, many of the natives collected together with the determination of killing me, and seizing the canoe with its contents, and they cast lots for my life, to see which of them should carry their design into execution.

El dia siguiente yo puse mi canoa á monte, y le eché una quilla postiza, y le dí su brea y sebo, y en la popa y proa clavéle algunas tablas para defensa de la mar que no se me entrase como hiciera siendo rasa; y púsele un mástil y su vela, y metí los mantenimientos que pude para mí y para un cristiano y para seis indios, que éramos ocho personas, y no cabian mas en la canoa: y despedíme de su Señoría y de todos, y fuime la costa arriba de la Isla de Jamaica, donde estábamos, que hay dende las naos hasta el cabo della treinta y cinco leguas, las cuales yo navegué con gran peligro y trabajo, porque fuí preso en el camino de Indios salteadores en la mar, de que Dios me libró milagrosamente. Y llegado al cabo de la isla, estando esperando que la mar se amansase para acometer mi viage, juntáronse muchos Indios y determinaron de matarme y tomar la canoa y lo que en ella llevaba; y así juntos jugaron

---

[1] Ferdinand Columbus says that the Indians called this eastern point of the island Aramaquique, and that it was thirty-four leagues from Maima, where the admiral was.

As soon as I became aware of their project, I betook myself secretly to my canoe, which I had left at three leagues distance from where I then was, and set sail for the spot where the admiral was staying, and reached it after an interval of fifteen days from my departure. I related to him all that had happened, and how God had miraculously rescued me from the hands of those savages. His lordship was very joyful at my arrival, and asked me if I would recommence my voyage; I replied that I would, if I might be allowed to take some men, to be with me at the extremity of the island until I should find a fair opportunity of putting to sea to prosecute my voyage. The admiral gave me seventy men, and with them his brother the Adelantado, to stay with me until I put to sea, and to remain there for three days after my departure; with this arrangement I returned to the extremity of the island and waited there four days. Finding the sea become calm I parted from the rest of the men with much mutual sorrow; I then commended myself to God and our Lady of Antigua, and was at sea five days and four nights without laying down the oar from my hand,

---

mi vida á la pelota para ver á cual dellos cabria la ejecucion del negocio. Lo cual sentido por mí víneme ascondidamente á mi canoa, que tenia tres leguas de allí, y hícime á la vela y víneme donde estaba el Almirante, habiendo quince dias que de allí habia partido: y contele todo lo sucedido, cómo Dios milagrosamente me habia librado de las manos de aquellos salvages. Su Señoría fue muy alegre de mi venida, y preguntóme si volveria al viage. Yo dije que sí, llevando gente que estuviese conmigo en el cabo de la isla hasta que yo entrase en la mar á proseguir mi viage. Su Señoría me dió setenta hombres y con ellos á su hermano le Adelantado, que fuesen y estuviesen conmigo hasta embarcarme, y tres dias despues. Y desta manera volví al cabo de la isla donde estuve cuatro dias. Viendo que la mar se amansaba me despedí dellos y ellos de mí, con hartas lágrimas; y encomendéme á Dios y á nuestra Señora del Antigua, y navegué cinco dias y cuatro noches que jamas perdí el remo de la mano gobernando la canoa.

but continued steering the canoe while my companions rowed. It pleased God that at the end of five days I reached the Island of Española at Cape San Miguel,[1] having been two days without eating or drinking, for our provisions were exhausted. I brought my canoe up to a very beautiful part of the coast, to which many of the natives soon came, and brought with them many articles of food, so that I remained there two days to take rest. I took six Indians from this place, and leaving those that I had brought with me, I put off to sea again, moving along the coast of Española, for it was a hundred and thirty leagues from the spot where I landed to the city of St. Domingo, where the Governor dwelt, who was the Commander de Lares. When I had proceeded eighty leagues along the coast of the island (not without great toil and danger, for that part of the island was not yet brought into subjugation), I reached the province of Azoa, which is twenty-four leagues from San Domingo, and there I learned from the commander Gallego, that the governor

---

y los compañeros remando. Plugo á Dios nuestro Señor que en cabo de cinco dias yo arribé á la Isla Española, al Cabo de S. Miguel, habiendo dos dias que no comiamos ni bebiamos por no tenello; y entré con mi canoa en una ribera muy hermosa, donde luego vino mucha gente de la tierra y trajeron muchas cosas de comer, y estuve allí dos dias descansando. Yo tomé seis Indios de allí, dejados los que llevaba, y comencé á navegar por la costa de la Isla Española, que hay dende allí hasta la Cibdad de Santo Domingo ciento y treinta leguas que yo habia de andar, porque estaba allí el Gobernador, que era el Comendador de Lares; y habiendo andado por la costa de la isla ochenta leguas, no sin grandes peligros y trabajos, porque la isla no estaba conquistada ni allanada, llegué á la Provincia de Azoa, que es veinte y cuatro leguas antes de Santo Domingo, y allí supe del Comendador Gallego como el Gobernador era partido á la Provincia de Xuragoa

[1] This cape is since called Cape Tiburon. Mendez does not speak of his arrival at the little island of Naraza, and other places spoken of by Ferdinand Columbus and Herrera.

was gone out to subdue the province of Xuragoa, which was at fifty leagues distance. When I heard this I left my canoe and took the road for Xuragoa,[1] where I found the governor, who kept me with him seven months, until he had burned and hanged eighty-four caciques, lords of vassals, and with them Nacaona, the sovereign mistress of the island, to whom all rendered service and obedience. When that expedition was finished I went on foot to San Domingo, a distance of seventy leagues, and waited in expectation of the arrival of ships from Spain, it being now more than a year since any had come. In this interval it pleased God that three ships arrived, one of which I bought, and loaded it with provisions, bread, wine, meat, hogs, sheep, and fruit, and despatched it to the place where the admiral was staying, in order that he might come over in it with all his people to San Domingo, and from thence sail for Spain. I myself went on in advance with the two other ships, in order to give an account to the king and queen of all that had occurred in this voyage.

á allanarla; la cual estaba cincuenta leguas de allí. Y esto sabido dejé mi canoa y tomé el camino por tierra de Xuragoa, donde hallé el Gobernador, el cual me detuvo allí siete meses hasta que hizo quemar y ahorcar ochenta y cuatro Caciques, señores de vasallos, y con ellos á Nacaona la mayor señora de la isla, á quien todos ellos obedecian y servian. Y esto acabado vine de pie á tíerra de Santo Domingo, que era setenta leguas de allí, y estuve esperando viniesen naos de Castilla, que habia mas de un año que no habian venido. Y en este comedio plugo á Dios que vinieron tres naos, de las cuales yo compré la una y la cargué de vituallas, de pan y vino y carne y puercos y carneros y frutas, y la envié adonde estaba el Almirante para en que viniesen él y toda la gente como vinieron allí á Santo Domingo y de allí á Castilla. E yo me vine delante en las otras dos naos á hacer relacion al Rey y á la Reina de todo lo sucedido en aquel viage.

[1] This should be Xaragua.

I think I should now do well to say somewhat of the events which occurred to the admiral and to his family during the year that they were left on the island. A few days after my departure the Indians became refractory, and refused to bring food as they had hitherto done; the admiral therefore caused all the caciques to be summoned, and expressed to them his surprise that they should not send food as they were wont to do, knowing as they did, and as he had already told them, that he had come there by the command of God. He said that he perceived that God was angry with them, and that He would that very night give tokens of His displeasure by signs that He would cause to appear in the heavens; and as on that night there was to be an almost total eclipse of the moon, he told them that God caused that appearance to signify His anger against them for not bringing the food. The Indians, believing him, were very frightened, and promised that they would always bring him food in future; and so in fact they did until the arrival of the ship which I had sent loaded with provisions. The Admiral, and those who were with him, felt no small joy at the arrival of this ship; and his lordship afterwards informed me

Paraceme que será bien que se diga algo de lo acaecido al Almirante y á su familiar en un año que estuvieron perdidos en aquesta isla: y es que dende á pocos dias que yo me partí los Indios se amotinaron y no le querian traer de comer como antes; y él los hizo llamar á todos los Caciques y les digo que se maravillaba dellos en no traerle la comida como solian, sabiendo como él les habia dicho, que habia venido allí por mandado de Dios, y que Dios estaba enojado dellos, y que él ge lo mostraria aquella noche por señales que haria en el cielo; y como aquella noche era el eclipse de la luna que casi toda se escureció, díjoles que Dios hacia aquello por enojo que tenia dellos porque no le traian de comer, y ellos lo creyeron y fueron muy espantados, y prometieron que le traerian siempre de comer, como de hecho lo hicieron, hasta que llegó la nao con los mantenimentos que yo envié, de que no pequeño gozo fue en el Almirante y en todos los que con él estaban: que

in Spain, that in no part of his life did he ever experience so joyful a day, for he had never hoped to have left that place alive: and in that same ship he set sail,[1] and went to San Domingo, and thence to Spain.

I have wished thus to give a succinct account of my troubles, and of my great and important services; which are such as no man in the world ever rendered to a master, or ever will again; and I do so in order that my sons may know these facts, and be encouraged to serve faithfully, and that, at the same time, his lordship may see that he is bound to make them a handsome return for such services. When his lordship came to the court, and while he was at Salamanca, confined to his bed with the gout, and I was left in sole charge of his affairs, endeavouring to obtain the restitution of his estate and government for his son Diego, I addressed him thus: "My lord, your lordship knows how much I have done in your service, and what trouble I am still taking, night and day, in the management of your affairs; I beseech

despues en Castilla me dijo su Señoría que en toda su vida [nunca?] habia visto tan alegre dia, y que nunca pensó salir de allí vivo: y en esta nao se embarcó y vino á Santo Domingo y de allí á Castilla.

He querido poner aquí esta breve suma de mis trabajos y grandes señalados servicios, cuales nunca hizo hombre á Señor, ni los hará de aquí adelante del mundo; y esto á fin que mis hijos lo sepan y se animen á servir, ó su Señoria sepa que es obligado á hacerles muchas mercedes.

Venido su Señoría á la Corte, y estando en Salamanca en la cama enfermo de gota, andando yo solo entendiendo en sus negocios y en la restitucion de su estado y de la gobernacion para su hijo D. Diego, yo le dije ansi: " Señor: ya vuestra Señoría sabe lo mucho que os he servido y lo mas que trabajo de noche y de dia en vuestros negocios: suplico á vuestra Señoria me señale algun

[1] On the twenty-eighth of June 1504; he entered the harbour of St. Domingo on the thirteenth of August, started for Spain on the twelfth of September, and arrived at San Lucar on Thursday, the seventh of November.

your lordship to grant me some recompense for what I have done." He cheerfully replied that he would do for me whatever I asked, adding that there was very great reason for his so doing. I then specified my wish, and begged his lordship to do me the favour to grant me the office of principal Alguazil of the island of Española for life; to which his lordship assented most cordially, saying, that it was but a trifling remuneration for the great services I had rendered. He also desired me to communicate his wish to his son Diego, who was very glad to hear of the favour his father had shown me in appointing me to the said office; and said, that if his father gave it me with one hand, he, for his part, gave it with both hands. This promise holds good as much now as it did then; but when, after I had succeeded, with considerable difficulty, in securing the restitution of the government of the Indies to my lord the Admiral Don Diego, (his father being then dead), I asked him for the provision of the said office, his lordship replied that he had given it to his uncle, the Adelantado, saying, however, that he would give me another post equivalent to it. I told him that he

---

galardon para en pago dello :" y él me respondió alegremente que yo lo señalase y él lo cumpliria, porque era mucha razon. Y entonces yo le señalé y supliqué á su Señoría me hiciese merced del oficio del Alguacilazgo mayor de la Isla Española para en toda mi vida: y su Señoría dijo que de muy buena voluntad, y que era poco para lo mucho que yo habia servido; y mandóme que lo dijese ansi al Sr. D. Diego, su hijo, el cual fue muy alegre de la merced á mí hecha de dicho oficio, y dijo que si su padre me lo daba con una mano, él con dos. Y esto es ansi la verdad para el siglo que á ellos tiene y á mi espera.

Habiendo yo acabado, no sin grandes trabajos mios, de negociar la restitucion de la gobernacion de las Indias al Almirante D. Diego, mi Señor, siendo su padre fallecido, le pedí la provision del dicho oficio. Su Señoria me respondió que lo tenia dado al Adelantado su tio; pero que él me daria otra cosa equivalente á aquella. Yo dije que aquella diese él á su tio, y á mi me diese lo que su

ought to make such a proposition to his uncle, and that he ought to give me that which his father, and he himself, had promised to me. But he did not do so; and thus I remained without any recompense for all my services : while my lord, the Adelantado, without having rendered any service at all, continued in the enjoyment of the dignity which belonged to me, and reaped the reward of all my exertions.

When his lordship arrived at the city of San Domingo, he assumed the reins as governor, and gave the post which he had promised to me, to Francisco de Garay, a servant of the Adelantado, to hold it for him. This took place on the tenth day of July of the year fifteen hundred and ten, and the office was then worth at least a million per annum. My lady, the Vicequeen, as tutress and guardian of my lord the viceroy, and my lord the viceroy himself, are really chargeable to me for this loss, and are debtors to me for it in justice and on the score of conscience. The post had been given to me by way of recompense, and nothing has been done in my favour towards the accomplishment of the Admiral's promise, since the day in which it was given, to this, the close of my life; if it had been given to me, I should have been the

---

padre y él me habian prometido, lo cual no se hizo; y yo quedó cargado de servicios sin ningun galardon, y el Sr. Adelantado, sin haberlo servido, quedó con mi oficio y con el galardon de todos mis afanes.

Llegado su Señoría á la Cibdad de Santo Domingo por Gobernador tomó las varas dió este oficio á Francisco de Garay, criado del Sr. Adelantado, que lo sirviese por él. Esto fue en diez dias del mes de Julio de mil quinientas diez años. Valia entonces el oficio á lo menos un cuento de renta, del cual la Vireina, mi Señora, como tutriz y curadora del Virey, mi Señor, y él me son en cargo realmente y me lo deben de justicia y *de foro conscientiæ*, porque me fue hecha la merced de él, y no se cumplió conmigo dende el dia que se dió al Adelantado hasta el postrero de mis dias, porque si se me diera yo fuera el mas rico hombre de la isla y mas

richest and most honoured man in the island; whereas, I am now the poorest, and have not even a house of my own to live in, but am obliged to pay rent for the roof over my head. As it would be very difficult to refund the revenues which this office has produced, I will suggest an alternative, which is this: that his lordship grant the rank of principal Alguazil of the city of San Domingo, to one of my sons, for his life, and bestow upon the other the rank of Vice-Admiral in the same city: by the grant of these two offices to my sons in the manner I have said, and by appointing some one to hold them on their behalf until they come of age, his lordship will discharge the conscience of the Admiral his father, and I shall hold myself satisfied, as duly paid for my services. I shall say nothing further upon the subject, but leave it to the consciences of their lordships, and let them do whatever they think proper.

Item. I leave as executors and administrators of my will here at the court, the bachelor Estrada and Diego de Arana, together with my lady the Vicequeen; and I beg his lord-

---

honrado; y por no se me dar soy el mas pobre della, tanto que no tengo una casa en que more sin alquiler.

Y porque haberseme de pagar lo que el oficio ha rentado seria muy dificultoso, yo quiero dar un medio y será este: que su Señoría haga merced del Alguacilazgo mayor de la Cibdad de Santo Domingo á uno de mis hijos para en toda su vida, y al otro le haga merced de su Teniente de Almirante en la dicha Cibdad: y con hacer merced destos dos oficios á mis hijos de la manera que he aquí dicho, y poniéndolos en cabeza de quien los serva por ellos hasta que sean de edad, su Señoría descargará la conciencia del Almirante su padre, y yo me satisfaré de la paga que se me debe de mis servicios: y en esto no diré mes de dejallo en sus conciencias de sus Señorías, y hagan en ello lo que mejor les pareciere.

Item: Dejo por mis albaceas y ejecutores deste mi testamento, aquí en la corte, al Bachiller Estrada y á Diego de Arana, junta-

ship to undertake this charge, and to direct the others to undertake it likewise.

Another clause. Item. I order that my executors purchase a large stone, the best that they can find, and place it upon my grave, and that they write round the edge of it these words: "Here lies the honourable Chevalier Diego Mendez, who rendered great services to the royal crown of Spain, in the discovery and conquest of the Indies, in company with the discoverer of them, the Admiral Don Christopher Columbus, of glorious memory, and afterwards rendered other great services by himself, with his own ships, and at his own cost. He died, etc. He asks of your charity a Paternoster and an Ave Maria.

Item. In the middle of the said stone let there be the representation of a canoe, which is a hollowed tree, such as the Indians use for navigation; for in such a vessel did I cross three hundred leagues of sea; and let them engrave above it this word: "Canoa."

My dear and beloved sons, children of my very dear and beloved wife Doña Francisca de Ribera,—may the blessing

---

mente con la Vireina, mi Señora, y suplico yo á su Señoría lo acepte y les mande á ellos lo mismo.

Otra cláusula. Item: Mando que mis albaceas compren una piedra grande, la mejor que hallaren, y se ponga sobre mi sepultura, y se escriba en derredor della estas letras: "Aquí yace el honrado caballero Diego Mendez que sirvió mucho á la Corona Real de España en el descubrimiento y conquista de las Indias con el Almirante D. Cristobal Colon, de gloriosa memoria, que las descubrió, y despues por sí con naos suyas á su costa: falleció, etc. Pido de limosna un Pater noster y una Ave María.

Item: En medio de la dicha piedra se haga una canoa, que es un madero cavado en que los Indios navegan, porque en otra tal navegó trescientas leguas, y encima pongan unas letras que digan: "Canoa."

Caros y amados hijos mios, y de mi muy cara y amada muger Doña Francisca de Ribera, la bendicion de Dios Todopoderoso,

of God Almighty, Father, Son, and Holy Ghost, descend
upon you, together with my blessing, and protect you, and
make you Catholic Christians, and give you grace always to
love and fear Him. My sons, I earnestly recommend you to
cultivate peace and harmony amongst yourselves, and that
you be obliging, and not haughty, but very humble and
courteous towards those with whom you have to do, so that
all may love you. Serve loyally my lord the Admiral, and
may his lordship grant you large recompense, considering
who he is himself, and by what great services I have deserved his favours. Above all I charge you, my sons, to be
very pious, and to hear very devoutly the divine offices, and
in so doing, may the Lord grant you long life. May it
please Him of His infinite goodness, to make you as good
as I wish you to be, and guide you always with His hand.
Amen.

The books which I send to you are as follows:

The Art of Well-dying, by Erasmus; a *Sermon*, of Erasmus, in Spanish; *Josephus de Bello Judaico*; the *Moral Philosophy*, of Aristotle; the books called *Lingua Erasmi*; the book of

---

Padre y Hijo y Espíritu Santo y la mia descienda sobre vos y vos cubra y os haga catolicos cristianos, y os dé gracia que siempre le ameis y temais. Hijos: encomiendoos mucho la paz y concordia, y que seais muy conformes y no soberbios, sino muy humildes y muy amigables á todos los que contratáredes, porque todos os tengan amor: servid lealmente al Almirante mi Señor, y su Señoría os hará muchas mercedes por quien él es, y porque mis grandes servicios lo merecen; y sobre todo os mando, hijos mios, seais muy devotos y oyais muy devotamente los Oficios Divinos, y haciéndolo ansi Dios nuestro Señor os dará largos dias de vida. A él plega por su infinita bondad haceros tan buenos como yo deseo que seais, y os tenga siempre de su mano. Amen.

Los libros que de acá os envio son los siguientes:

Arte de bien morir de Erasmo. Un sermon de Erasmo en romance. Josefo de Bello Judaico. La Filosofía moral de Aristóteles. Los libros que se dicen Lingua Erasmi. El libro de la

The Holy Land;[1] *The conversations of Erasmus; A treatise on the Complaints of Peace; A book of Contemplation of the Passion of our Redeemer; A treatise on the Revenging of the Death of Agamemnon;* and other small tracts.

I have already told you, my sons, that I leave you these books as heir-looms under the conditions described above in my will, and I wish them to be put together with my other documents, which will be found in the cedar box, at Seville, as I have already said; I wish also the marble mortar should be placed in it, which is now in the possession of Don Ferdinand, or of his major-domo.

I, Diogo Mendez, affirm that this document, contained in thirteen sheets, is my last will and testament, for I have dictated it and caused it to be written, and have signed it with my name; and by it I revoke and annul any other will or wills whatever made by me at any other time or place, and I desire that this only be considered valid. Made in the city of Valladolid, the nineteenth day of June, in the year of

---

Tierra santa. Los coloquios de Erasmo. Un tratado de las querellas de la Paz. Un libro de Contemplaciones de la Pasion de nuestro Redentor. Un tratado de le venganza de la muerte de Agamenon, y otros tratadillos.

Ya dije, hijos mios, que estos libros os dejo por mayorazgo, con las condiciones que estan dichas de suso en el testamento, y quiero que vayan todos con algunas Escrituras mias, que se hallarán en el arca que está en Sevilla, que es de cedro, como ya está dicho: pongan tambien en esta el mortero de mármol que está en poder del Sr. D. Hernando, ó de su mayordomo.

Digo yo Diego Mendez que esta Escritura contenida en trece hojas es mi testamento y postrimera voluntad, porque yo lo ordené é hice escribir, y lo firmé de mi nombre, y por él revoco y doy por ningunos otros cualesquier testamentos hechos en cualesquier otros tiempos ó lugar; y solo este quiero que valga, que es hecho en la villa de Valladolid en diez y nueve dias del mes de Junio,

[1] By B. von Breydenbach.(?)

our Redeemer one thousand five hundred and thirty-six.—
DIEGO MENDEZ. And I, the said Garcia de Vera, scrivener
and notary public, was present at all which has been herein
said; and it has all been set down by me by order of the
said lord-lieutenant, and by request of the said Bachelor
Estrada, forming the testament in these twenty-six leaves of
folio paper, as is here seen. I caused it to be written as it
was presented and laid before me, and have kept the original
in my possession. And to this effect I have here placed this
my seal *(here was placed the seal)*, in testimony of the truth.—
(Signed) GARCIA DE VERA.

*This agrees literally with the clauses copied from a will
sealed and signed by the said scrivener, Garcia de Vera, the
original of which is in the archives of the most excellent the
Admiral Duke of Veraguas, from which I copied it in Madrid
on the twenty-eighth day of March, in the year eighteen hundred and twenty-five.—Thomas Gonzalez.*

Note.—*The other clauses of this will of Diego Mendez, refer
to his funeral arrangements, and the declaration of debts, due*

---

año de nuestro Redentor de mil quinientos treinta y seis años.
Diego Mendez. E yo el dicho García de Vera, Escribano Notario
público, presente fui á todo lo que dicho es, que de mi se hace
mencion, ó por mandado del dicho Sr. Teniente ó pedimento del
dicho Bachiller Estrada, este testamento en estas veinte é seis hojas
de papel, pliego entero, como aquí parece, fice escrebir como ante
mí se presentó é abrió, ó ansi queda originalmente en mi poder.
E por ende fice aquí este mi signo tal en (*está signado*) testimonio
de verdad. García de Vera. (*Está firmado.*)

*Concuerda literalmente con las cláusulas copiadas de un testimonio
signado y firmado por el expresado Escribano García de Vera, que
obra originalmente en el Archivo del Excmo. Sr. Almirante Duque
de Veraguas, de donde lo copié en Madrid á veinte y cinco dias del
mes de Marzo de mil ochocientos veinte y cinco años.—Tomas
Gonzalez.*

both to him and by him, in Spain and in the island of Hispaniola, as well as other matters purely personal, and relating to his family; but they bear no reference or allusion to the Admiral Columbus, or to his voyages and discoveries, and therefore have not been copied.

FINIS.

INDEX.

ADDA (MARQUIS D'), his reproduction of the printed text of the first letter, cxxv
Adelantado, *see* Bartholomew Columbus,
Adelphus (John), his connection with St. Dié, lxxxvi
Ages. a kind of turnip used by the Indians, 63, 68
Aguacadiba, village in Jamaica, 223
Aguado (Juan), recommended to the notice of the King and Queen, 93
Aguja (Punta de la), Needle Point, 125
Ailly (Cardinal Pierre d'), his Imago Mundi studied by Columbus, xlv
Alcatraz (Point), 125
Alfragan, the Arab astronomer, his influence on Columbus, xlvii
Aloes, found in Española, 67
Ameyro (The Cacique), his friendship for Diego Mendez, 225
Animals in Española, 42
—— of Cariay, 200
Antillia, supposed island of, xxvi
Appianus, his Mappemonde bearing the name of America, lxxxvii
Arabian expedition to America, xix
Arana (Diego de), Governor of Española, 12
—— (Pedro de) commander of one of the ships sent on by Columbus to Española in the third voyage, 115
Arenal (Point of), 119
Arguin, called by Columbus Hargin, 136
Arin, Island of, 135
Arrows used by the Caribbees, 31
Astrolabe rendered useful for seamen, li
Atlantis, spoken of by Plato, v
Australia discovered by the Portuguese within one hundred years of the rounding of Cape Bojador by Prince Henry's navigators, i

Avan, a province of Juana, 10
Ayala (Pedro de), on the supposed islands in the Atlantic, xxvi
Ayay, one of the Caribbee Islands, 31
Axes made of stone used by the Indians, 68
Azoa, Province of Española, 232

BACON (ROGER), his *Opus Majus* supplied the portion of the *Imago Mundi* which is supposed to have inspired Columbus with the idea of discovering America, xlvii
Bardson (Heriulf), establishes himself at Heriulsnes in Greenland, x
Barrow (Sir John), his account of Cortereal's expedition, xxvii
Bastimentos, harbour of, 184
Becher (Captain) agrees with Muñoz on the landfall of Columbus, lx
Behaim (Martin), on the supposed islands in the Atlantic, xxvi; said to have discovered the Azores, xxx; the evidence of his globe, xxxi; in conjunction with Roderigo and Josef, renders the astrolabe useful for seamen, li
Belem and Belpuerto, disabled ships left there, 193
—— or Yebra, river, 213
Beltran, recommended to the notice of the King and Queen, 92
Bianco (Andrea), his map, on which is the word "Antillia," xxvi
Bibliography, cviii
Birds' nests in Española at Christmas, 42
Bobadilla (D. Francisco de), his infamous treatment of Columbus, lxxi; his death, lxxvi
—— Columbus's account of his arrival in Española, 159; his conduct, 160; arrests Columbus, 167; seizes his house and papers, 173
Bohio discovered, lxiii

Bohio, a province of Española, 41
Bojador (Cape), rounded by Prince Henry's navigators in 1434, i
Bonacca, *see* Guanaga
Brazil, supposed island of, xxvi
Bremen (Adam of), makes the earliest allusion (*printed*) to the colonization of America by the Scandinavians, viii
Brerewood (Edward), derives the Americans from the Tartars, vi
Burenquen(PortoRico)discovered, 39

CABOT (JOHN), his zeal for the discovery of the supposed islands in the Atlantic, xxvi
——— (Sebastian), his discovery demonstrated, xxviii
Cabras, Goat Island, 43
Canaanites supposed to have peopled America, vi
Cannibals, Caribbee, 26, 29
——— in Cariay, 201
Canoes, 9, 10
Caonabó, a chief in Española accused of having burned the Spanish settlement, 48; gold mines in Niti belonging to him, 64; his bad disposition towards the Christians, 77
Cape Gracias a Dios, 178
Cape Honduras, clxxvii
Cape Verde Islands discovered by Diego Gomez (see *Life of Prince Henry the Navigator*), 115, 116
Capitana ship, the captaincy given to Diego Mendez, 222
Carabajal, Alonzo Sanchez de, commanded one of the ships sent on by Columbus to Española in the third voyage, 115
Caracol, Bay of, in Española, 47
Caradoc of Llancarvan's account of the Welsh expedition, xxi
Carambaru, golden mirrors worn by the Indians, 180
Cariay, Columbus arrives there in his fourth voyage, 180; enchanters, 199; sepulchre, 199; animals, 200; cannibals, 201; copper mines, 201; cotton beautifully worked, 201
Caribbee Islands discovered, 25
Caseneuve (Guillaume de), his name confounded with that of Columbus, xxxviii
Cathay, Northern China, 194
Cazadilla, bishop of Ceuta, condemns the proposed enterprise of Columbus, lii

Celts supposed to have peopled America, ix
Ceyre, Cayre or Charis (Dominica), 31; said to abound in gold, 37, 38
Chanca's (Dr.) letter, iii; history of, cxxxviii, cxl; physician to the fleet of Columbus, in his second voyage, his letter, 19; mentioned in the memorial of Columbus, 93
Chinese supposed to have reached America by the north, vii
Ciamba, province of, gold mines, 180
Cibao, gold mines of, 69
Ciguare, dress and customs of the people, 181
Cladera (Don Cristóbal) refutes the statements respecting Behaim, xxx
Cobrava Aurira, province, 214
Columbus (Bartholomew) sent by his brother to Henry VII, lvi; arrested by Bobadilla, 167
Columbus (Christopher) derives the idea of explorations to the West from Prince Henry's researches into the Atlantic, i; the importance of his original letters, ii; the pathos and dignity of his complaints, iii; the evidence of European adventurers having visited America before his time, does *not* detract from his merit, xxxi; every previous discovery having been accidental, xxxii; his parentage and date of birth, xxxii, xxxiv; birthplace, xxxv; education, xxxv; his connection with Guillaume de Caseneuve discussed, xxxvii, xlii; his sojourn in Portugal, where he first receives the inspiration of his great discovery, his marriage with the daughter of Perestrello and consequent inheritance of his papers, etc., xlii, xliii; the facts and signs which convinced him there was land to the West, xliii, xliv; his studies, xlv; influenced by al Fergani or Alfragan, xlvii; Marco Polo and Sir John Mandeville, xlviii; his letter to Toscanelli and the answer, xlix; his patience in biding his time for application to the King of Portugal, l; his letters of 1477 quoted by his son, l; his audience with the king, li; his enterprise condemned by the Council, lii; his unworthy treatment, lii; and de-

parture, liii; conjectures respecting his subsequent history, liii; his visit to the Convent of Rabida, liv; his various fortune at the Court of Spain, liv, lvii; sets out on his first great voyage, lvii; discovers the Island of San Salvador, etc., the true land-fall discussed, lviii-lxiii; establishes a colony in Hispaniola, lxiii; his stormy passage home, lxiv; reception at the Azores, lxiv; arrives at Lisbon, lxv; and reaches Spain in safety, lxvi; his triumph at Barcelona, lxvi; the Papal bull obtained, lxvii; his second voyage, lxviii; and return, lxix; third voyage, lxix; his cruel treatment, lxxi, lxxii; arrives in Spain and is honourably received by the sovereigns, lxxiii; his fourth voyage, lxxiv; and return, lxxix; his sufferings till death, lxxx; his first letter addressed to Raphael Sanchez, 1; discovers San Salvador, Santa Maria de Conception, Fernandina, Isabella and Juana, 2; sees another island and names it Española, 3; takes possession of Española and builds the fortress of Villa de Navidad, 11; describes the benefits to be derived from his discoveries, 15, 16; leaves Cadiz for his second voyage, arrives at the Great Canary, Gomera, 20; Ferro, 21; discovers Dominica and Marigalante, 22; discovers Guadaloupe, 24; discovers Montserrat, Santa Maria la Redonda, Santa Maria la Antigua, and St. Martin, 34; discovers Santa Cruz and St. Ursula, 38; discovers Porto Rico, which he names St. John the Baptist, 39; arrives at Espanola, 41; receives a deputation from Guacamari, 44; finds the settlement destroyed by fire, 51; goes to visit Guacamari, 54; selects Port Isabella for the new settlement, builds the City of Marta, 62; sends two parties in search of gold mines, 69; his memorial to the King and Queen of the results of the second voyage, 72; refers to Gorbalem and Hojeda for an account of the gold to be found, 74; describes the difficulties and dangers to be encountered, 75, 81; describes the fertility of the country, 81; asks for supplies, 82, 84; asks for the confirmation of Antonio de Torres as governor of the City of Isabella, 92; recommends to the notice of the King and Queen Messire Pedro Margarite, Gaspar, Beltran, and Juan Aguado, 92, 93; also Dr. Chanca, 93; Coronel, 95; also Gil Garcia, 96; complains of the conduct of Juan de Soria, 98; asks for further assistance and stores, 100, 104; recommends Villacorta, 105; his narrative of his third voyage, 108; his address to the King and Queen, 108, 114; sails from San Lucar, 114; discovers Trinidad, 118; describes Indians in a canoe near the point of Arenal, 119; violent currents near the Point, 122; beauty of the country at the Punta de la Aguja, 125; conjectures respecting the violent currents, 130; the north star, 133; form of the earth, 134, 135: describes the Gulf of Pearls, 139; his conjectures as to the situation of Paradise, 141, 146; letter to the nurse of Prince John, 152; describes his troubles on arriving at Española, 155, 156; conduct of Hojeda and Vincent Yañez, 156; of Adrian Mogica and Don Ferdinand, 157; describes Bobadilla's arrival, 160; his arrest by Bobadilla, 167; his house and papers seized, 173; letter to the King and Queen on his fourth voyage, 175; his reception in Española, 176; dreadful storm, 176, 178; his distress on account of his son and brother, 178, 179; arrives at Cariay, hears of gold mines in Ciamba, goes to Carambu, 180; describes the people of Ciguare, 181; his conjectures with regard to the earth, 183; reaches the harbour of Bastimentos, 184; his suffering during an awful tempest, 185; returns to Puerto Gordo, 186; reaches Veragua, 187; finds gold mines, 188; deceit of the Cacique Quibian, 188; establishes a settlement, 189; takes the Cacique prisoner, 189; describes pathetically his misfortunes on this coast, 190; his dream, 191, 192;

supposes himself in China, 194; reaches Jamaica, 195; repeats the course of his voyage, 196, 197; describes the enchanters of Cariay, 199; sculptured sepulchre, 199; animals, 200; products, 201; abundance of gold in Veragua, 202; conjectures concerning the gold of Solomon, 204; his distress for the condition of Española and Paria, 206; his touching complaint of cruel treatment, 209, 211; his conference with Diego Mendez related by the latter, 226

Columbus (Diego), information given by him to Las Casas respecting his father, xliii; leaves Lisbon with his father, liii; his father's anxiety about him, 179

——— (Juan Antonio) commanded one of the ships sent on by Columbus to Española in the third voyage, 115

——— (Ferdinand) on the subject of his father's parentage and date of birth, xxxii; on the subject of Caseneuve, xxxviii; on the subject of his father's first thoughts of his great discovery, xlii; relates the facts and signs which led him on to the West, xliii; collects his father's books and bequeaths them to the Cathedral of Seville, xlv; speaks of the influence of Alfragan, xlvii; quotes a letter of his father's, 1; his statement that his father went to Spain in 1484, liii

Copper mines in Cariay, 201

Coral ornaments worn by the Indians of Ciguare, 181

Cordeiro quoted by Sir John Barrow, xxvii

Coronel recommended to the notice of the King and Queen, 95

Correa (Pedro), brother-in-law of Columbus, confirms his idea of land to the West, xliii

Cortereals, the Portuguese explorers, xxvii

Cosa (Juan de la), his map, lxi, lxii, lxxxix

Cosmographiæ Introductio, of Waldseemüller, lxxxiv

Cotton worn by the Indian women, 6; great quantities in the islands, 15; found in Guadaloupe, both spun and prepared for spinning, 25; spun and woven into sheets by the Caribbees, 29; worn in bands round the knee and ankle by the Caribbee women, 30; hammock of, 56; worn by the Indian women, 64; trees of in Española, 66; worked in colours and worn by Indians near Point Arenal, 120; beautifully worked in Cariay, 201

Crantor confirms the story told by Plato, v

Cuba, *see* Juana

Cubagua discovered, lxx

Dati (Giuliano), his poem, xc, cvii

Dauphin (Port) in Española, 60

De Murr, his evidence on the subject of Behaim, xxxi

De Guignes, states that the Chinese reached America by the north, vii; his opinion on the Arabian expedition, xix

Deza (Diego de), the faithful friend of Columbus, lv, lxxx

Documents—Columbus' letter on the first voyage, 1; Dr. Chanca's on the second voyage, 19; Memorial of Columbus on the second voyage, 72; letter of Columbus on the third voyage, 108; his letter to the nurse of Prince John, 152; his letter on the fourth voyage, 175; narrative of Diego Mendez, 212

Dogs in Española, 42

Dominica, Island of, discovered, 22; described in second voyage, 31; report of gold there, 37

Dragon's mouth, 139

Ducks found in Zuruguia, 13

Editio princeps of first letter of Columbus, the rival claims discussed, cxxii, cxxxviii

Edrisi on the Arabian expedition, xx

Egyptians supposed to have colonised America, etc., vi

El Retrete, lxxviii

Engaño, Point, Española, 41

Eric the Red colonises Greenland, x

Eric, Greenland Bishop, visits Vineland in 1121, xvii

Escobar, companion of Diego Mendez, 217

Escobedo, Rodrigo de, lieutenant to the governor of Española, 12

Española (St. Domingo) seen from Juana, 3; scenery, harbours, vegetation, spices, gold and other

metals, 4-5; inhabitants, 5-9; great size, 11; town of Villa de Navidad, 11; manners and customs, 12-14; products, 15; arrival of Columbus on his second voyage, 41; its division into provinces, 41; country described, birds and animals, 42-43; harbour of Monte Cristi, 45; river Yaque, 45; Bay of Caracol, 47; Port Dauphin, 60; Port Isabella, 62; city of Martn, 62; vegetation, 63; the people, 64; gold mines, 64; products, 66-68; abundance of gold, 69-70; Columbus finds the colony in a state of revolt when he arrives there in his third voyage, 155; Bobadilla's arrival, 160; reception of Columbus on his fourth voyage, 176

Evangelista discovered, lxviii
Exuma discovered, lxiii

FERNANDINA (Great Exuma) discovered, 2
Fonseca (Juan Rodriguez), Bishop of Badajos, his enmity to Columbus, lxviii and 156
Fortress built at Villa de Navidad, 11-12

GALEA, CAPE, now Cape Galeota, the south-east point of Trinidad, 118
Gallardo (Don Bartolomé), the *Imago Mundi* not mentioned in his list of books in the Columbian library, xlvi
Gallega Island, 177
Garcia, land of, 121; violent currents between it and the I. of Trinidad, 123
Garcia (Gil), recommended to the notice of the King and Queen, 96
Gardar, a Dane, discovers Iceland in 863, x
Gaspar recommended to the notice of the King and Queen, 92
Genoa, birthplace of Columbus according to his own assertion, xxxv
Ghillany's (Dr. F. W.) copy of Martin Behaim's globe, xxxi
Gibbs (Mr.) confirms Navarrete on the landfall of Columbus, lviii
Giocondi (Fra Giovanni) translated Vespucci's letter into Latin, lxxxiv
Globus Mundi, lxxxv
Gold and other metals in Española, 5, 15; report of large quantities

at Cayre, 37; ear-rings and necklaces worn by the Indians, 44; masks sent as presents by Guacamari, 48; beaten into thin plates by the Indians, 55; mines at Cibao and Niti, 69; great quantities found by Gorbalan and Hojeda, 74; ornaments of, worn by the Indians of Paria, 125; Indians direct Columbus where to find it, 128; seizure of, by Bobadilla, 167; gold mines of Ciamba, 180; mirrors of, worn by the Indians of Carambaru, 180; ornaments of worn by the Indians of Ciguare, 181; mines of Veragua, 188; abundance of, in Veragua, 202; of Solomon, 204
Gomara on the subject of the Polish pilot, xxix
Gorbalan, his discovery of gold, 74
Greenland discovered and colonised, x
Grotius (Hugo) describes America as peopled from Norway, ix
Grüninger (Johann) of Strasburg, his edition of the *Cosmographiæ Introductio*, lxxxv
Guacamari sends a deputation to Columbus, 44; sends his cousin with an account of the destruction of the Spanish settlement, 48; receives Melchior and his party, 54; his interview with Columbus, 56; his hammock of cotton network, 56; his pretended wound, 58; his disappearance, 60
Guadaloupe, Island of, discovered, 24; immense waterfall, 25; deserted houses, 25; the inhabitants, 27; their arts, 29; manners and customs, 30-32
Guanaga Island discovered, lxxvii
Guanahani (San Salvador, now Watling's Island) discovered, 2, lxi
Gunnbiorn discovers Greenland in 877, x
Gutierrez (Pedro), lieutenant to the governor of Espanola, 12

HAIR, various ways of wearing among the Indians, 37
Hammocks used in Española, 56
Hatchets and axes made of stone, 68
——— etc., made of copper in Cariay, 201
Hayti, a province of Española, 41
Helgason (Adalbrand and Thorwald), Icelandic clergymen and explorers in 1285, xviii

Henry VII. willing to accept the services of Columbus, lvi
Herrera on the signs which led Columbus to the West, xliv; his map, its evidence on the landfall of Columbus, lx, lxii
Hispaniola, see Española
Hojeda (Alonzo de) sent by Columbus to examine gold mines, 74; causes great trouble to Columbus in Española, 156
Homo, province of Cuba, 222
Honey found in Española, 5
Hornius, his treatise "*De originibus Americanis*, vi
Huarco, Cacique, 224
Humboldt's answer to the theory of De Guignes, viii; his assertion respecting Ortelius, viii; his opinion on the Arabian expedition, xx; on the subject of the Polish pilot, xxix-xxx; on the date of the *Imago Mundi*, xlvi; on Roger Bacon, xlvii; on the landfall of Columbus, lviii; his testimony to the glory of Columbus, lxxxviii
Hylacomylus, see Waldseemüller

ICELAND discovered and colonised, x
Idolatry not practised by the Indians, 8
Imago Mundi, studied by Columbus, xlv; dates assigned to the first edition, xlvi
Indians, their weapons, 6; their want of courage, 7; simple, honest and liberal, 7; not idolaters, 8; very intelligent, 9; their canoes, 10; manners and customs, 13-14; deserted houses in Guadeloupe found to contain cotton and human bones, 25; Caribbee, their characteristics, 29-30; their customs, 31-32; dress, 37; miserable hovels in Española, 52; their manner of working gold, 55; join readily with the Christians in their acts of worship, 65; tools made of stone, 68; their food, 68; of Paria, description of, 119, 124; their houses, food, etc., 126; dress, 128; tell Columbus where to find gold, 128; of Trinidad described, 137; of Carambaru wear golden mirrors round their necks, 180; of Ciguare, dress and customs, 181; of Cariay, enchanters, 199, 201; of Veragua, 215, 217; conflict with, 219, 221; refuse to supply Columbus, but are frightened into obedience by the prediction of an eclipse, 234
Ingolf, a Norwegian, colonises Iceland, x
Ires (William), native of Galway, one of the men left by Columbus in Española, 12
Iron not known by the Indians, 6
Isabella, her sympathy with Columbus, lxxiii; her death, lxxx
——— (Saometo or Crooked Island) discovered, 2
——— city, river, and port of Española, 62
Isle of Pines, see Evangelista
Isla de las Bocas, 197

JAMAICA, letter on the fourth voyage dated from, 211; Diego Mendez treats with the natives, 223
John, King of Portugal, grants an audience to Columbus, li; calls a council to consider his proposition, li; yields to the unworthy advice of his enemies, lii
Josef and Roderigo, with the assistance of Behaim, render the astrolabe useful for seamen, li; condemn the proposed enterprise of Columbus, lii
Juana (Cuba) discovered, 2; its size, 10; contained two provinces, 10

KARLSEFNE (THORFINN), distinguished early discoverer, xiii
King's Garden (The) discovered, lxiii
Kircher (Athanasius), his conjectures concerning the colonisation of America, etc., vi
Klaproth, his answer to the theory of De Guignes, vii
Kohl, on the Venetian expedition, xxv

LAJES (TALLARTE DE), an Englishman, one of the men left by Columbus in Española, 12
Lambinet on the date of the *Imago Mundi*, xlvi
Landfall of Columbus discussed, lviii, lxiii
Las Casas, his evidence respecting Columbus and Perestrello, xliii
Lannoy (Jean de), on the date of the *Imago Mundi*, xlvi
Leibnitz acknowledges that he had

INDEX. 251

erroneously inserted the name of "Christophorus" into the letters supposed to refer to Columbus, xxxvii-xxxviii
Lescarbot (Marc) derives the Americans from the Canaanites, vi
Lief, son of Eric the Red, discovers Newfoundland and Nova Scotia in the year 1000, xi; also New England, xii
Li-Yen, Chinese historian quoted by De Guignes, vii
Lizards, an Indian luxury, 43
Lud (Walter), canon of St. Dié, his college and printing press, lxxxiv

MACAO (Point), Española, 41
Mackenzie (Commander Alexander Slidell) on the route of Columbus, lxii
Malte Brun on the Arabian expedition, xx
Manchineal, fruit of, 24
Mandeville (Sir John), influence on Columbus, xlviii
Mangi, name given to Southern China by Marco Polo, 194
Maps: by Nicolò Zeno, xxv; anonymous, xxvi; by Andrea Bianco, xxvi; the earliest MS. bearing the name of America, lxxxvii
Mappa Mundi, by Pierre d'Ailly, treats of Alfragan, xlvii
Mappemonde, by Appianus, bearing the name of America, lxxxvii
Marchena (Fray Juan Perez de), his interest in Columbus, liv
Marco Polo, influence of his work on Columbus, xlviii
Marcolini (Francesco), his account of the Venetian expedition, xxii
Margarita, Island, discovered, 156
Margarite, Messire Pedro, recommended to the notice of the King and Queen, 92
Margry (M.), his pretension founded on the fondness of Columbus for the works of Pierre d'Ailly, xlv; disproved, xlv
Marigalante (Island of) discovered, 22
Marquez (Diego) and his party lost for four days, 27, 28
Marta (City of), Española, 62
Martin (Andreas) his respectful treatment of Columbus in his trouble, lxxii
Martin (Fernam) his correspondence with Toscanelli, xlix

Masks of gold made by the Indians, 55
Mastic found, 15
Matenino (Martinique), 14
Mayaguana, supposed by Varnhagen to be the landfall of Columbus, lx
Mayreni, a chief in Española, accused of burning the Spanish settlement, 48
Medici (Lorenzo di Pier Francesco de'), letter to him from Vespucci, lxxxiii
Melchior and his party received by Guacamari, 54
Melilla, 224
Memorial of Columbus on the second voyage, 72
Mendez (Diego), extract from his will, iii; his devotion to Columbus, lxxviii, lxxix; his narrative, 212; renders assistance to Columbus at Veragua, 213; his reception by the Indians, 216; conflict with, 219; made captain of the ship *Capitana*, 222; goes to treat with the natives of Jamaica for food, 223; goes to Española and purchases a ship for Columbus, 233; his interview with Columbus and promised reward, 235, 236; his disappointment, 237; directions respecting his grave, 239
Mendoza, archbishop of Toledo, adopts the cause of Columbus, lv
Mogica (Adrian), one of the rebels in Española, 157
Mona, 41
Monte Cristi, harbour in Española, 45
Montserrat (Island of), discovered, 34
Mundus Novus of Johann Ottmar, lxxxii
Muñoz, his opinion that Columbus went to Genoa from Lisbon, liii; his opinion on the landfall of Columbus, lviii
Mylius (Abraham) supposes America to have been peopled by the Celts, ix

NARRATIVE by Diego Mendez, 212
Navarrete on the landfall of Columbus, lviii
Navidad, villa de, town and fortress in Española, 12
New England discovered, xii

Newfoundland discovered A.D. 1000, xi
Nightingales and other birds singing in November in Española, 4
Niti, gold mines of, 69
Norwegians supposed to have peopled America, ix
Nova Scotia discovered in the year 1000, xi

ODJEIN or Ougein, 135
Opus Majus of Roger Bacon supplied the portion of the Imago Mundi which is supposed to have given Columbus the idea of discovering America, xlvii
Oronoco, confluence of the, with the sea, 123
Ortelius, not the first to recognize the discovery of America by the Northmen, viii
Ottmar (Johann), his Mundus Novus, lxxxii
Otto (Mr.) of New York, his assertion respecting Martin Behaim and the Azores, xxx
Ovando (Nicolas de), the governor of St. Domingo after Bobadilla, lxxiii

PALM-TREES, very fine in Española, 4, 5
Paracelsus, his statement of the peopling of the New World, vi
Paradise, supposed situation of, 141
Paria, coast of 121
Parrots found in deserted houses in Guadaloupe, 25
Pearls, Gulf of, 139
Pearls, bracelets of, worn by the Indians of Paria, 125 ; Columbus leaves orders with the people in Española to fish for them, 155
Pelicans show that land was near, 40
Pelican (Point), 125
Peña Blanca (Point), 123
Pepper plant, known to the people of Ciguari, 181
Perestrello (Felipe Moñiz de), wife of Columbus, and daughter of Bartollomeu Perestrello, xlii
————— (Bartollomeu), received the commandership of Porto Santo from Prince Henry, his widow gives up his papers, etc., to Columbus, xlii, xliii
Perez (Alonzo), the first to see land in the third voyage, 118

Philesius, pseudonym of Ringmann, lxxxiv
Pilot of the ship Capitana first to see land on the second voyage, 21
Pinzon, his jealousy of Columbus, lxvi
Plato speaks of an island called Atlantis, v
Polar star, observations of Columbus on, 133
Pomponius Mela, edited by Vadianus, lxxxvi, lxxxvii
Porto Rico, named by Columbus St. John the Baptist, discovered, 39
Portuguese expedition to America, xxvii
Prince Henry originates the researches into the Atlantic which led to the discoveries of Columbus, i
Puerto Bello discovered, lxxviii
Puerto Gordo, 186

QUEEN's Gardens discovered, lxviii
Quibian, the Cacique, attempts to deceive Columbus, 188 ; taken prisoner, 189 ; advice of Columbus respecting him, 205

RABIDA (Convent of Santa Maria de), Columbus's visit there, liv
Rafn (Professor), his work Antiquitates Americanæ, ix; his collection of MSS. on the discoveries of the Northmen, and his inferences, ix, xviii
Reeds used as Indian weapons, 6
René II, Duke of Lorraine, patron of Walter Lud, lxxxiv
Reptiles eaten by the Indians, 68
Rhubarb and other drugs in Española, 15
Ringmann (Mathias), his admiration of Vespucci, lxxxiv; suggests the name of America, lxxxv
Roderigo and Josef, with the assistance of Behaim, render the astrolabe useful for seaman, li; condemn the proposed enterprise of Columbus, lii
Roldan, the enemy of Columbus, perishes in a storm, lxxvi

SAIS, priests of, their story of the Island of Atlantis, v
Sandy Point (Punta del Arenal), 119
S. Brandan, supposed island of, xxvi
St. Catherine discovered, lxiii

St. Domingo, see Española
St. Martin (Island of) discovered, 34
St. Ursula and the eleven thousand virgins (Islands of) discovered, 38
San Miguel (Cape), 232
—— Salvador (Watling's Island), name given by Columbus to Guanahani, 2
Santa Cruz (Island of) discovered, 38
—— Maria la Antigua (Island of) discovered, 34
—— Maria de Concepcion (Long Island) discovered, 2
—— Maria la Redonda (Island of) discovered, 34
Santander (Serna) on the earliest date of the first edition of the *Imago Mundi*, xlvi
Scandinavians supposed to have peopled America, viii
Sepulchre in Cariay, 199
Serpent's mouth, 123, 139
Snakes in Española, 42
Soderini (Pietro), Vespucci's schoolfellow, the letter intended for him, lxxxiv
Solon, remarkable story related to, v
Soria (Juan de), the complaint of Columbus respecting his conduct, 98
Sousa, Faria y, silent respecting the Cortereals, xxviii; supposed discovery of Newfoundland,
Spice in Española, 5; trees, 67
Spinning and weaving among the Caribbees, 29
Sugar canes, 81
Sumner (Mr. George), his search in the archives of Aragon and Barcelona for records of Columbus, lxvi
Szkolny (John), Polish pilot said to have discovered America in 1476, xxix

TALAVERA, his opposition to the projects of Columbus, liv
Tartars supposed to have peopled America, vi
Terra firma, note on the supposed discovery in the second voyage, 110; discovered in the third voyage, 121
Theopompus, his story relating to the "New World", iv
Thorwald, Lief's brother explores the coast of America, xii

Toinard (Nicolas), his correction of Leibnitz, xxxviii
Torfæus (Thormodus), Norwegian historian, relates the discovery of America by the Northmen, ix
Torres (Antonio de), Columbus begs the King and Queen to confirm his appointment as governor of the city of Isabella, 92
—— (Doña Juana de la), letter of Columbus to, lxxii, 152
Toscanelli (Paolo), his correspondence with Martins and afterwards with Columbus, xlv, xlviii, xlix
Trinidad, Island of, 121; violent currents between it and Garcia, 123; city of, 222
Tristan (Diego) killed by Indians, 220
Turk's Island, supposed landfall of Columbus, lviii
Turner's (Sharon) curious surmise respecting Columbus, liii
Turuqueira and Ayay, probably the two islands which form Guadaloupe, 31
Tychsen's opinion on the Arabian expedition, xx

VADIANUS (JOACHIM) uses the name of America in 1512, lxxxvi
Varnhagen (Señor de), his opinion on the landfall of Columbus, lx; proved to be mistaken, lxii; referred to on the subject of the earliest edition of the first letter, cxxv, cxxvii
Venetian expedition to America, xxii
Veragua, Columbus arrives there in his fourth voyage, 187; gold mines, 188; custom with regard to burial of the chiefs, 203
Vespucci (Amerigo), his letter addressed to Lorenzo di Pier Francesco de' Medici, lxxxii; the question of his voyage discussed, lxxxiii; the way in which his name was given to America, lxxxv
Vicente (Martin), Portuguese pilot, confirms Columbus in his idea of land to the West, xliii
Villacorta recommended to the notice of the King and Queen, 105
Vineland, New England, xii
Vitalis (Ordericus) speaks of the country visited by the Scandinavians, ix

WALDSEEMÜLLER (MARTIN), his *Cosmographiæ Introductio*, lxxxiv
Washington Irving on the landfall of Columbus, lviii; disproved, lxii
Watling's Island proved to be the landfall of Columbus, lxi
Watt (Joachim), *see* Vadianus
Welsh expedition to America, xx
Williams (Dr) advocates the truth of the Welsh expedition, xxii

XAMANA, a province of Española, 41

Xuragoa (Xaragua), 232

Yams in Española, 63
Yanez (Vincent) helps the disaffected in Española, 156
Yaque (River) in Española, 45

ZENO (NICOLÒ AND ANTONIO), Venetian nobles, their expedition, xxii, xxiv; map published by their descendant, xxv
Zuruguia, ducks found there, 43

www.ingramcontent.com/pod-product-compliance
Lightning Source LLC
Chambersburg PA
CBHW022115290426
44112CB00008B/684